Diamonds
and
Deadlines

Diamonds and Deadlines

A TALE OF GREED, DECEIT, AND A FEMALE TYCOON IN THE GILDED AGE

BETSY PRIOLEAU

ABRAMS PRESS, NEW YORK

Library of Congress Control Number: 2021946806

ISBN: 978-1-4683-1450-2
eISBN: 978-1-4683-1451-9

Printed and bound in the United States
10 9 8 7 6 5 4 3 2 1

ABRAMS The Art of Books
195 Broadway, New York, NY 10007
abramsbooks.com

*To Addie Austin and the mothers and grandmothers
who broke the mold:
Harriet Mason Stevens, Adeline Green Howle,
Claudia Miles Stevens, Sarah Parsons Prioleau,
Adeline Howle Stevens, and Phoebe Gibson Prioleau*

"I want admiration, I want excitement,
I want money, yes, money!"
—LILY BART, EDITH WHARTON, *HOUSE OF MIRTH*

"Newspapers have become the mirror of the world."
—WALT WHITMAN

"Mystify, mislead, and surprise."
—STONEWALL JACKSON

CONTENTS

INTRODUCTION

THE AMERICAN GILDED Age was an era of overscale, colorful personalities—John D. Rockefeller, Mark Twain, Theodore Roosevelt, Victoria Woodhull, Nellie Bly, Isabella Stewart Gardner, and other banner names. Among them is a forgotten figure: Mrs. Frank Leslie. In her day, she was legendary, one of the most famous, influential, and remarkable women in America. When women were confined to the private sphere, marginalized, and denied financial autonomy, Mrs. Leslie ran the largest publishing empire in the country in a male-only preserve. A female captain of industry was unthinkable, never mind a successful one. She had a brilliant head for business, steered Frank Leslie Publishing to nationwide eminence, and made a fortune. What she did with that fortune is more astonishing still. Although an unsung heroine in feminism, she left her entire estate—the equivalent of $22 million today—to women's suffrage, a donation never equaled that proved essential to the passage of the Nineteenth Amendment.

Mrs. Leslie herself was stranger than fiction, a diva who tore up the script and suited the world to her purposes. She misbehaved, flouted accepted mores, and played the system. A master of self-presentation, she adopted the persona of the perfect Victorian lady, marketed it through her media, and did as she pleased. To American women she incarnated the ideal "womanly woman" and dictated style with her fashion-forward couture wardrobe. Men, cozened by her façade, didn't see the hard-knuckled business commanda at the controls. She was under deep cover, a woman of multiple self-created identities with eight different names over a lifetime.

Hidden within all these personas were secrets Miriam Leslie would rather not talk about. Her life wasn't the "romance" she promoted, the moon-and-magnolias plantation childhood and kid-glove aristocratic upbringing. Instead, it was the stuff of dime novels. Illegitimate and probably biracial, she grew up in a hard school, with an absentee, bankrupt father and a pillar-to-post youth spent in poverty. Early years in the theater and sex trade weren't the end of her secrets. Over her long career she concealed misadventures that would have appalled Victorian Americans, including lovers, adulterous affairs, three divorces, and a ten-year ménage à trois. All the while, she maintained a bulletproof front and kept her head on her shoulders.

Whip-smart and fluent in four languages, she wrote six books and a play, lectured professionally, and hosted a celebrated salon outside office hours. Napoleonic in her ambition, she stopped at nothing in her lunge for wealth, fame, and rank, and died with a bogus title, the "Baroness de Bazus." Like many grandiose, complex personalities, she contained massive contradictions—notably a conflict between autonomy and male adoration, louche and high society—that were never resolved.

Both of her time and ahead of it, Mrs. Leslie makes a riveting subject. Her passions and prejudices reveal the pulse of her century, and her power seat in the media provides a privileged window onto the era, a seismic epoch in American history. She is witness to an era of unprecedented upheaval and tumult: the explosive growth of industry, technology, transportation, immigration, big business, and megarich tycoons. It was an age of surface glitz, imposture, spectacle, runaway consumption, and ill-gotten fortunes. Money was king, morality elastic, and the country on the make and move.

For a fraction of the country. Over 90 percent of Americans lived in desperate poverty, prey to capitalistic exploitation and successive financial panics. Three-quarters of New Yorkers lived in "packing house" tenements, often five families to a room. Unparalleled labor and class violence resulted in a chain of riots through the decades that brought the country to the brink of anarchy. Few periods in America have been as convulsive and polarized.

Mrs. Leslie was in the thick of it, a recorder and product of the Gilded Age. She was of a piece with the large self-fashioned figures of the day; her money fever, ostentation, and ambition were the coin of the realm. Many of her values—distasteful now—reflect cultural norms: the worship of aristocracy, disdain for the poor, and prejudice toward African Americans and other minorities.

For all that, she was light-years ahead of her time. A law unto herself, she smashed the feminine mold, jettisoned the rule book, and built her own empire, in command of herself, her narrative, and her money.

She also presaged the future. Her character and career address concerns central to women today: the glass ceiling, female leadership, sexual agency, and image management. She was a high-handed grande dame with serious failings, but she suggests how a woman of grit and swish can live large, attain unimagined heights in a hostile world, and have men at her bidding in the bargain.

In telling her story, I've tried to create a faithful portrait of Mrs. Frank Leslie. Although she shrouded herself in mystery, her life is surprisingly well documented through countless newspaper accounts, her own writing and correspondence, interviews, and court dockets. Previously undiscovered records shed light on darker, more concealed corners of her past. Many biographies, histories, and contemporary chronicles, guides, journals, and diaries contribute to the larger cultural picture.

I've hewed as close as possible to the facts—invented no key events, dialogues, interior monologues, or characters. Occasionally I reconstruct scenes with a weave of available data and period details and "dress" Miriam (if not recorded) based on her descriptions of gowns and those of her favorite couturiers. I've also used "inspired conjecture" throughout to help decipher her psyche, motives, and conflicts. Otherwise, Miriam's life unfolds just as it happened, in all its color, drama, and incredible futuristic storyline.

THE EMPRESS OF JOURNALISM

ON THE EVENING of June 7, 1898, Mrs. Frank Leslie had every reason to rest on her laurels. She had "met the world and conquered it." She was rich and powerful, an international celebrity. The Gilded Age—one of the most dynamic, volatile, and boom times in American history—created a free-for-all for fortune seekers and business barons like Vanderbilt, Gould, and Rockefeller. With hustle and ingenuity, the culture proclaimed, anyone could cash in. Unless you were the wrong color or sex. But here she was, if rumor served, wrong on both counts and an industry titan. She had captained the nation's largest publishing house for fifteen years, beaten cutthroat competition on male turf, and rescued the Frank Leslie company from financial ruin, turning it into a multimillion-dollar enterprise.

For three years she had been on a well-earned sabbatical on a tide of prosperity. Before her "long vacation," she'd leased *Frank Leslie's Popular Monthly* for a princely sum to a syndicate run by the capable Frederick L. Colver and invested $100,000 in *Frank Leslie's Illustrated Newspaper*, operated by Arkell publishing. Everything tacked down and in excellent hands, she could rest assured.

Tonight, she stood at the summit of her fame, an acclaimed author, social figure, and "newspaper queen." Prospects had never looked brighter. She was in her Manhattan suite on the eve of another European holiday, reinvigorated in mind, body, and morale, with the harried mid-nineties behind her and best forgotten.

A NATIONAL TREASURE and the legend of Publishers' Row, Mrs. Frank Leslie was the darling of the press in 1898. The public devoured stories about her—her glamorous high life, fabled career, soigné costumes, and whispered indiscretions. She was "consecrated as [a] public idol," the "most talked of and most photographed woman in America."

She was also the country's great conundrum. After all, a woman's position was ironclad. By cultural decree, middle-class women were confined to the private sphere, "angels in the house" dedicated to home, family, and good works. Fragile and ethereal with "smaller" brains, they obeyed the master sex with docile modesty and knew their place. Public life was forbidden territory. If a woman stepped into the brawl of the marketplace, ruin followed. "Should women make speeches, edit papers, and hold office," warned the editor of *The Household*, they unsexed themselves, invited "nervous bankruptcy," and faced social exile and disgrace. It baffled the best minds: How did Mrs. Leslie get away with it?

More confounding was the affront to women's most sacred attribute—female purity. A "true woman," declared authorities, was a disembodied passive flower devoid of "sexual feeling of any kind." She shrank from the lusts of the flesh and endured her husband's embraces with stoic fortitude. The presence of female desire bespoke disease and manliness, and stern remedies were meted out, from opium enemas to clitoridectomies. To fool around, dishonor the marriage bed, or divorce was to fall into the pit of infamy. "The Rubicon of chastity once passed, the moral descent is rapid," inveighed Dr. Elizabeth Blackwell, the first female doctor in America; illicit intercourse was "a loathsome ulcer eating at the heart of civilization."

Yet Mrs. Leslie was a flagrant "free luster." She traded sex for favors in her youth, lived ten years in an open ménage à trois, divorced three of her four husbands, and took lovers with impunity, including an adulterous affair with the "Byron of the Rockies," poet Joaquin Miller, which, according to hearsay, was ongoing.

How she pulled it off, she'd be the first to agree, was a masterpiece. An adept of self-presentation with the press at her service, she manufactured a persona that ran rings around the gender police and public censure. She assumed the role of the ultrafeminine Victorian lady, reinvented a highborn past, laundered her amorous escapades, disdained gossip, and cloaked herself in mystery. Who could possibly have detected a "free luster" and high-powered tycoon under the "gracious garments of womanliness?"

"I imagined," recalled a reporter, "a sort of manly, independent woman's rights sort of woman of the most advanced type." Instead, Mrs. Leslie epitomized the belle ideal—"delicate, womanly, and refined," with "pretty" gestures, a "delightful voice," and ingratiating manner. Her wardrobe was the last word in feminine finery, couturier gowns that accentuated her "perfect" Gilded Age figure: a prodigious bosom, wasp waist, and plump derriere. She'd used the master's weapons to invade the master's terrain—a strategy worthy of her idol, Napoleon.

She managed her private affairs with the same finesse. Even now, over sixty, she had suitors and an erotic history that would be a *grande horizontale's* envy, complete with duels and "Wertherlike tragedies." Beneath the ladylike façade, she deployed established courtship conventions and the arts of the courtesan to govern her love life. She possessed a professional's expertise: captivating conversation, "sympathy," "animation," and the nuanced interplay of delight and difficulty. A woman who understands the craft of "fascination," she advised, wields a "fatal power" before which others "must wane and pale." As for pedestaled femininity, she turned that to her advantage, too. "Never come down from your throne," she instructed. "Become queen of your position and [a man] will make you queen of his."

Only one throne eluded her: a "high seat" in Society. The overnight explosion of new fortunes sowed confusion in the social firmament and the ranks closed. The power elite established an exclusive inner circle that mandated pedigree, chaste comportment, intricate etiquette, and rigid conformity and guarded the citadel against undesirables. They numbered among the uber-rich who owned a sixth of the national wealth while the majority lived below the poverty line on an average annual income of $360. These cliquish patricians were America's first celebrities, the envy, style-setters, and aspiration of the masses.

Mrs. Leslie had aspired to join them and had been cruelly cut. Ladies in business tarnished with divorce and dubious intrigues and ancestry need not apply. But she'd risen above it. Excluded from the select two-hundred-member Thursday Evening Club, she opened an alternative Thursday salon that became "one of the institutions of the city." She provided music and entertainment, caviar and strong punch, and conversation in four languages, and drew the cultural and literary luminaries of the day. Just moments ahead lay a gala Thursday soirée, a reception and musicale to mark her departure the next day for her annual summer abroad.

THAT NIGHT THE weather could not have been lovelier—a balmy eighty degrees with a gentle breeze eddying through her boudoir. Mrs. Leslie occupied the "choicest" of French flats in the Gerlach Hotel, the premier apartment building in Manhattan that featured an eleventh-floor roof garden, a dining room with two orchestras, and deluxe accommodations. She sat at her Venetian toilet table filled with monogrammed brushes, sliver boxes, jars, and vials and regarded her vermeil mirror.

Although she touted the advantages of age and insisted a woman was only as old as she felt, she could not have been pleased by her reflection in the glass. At sixty-two she looked "no longer young." Her famed porcelain skin had creased, and her strong features sharpened as if drawn by a hostile caricaturist. Her Roman nose bulked large over a pinched mouth bracketed by marionette lines, and her bulging eyes were undershadowed by violet half-moons.

Miriam Leslie, however, trusted in artifice, the "little deceptions" that "defeated time and raised a woman above nature, the better to subjugate hearts and stir souls." She had also learned more than she cared to admit during carefully concealed adventures on the stage and the wrong side of the street.

A cape drawn over her shoulders, she lifted her hair to her crown, coiled a long artificial switch around a French twist, and pinned a fringed front to her bangs for a perfect "Newport knot." With touches of burnt sienna pomade she covered the gray streaks in her chestnut rinse. Next, her face. Applying a layer of Leichman's theatrical greasepaint foundation, she dusted her cheeks, nose, and chin with pearl powder to achieve the desired milk-white effect. (An effect that masked a darker hue, later a cause célèbre in court.) She then extracted rouge from a crystal pot, charcoaled her lids and lashes, brightened her eyes with belladonna, and glossed her lips with carmine-tinted balm.

As a finishing touch, she reached for one of the spiral-stoppered perfume flacons on her table. In the late nineties, Parisian perfumeries—Guerlain and François Coty—collaborated with master glass blowers to produce bottles that were ornate works of art. At the same time, they invented complex, sophisticated fragrances, which were considered aphrodisiacs and the province of the demimondaine. Mrs. Leslie wouldn't have only scented her fan and gloves in the "respectable" fashion. Instead, she likely picked the most potent of the new scents—"Jicky," an aromatic mélange of lavender, citrus, amber, musk, and civet—and doused it on her pulse points as courtesans did.

With luck, Annie Simons, her cousin and companion who "dressed and undressed her" for years, was on hand for the most important part of the toilette. Mrs. Leslie found servants "as little helpful as possible," especially for this complicated and arduous rite.

The staging ground was her bedchamber, a "fairy-like" sanctum upholstered in blue and amber with an en suite bathroom fitted in matching tiles and silver fixtures. She'd soaked there earlier in the porcelain tub after a dumbbell workout in her adjacent gym. Around her in the boudoir hung "rare paintings"—nude studies, a Renaissance "chaste Lucretia"—and a silver crucifix from "the late Pope." A miniature malachite clock ticked on the bronze mantelpiece. At the center of the room stood a canopied brass bed draped in guipure lace and covered with a white satin spread appliqued with violets. On the bedside table were a prayerbook and an ivory-handled pistol.

From the chiffonier, she extracted the core of a woman's wardrobe, the corset. At first glance, it seemed a dainty piece of lingerie, a rose-embroidered, lace-trimmed silk bodice. But it was a brutal piece of combat armor. Improving on the earlier whalebone foundations, the "metallic age" fashioned steel-springed corsets with a dozen grommets that fastened in front, a curved busk (a sort of push-up bra), and an elastic harness with a belaying pin that squeezed waists to achieve the desired hourglass silhouette: a mere twenty-two inches for a full-figured woman like Mrs. Leslie.

The gown, though, was the centerpiece. For Victorian Americans, clothing was invested with almost "religious reverence." During this era of appearances, what you wore defined and placed you. An elegant turnout could transform a plain woman into a "beauty," transcend age and flaws, and confer social renown. Mrs. Leslie, with her patently so-so looks, was a showcase exhibit. Despite her indifferent looks, she was widely regarded as the "reputed beauty of her times." In column after newspaper column, she talked up the advantages of "becoming female attire." Fashion could take you everywhere and procure rank, regard, and "power over the other sex."

Tonight required "royal apparel." Spread across her bed was a pièce de résistance from Worth's, the storied Parisian couturier— surely one of his prize reception gowns, close-cinched at the waist, with butterfly sleeves, a trained ecru lace overskirt, a double ruffle of mousseline de soie, and a low décolleté neckline designed to display her ample cleavage. The first order of business was the underskirt—hoisting a flounced batiste petticoat over the head and draw-stringing it in back. Then the tiny buttons of the camisole had to be fastened; the heavy brocade skirt and train, attached; and the tight bodice clasped with strong hooks and eyes. Finally, Mrs. Leslie slipped on her size-one satin slippers (tiny feet, "trilbies," were the rage) with French heels and pointed toes. The complete ensemble, with customized accessories, had set Mrs. Leslie back close to $20,000 in today's money. But she could afford it.

At last, the moment she relished most—her bijouterie. One by one, she carefully lifted the priceless pieces from her antique jewelry stand. "Jewels," she decreed, "are one of the badges and hall-marks and certificates of position in society." And her collection was unrivalled; the Society "firsts" had nothing on her. Decked in precious gems from head to toe, she "flashed and sparkled and scintillated with every movement."

After she attached her "nickel"-size diamond earrings, she pinned glittering broaches and sprays on her bodice, drew gold bangles etched with her name in diamonds on her wrists, stacked rings on her fingers, placed a diamond Spanish comb in her chignon, and hung a Renaissance heirloom around her neck that once belonged to Catherine de' Medici's lady-in-waiting: a jeweled bird with a secret chamber for poison, suspended on a chain of three thousand diamonds set in turquoise roses.

Beyond the door she heard the preparations in the front parlor: the murmur of the Gerlach Hotel staff, the chink of crystal cups set beside the repoussé silver punchbowl. Platters clunked on the buffet table loaded with caviar biscuits, cut cake, and finger sandwiches; party chairs scraped across the parquet floor; the doorbell chimed, followed by the pit-a-pat of Mrs. Leslie's hall boy "in buttons and white broadcloth" who scurried to greet the deliveryman with the hothouse flowers.

In half an hour, her salon guests would start to arrive. She swept her court train to the side, threw back "her beautiful shoulders," and

smoothed her waistline, which could be "spanned by a necklace."
Her admirers didn't lie. She could pass for forty-five, or perhaps even
younger in the right light. She stepped through the boudoir archway,
flicked on the ten-watt gilt sconces, and regarded herself in the rose-
ate glow of the full-length Venetian mirror. She looked every inch an
Empress of Journalism. Nothing suggested the June evening would
be anything but a triumph.

It would be a calamity.

CHAPTER ONE

"DELICATE HUGUENOT EXOTIC"

New Orleans, 1883

IN THE VIEUX Carré stood a clutch of curious spectators: families in satin waistcoats and "flower show dresses"; *marchandes* with reed baskets on their heads; and assorted children, dogs, and tourists. Sunday, February 26, 1883, was unseasonably raw for New Orleans, with a wintry northwest wind gusting in from the Gulf. A gray mist shrouded the corner of Dauphine Street.

The woman they were watching struck a dramatic figure in front of LePretre Mansion, the city's showplace. Though not tall, she held herself high and wore a regal walking costume, a "widow's peak" bonnet and black cashmere gown with a tight, brocaded jacket and an apron overskirt drawn back in a bustle that cascaded to the sidewalk. Everyone could see she was "much affected" by the sight before her. Perhaps she drew a lace handkerchief to her eye; perhaps she clutched the cambric cravat at her throat.

Mrs. Frank Leslie was revisiting her childhood home for the first time in nearly forty years. With her were her best friend, Jane G. Austin, the popular novelist and descendent of Myles Standish, and her newspaper "corps," writer Joseph Nagle and artist Charles

Upham, who were there to record the trip. The Dauphine Street mansion couldn't have failed to impress them. The elaborate building of lime-washed stucco, enwrapped in tiers of lacework balconies and hung with flower baskets, rose three and a half stories, towering over the low neighborhood houses.

As they continued down Orleans Street toward the French Market, they could see the Queen City's glory days were past. Rusted gates sagged on broken hinges, and stain-blotched buildings in various stages of disrepair lined streets filled with litter and pools of stagnant water. The once-manicured Jackson Square, where they veered off toward the Rue de la Levée, had become a "Dusty Place peopled with phantoms."

The French Market, though, was as Mrs. Leslie remembered it, only more so. An iron edifice half the length of a football field (designed by pioneer African American architect Joseph Abeilard) covered the Bazaar, and two hundred booths sprawled over the grounds outside. The market seemed bigger, busier, and noisier. Over the clatter of mule-drawn carts rang the cries of peddlers—"*Calas! Tout chaud!*" (hot rice cakes); a babel of French, Spanish, "Gombo," and German; and the *boom-boom-tika-boom* of spasm bands.

Mrs. Leslie knew good copy when she saw it and dispatched her staff. Artist Charles Upham hoisted his pochade box to his lap and Joseph Nagle strolled off with his notebook into the seething "curiosity shop." Beneath tented booths were clotheslines strung with pants for fifty cents and ropes of jalapeños and onions; open tables displayed palmetto fans, toys, alligator skins, and "snowy plantation cotton"; hagglers bickered beside sugar cane stalks; and Choctaw Indians with babies on cradleboards sat in a semicircle with sassafras and roots next to a parrot on a stand.

The ladies departed early. Mrs. Leslie had taken rooms at the St. Charles Hotel, a Corinthian-columned palace that one British traveler compared to St. Peter's in Rome. In her suite later that evening she received the press. Reporters found her "middle-aged" but a "handsome lady" all the same, cast in the "Creole mold" with "brilliant dark eyes," dark brown hair, and a slight "olive" complexion—a description unlikely to please her.

Yes, she exclaimed, she was forever a "woman of the South in heart and feeling." "This is my home," she continued, "I was born in a house somewhere on Dauphine Street, [and] raised until I was twelve years old partly in the city and partly on a plantation," nursed by a dear "old mammy."

The account varied at each telling but adhered to the same theme: class. She was "born to it"—a "delicate Huguenot exotic" of patrician pedigree. Brought up in "somewhat formal courtesy" by genteel parents, she learned social graces from her Bostonian mother and world culture from her "punctilious and scholarly" father, a prominent cotton broker. His forebears were illustrious: noble Huguenot émigrés from royalist France who made a fortune in the French Caribbean.

The aristo-narrative was impressive, and believed verbatim by biographers. The truth, however, was much stranger and more tangled.

THE STORY GOES this way, instead. Her father's family, the Follins—neither aristocratic nor Huguenots—appear to have been lured from Picardie, France, to Saint-Domingue around 1764 with promises of free land in the new colony with sugar plantations worked by African slaves. In a pattern to be repeated by generations of Follins, Miriam's great-grandfather was scammed. The government needed manpower to build a naval base, and the recruits found themselves in a "work camp" at Môle St. Nicolas on the northern tip of the island, living in makeshift tents, on short rations, and clearing the jungle.

Some workers, including the Follins, deserted and established small farms where they grew sugar, indigo, and cotton, often with slave labor. A surreal colonial culture evolved: carnal excess and savagery toward the enslaved population overlaid by a veneer of French refinement. Due to a shortage of white women on the island, sexual license and mixed-race unions flourished. All the while Black rage mounted against the colonists.

Miriam's grandfather, Auguste-Firmin, was born into this culture and spent his formative years and adolescence in Cap-Français, the "Paris of the Antilles." Until one day it wasn't the old Paris anymore. As France devolved into revolution in 1791, the brutalized Black majority, who outnumbered whites four to one, rose up in revolt. Cities and plantations were torched, wells poisoned, and colonists raped, dismembered, and massacred. The Follins were among the first to escape—but not, as Miriam fantasized, with "five vessels loaded with [goods]" from vast Dominican estates.

The family patriarch, Francois Michel Follin, fled to Charleston, South Carolina, with his wife, four children, and a mixed-race boy (origin unknown), opened a tobacco shop on King Street, and attended St. Mary's Catholic Church. His eldest son, Auguste-Firmin, married a Frenchwoman, Melanie Noel, and moved to Philadelphia around 1810 with his first son, Charles—Miriam's father. In Philadelphia, a thriving asylum for French refugees from the Revolution and Saint-Domingue, he started a candle factory on borrowed money. The business failed within five years. True to Follin tradition, he then embarked on a doomed scheme, a utopian experiment in the Alabama hinterlands. Known as the Vine and Olive Colony, the group of sixty-nine planned to cultivate a stretch of wilderness at the junction of the Tombigbee and Black Warrior rivers and produce wine and olives for export.

The venture passed into Alabama lore as an arcadian idyll where ladies and gentlemen battled the elements in Parisian silks and satins by day and danced minuets at night. Miriam's incurable romanticism supposedly stemmed from these tales, but the colony was a blunder from start to finish. The journey upriver from Mobile proved a nightmare, marred by shipwreck, exhaustion, and disease. When the settlers, "none of noble birth," finally arrived, they found they'd landed in the wrong place due to a surveying error, and had to decamp from a fertile riverside to the less hospitable Aigleville.

Auguste-Firmin, along with an uncle, two brothers, a wife, and soon-to-be eight children, occupied plot number 27.

During the next decade, every effort at self-sufficiency failed. The sheltered homesteaders weren't prepared for the challenges of the frontier. They built rickety sixteen-by-twenty-eight-foot log cabins of poor lumber, lost their grapevines and olive grafts on voyages from France, suffered repeated crop failures and epidemics, and generally labored to no end. Life was harsh, morale sank, and morals deteriorated.

Auguste-Firmin resorted to animal doctoring on the side, and no telling how Charles, in the flush of manhood, spent his time. Irregular free sex was the norm, and "women of easy virtue" and mixed unions abounded. (Two resident Follin family members married "Creoles," a common usage then for interracial people.) Rather than dancing quadrilles in the evening, male rowdies roistered through Aigleville and traded sexist anecdotes, like the one about the man "who beat his wife to make her spin." One inhabitant summed up the whole Vine and Olive fiasco: "Here my only pleasure is the hope that I cannot ruin myself." By the late twenties, Miriam's grandfather, Auguste-Firmin, did ruin himself, and back-trailed with his large brood to Mobile, where he died in 1833 at age fifty-six.

Miriam's father at this point wound up in Charleston, in a lower class, mixed-race quarter above Calhoun Street. America's tenth largest port, the city at the end of the 1820s was both a magnet for ambitious merchants and the home of Follin cousins with business ties. Charles's timing, however, was inopportune.

The Charleston "Golden Age" had begun a slow decline, and the Federal tariff of 1828, a 50 percent tax on foreign goods and local raw materials such as cotton, dealt a body blow to Lowcountry commerce. Profits sank, and Carolinians feuded with each other and the government over the "tariff of abominations"—almost to the brink of civil war.

To break even under such conditions must have been a challenge for Charles—never mind mastering cultural history, philosophy, music, and modern languages, as Miriam claimed. Regardless, he should have been paying attention to his account books. Charleston records show him in "very heavy" debt in 1830. He was thirty-one, and according to a passport description, easy on the eyes—five feet seven inches tall, with an oval face, dark brown hair, gray eyes, a straight nose, and rounded chin.

That year he set his sights on a wealthy widow, Caroline Carrere Trescot, who owned a valuable rice plantation bequeathed to her and her two young daughters. After her husband Dr. John Sen Trescot's death in 1820, the resourceful Caroline sought and gained administration of Hickory Hill, a 490-acre "tide swamp plantation" on the Ashepoo River with fifty-eight enslaved people. In her marriage contract with Charles Follin she took similar measures to look after herself. She must have had suspicions about Charles, as she appointed a trustee for her estate who held the purse strings and insured that she retained "full power and authority" over her property and was in no way responsible for Follin's debts.

Despite her precautions, Charles's debts soon became her problem. Two months after their marriage she prevailed on her trustee to liquidate the plantation down to the last rice sickle and hoe and auction forty of the fifty-eight slaves. They realized $10,780.90, largely consumed by Charles's "very heavy debts." In 1832 he took the remaining assets to New Orleans with a large entourage—Caroline, their infant son Ormond, the two Trescot daughters, an inexplicable five-year-old son Noel, and six or more slaves. These slaves would prove a future powder keg—the buried secret to Miriam's parentage.

OF ALL THE enigmas in the Follin family, Miriam's birth is the most tantalizing. After Caroline died in New Orleans in 1833, little is known of Charles and his ménage except that he ran up further financial losses in business speculations. Around 1836 a daughter, Miriam Florence, joined the family. It's anyone's guess who her mother was. What's certain is that she was illegitimate, and her Vieux Carré birthplace a fiction. LePretre Mansion, which she remembered so fondly, was built by wealthy investor Joseph Gardette in 1836. Her official mother, Charles's common-law wife Susan Danforth, lived in New York, "her city," and didn't visit New Orleans until 1842, when Miriam was six.

Susan Danforth was a riddle in her own right. She left no paper trail. Unmentioned in either census rolls or newspapers, she wasn't "old Boston." Miriam liked to trace her mother's ancestry to Revolutionary War hero Samuel Danforth, but he had four children—none named Susan. Another possible Samuel Danforth was a lowly foot soldier from Shrewsbury with eight children, one of whom *was* a Susan.

But that raises many questions, such as her presence in New York and independent income. While in the city, she sent care packages of "Gloves, Flannel," and the "finest linen" to Charles and dresses to his mother. How did a single woman without an inheritance manage so well in a hostile, sexist metropolis? Manhattan wasn't known as the "City of Eros" for nothing, with its large "whorearchy" of brothel keepers who often did "extremely well." (Susan's profession later became more than a conjecture.)

The more likely candidate for Miriam's birth mother is one of the enslaved women Charles brought with him to New Orleans, as contestants to Miriam's will charged after her death. The Follins and Miriam had every reason to suppress the evidence. The mere hint of "tainted blood" would have been a matter of deepest secrecy. Antebellum New York City—not to mention the slaveholding South—was violently racist. African Americans were regarded as nonpersons, and the stigma of "miscegenation" was second only to incest. The slightest suspicion of racial mixture was enough to label a woman a "Negress," to stereotype her, and exclude her from polite society.

Yet a number of clues point to Miriam's biracial parentage. No birth certificate exists, as was customary for mixed-race babies, and throughout her life, Miriam's Creole features attracted comment and

speculation. Charles would have been no stranger to interracial cou-
plings, both from his Alabama adolescence and the accepted preroga-
tive of white slaveowners to avail themselves of their property. The
practice was endemic and ubiquitous in the antebellum South—"the
thing," wrote diarist Mary Chestnut, "we cannot name."

Records have recently come to light that point to several female
slaves who might have been Miriam's mother. By the mid-nineteenth
century nearly all enslaved African Americans possessed white
blood, so Charles's offspring could well have passed as white, especially with the aid of pearl powder and "Creole freckle paste." The
1831 Follin slave auction documents suggest a number of maternal
possibilities. Of the eighteen unsold Trescot enslaved people, at least
six were women of childbearing age. Hester, Caroline's favorite, was
among them, but there were other candidates in the group Charles
took to New Orleans—Fanny, Jenny, Betty, May, and Sally.

In the absence of DNA evidence, the identity of Miriam's birth
mother may never be known, but chances are good she was one of
the enslaved women. Even Charles's stepdaughter, Amelia Trescot,
who was on the scene at the time, insisted Mrs. Leslie "was the illegitimate daughter [of] one of the female slaves belonging to [the
Trescot estate]" and had "Negro blood."

WHEN MIRIAM WAS about a year old, her father declared bankruptcy. He was not alone. In 1837 European markets contracted and
the American economy tanked, triggering a nationwide panic that
dragged on through the early forties. Worst hit was the Cotton Belt,
where cotton brokers like Charles found their produce worthless.
Insolvent and without prospects in New Orleans, Charles tried to
redeem himself in Manhattan. He little reckoned on the wreckage
there: business stagnation, crime, civic corruption, financial chicanery, and thousands of jobless paupers on the prowl with the "air
of famished wolves." *Longworth's American Almanac* of 1839 locates
Charles on 139 Crosby Street, a low-rent residential quarter inhabited

by French and Irish immigrants, rather than the business district. Conceivably, he worked from home—a cramped flat with Susan and three children underfoot.

By 1840, they relocated to another poor neighborhood in the Fourteenth Ward, where an "unidentified female" in her twenties joined the household. Given the dismal state of the Follin finances, a servant was unlikely—a rumored "Aspasia" (a byword for prostitute) under the roof more plausible. Miriam drew her first impressions of life from these harsh, lean years. She would never get over them.

Nights in the Fourteenth Ward would have been full of menace and uproar. Before bedtime, she and her mother picked their way by candlelight past haunted faces to a communal privy shared by forty tenants. In the dark and bitter cold, Miriam heard the tumult outside: "Millerites" (followers of prophet William Miller) bellowing that the end was near; thugs battling with sticks and brickbats in the street; and bells clanging for fires followed by loud cries and crashing wheels.

By day, the city was just as forbidding. On sidewalks piled knee-deep in garbage, pedestrians held camphor-soaked handkerchiefs to endure the stench of raw sewage, rotting horse carcasses, and a putrid "corporation pudding" of factory waste. Feral hogs stampeded down streets and beggars and homeless urchins crowded and heckled small children.

"Floy," as her parents called her, would also have sensed, with a child's antennae for the emotional terrain, the distress at home. There must have been anxious talk of robberies on the rise, racial violence, gangs of "brothel bullies," and the shocking murder of prostitute Mary Rogers, the "Beautiful Cigar Girl." Family shame, too, would have been palpable. Mid-nineteenth-century Manhattan vilified people like her father; poverty denoted depravity, and a man was poor through vice and moral failure. Charles's conduct past and present hadn't been exemplary, and nothing had come of his attempts at solvency.

After less than a year on Bond Street, he left Susan to fend for herself and headed back to New Orleans to seek his fortune. He had no better luck there. His letters to Susan from 1840 to 1842 were a long lamentation. He was "without a home," unable to send "little Miriam" the books he promised, and weary of his "late absences." He would, however, provide Susan with a *"comfortable* living" if only he could recover from a dubious stock investment, and if only she would advance him the money to buy a house in New Orleans. "Time, my dearest," he wrote, *"will* and *must* come to the rescue."

Time, though, didn't cooperate. Soon he received a subpoena to appear in court in South Carolina on charges of reckless misuse of Caroline Trescot's estate. Perhaps this was the moment Susan agreed to the house. In 1842, Charles summoned his family to New Orleans—beyond the reach of the law and closer, he thought, to renewed prosperity.

New Orleans should have been the childhood idyll Miriam pictured for the press and her readers. She now lived in a house with a yard and balcony (possibly at 149 Dauphine Street, occupied by "Follins") and had the company of both a friendly stepbrother, Ormond, and her father, who reminisced about those "happy days." She nostalgically recalled daydreams about the "Gentlemen of Benjamin" over the family Bible, lessons in deportment from her mother on plantation visits, her father's gift of a "lovely French doll," and devoted servants.

There *was* a lot for a young girl to love in 1840s New Orleans. Children played unsupervised, crawfishing in ditches, romping in the "neutral land" (a vacant city lot), buying popcorn tictac balls for a picayune, and watching parrots and monkeys at the "bird store" near the cathedral. With a parent, she could visit the French Market with its kaleidoscopic array of vendors, booths, and nationalities.

En route was a display of street theater that would leave an indelible impression. Proud, gorgeously appareled mixed-race mistresses of wealthy planters paraded down thoroughfares, and elegant prostitutes, schooled in disguise, refinement, and seduction, flaunted themselves in doorways without censure. Here were alternative, glamorous role models for a girl, and the most sexually relaxed climate in America. On Sundays, the city became a bacchanalia of carnival license and spectacle, with masquerade balls, French operas, horse races, circuses, and blood sports.

The New Orleans years, however, weren't as halcyon as Miriam pretended. Before she died, she admitted: "I never had any childhood, for the word means sunshine and freedom from care. I had a starved and pinched little childhood as far as love and merriment go." Her father might have reminisced about "happy days," but his continued insolvency cast a pall over the household. The Parisian doll must have been a fantasy, like the plantation and the rest. Charles lost an investment in a Mississippi land speculation and, by 1844, had to borrow $4,000 to $5,000 from his cash-strapped mother.

He liked to remember the Louisiana "old-time dinners" and "pleasant" days on the veranda. Susan, though, bore the brunt. Without servants, housekeeping was brutal, perhaps inspiring Miriam's lifelong horror of domesticity. One of his "old-time dinners" demanded Sisyphean labor: a daily slog to the market for provisions (ice was a luxury), followed by hours of preparation—cones of sugar to be chipped and pounded and kettles boiled on "spiders" in the kitchen fireplace. Since gas lamps didn't arrive in New Orleans until the late forties, her mother cleaned, washed, and stitched endlessly by candlelight.

There were also humiliations to endure. A Mr. Ogden, presumably of the Ogden Southgate Law Firm, insulted Charles with a "coarse expression" in front of Susan and Miriam—doubtless a cringe moment for his daughter. The exclusion from the "best society" must have smarted, too. Miriam knew about the New Orleans elites—the Eustises, Doswells, and Swilers—and knew she was cut. She failed to make any of the select guest lists or private school rolls. Girls from "good families" attended Granet's School for Girls and Professor Devoti's, where they learned feminine gentility: how to dance, draw, sing, stitch, and gracefully "rise, bow, and receive a book."

Instead, Miriam went to a neighborhood schoolhouse, probably one of the free public schools that became available in 1842. She might have resented it at the time, but she was spared the standard insipid fare for Southern girls and became an excellent student. And despite his derelictions, Charles became her greatest booster, rare among American fathers in the mid-nineteenth century, when daughters with book learning were a liability. Very likely, his motives were mixed; he dwelled a little too insistently on the "high position" and "rich rewards" she would gain through knowledge, as if he imagined her marrying up abroad and salvaging the family.

Whatever his object, his encouragement had the desired effect. She paid "proper attention to [her] studies" as he wished and recited her lessons "well." Her grandmother, who tutored her in French by mail, congratulated her in 1844 on winning a prize at an examination. Later Miriam preened herself on her erudition: "I was," she said, "the worst, most tiresome pedant in the world."

For all her unresolved contradictory feelings toward her father, she never ceased to credit him for the cultivation of her mind. The educational advantages he gave her, she wrote, endowed her with "a sense of security and serenity which nothing else can give; [you feel] you have the right to stand uncovered before the king."

It also endowed her with a core sense of strength when she was most vulnerable, as well as self-worth, pride, grit, and drive. For the struggle ahead, she would need everything brainpower conferred. At the end of 1844, Charles's affairs deteriorated further, and in desperation, he drifted back to Manhattan in a last-ditch effort to make ends meet.

Left in the lurch, Susan collected the ten-year-old Miriam and relocated to Cincinnati in 1846, where Charles's mysterious progeny Noel had settled and become engaged to a pork heiress, Caroline Redder. Miriam typically made a romance of this move. Her family, she claimed, had been driven to Ohio by marauding Yankees who plundered their estate and looted the Follin fortune. (In fact, the only war in progress was the Mexican conflict.)

At one level, the "Queen City of the West" was an upgrade. Charles Dickens, a visitor at the time, praised the prospect—the paved streets, excellent "free schools," and neat red and white houses. Miriam occupied one of these houses with a pretty grape-vine at the window, and acquired a pet, Beppo (a show-off allusion to Byron's poem), the first of many dogs. Like the New Orleans interlude, nothing about her time there is certain since censuses contain no "Follin," but letters convey a general idea of Miriam's existence: She attended a regular (perhaps "free") school, read such edifying works as *Heroes of the Revolution*, made friends, and hosted little parties.

But Cincinnati was still Porkopolis—a raffish, rough-edged boomtown. Men, complained Dickens, spit to punctuate sentences, and throngs of transient dockworkers, drawn to the "fastest growing" port city, drank to excess, caroused unchecked through the streets, and displayed a "universal want of manners." Culture was lowbrow; ventriloquists, banjo players, and magicians shared the bill with Irish melodists and "Mrs. Cook! Danseuse" at the popular Shires' Garden. Local gentry were apt to reprimand outsiders: "Shakespeare, Madame, is obscene."

At the same time, racial strife wracked the city, with repeated attacks on African Americans by immigrant mobs, and worsened cruelty toward slaves on the levee and elsewhere. Both Stephen Fos-ter and Harriett Beecher Stowe, residents during the forties, docu-mented the Black misery they witnessed; Foster in his ballads, Stowe in *Uncle Tom's Cabin*, which she researched in Cincinnati. Beneath Dickens's "private residences" ornamented with "trees and flowers" stood the shacks of "Rat Row" crammed with the down-and-out, desperate, and dangerous.

Miriam's father must have had an inkling of this climate and its dangers because his letters to her over the next three years sound a strong cautionary note. He lectured her on morality: She should in all matters consult her God-given good sense and cultivate "the ability to judge right and wrong." A "crime of omission," he warned, was as odious as one of "commission." As for those parties with schoolmates, she should avoid the merest hint of "vulgarity" or "dissipa[tion]."

"I am sure," he wrote, your "kind mother's ability to entertain" will make your gatherings "most fastidious." She should also assume a "chaste, appropriate, and lady-like" appearance. "These qualities are much more desirable," he directed, and "are always more approved than is the display of gay colors and a superabundance of jewelry, always the mark of vulgar taste."

Above all, she should attend to her studies. Enter classes, he coached, where you can advance quickly rather than "go into the highest" and be ill-prepared. The key was not "to get *many* and *long* lessons, as to know them *well*." He quoted her grandmother's letters in which she praised Miriam's fluency in French and her vignettes of Cincinnati. However fortifying, Charles's encourage-ment wasn't enough.

In New York he was foundering. With his brother Aristede he set out for the tropics to recoup his fortunes, but business remained "very bad" and he "fail[ed] again" in 1846. At a loss, he opened a Bond Street boarding house—perhaps with Susan's assistance. Nev-ertheless, he fell deeper into debt; by 1848 creditors seized his assets and took him to court five times for unpaid bills. Grandmother Fol-lin in Mobile had some words for her son. He "should have more fortitude and surmount his troubles," she wrote Miriam. "There is no dishonor in working."

If Miriam had not questioned him before, she must have now. Bad enough that he had been an absentee father and nonprovider, but the hypocrisy was patent. The very transgressions he warned Miriam against, he committed himself, first his questionable chas-tity, and now the great sin of omission—failure to honor his debts. A note of pique entered her letters; he'd made her feel "muggy" over a contretemps and she had a quarrel "to pick with him." She was forced to take comfort in her grandmother's home truth: "We must bear what we cannot prevent."

Bearing up, though, grew more difficult. Noel, the hope of the family, "gave up" a dentistry career, and seemed to be without purpose or income, dependent on his wife's dwindling resources. Miriam's cousin, Charles, couldn't cover a bill she sent him, her stable Uncle Adolphus contracted bronchial trouble, and her mother came down with an "indisposition."

Then her father required their presence in New York, ostensibly for housekeeping assistance. Once more, the move received the romantic treatment. In Miriam's version, Susan departed in a blaze of largesse, bequeathed the Cincinnati house, furnishings, and ancestral silver to Noel, and joined her husband in an upscale rooming house, leasing apartments to "reputable gentleman." That story would raise many eyebrows down the road.

After an arduous journey via the Erie Canal at ten miles an hour, Miriam and her mother found themselves in an alien, unruly city. Dockside they were greeted by chaos and uproar. Crowds of passengers, seamen, and longshoremen jostled on wharves cluttered with cotton bales and boxes; wagon drivers collided and cursed; hacks thundered over cobblestones. "The throng and rush of traffic," wrote a British tourist, "is astonishing even for London."

Gotham had exploded since 1842. In a decade, the city had become the nation's leader in banking, manufacturing, media, transportation, and a donnybrook of free market capitalism. Irish and German immigrants poured in by the thousands in a mad scramble for wealth, doubling the population to half a million. Sharpers and con artists plied the waterfront with bogus deals for newly-arrived "pigeons to be plucked." Cabbies cried, "Carriage, ma'am, take you for a dollar,"—extortionist rates; dressmakers made less per week.

But Miriam and her mother must have brought hopes for better prospects to the bedlam. The drive downtown to Bond Street, though, was not designed to console them. First, the new Gold Coast scrolled past: rococo mansions on Tenth Street and Fifth Avenue, gleaming four-in-hand carriages, palatial department stores, banks built of white Tuckahoe marble, and men with ram's-horn mustaches and gold-tipped canes on leafy boulevards.

As they veered further south, however, the vista abruptly changed. Flocks of women in feathers and bright chintz idled beside oyster saloons, rag peddlers plowed through packed streets with pushcarts, and stooped women swept mud and manure at intersections, begging for pennies.

The sight of 55 Bond Street couldn't have lifted their spirits. Instead of the respectable address they expected, they found a squat row house in a borderline neighborhood next to furnished rooms for dockhands, a dance academy, a storefront church of "Primitive Christians," a grocery, and a homeopathic dispensary. The infamous Bowery loomed right around the corner.

How they reacted to the boarders Charles assembled on the premises can only be conjectured. With him were his brother, Adolphus; a man named Richard Brooks from Louisiana; a five-year-old cousin, Virginia; and four mysterious women: Emma Wright of New Orleans, and three Irish teenagers, Margaret Crowlin, Mary Westeroelt, and Margaret Murphy. In view of her father's insistence on chaste, "lady-like" refinement, Miriam must have wondered about this troupe of young women.

They might well have sewn cuffs and trimmed hats for their keep. Or they might not have. One contemporary source maintained that Charles, a "sort of adventurer," had "no business" except "living with"—perhaps off of—"other women." If so, it explains Susan's reputation as a "proprietor" of "a house of ill fame [in New York City] about the years 1846–1854" who "let rooms to single gentlemen by day or week no questions asked."

At any event, Bond Street didn't pay. Charles couldn't bail himself out, borrowed $5,100 from his brother Adolphus, and made himself scarce. Miriam struck back. With a cool appraisal of the situation and spunk beyond her years, the fourteen-year-old petitioned the court to make her Uncle Adolphus legal guardian in the absence of "some proper person" to look after her.

Adolphus, ironically, the sickest of her uncles, gave substance to her father's dreams of Miriam's intellectual promise. For two years, he subsidized her studies. He hired language tutors and a drawing master, paid for an uptown school, and saved her, so far as possible, from the undertow of the Bowery.

During this reprieve, Miriam armed herself with more than her lessons: grandiosity. She might have taken her cue from Manhattan, a vanity fair of outsized personalities and self-puffery, and/or compensated for feelings of inferiority. She now professed to be a prodigy who at age fourteen authored a front-page story, "Life of General Paez," in the *New York Herald Tribune*— actually the work of the newspaper staff. She channeled Napoleon. "A woman with brains and energy," she boasted, "knows what she means to attain and is as unscrupulous as the great Napoleon in attaining it." It was a case, psychoanalysts might say, of "life-saving grandiosity."

MIRIAM WOULD SOON require every ounce of "unscrupulous" drive and imagined supremacy. In 1852, the wolf was at the door. Her father and her half-brother Ormond plunged further into arrears somewhere south of the border; Noel lost his shirt in another venture; and Susan was in debt to a Mrs. Carpenter and couldn't pay the rent. They were forced to vacate Bond Street and find still cheaper quarters.

Although apologists after Miriam's death made much of the respectability of the neighborhood, 319 East Tenth Street was a decided step down, a seedy and remote enclave a mile from the busy intersection of Broadway and the Bowery. The houses across from Tompkins Square had been converted to tenements by mid-century and held ten to twenty families in four apartments of two or three ill-ventilated rooms.

Uncle Adolphus seems to have relinquished the role of guardian and settled at 95 Green Street. Miriam, in any case, was an adult by the standards of the day, nearly seventeen. What happened next would occupy gossips for decades.

Her father and half-brother continued to cheerlead her mental cultivation. From nether Mexico, Charles insisted she "improve [herself] practically." "Think for a moment," he counseled, "of your ability to converse in the four most important living languages together with a perfect knowledge of Latin; think of the rich lore of literary works which will be open to you." Ormond joined the chorus. "To see you the most educated, the most talented, the most refined, the most noble of women is your brother's hope," he rooted. "You are my idol and were it possible I would have you perfect."

Talk was cheap, however, and neither could pay the rent. Unless she and her mother had an unnamed source of income, they were cast helpless on their own resources. They had to get their living for themselves. Someone had to be the man in the family.

Miriam's choices were stark. Little wonder she came to believe that "life [was] cruel and experience [was] pitiless," or that she lamented the plight of "the unprotected girl" in America and sought "loyal and manly protection." Opportunities for women in the early fifties in Manhattan were few and thankless. Seamstresses, flower-makers, map-colorers, straw-braiders, and book folders endured "never-ending daily toil" under harsh bosses for as little as seventy-five cents a week. Volunteer societies like the House of Industry and Home for the Friendless aided destitute women by reading them scripture and teaching these thankless trades.

Sex workers, on the other hand, earned an average of five dollars a night and enjoyed a modicum of autonomy, especially if they freelanced part-time, which many did. An estimated fifty thousand women practiced prostitution in the city mid-century—20 percent of the female population. Successful demimondaines with sobriquets like "Princess Anna" and "Aspasia" promenaded down Broadway dressed in tight-corseted gowns of frilled ribbons and flounced satin petticoats in the latest French fashions.

There's an off chance Miriam resisted the call. Investigative reporters, however, entertained no doubts: She was, they charged, a conspicuous "lais" (prostitute) who spent a "fiery youth" on the town and engaged in "wanton" doings. Everywhere "stories [were] afloat about her."

She leaked as much in her work. Girls in big cities can be corrupted, she wrote, adding that they could still be "lad[ies]," although "bad." Her sympathies were always on the side of demimondaines, women "with some spot on their name," and claimed they were "not impossible in America." New Orleans must have primed her for the profession—as well as the Follin tradition of lax sexual mores.

When she looked in the mirror, she must have seen her qualifications. She wasn't conventionally pretty; she had a hooked nose, a square masculine jaw, a wiredrawn mouth, and protrusive eyes. But she had filled out and boasted a figure that was the mid-nineteenth-century ideal: full, voluptuous breasts, a wasp waist, and tiny hands and feet. Plus masses of thick, dark fusilli curls. And whether she admitted it or not, she possessed a dusky, exotic "unfamiliar type of beauty."

Her theatrical flair, fostered by New Orleans and her home life, would also have served her well. Putting identities on and off, performing a part, and "staging" herself came naturally. She had, too, the necessary do-or-die ambition, sharpened by want, fear, underclass spite, and rage for riches. There was much cash could rectify besides rent, such as shame and social exile.

But she needed guile to navigate New York's mean streets and byzantine underworld. Dissimulation and appearance ruled in this subterranean Gomorrah, and costume was required armor—an explanation of Miriam's celebrated fashion savvy. She quickly discarded her father's admonitions on the "superabundance of jewelry" and ostentatious dress and changed her name to "Minnie."

Entry into the trade would have been easy. A Dr. Collyer on Broadway hired women to pose in "tableaux vivants," after which the "model-artists" could arrange rendezvous with spectators at the Bowery Hotel, "no references required." Popular assignation places, some semi-respectable, abounded: "naughty third tiers" in theaters, restaurants with private rooms, ice-creameries, concert halls, evening art galleries, and dances.

Each night an ambitious "Aphrodite" could choose from a dozen large public balls. Early in the fifties, Miriam's half-brother, Noel, remarked on her attendance: "I am glad to hear you so enjoyed the balls you attended." But, he teased, "you did not name your escort," and suggested several candidates: "our friend Lamp Umbrella or Mr. Denpexter or . . . [men] (of the like kind)." Clients she joked about?

He continued in a more mercenary vein. Be assured: She was "well up in the market. I cannot say less than two hundred thousand for you. If you are in luck you may catch half a million." No mention of her Latin lessons. Susan, meanwhile, spoke often to her daughter "about [her] beaux." They might have been their sole support. In 1854, her father abandoned all pretense of business.

WHY MIRIAM EMBROILED herself in a scandal at this moment is a mystery. Contrary to her father's admonition against "vulgar" bijouterie, she developed a passion for expensive jewelry. The recently built Tiffany might have been the catalyst—a white marble palazzo at 550 Broadway owned by the "King of Diamonds" whose show windows glittered with parures, bandeaux, rings, pendants, and corsage ornaments mounted on springs to increase the sparkle. For "Minnie" these gems assumed a talismanic significance, incarnating status, distinction, and wealth. "Within the heart of a diamond," she maintained, was "a soul," a glorified image of her own.

She didn't pass Baldwin & Co. jewelers on Broadway without stopping. Inside, she met the dapper clerk, David C. Peacock, a "gay young fellow," and one thing led to another. A bit of negotiation followed: favors in exchange for the loan of certain diamond pieces in the display case. This continued until her mother pried out the truth and revealed a side of herself at variance with a "very refined and cultured gentlewoman." She advanced on City Hall and demanded Peacock be arrested for criminal seduction. As of 1848 in New York State, "sexual intercourse by the defendant under promise of marriage" was a misdemeanor, punishable by up to five years in the Tombs, Manhattan's foulest prison.

When David Peacock received the arrest warrant the night of March 24, 1854, he expressed disbelief. He protested his innocence, grew "agitated and excited," and asked to see his lawyer. Susan and the sheriff seemed to have anticipated this. Unfortunately, the lawyer couldn't be reached, nor could Peacock "procure the $3,000 bail" (provided the sum existed) since banks were closed. Besides, the sheriff admonished, he had committed the crime of "carnal connection" with an unmarried female of "previous chaste character," and would pay. Newspapers would publish the offense; he would lose his job and be locked in jail. Ruined.

However, the sheriff indicated, he could save himself. All would be forgiven if he married the young lady that night. Peacock recoiled and requested "time to consider the matter." At this, the sheriff pulled him aside and impressed upon him the liberal terms: He didn't have to cohabit with Miss Follin, support her, or see her again, and he could annul the union after two years. The lady just wanted his "name" and a marriage certificate. Still resistant, Peacock was taken from his rooms on Broome and Broadway and frog-marched to Tenth Street.

The night life in Tompkins Square was at its usual pitch when they arrived: drunks bawling "no, nay, never, no more"; a g'hal crying, "Oh git out—you Mose!"; and a night cart of latrine waste drawn by Black men in bandannas lumbering by. When they reached number 319, "the mother of the girl appeared" and ushered them into a dim front room. She summoned her daughter and an awkward moment ensued. In the preparations, someone had forgotten to hire a justice of the peace. At last, Alderman Nathan C. Ely appeared on the stoop, and the ceremony began.

"Do you take this woman your lawful wife?"

No reply.

Nevertheless, the ceremony proceeded. The bridegroom sealed the "terms" with a dollar and left without a word to Miriam. From then on the couple "passed each other in the public street without any recognition."

Although the arrangement seemed a net loss for Miriam, there were benefits. Marriage in the 1850s offered few advantages; under the rule of coverture, women submitted to male authority and lost both "title to their earnings or property" and their independence. By living apart, Miriam preserved her autonomy and obtained marital status, which supplied instant respectability. In the world of strangers, establishing a good reputation was a crucial survival skill. And the "seduction" charge helped in another way. Since Peacock couldn't be guilty unless Miriam was of "chaste character," she was re-virginated overnight.

AS IT TURNED out, though, Miriam might have congratulated herself too soon on her shotgun marriage. The frigid winter of 1854–55 (temperatures dipped below minus ten degrees) coincided with a recessionary crisis, massive layoffs, and an onslaught of immigrants, more than had ever been recorded—428,000. Unable to cope, the city devolved into chaos. The treasury was empty and the municipal police force disbanded under Mayor Fernando Wood's "rum and rowdyism" regime. A "miscellaneous assortment of suckers, saplocks, Irishmen, and plug uglies," wrote George Templeton Strong, officiated "in a guerilla capacity," and street violence soared.

In addition, Mayor Wood launched a crusade against prostitution and unleashed his vice squad on suspects. In a daily struggle against ruin, women resorted to more dangerous recourses and scarcer, worse-paid factory jobs. Two German sisters, Cecilia and

Wanda Stein, discharged as embroiderers and unable to find employ-
ment, spent their last penny on flowers, swept the room, and drank
a fatal dose of prussic acid.

Around Tompkins Square, no one "seemed safe anymore," and
pedestrians began to carry revolvers. Unemployed, angry day laborers vented frustration on women with increasing incidents of harass-
ment, physical abuse, and rape. Catholics, foreigners, and especially
Blacks were targets of marauding malcontents. With the Fugitive
Slave Act of 1850 and bounty hunters on the loose and a surge of
racism fueled by Mayor Wood, it was perilous to be "colored." In
Brooklyn, the Reverend Henry Ward Beecher held mock auctions for
"light-skinned" African Americans to dramatize the crisis.

Miriam's "Creole" looks couldn't have helped, nor the attentions of a prominent public figure and connoisseur of women "with
a tinge of color," Ephraim G. Squier. This famous anthropologist
and scholar, destined to resurface so fatefully in her life, called her
"La Niña" and hinted at a sexual liaison. After he left for Central
America, Squier's friend, Amory Edwards, wrote of her intrigues in
the city and chided, "Don't get your pecker skinned so far that you
cannot get it back for the Niña will want some."

Rumor had it that she got more than "some" while he was away
and committed many "misdeeds." The new World's Fair and the
attendant tourist trade must have aided her. Crowds of visitors—up
to four thousand a day—flocked to the great Crystal Palace at Forty-
second Street, where exhibitors from twenty-four nations displayed
the "miracles of the age" beneath a 148-foot glass dome faceted with
enameled glass panes. As "Minnie" scanned displays of marble
sculpture, photography equipment, and machines for everything
from pumping water to washing gold, she might have passed a raw
country boy her own age and moved on. He wasn't to her taste and
never would be: Romantic cavaliers with pedigree and deep pockets
were more her style.

Samuel Clemens, fresh from Hannibal, Missouri, couldn't
have missed her—an overdressed, bosomy head-turner sheathed

in silk, laces, and ruffled petticoats that billowed over the aisles. Perhaps she contributed to his view of the fair as a "perfect fairy palace—beautiful beyond description." All too soon, though, the bubble burst, even under the aegis of impresario and showman P. T. Barnum, who introduced a six-hundred-voice choir and daredevil balloon ascensions. Receipts dwindled, and the fairground closed at a loss.

Fortune wasn't favoring Miriam, either. On March 6, 1856, David Peacock, deaf to her half-brother's entreaties to "make his sister an honest woman," called in his dollar pledge and initiated annulment proceedings. The Brown, Hall, and Vanderpoel attorney laid out the case detail by sordid detail, and the motion passed without an "answer or demurrer" from the plaintiff.

Peacock timed his suit to malign perfection. Society was leveling its wrath on divorcées. A "Divorce Controversy" consumed the country, and separated or divorced women were calumniated and denounced in papers, churches, and public places as "infidels" like Mary Gove Nichols, who celebrated broken marriages in her autobiography, *Mary Lyndon*. Miriam's marital maneuver seemed to have backfired.

Familial support eroded further. About this time, her father deserted permanently to live with his mother in Alabama; Ormond vanished into Mexico; Uncle Adolphus sought $500 "to keep soul and body together"; cousin Charles begged for advances against his salary; and Noel seemed to have gone completely off the rails. After abandoning his wife and two children in Cincinnati and scrambling for a livelihood in California, he was at his wit's end. "Desolate and hopeless," he drifted to Sacramento, where a "financial crisis" overwhelmed him like an "avelanch [*sic*]."

Noel's letters suggest that Miriam and her mother had their own difficulties. "What are you all doing? How are money affairs with you?" he wrote. "Did Uncle Augustus [a prosperous great uncle] do ought for mother?" You keep a "studied silence about your husband," he persisted. She might have spared him other details as well, such as a possible recourse to "concert saloons," where "waiter girls" serviced men upstairs between musical acts.

Exacerbating her plight were mounting anarchy in the city and rumors of war. Without municipal protection, criminals took possession of lower Broadway, and gang hostilities raged. A sense of imminent disaster suffused public and private life. The build-up to civil war seemed inevitable and irreversible as violence worsened by the day.

Pro-slavery armies rioted in "Bleeding Kansas" with growing casualties, and South Carolina Congressman Preston Brooks caned antislavery advocate Senator Charles Sumner so viciously that Sumner couldn't return to work for three years. New Yorkers were at daggers drawn during an election year—the Dixiecrats, whose fortunes and sympathies were tied to the slave trade, versus the Republican abolitionists. Amid hardship on the home front and dissension and chaos in the nation at large, Miriam and her mother must have felt the bottom dropping out.

UNTIL ALL AT once, hope. Noel seemed to have turned a corner at last. He was on a "good road," he announced. He had found a protectress—none other than Lola Montez, the world-renowned stage star and manslayer. Her history beggared fiction. Born Eliza Gilbert in 1821 to a fourteen-year-old mother and British petty officer in County Sligo, Ireland, she eloped with her mother's lover at sixteen and launched a career of wholesale seduction and theatrical imposture few women have equaled.

A dramatic black-Irish beauty with long-lashed blue eyes, a "perfect form," and breasts "that made madmen everywhere," she reinvented herself as a Spanish noblewoman, Maria Dolores Montez, and danced to worldwide fame, performing a lascivious tarantella in which she chased an imaginary spider up her skirts. In the process, she burned through men. She was, wrote the press, "merciless in her man-killing propensities." She enamored kings, emperors, and leading lights such as Franz Liszt and Alexandre Dumas, Jr., and caused Ludwig I's abdication from the throne of Bavaria.

Miriam must have heard of this notorious siren/adventurer. Four years earlier, Lola had mounted a five-act spectacular, "Lola Montez in Bavaria," in Manhattan. Her risqué spider dance and dramatized feats created a sensation, grossing $1,000 a week. She was more talked about than the "race for presidency." On tour, she dashed from scandal to scandal. She slapped a prompter in Boston, smoked cigarettes on railroad cars, battered her maid in New Orleans, and bit and kicked the officer who tried to arrest her.

When Noel encountered her, she had discarded three husbands and settled temporarily in the mining town of Grass Valley, California, with a grizzly cub, assorted pets, and a coterie of male admirers. Noel was soon "under her spell." At her prompting, he changed his name to Frank Folland and became an actor. She had marked him out for "special favor," he wrote Miriam—she'd cooked a dinner for him "by herself" and conversed in five languages. Lola was to take him on a two-year barnstorming tour of Australia, China, and Europe. She was rich; he stood to gain at least $5,000. All would be well.

At the Tenth Street tenement there must have been a collective sigh of relief. Deliverance. Finally a male Follin who stepped up to the plate. They little guessed how the adventure would unfold. Lola couldn't help trailing disruption in her wake. Dumas alerted his fellow victims: "She has the evil eye, and is sure to bring bad luck to anyone who closely links his destiny with hers."

At first, Frank Folland thrived as Lola's costar in a run of light romantic comedies. Australian critics and the public loved him. Then Lola began to be Lola. She disbanded the troupe in Melbourne without payment, greeted the bailiff nude, and attacked an unfriendly journalist with a whip. Folland came to her defense and drew a pistol on the journalist. But his chivalry was losing its luster with the capricious Lola. They quarreled, he refused to go onstage at a benefit, and during one spat, Lola lunged at him with a dagger.

In the end, Lola canceled the rest of their engagements and they set sail on the *Jane A. Falkenberg* for the two-month voyage back to California. On board, the disputes continued. On July 7, 1856, the ship made an emergency stop in Honolulu, and when Lola disembarked, observers noticed her "careworn" countenance. However, that night she threw a fête for her lover's twenty-ninth birthday, with champagne and toasts that lasted well into morning. It was uncertain what transpired afterward, except that Frank Folland abruptly left the party and staggered to the "deck to clear his head."

In the summer of 1856 yellow fever ravaged New York. Seven infected vessels rode at anchor off Staten Island, and escapees filtered into the city by the dozen each night. Hearses rumbled "unceasingly" over flagstones, and the stench grew unbearable. In mid-July a record heatwave struck. Temperatures hovered in the high nineties, and on the eighteenth, the day the letter probably arrived, six people died of sunstroke.

Susan and her daughter doubtless stood at the one tenement window stirring the sultry air with newspaper-pleated fans when they opened the envelope and found the clipping from the *Pacific Commercial Advertiser*. At the first line, Susan, a "true mother" to Noel, must have reeled. Noel had drowned July 8; no one knew quite how. One theory was that a lurch of the boat pitched him overboard in his sleep; another, that he jumped to his death after a violent fight with Lola. Either way, their lifeline snapped—their hope of ready money and relief destroyed. Miriam was a streetwise survivor armed with brains, cunning, nerve, and Napoleonic drive and hubris, but forces beyond her control seemed aligned to defeat her.

She could not do piecework or housework, and street work posed fresh dangers in a world of tightened surveillance, angry johns, and disease. She was out of options, out of ideas—in a torrid tenement room that smelled of something sick in the hall, and waves of street noise welling up from below: the rattle of drays, the knife-grinder's bell, the cries of vendors "old clo, any old clo!," and a distant hot corn girl, "hot corn/all hot, just came out of the boiling pot."

CHAPTER TWO

DEMIMONDE
1856–60

WHEN LOLA MONTEZ, the notorious beauty and stage sensation, stepped off the gangplank in San Francisco on July 26, 1856, she was unrecognizable. Grief, reported the papers, had disfigured her features, "unsettled her reason," and unhinged her mind. Shattered by the death of her lover Noel Follin on the return voyage of her theatrical tour, she declared that the young actor was "the only man she ever loved" and vowed to reform.

She repudiated her past and converted to spiritualism, a widespread nineteenth-century belief in contact with the otherworld and occult guidance. The spirits instructed her to repent and recompense the Follin family. Broken and bereaved as she was, she mounted a whistle-stop tour of California, reprising her spider dance and attracting "overflowing houses." She sold her Grass Valley home, auctioned her prize jewelry collection, and in all, raised $23,000 to benefit the Follins. To no purpose; his widow in Cincinnati flatly refused the money. Lola, however, would soon find a less fastidious recipient elsewhere.

* * *

HOW SUSAN AND Miriam scraped by in the Tenth Street tenement throughout that long fall can only be imagined. It was the season of rising discord—frayed nerves, intolerance, and conflict. Opposing camps in the 1856 presidential election revealed a nation on the brink. Antislavery Republicans for John Fremont waged open war on Democratic appeaser John Buchanan (who won), and hatemongers of the Know-Nothing American Party, which carried New York, fomented attacks on Blacks, immigrants, and Catholics.

Against this fractious backdrop seethed an unquiet city. The yellow fever plague persisted into September and October; a mob of firefighters rioted unchecked by police on Duane Street; workingmen swarmed City Hall agitating for the rights of "the white man"; and angry feminists converged on the Broadway Tabernacle. At the Seventh Annual Women's Rights Convention, activists read the riot act. "Give us liberty or give us death!" harangued Mrs. Mary F. David. "Woman is, in everything, in bondage," she charged, to man-made laws that forbid education, economic independence, and equal representation, and enforce marriage—nothing less than "legalized prostitution."

Such rhetoric would have fallen on deaf ears at the Follin household. Survival was at issue and a crackdown on illegal prostitution the concern. The stakes rose daily, and the vise tightened. On October 20, six plainclothes policemen infiltrated Franklin's Museum on Grand Street and arrested five ingenues who performed tableaux vivants clothed in flesh-colored tights to a "crowded and admiring" audience. At the station house, the girls "wept bitterly" and protested that they had led virtuous lives and only modeled to gain a livelihood. One supported her parents, a husband, and a three-month-old child; two others lost jobs as a tailoress and paper-box maker. The pay at Franklin's ranged from four to eight dollars a week, depending on "the difference in good looks."

Miriam must have felt two steps from the almshouse. Winter was bearing down, and the neighborhood was on edge. The din of repaved streets on nearby Broadway thundered and clanged through

Tenth Street, accompanied by the incessant, off-key "Casta Diva" of organ grinders, peddlers' shrieks, and tenement screaming matches.

Miriam and her mother would have been at the end of their patience and resources. It was late December when the note from Lola Montez arrived, inviting them to her hotel suite. The woman who greeted them bore little resemblance to the "world-conquering siren" of popular renown; her plain dress was a drab Quaker gray and her celebrated "sorceress" eyes were dark-rimmed and unpenciled. But she hadn't lost her flair for melodrama. As soon as they entered the room, she fell on her knees and flung herself at their feet. "I have killed your son! I have killed your son!" she sobbed.

She would atone, she pleaded. She would endow them, adopt Miriam as her protégée, and train her as an actress for the stage. She was assured of the girl's promise. In Grass Valley Noel had shown her Miriam's daguerreotype, and she had been won over. "Una cara tan inteligente tan linda" (Such a pretty and intelligent face), she had said, and pronounced herself "in love with" her.

Miriam's astonishment must have been profound. Here was one of the most famous celebrities alive—comparable to a media superstar today—with a beyond-belief proposition. Neither she nor her mother hesitated, despite the low repute of women in the acting profession and Lola's dissolute past.

OVERNIGHT THEIR FORTUNES changed. Lola transported the Follins from Tenth Street to "private apartments in an elegant style" on Stuyvesant Place and began Miriam's makeover. This would be the most formative tutorial of Miriam's life and Lola, her most influential mentor and role model. The two women shared much in common: intellect, ego, vaulting ambition, theatricality, brawn, and dysfunctional backgrounds. Both were born illegitimate and grew up on the margins without money or dependable men.

For Miriam, Lola was an object lesson on how she, too, might rise in the world. Lola had beaten the odds, stormed past obstacles, manufactured a new identity as a Spanish noblewoman (among other personas), and won fame and adulation through her wits. And to a provincial New Yorker, Lola possessed a coveted continental gloss. She had navigated the throne rooms of Europe, slept with the international crème, and circulated in elect salons with such luminaries as George Sand. She could teach Miriam a lot.

Time was short. Lola had little over a month to transform Miriam. Her program was extensive—the accumulated wisdom of a lifetime, which she published a year later in *The Arts of Beauty*. With her charge, she must have started with the "secrets of a ladies' toilet": eye paint, beet-juice rouge, pearl powder to whiten skin (Miriam's most important aid), and potions for the bosom, "the greatest claim of a lovely woman." She then taught Miriam the value of "elegant" dress and accessories and revamped her wardrobe. Voice training followed, along with expressive facial skills, carriage, and "graceful and fascinating deportment."

Just as significantly, she fortified Miriam's spirit for the stage—and life. Everything, she pronounced, should be carried off with no-apologies panache. In addition, a woman must develop "the quills of a porcupine" combined with the wisdom of the serpent. Lola instructed by example; she was highly charismatic and contagious. She stepped out boldly, defied social mores, and got her way with impunity. "I am a free independent woman," she taunted, "subject to my whims and sensations alone."

Finally Lola readied Miriam for her theatrical debut. She gave her a script to prepare, a two-act melodrama, *The Cabin Boy*, and a new identity as "Minnie Montez," her sixteen-year-old (shaving off four years) sister. The work had gone well. Lola was pleased—so pleased that Pygmalion-wise she grew infatuated with her product. "I could give you a true sister's love, pure and devoted," she gushed, "for you have made me love you—you *little witch*." By now Miriam should have been wary of Lola's love.

* * *

THE "SISTERS" OPENED February 2 at the Green Theatre in Albany, a "neat little temple of drama" with a mirrored curtain that reflected the audience. The house was full. "Minnie" played the apropos part of Jenny LaRouche, a Dominican orphan of mysterious origins who is plagued by a bankrupt plantation and doomed to penury. Beneath the main action—Jenny's pursuit by a lecherous debt collector—there's a racial subplot. Jenny, it seems, is the illegitimate daughter of a planter and his slave. "This," Jenny cries (surely with a personal resonance for "Minnie"), "this is my mother's secret!" In a finale worthy of Miriam's childhood fantasies, a hero rides to the rescue, frees Jenny from slavery, and sweeps her off to married bliss.

The next stop on their theatrical tour was Providence, Rhode Island. If Providence hadn't heard of Lola, she made sure they did in one of her signature publicity stunts. The night before their departure on February 8, they were awakened by a thunder crack, followed by loud snaps and booms, fire alarms, screams, and pandemonium. In the worst flood in memory, cataracts of floodwater tore through the ice-sheeted Hudson and roared into the city, rising three feet into homes and stores and submerging the railroad tracks, the only escape route. Lola and Minnie found themselves at the heart of "the great inundation."

Undeterred, Lola paid three boatmen a hundred dollars (a month's salary for each) to cross the raging river clogged with dead cattle, wrecked homes, timber, and broken shards and columns of ice, some twenty feet high. The crew nearly lost their lives on a return trip with her trunks. As expected, the press was there to record the feat, and pictured the "indomitable Lola Montez (and her sister)" fording the treacherous waters on their way to "their next theatrical engagement" in *Frank Leslie's Illustrated Newspaper*. Lola's spirit guides should have tipped her off; the paper presaged Miriam's future.

Predictably, the Providence engagement sold out. More than two thousand spectators crowded the Forbes Theater for the first performance, and hundreds were turned away each night. Lola gave them their money's worth with her extempore tirades and her sister act. The audience and critics loved Minnie. "The younger sister," wrote a reviewer, "is quite as attractive a personality as she was represented to be, and acquits herself well on the stage for a novice." Such plaudits make Miriam's next step all the more puzzling.

William M. Churchwell was not new on the scene, and somehow seems to have turned up on the tour. Miriam's liaison with the married Tennessee congressman, bank president, and railroad baron went back several years. In 1855, illustrator Dewitt Clinton Hitchcock informed friends that Miriam was "privately kept" by a tall "gent" named Churchwell with "black mustaches" who was giving her a "general good time." He was, noted others, the "sort of man she was looking for, as he had the gold and precious stones."

Whether Miriam expected Churchwell in Providence is another matter. But his presence would not have been welcome to the redeemed Lola, who had renounced the sins of the flesh and a "life of evil." When she caught the two together and "received ocular demonstration that Miriam was not an innocent miss," she exploded. In an instant, Miriam fell from grace and lost the chance of a lifetime. She also lost a fortune. As Lola barnstormed through the Midwest, she took time to write Miriam out of her will—a sizable estate.

However, all was not lost. Miriam kept the good graces of Churchwell, who bought her a townhouse at 37 Seventh Street where she and her mother spent the spring and summer. And thanks to Lola's tutelage, she secured the title role in another melodrama and returned to the Green Theatre in Albany for the June premiere of *Plot and Passion*.

Once more she played an apt role. The heroine is Mme. de Fontanges, a young, widowed seductress with a taste for intrigue, mystery, and money. When act one opens, she has been ruined at the gaming table through her avarice. She hectors, pleads, and threatens Fouché, the villainous constable: "The money, man, the money! Or there is laudanum."

Fouché comes to terms on the condition that she become his secret agent and hunt down a certain traitor. In disguise, she pursues the felon, but she falls in love with him instead and joins him in a plot to expose Fouché, a procurer of destitute girls. Cornered at last, Fouché wheels on Madame de Fontanges: "You would have made a capital actress!"

According to the reviews, she might have. The Washington *Evening Star* hailed Minnie's "success" in Albany, and local papers praised her "fascinating personal charms [and] rare talents." Yet Miriam, for reasons never fully explained, decided otherwise.

Ephraim G. Squier, an erstwhile beau, resurfaced in New York in August after a long absence abroad. His colleagues had kept him apprised of Churchwell's advances, and Squier was a competitive man. He was also a family favorite; both Miriam's nephew and uncle worked for his Honduran Interoceanic Railway (HIR), an ambitious scheme to link Central America by rail that promised millions. Susan might well have pressed his case since finances were precarious and she was "fretting about their affairs." By early September, he was well ensconced; Churchwell had ceded the field and gone to Mexico, and Miriam had sold the townhouse for $9,000.

E. G., as he preferred to be called, seemed a sterling choice. At thirty-five, fifteen years Miriam's senior, he was already a prominent figure—an authority on indigenous peoples, author of six archeological books, and a former chargé d'affaires to Central America. His venture as a railroad entrepreneur further enhanced his résumé. "My present purpose," he announced in 1854, "is to make money." He could be charming when required and speak fluently on nearly any subject. Like Miriam, his background was impoverished and his ambition, titanic. And he cut a respectable figure with his classic Grecian profile, Prince Albert beard, and short, trim, somewhat androgynous build.

But he was not her "sort of man"—a romantic paladin and plutocrat who was "faithful and gentle and yet a very tower of strength and defense." By nature choleric and thin-skinned, he brooked no criticism and hurled "invective at those who disagreed with him." His professional ethics weren't above reproach, either. He misrepresented facts in his books, failed to give others credit for work, and engaged in slippery financial practices. Novelist Anthony Trollope, who met him in the British West Indies, drew a thinly-disguised portrait of E. G. in *The Way We Live Now* as Hamilton K. Fisker, the glib, double-dealing peddler of a phantom railroad, bedecked in "a silk waistcoat and chains." In addition, E. G. had a poor head for business, a trait unlikely to endear the fiscally astute Miriam.

E. G.'s fiancée might have had another, more troubling cause for concern. Beneath his cultivated façade lurked a Hydesque side. Although he championed—as per racist dogma—the superior sexual purity and instinctual restraint of whites over the "debauch[ed]," "brown" population, he had a known predilection for debauch himself. It was an open secret among his confreres: his love of "houses of convenience," drink, and "maidens with a hint of color." He also favored men, especially indigenous boys.

Miriam must have gathered as much if she read E. G.'s 1855 novel, *Waikna*. Artist Sam Bard, the narrator, recounts a long homoerotic idyll in the Nicaraguan outback with two Indian guides: a "perfect[ly] form[ed]" nude Poya boy and the heroic Antonio, who sleeps beside him, carries him naked on his shoulders, and leaves him weeping at the end. Possibly Miriam knew, at least partially, what she was getting into.

On September 10, 1857, E. G. notified his parents of his engagement. He told them he was now well-positioned to marry—on the cusp of "being what most men call rich." His fiancée, he wrote, was "young, not yet 21, highly educated and very beautiful. I am not aware that she has a dollar or the expectations of one." He "cordially dislike[d]" her family, "except her mother." He had known Minnie for three years, neglecting to add that she had been his on-and-off mistress or where they probably met: Castle Garden on the Battery, an entertainment center frequented by "unattended women" to flirt and "arrange trysts."

The wedding date was set for October 15 in Providence, at a safe remove from New York City gossips. By the eighteenth, though, the ceremony still hadn't taken place. Miriam lay closeted in a dark room with a "severe cold" and "inflammation of the eyes," surrounded by vinaigrettes, scent bottles, and Ayer's pills. Since Victorian women traditionally expressed unacceptable feelings, such as distress and revolt, through illness, Miriam might well have had reserves about her future husband and marriage. She'd had a close shave with matrimony before.

E. G., no friend to "Women's Rights," would have expected her to fill her prescribed marital role. And the role of a wife in 1857 was severely circumscribed. Confined to the domestic sphere and the monotony of household management, a married woman couldn't—on pain of social exile—partake in public life. Husbands ruled the roost and expected deference and respect. "She who makes her husband happy," preached high priestess Mrs. Beeton, "is of much greater character than ladies described in romances, whose whole occupation is to murder mankind with shafts from their quiver, or their eyes." Yet that had been Miriam's occupation thus far—not submission, servitude, constraint, and domestic lockdown. As she perhaps feared, it would be a difficult fit and not her last illness with E. G.

The wedding finally went off without incident on October 22. Polite society filled the pews, the Bishop of Rhode Island officiated, and Governor Henry Bowen Anthony, E. G.'s longtime drinking companion, gave Miriam away in the absence of her "unavoidably absent" father. The couple settled at 52 St. Mark's Place, a row house of Flemish brickwork with a high stoop and parlor-floor windows in a mixed-residential neighborhood. Miriam's mother conveniently kept house for them, and her uncle's wishes for "future felicity" seemed within reach.

The marriage, however, was off to a rocky start. E. G., who had fully expected to be "what most men call rich" by fall, was sideswiped by the Panic of 1857, the worst economic downturn in twenty years. Overspeculation in land and railroads, combined with a trade deficit and gold drain, toppled the stock market, destroying thousands of businesses and construction projects like E. G.'s Honduran railroad. "Financially, affairs are in the worst state possible," he complained to his family; "all public enterprises are suspended and money almost impossible to be had for any purpose." An estimated one hundred thousand people were out of work in Brooklyn and Manhattan, and a hungry mob of four to five thousand unemployed laborers invaded Miriam's old Tompkins Square neighborhood, raiding stores and bakers' wagons in what became known as the "Bread Riots." It took two days for the state militia to disperse them. Worst hit were women, whose jobs evaporated and whose options narrowed to prostitution.

Given the alternative, Miriam must have resigned herself to an increasingly "ill-natured" E. G. Freed from household cares by her mother, she returned to her studies. She hired a German tutor, a Mr. Schlumpf, and brushed up her algebra, Spanish, and French. For practice, she translated Alexandre Dumas Jr.'s play *The Demi-Monde*, a risqué comedy about Parisian courtesans, "falsely positioned women who assume to be other than what they really are, and wish to conceal their true character"—a theme she could warm to. In the play, Susan, Baroness d'Agne, the feisty, clever heroine, has slept her way via a marquis to a fortune and title, but she now seeks the respectability of marriage. An old lover who tries to thwart her plans to ensnare a nobleman gets his comeuppance. "You should not attempt to outwit a woman," she triumphs. "Even the most stupid woman of the world is a thousand times shrewder and more adroit than the most sensible man."

E. G. apparently wasn't listening. "We passed a very quiet Christmas," he assured his parents, "and altogether are getting on 'quite as old folks," an unpropitious note. Then fresh troubles struck: E. G.'s agent and close friend, George Gliddon, died of yellow fever in Panama; his half-brother Charles, sent south on a surveying mission, declared the terrain impractical for a railroad line; and the Honduran investors dried up. Miriam "complain[ed]" and grew ill.

* * *

EITHER TO APPEASE Miriam or to search for bondholders—
perhaps both—E. G. launched a European trip in the new year. They
left May 12 on the *Arabia* and were away nearly a year—not all of it
smooth sailing. Wealthy backers for his railroad failed to materialize as he had anticipated. "Money is very cheap and abundant," he
groused, "but people are very careful about parting with it." To tide
him over, he borrowed £350 from a British creditor at the Honduran
company, a loan he would later repent.

During their Grand Tour of the continent—Paris, London,
Brussels, and Switzerland—Miriam came down with one of her
mysterious maladies. Possibly she became pregnant. E. G. alerted
his father from Lucerne that she was "rather delicate 'for cause,'"
"and no accident intervening, [would] probably make [him] a grandfather before many months." If she did miscarry, she remained unwell through the fall, staying in Paris while E. G. scouted clients in
London, which did "not agree with her."

By the time they arrived home at the end of January 1859, neither was in high spirits. Miriam still "suffered a good deal," and E. G.
grew testier by the day about finances and the "abominable railroad,"
which he "longed to have it out of [his] way." The tension in the household must have been acute. Miriam, however, a veteran of Follin ill-
usage and Manhattan's mean streets, had studied self-preservation.
She took solace in pets, a cockatoo named Peter and a "quaint dog,"
and the "comfort" of clothes—women's "inherent love of dress and
self-ornamentation." In a contemporary photograph, she sits beside
the diminutive E. G. in drop earrings and a voluminous white satin
dress with a Valenciennes lace overskirt and puffed pagoda sleeves.

She also returned to her writing desk. Although perhaps not her
first choice, she helped promote E. G.'s Honduran venture by translat-
ing Arthur Morelet's *Travels in Central America* from the French—a
four-hundred-page tome replete with technical jargon, exotic fauna
and flora, arcane tribes, and convoluted topography. In another publicity effort, she edited a Spanish newspaper for Central and South
American readers, *El Noticioso de Nueva York*. The *New York Herald*

praised the paper for its "bright, business look" and "sharp lookout for the news," and predicted *El Noticioso* was on the right track. But it wasn't. Like everything seemingly under E. G.'s management, the newspaper failed. To "keep the pot boiling," he started submitting travel pieces for publication. Again, he reported, "Minnie [was] not very well."

THIS TIME MIRIAM discovered an anodyne—one she recommended to physicians: "no matter what the ailment," she advised, the patient should "try a change of air." The change, in this case, was Saratoga Springs. In August, E. G. brought her to the "Queen of Spas," an untrammeled parallel universe where guests could strike off the fetters of social convention and indulge. Starting with the ritual procession each morning for dippers of mineral water, life was dedicated to hedonism, play, leisure, and parade. Women promenaded in flashy finery, flirted, and shed inhibitions. There was nonstop entertainment—orchestra music, lawn games, picnics, carriage rides, nine-course culinary spectacles, and after-dinner "hops." On verandas, guests milled thorough the night and coquetted with strangers.

It's possible Miriam coquetted with someone there on a newspaper assignment—Frank Leslie. He certainly would have attracted Miriam's attention: a short dark-bearded man with a boxer's physique, eyes that sparkled like black mica, and a dynamic presence. He radiated exuberance, self-confidence, and derring-do—his bold "unruly talk" ringing out over the room in a British-inflected baritone. He couldn't have remembered the "Minnie Montez" of the Hudson River stunt two and a half years earlier. But she may be "the mysterious married woman leaning on the arm of her husband" in his *Illustrated* feature. "Her carriage is royal," effused the writer, "her step a queen's; her dress a splendid silk."

Frank Leslie was an exceptional catch. Already a household name, he had built a publishing company from the ground up and knew how to turn a profit. He published the lucrative *Frank Leslie's Illustrated Newspaper* and four other papers, and had grandiose plans for the future. A self-made man, he left England at twenty-seven in 1848, with only his skill as an engraver and his colossal ambition. He changed his name from Henry Carter to Frank Leslie and lucked into an alliance with P. T. Barnum, the advertising wizard and "king of humbugs," who took him across the country as his publicist on his Jenny Lind tour. When Leslie finally set up shop on his own, he put Barnum's lessons in promotion and American taste to use and published the popular *Ladies' Gazette of Fashion and Fancy Needlework*, followed by *Frank Leslie's Illustrated Newspaper*.

He blazed new journalistic territory. Nothing like this had ever been seen in America—general interest publications geared to average readers with entertaining copy "floated" on copious pictures. With his clairvoyant grasp of the market, he appealed to a newly literate mass public, eager for amusement, sensation, national news, and escapist stories. His governing principle: "Never shoot over the heads of a people."

He was also a pioneer in print technology. He introduced "overlaying," a sophisticated shading method, and invented a technique of divisible blocks so that twenty artists could work on the same engraving and produce a woodcut in a day instead of a week. His "perfecting press" printed 1,200 sheets a minute, which, combined with cheaper paper and improved transportation, decreased costs and increased distribution.

By 1859, Leslie's numbers and prospects were on the rise. Unlike most publishers, he had weathered the 1857 panic, providing graphic pictorial reports of the depression and punching up sensational content with accounts of crimes, sex scandals, and civic corruption, such as his famous "Swill Milk Campaign" that exposed New York City's polluted dairies. Circulation shot up to one hundred thousand and kept growing. Leslie already netted $500,000 a year and owned a yacht. His motto was "Excelsior"; his vision, stratospheric. He was destined to become America's first publishing tycoon, with a vast empire of magazines, newspapers, and books.

THAT FALL, THOUGH, it must have been hard for Miriam to remember Saratoga. Her father died November 18 in Mobile, Alabama, in debt and without acknowledging Miriam as his daughter. According to the death notice, Charles Follin "left no widow and but one child, a son, named Ormond." The news must have galled. She didn't attend the funeral, nor did she ever put a stone or monument over his grave in the Catholic cemetery. E. G. disappointed as well. His Honduran Interoceanic Railway project was unraveling, and his next scheme seemed equally unpromising—a plan to colonize Central America with white cotton plantation owners. Miriam, once more, became "quite ill."

In a last-ditch bid for income, Squier set his sights on Cuba. With talk of American annexation and profits to be made from the world's largest sugar producer, Havana seemed ripe for investment. In the spring of 1860 he and Miriam headed south, despite memories of their trying year abroad and the recently publicized Cuban travel advisory. In *A Trip to Cuba*, Julia Ward Howe trashed the country: the gaudy women of easy virtue, mosquitoes, stench, heat, and (strangely, for the author of "Battle Hymn of the Republic") the "chattering of Negroes," "ugly as Caliban, lazy as the laziest brutes."

By contrast, Miriam enjoyed Cuba. She even "bore the passage very well," a voyage notorious for cramped quarters and seasickness, the "green monster." Once there, she discovered a lenient, vibrant culture similar to the New Orleans of her youth, where a farrago of races mingled easily in a colorful, raucous laissez-faire society. Driving through the Plaza de Armas, she would have seen a clamorous street fair in progress. Amid throngs of soldiers, naked children, and women with baskets of oranges on their heads, hawkers cried "*te fuma?*," vendors peddled fried cakes, plantains, and onions from sidewalk braziers, derelicts shouted obscenities, and guitars twanged, accompanied by the *chick-a chick, chick-chick* of gourds.

The place to do business was Dominica's Café—the "great café of Havana." Customers left the glare of the street and entered a shadowy, smoke-filled room furnished with a tiny fountain, attended by waiters who darted in and out with chafing dishes to light cigars and take orders for coffee and iced orange *granizadas*. Women were welcome, and wove through the round and square marble tables, as Miriam undoubtedly did, in ornate gowns and "audacious bonnets." She must have winced when she heard E. G. negotiate the purchase of a cattle transport steamer. With her sharp eye on the "value of a dollar," she had to have seen that business in Cuba was "most unfavorable" and money becoming tighter.

At home, the Squiers found the city in the grip of its own financial crisis—shuttered banks, ruined merchants, and tightened belts. Forced to economize, they moved from St. Mark's Place to 205 East Tenth Street—a transitional neighborhood comprised of Greek revival row houses (some owned by old-guard holdouts), new tenements, and McLaughlin's Bear Pit on the corner. Although E. G.'s colonization project garnered $10,000 from Congress, he remained short of funds, and signed on to write about Central American affairs for *Frank Leslie's Illustrated Newspaper*.

The paper had bigger stories to handle in 1860. No presidential election year was as inflammatory. The parties split on the slavery question, and sectional hostilities escalated—all intensified by the media, Leslie's pictorial coverage included.

Manhattan was a flashpoint. The majority of New Yorkers opposed Lincoln and supported the South where it did business. New York earned forty cents of every cotton dollar, underwrote slaveholders with tens of millions in loans, and participated in the illegal slave trade to the tune of roughly $900,000 between 1859 and 1860. Poor whites believed cheap Black labor would destroy jobs. So rabid was the opposition to Lincoln that pro-Confederate Mayor Fernando Wood proposed that Manhattan secede from the union as a "free city." Otherwise, warned his camp, "we shall find negroes among us thicker than blackberries swarming everywhere." In October of 1860 thousands cheered a torchlight parade to Union Square where bands played "Dixie" and exploded rockets through the night.

Frank Leslie positioned himself as nonpartisan "without bias and without feeling," yet he continued to appease Southern readers. As for the Squiers' sympathies, with E. G.'s acknowledged racism and Miriam's slaveholding cousins and background, we can only guess. But after Lincoln's election and South Carolina's secession, all three swung over to the party in power. "We must go," said the prudent E. G., "where our business lies." His old comrade, Henry B. Anthony, had been elected a Republican senator and procured two tickets for him to the Inaugural Ball. Frank Leslie received one, too, perhaps through E. G., his editor and new friend.

"THE MOMENTOUS QUESTION of war"—the keynote of Lincoln's Inaugural Address—brooded over the March 4 celebration ball. During the election, the South had warned of military action, and with the formation of the Confederate States of America a month before, it was just a matter of time. When Lincoln entered the ballroom, a temporary hall decorated like a "white muslin palace of Aladdin," he looked noticeably "fatigued" and "distracted." Miriam was twenty-five and impervious; she had fought too hard for this night. She would take the stage; she would shine.

Lola's training bore fruit. She wore a six-flounced décolleté white illusion dress that weighed twenty-nine pounds, with puffed sleeves, a satin-quilled bodice, and a cherry overskirt looped up with white roses. Choice accessories completed the effect: an ivy chaplet, opal and diamond jewelry, and a gemmed crucifix at her throat. She went "through the whole performance," boasted E. G., "with great éclat [and] took down all the other girls present." Her past must have made that easy. Wise in the ways of seduction, she flirted with foreign diplomats, such as Señor de Figaniere and Baron Stoeckl, in Spanish and German, and danced an expert "gallop" (a Saratoga specialty) throughout the night with Union officers and swallow-tailed congressmen.

Nothing was lost on the observant Frank Leslie. His account of the evening in the *Illustrated Newspaper* included a description of "Mrs. E. G. Squier's" gown, her "personal attractions," and the droves of distinguished men drawn to her "sprightly and intellectual conversation." He pictured her front and center in a lineup of eight women on page one and pronounced her "the acknowledged belle of the ball." He took note of E. G., too—alone on the sidelines, supported by a cane.

Not coincidentally, Frank made E. G. editor of the *Illustrated* six months later. With the Confederate bombardment of Fort Sumter on April 12 and the onset of the Civil War, Leslie could argue that he needed a credentialed scholar and author to cover the hostilities. And E. G. obviously needed work—finances were tight, aggravated by the necessity to outfit his two brothers for service with uniforms and gear.

He himself was too sick to serve. Since January his health had been deteriorating, with symptoms suspiciously consistent with syphilis. Although diagnosis was in its infancy in 1861, the disease was rampant (roughly 17 percent of the male population in New York), and E. G. was a likely candidate with his record of youthful license. As early as 1849 he complained of a telltale rash, followed by temporary blindness seven years later, and then, typically, a latency period. (This might explain Miriam's 1858 "miscarriage," since spontaneous abortions can accompany syphilitic infections.) By 1861, the characteristic signs were back: spinal cord degeneration and the "awful attack[s]" which left him with atrophied legs, dependent on a cane. Frank Leslie's offer could not have come at a better time.

Or so E. G. thought. Almost as soon as he began work, Leslie left his wife and asked if he could board with the Squiers. The extra income was a consideration—twenty dollars a week. In hindsight, E. G. should have reconsidered. Once ensconced, Frank set his sights on Miriam. The choice between the two men must have been blatant: one a buff, rich "fireballer" in full courtship mode; the other a querulous invalid with "wasted legs" and dwindling resources.

Miriam, no stranger to sexual intrigue, seems to have readily succumbed to his advances. A door separated Frank's and Miriam's bedrooms, and E. G., perhaps in secret collusion (his sexual orientation, after all, was complicated) or in resignation, followed the pair everywhere. A coachman who drove them from the theater one night recalled how "Mrs. Squier" and the publisher had leaped out of the carriage and let E. G. ride home alone. The next morning, Leslie's eyes were "black" from a sleepless night.

BENEATH A FAÇADE of Victorian bourgeois respectability, the Squier household harbored an open ménage à trois. Both men escorted Miriam to Mrs. Lincoln's Grand Presidential Party on February 4, 1862, where Frank's overt attentions would have maddened a less compliant husband. He placed a woodcut of Miriam on the first page, accompanied by a fulsome tribute: Among "the nation's most beautiful and brilliant women," Miriam reigned supreme in a "pink swansdown-trimmed gown [which] well accorded with her soft and *spirituelle* beauty."

Regardless of E. G.'s reaction, Frank held the purse strings. He paid E. G.'s salary, fronted $24,000 for the purchase of a "big house" at 13 East Thirty-eighth Street (presumably with freer access to Miriam), and was reaping a journalistic bonanza through his Civil War coverage. Five months after the Battle of Bull Run, the surprise Confederate victory, circulation rose to an "exceedingly profitable" two hundred thousand. To cinch his financial hold on the Squier ménage, he put Miriam on the payroll. After the editor of the new *Frank Leslie's Lady's Magazine* died, he asked Miriam to fill her shoes and escorted her to work each day by carriage while E. G. walked or took a cab. E. G.'s health had not improved; his eyesight deteriorated (a classic mark of tertiary syphilis) and he "could read but little."

Miriam, on the other hand, thrived. She found her métier and a longed-for engagement with public life. With her business acumen and antennae for what people want, she turned the ailing magazine around. She eliminated dismal war stories and proclaimed 1863—the terrible year of Gettysburg and Chancellorsville—"the year of fashions." A crass choice, but she perceived that her readers were "harrowed by real life"—news from the front, privations, unspeakable horrors, and personal tragedies—and craved escape. They wanted to be told "what should be worn and what should not," to envision walking dresses of "Napoleon-violet piped in black taffeta," and to read about the Duchess de la Tré's satin gown trimmed in marabou feathers that produced "a beautiful effect impossible to describe." They wanted to lose themselves, however briefly, in fantasy—fashion, sentimental stories and poetry, travel adventures, historical biographies, and embroidery patterns. Profits surged. Soon Miriam was garnering $39,000 a year.

JUST AS MIRIAM hit her stride, E. G.'s luck turned. He got a job as a claims commissioner in Peru with a $5,000 stipend and insisted Miriam accompany him. Perhaps in a bid to lessen Frank Leslie's financial grip, he also demanded they economize and move to cheaper lodgings—a rental at 105 East Thirty-ninth Street. Miriam responded by becoming "very ill" and stalling for time. Eventually she agreed to meet him in Central America three months later, at the end of June. Neither "would have very pleasant memories of this trip."

After a grueling eighteen-day voyage, Miriam met E. G. in Colón, Panama, where they crossed the Isthmus and boarded the *Bogotá* for a rain-drenched journey to the "filthy," "tumble-down" port of Callao. Lima, six miles distant, offered another dismal prospect. Shrouded in a dank fog during the June to December winter season, the city was unkempt and derelict, with "low irregular" buildings constructed of poles and mud and stuccoed to resemble stone. "Under a brisk shower," Miriam observed wryly, "the whole city would melt away, leaving only a withered canebrake in a gigantic mud puddle"—an apt metaphor for the Squier marriage, which nearly dissolved in Lima. When she arrived, Miriam discovered such conditions that "she could have got a divorce" (the only grounds being adultery), and from then on, things went from bad to worse.

E. G.'s health continued to plummet. He lost use in one eye and faced total blindness, declaring that he would give up all literary labor entirely—their major source of income. "Scarcely ever free from pain," he couldn't sleep and dragged himself to the negotiating table each day to referee disputes over the price of guano and warship reclamations. Miriam contracted another of her undetermined ailments and withdrew to her sickbed in a suite of rooms at the American Legation. There she received a local doctor who doted on his "neglected" patient and very possibly slept with her. She teased him about his morning-after "pallor and heavy lids."

When she recovered, she attended official functions, dining on dishes like *puchero* (a yucca, sausage, and cabbage stew), which required "extraordinary powers of digestion." Off duty, though, she found something to admire in Lima. As she explored the paseos, she noticed a striking group of women swathed in long mantos that concealed everything except their jeweled hands, braceleted arms, and black, burning, straying eyes. Without arousing their husbands' suspicions, these camouflaged señoras arranged assignations with lovers in the public square. The Limeñas, noted Miriam, were "privileged character[s]" who never—as she could appreciate—"willingly renounce[d] their disguises." When the Commission's work ended in November, she pleaded an indisposition and set off for New York alone, leaving E. G. to explore the "land of the Incas" with his crew of boon companions.

E. G. WAS UNEASY about Miriam in Manhattan. "Poor girl," he told his parents, "I dread the effect of the winter on her enfeebled constitution." Far from unwell, Miriam flourished. She had missed New York at its worst—the spate of ugly strikes and the three-day draft riot that ignited anarchy in the city and resulted in fifty Black lynchings, one thousand deaths, and two million dollars in property damage. Instead, she came back to a city on a crest of postwar prosperity and the rewards of a challenging career and an attentive lover.

Without E. G. in the way, the affair intensified. Frank stopped financial support of his estranged wife until she divorced him and squired Miriam around as her *cavalier servente*. They frequented Delmonico's at the Grinnell Mansion (where the price of dinner could support a soldier's family for a year), attended supper parties together, and vacationed in Saratoga, Miriam's favorite resort.

At A. T. Stewart's Department Store, a five-story Venetian-style fortress, and Ball, Black & Company's "Diamond Palace," a shopping binge was in progress. And to judge by an *Illustrated* write-up, Miriam, flush with Leslie largesse, joined the spree. "Mrs. S-r, just from Peru," ran the report, "wore a dress of richest white rep silk, which hung in classic folds upon her slight and elegant form. Her hair, which fell in rippling ringlets to her waist, was confined at the back of the head with a barbe of point lace fastened with a diamond star. A parure of diamonds and opals completed [the] toilet."

Frank could indulge her whims. The Civil War, which dragged on with mounting horrors—the Battle of the Wilderness (thirty thousand casualties), the burning of Atlanta, and Sherman's scorched earth "March to the Sea"—was making him ever wealthier. By December 1864, he had published three thousand pictures of the conflict and sent sixteen artist correspondents into the field (twice as many as his competitors) and planned a profitable *Pictorial History of the Civil War*. And he had not begun to cash in on the postbellum boom.

An increasingly restive Miriam fired off a nine-page screed to E. G. in April. Why, she needled, did he prolong his "hideous" foray in Peru unless he preferred behaving like "a boy again?" She doubted "[their] future" and expected him to earn more, much more, to support their "luxurious tastes and habits." He shouldn't have passed up a partnership with "Mr. Leslie." Nor should he expect another Penelope on the home front. "If [a man] does not make love to his wife," she cautioned, "someone else will do it for him," and she left little doubt who that "someone" was. The arrangement on Thirty-ninth Street was too irregular, she told him, for his brother to visit: "Our hours of rising and slightly Bohemian mode of life [aren't suitable] for one beginning life with scanty experience."

In January 1865, fifteen months after Miriam left Lima, E. G. suddenly reappeared, $16,000 out of pocket and freighted with baggage. He brought a hundred cases of pottery, stone carvings, Incan skulls, drawings, and photographs, and a Peruvian youth named Juan, a tribute to his abiding "interest in Indian boys." His idea was to capitalize on his trip through travel essays and show-and-tell lectures, and for a while it seemed to pay off, with a series in *Harper's New Monthly Magazine* and bookings with scientific societies. Whatever his disease, it was in remission for the moment. If only he hadn't miscalculated and neglected to credit Dewitt Clinton Hitchcock for his engravings and archeologist Augustus Le Plongeon for his photographs in his Peruvian essays. He would pay for both later—and Le Plongeon's plagiarism lawsuit was the least of it.

E. G.'s renewed presence seemed to have little effect on the triangular household. Frank kept Miriam as "spoiled" as before and her "vanity" and ambition stoked. In the spring, with perfect timing, he gave her a second magazine. The war had ended and left the nation lacerated and reeling. After Lee's surrender at Appomattox on April 18, a grim reckoning followed: The death toll climbed to 1.1 million, the defeated South retaliated with the Ku Klux Klan and "black codes," and John Wilkes Booth assassinated President Lincoln at Ford's Theater on Good Friday. The country was ripe for the balm of sentiment, for the "aurora of peace," the home circle—"a real family newspaper." Miriam's *Frank Leslie's Chimney Corner*, which debuted in June, struck the perfect note—a soothing potpourri of popular science, history, serialized light fiction, biographical sketches, stories of "boys who rose to fame," and a women's column—"The Ladies Conversazione."

The column, which lasted five issues, signaled a new direction for Miriam, albeit tentative. Behind the persona of guardian of the "domestic altar," she hosted an incendiary forum of feminine resistance. In letters to "Mr. Editor" (some written herself), she aired a constellation of female grievances against the male establishment— among them, women's lack of meaningful work and maternal/marital miseries. "M.A.L." wrote that the cares of motherhood made her wish she "was lying in the graveyard opposite, with [her] baby in [her] arms"; "Viola Treadwell," that her husband abused her physically and mentally. What could she do? "Mr. Editor" responded, as if in anticipation of the future: "Who knows what pistols and threats such men might use." Remain with him, she advised, and try to make him ashamed of himself. "That is all an ill-used wife can do in the nineteenth century."

Yet Miriam was proof that was *not* all an ill-used wife could do. Using propriety as her ally, she pursued a forbidden love life and profession in the guise of the perfect lady. At work she proved equally adroit. Managing a large force of male employees—artists, engravers, reporters, editors, typesetters, foremen, accountants, and distributors—was an inconceivable challenge for a woman in 1865. Miriam's approach was an executive tour de force. She cunningly appropriated the nineteenth-century idealized model of womanhood and played on her pedestaled position, privileged "higher" nature, inborn coquetry, and right of chivalric protection to command the staff. Circulation rose to eighty thousand, and her clout and confidence with it. She was soon bringing in $72,000 a year. No small achievement considering the entrenched taboo against women in newspaper work at the time, not to mention a woman at the helm.

E. G. was faring less well. His Peruvian boy betrayed him. He apprehended Juan in the "dead of night" with a hundred dollars he had filched from E. G.'s pocket and dispatched him to China.

Then, in a gesture hard to interpret (except as another perverse collusion), he prevailed on Senator Anthony to have Leslie appointed a commissioner of the 1867 Paris Exposition, fully aware "he and Miriam [were to] accompany him." It was a favor he would live to regret. Moreover, his symptoms recurred—"extraordinary complaints" that now included "disarrangement of the bowels." Nor did his finances improve.

By contrast, Frank Leslie came out of the Civil War roaring. The year 1866 ushered in the "Flash Age," an era of wildcat industrial and urban expansion, mercenary fever, and overnight fortunes. Consumerism swept the country, particularly the consumption of news. The public appetite for pictured events and explanations of a chaotic postbellum reality exploded. Leslie was not only a representative man of the age—supersized and driven—he was in the publishing vanguard. He depicted the postwar upheavals in graphic mini-narratives that gave readers a coherent read on the changing world, complete with drama and double-page engravings. He was unrivaled in his coverage of the key stories of the day: the backlash race riots in the South; the gangster-style takeover of Tammany Hall by Boss Tweed and his minions; the brigandage of money lords like Jim Fisk; and "the Calamity of Johnstown, Pennsylvania," in which a crowded railroad bridge collapsed during President Johnson's visit, injuring 350 and killing four. Leslie was quickly becoming an industry titan. Within the next five years, he expanded his company to include fourteen magazines, three almanacs, and, anticipating the scandal sheets, a gossipy, off-color *The Days' Doings*.

IN FEBRUARY 1867 Frank and the Squiers embarked on the trip E. G. had unwittingly set in motion. "Minnie," he noted without irony, "thinks she will appreciate the old world more than before." He seems to have had no premonition and boarded the *Australian* for England in a state of apathetic resignation: The trip, he sighed, was "not of much consequence. I am too old a traveler to be much elated or depressed about anything." His apathy didn't last.

The crossing proved uncommonly rough. Water poured over the deck in floods as the ship lurched, bucked, and plunged through high seas, causing stage-four seasickness and saturating staterooms with mold and rot. In his misery, E. G. failed to appreciate a sinister figure on board—a lantern-jawed stranger with mutton chops and a "yellow-green" complexion who eyed him knowingly in the dining saloon. When they reached Queenstown, E. G. watched the stranger send a dispatch to Liverpool and thought nothing of it.

Most accounts of this transaction implicate Frank Leslie (as E. G. later did) and claim he either hired a proxy or did the deed himself. Frank's behavior at the dock in Liverpool was admittedly odd. Smiling broadly, he welcomed the police officer on deck and led him to E. G. When the constable arrested E. G. in the name of her "Majesty the Queen," Frank joked, "The Queen? Well how *is* the old girl?" E. G., it turned out, had failed to pay the £350 debt he contracted on his 1858 tour with Miriam. He was summarily sent to debtor's prison, where he spent the next two weeks behind bars in the Liverpool "British Bastille."

Leslie appeared to be "overwhelmed with remorse" at the incident, but somehow he couldn't find the money to bail E. G. out. Nor could Miriam, who produced "a roll of notes" from her bodice, apologized, and said the funds were for her Paris trip. Afterward the two departed for a London holiday.

They checked into Claridge's, a hotel not patronized by Americans who might recognize them, and dropped precautions. Frank's sister, Mrs. Mary Ann Jubber, who visited them, sniffed that their "conduct was such as one would expect between man and wife." She witnessed their shared "chamber," and watched Frank "unpack Mrs. Squier's big box" and fasten her boot, "which she placed for him to do on his chair, the heel of her boot between his two legs." By day, they attended picture exhibits, inspected the world's first underground railway with Mrs. Jubber, and bought printer's paper and a five-sovereign care package for E. G. "That will keep him quiet," declared Leslie. "Yes," replied Miriam, "that would amuse him till we go to Paris."

In his collected papers, E. G. preserved dozens of news clippings about his imprisonment and the "liabilities" connected with his "oceanic scheme." Although he portrayed his incarceration as a Gilbert-and-Sullivanesque farce in his Liverpool memoir, this proud, tetchy man must have felt mortified. He thanked Miriam with uncut sarcasm for the "box of goodies" and told her to "have a good time." Miriam riposted on Claridge's gold-embossed stock: "My darling, the hours you have spent in that horrid place [must] bear fruit; may they teach you that money is the all in all of our existence."

When the three reunited in Paris, there was a scene. Mrs. Jubber, who delivered E. G.'s bail, recorded it all. She heard "loud talking" in Mrs. Squier's bedroom, followed by Frank's stentorian threats and E. G.'s face-off with him: "If you had let me come by way of Southampton," he flared, "as I wanted to, the arrest would not have happened. I thought it would be so."

But E. G. had signed on for the expedition and couldn't back out now. Once in Paris, he contracted "a cold caught in that infernal country England," and watched Frank's ceremonial rounds and courtship of his wife from the wings. And court her he did. A profligate spender, Leslie lavished Miriam with the "love gifts" she'd always desired. The lesson couldn't be plainer: "Money [was] the all in all."

The 1867 *Exposition Universelle* was a mammoth shrine to global capitalism and Napoleon III's Second Empire, and the largest World's Fair ever staged. The fair covered 150 acres in the center of Paris and featured a gigantic elliptical hall of iron and glass that held galleries with exhibitors from forty-two countries. Booths displayed a dizzying array of products, ranging from Turkish water pipes and Japanese enamel to paintings, porcelain, and livestock. Also on exhibit were industrial innovations such as an elevator that lifted passengers eighty-two feet in two minutes and the ill-omened fifty-ton

Krupp cannon, which would batter Paris into submission three years later with its thousand-pound shells. A vast amusement park surrounded the hall. Visitors entered the grounds to find fiddlers, sword-swallowers, chocolate vendors, Arabs in burnooses, tattooed South Sea Islanders, and jostling tourists in a surreal landscape. Paths led to an underground aquarium grotto, past ornate kiosks, to a vista of full-scale models of an Egyptian temple, a fifty-foot lighthouse, a Tunisian palace, and a rustic American schoolhouse. Record crowds poured in at the rate of eleven thousand an hour.

As P. T. Barnum's pupil, Frank Leslie should have appreciated the production. But like many Americans in 1867, he had a cultural chip on his shoulder. There was the problem of an effete Old World civilization, French flamboyance, a crested nobility, and the language. It was easy to feel like a rube in Paris.

Leslie's dispatch to the *Illustrated Newspaper* struck back. "The Great Exhibition," he inveighed, was a "sordid" "Peep Show" designed to lionize worthless dukes, fleece the public, and extol the French, "the smallest and puniest people in Europe," who have given the world nothing but "feminine gimcracks, good wine, scientific fancies, and dancing-masters, to say nothing of the lofty style of literature known as yellow-covered." Paris, he concluded, was "only a Babel or rather a den of thieves."

Miriam, on the other hand, must have felt on home ground. She was fluent in French, steeped in the culture and "yellow" literature, and enamored of Parisian aristocracy, fashion, and *le style*. With a "roll of notes" in her bodice, she meant to revel in it. Since her last visit, Baron Haussmann had clear-cut through the tangled *quartiers* and opened up broad geometrical avenues that housed the new department store, Printemps, and rows of chic boutiques. With Frank in tow, she bought costly souvenirs at a Palais-Royal jewelry shop and a complete wardrobe of Maison Worth gowns, each of which started at a thousand dollars, about $17,000 today.

To climax her Parisian extravaganza, Frank escorted her to Napoleon III's party for the Russian czar, one of the most magnificent fêtes of the Second Empire. Leslie had been singled out, among the ten commissioners, for an invitation, but his antipathy to French "clap-trap show[s]" rendered him indifferent to the "distinction." E. G. had to tog him out in the required black britches, black dress coat, and silk stockings, "much against his will."

For Miriam, though, this must have been a supreme moment— her snub to Dauphine Street and entrée to titled glory. At ten P.M. she entered the Tuileries Palace on Leslie's arm in a Worth's confection of Empress blue silk and greeted the American ambassador, General Dix, who ushered them through a receiving line of notables. "All the people you have read about for years," reported the *New York Times*, "were there: the Prince of Wales, Count Bismarck, the King of Prussia, and [assorted] dignitaries."

The evening proceeded from spectacle to spectacle. Guests descended a staircase modeled on Fontainebleau and discovered "a sight that surpassed the imagination"—a garden illuminated with gas-lit festoons of colored lights, Chinese lanterns, and tinted fountains, which stretched down the Grande Avenue to a blazing starburst in the distance. Hidden orchestras serenaded partygoers who drifted in and out of the ballroom before sitting down to a "splendid supper" in an old Tuileries theater transformed into an "immense festive hall." "Only the pen which wrote *The Arabian Nights*," raved a guest, "could adequately describe the [evening]."

E. G., who had been excluded and exiled to his hotel room, could not have relished these descriptions. The next day he wrote his parents: "Paris is odious. I am sorry I ever came. I want to go home!" Instead, the unwilling Squier had to spend another month abroad with his wife, his employer, and the ever-present Mrs. Jubber. As they toured Italy, from the Florentine Pitti Palace to the Roman ruins, E. G. strode with his Murray (a guidebook) a "long way in front."

The lovers grew more heedless. At the Hotel de Malta in Genoa, Miriam and Frank shared adjoining rooms and shopped alone for velvet and filigree work "the whole day." In Rome they nearly missed the omnibus, sauntering down "the middle of the street" and laughing that they'd kept them waiting. "Here they are," E. G. sneered, "she is always after him." Miriam appeared unfazed. When Mrs. Jubber asked her about "home in New York," Miriam replied blithely that "she should be the second Mrs. Leslie when he got a divorce." Pity, she said, "nothing could be found against the first wife." Mrs. Jubber thought she was joking.

Divorce was no laughing matter in 1867. The subject was unmentionable in polite society—a disgrace to the family, a "scandal and severe humiliation" for women, as Miriam herself decreed. Even if the wife wasn't guilty, she became a social outcast and "fallen woman." For someone so attached to rank and reputation, Miriam's remark seems puzzling. The practical difficulties alone, especially the disposal of E. G., were formidable. Mrs. Jubber, though, was wrong not to have taken her seriously. Miriam had weighed her chances and placed her bets. She was tenacious and shrewd and learning to bend the world to her will by fair means or foul. Many would say foul in the next four years.

CHAPTER THREE

"DOMESTIC TREACHERY"
1867–68

ON A GRAY October afternoon in 1867, the *Saint Laurent* nosed
into the Hudson River from Le Havre. Miriam Squier would have
been on deck watching the approach to the city—the sloops, tug-
boats, clipper ships, and schooners darting like water striders
against the low, jagged skyline. She doubtless wore a dernier cri
traveling costume, Worth's "Tallien Redingote," a long fitted coat
of brown and gold *drap d'or* over a trained underskirt tied behind
with a satin sash. In the hold, her trunks bulged with spoils from
their eight-month European tour—Exposition souvenirs, paintings,
Genoa velvets, clothes, and jewels.

At the ship's rail, she could see hoisting tackle lower her
heaped luggage in a rope net to the crowded dock below. Miriam
and Frank, followed by E. G., descended into the maelstrom. Arriving passengers fought through a swarm of baggage porters amid a
din of shouts, curses, whip cracks, rattling winches, and screaming
boat whistles. Harbor thieves, who lived beneath piers in flatboats,
zig-zagged through the crush hawking fenced goods. The stench
was overpowering—a compound of bilge, tar, animal rot from offal
barges, and the reek of the Manhattan Coal Works.

With their baggage claimed and counted, the three flagged a hack passenger wagon fitted with thoroughbrace shock absorbers. The pitch and heave, though, up Fulton Street was jaw-jolting, and at Washington Market the wagon shuddered to a stop. The busy market square, filled with rickety stalls half-covered by collapsing roofs, was a bottleneck of wagons heaped with vegetables, fruit baskets, and crates of honking geese and clucking chickens. Flies swarmed. Rats the size of squirrels scuttled on the wet cobblestones. At a cellar door, old women smoked pipes beside tinware for sale; a knot of workmen pored over the *Police Gazette* at a newspaper stand; a constable chased a barefoot boy with a stolen pocket watch across the road. It wouldn't have been unusual to wait over thirty minutes for the path to clear.

From there, the passenger wagon lumbered through the poor wards, past tenements above oyster cribs where shutters dangled from windows, past pig sheds surrounded by pools of swill and garbage dumps overrun with women and children scavenging bones, coal, rags, and old metal. Further on toward Broadway, the scene changed dramatically. "Wealth and poverty," observed a Boston tourist, "jostled cheek by jowl" in Manhattan.

Around the corner from the squalid third and sixth precincts stretched a golden corridor. In Miriam's absence, the postbellum boom had accelerated. Behind the old City Hall gaped the massive foundations for a grander, larger building now crawling with workers. As the wagon trudged uptown, a stream of white-columned edifices filed past: high-end art galleries, fur and leather emporiums, and the six-story "Diamond Palace of Broadway," Ball, Black & Company jewelers, with its Carrara staircases, bronze chandeliers, and $50,000 diamond parures displayed in nine-by-fifteen-foot windows.

After the "established repose" of the high-stooped Washington Square brownstones, another luxe commercial district reared up: the colossal A. T. Stewart's department store, with a line of carriages in front, and Delmonico's at Union Square, Miriam's favorite

restaurant, where magnates and dealmakers dined on Lobster New-
burg, baked Alaska, and champagne cocktails. Soon the massive
Fifth Avenue Hotel loomed on Twenty-third Street, the resort of millionaires, next door to Leonard Jerome's balustraded mansion with
its private theater and breakfast room that seated seventy.

Just to the northeast rose the residential neighborhood of Murray Hill. The Squier house at 135 East Thirty-ninth Street no longer stands, but it likely resembled the others in the upper-middle
class Churchill development—a twelve-foot façade with two bays, a
mansard roof, and twelve rooms. Home, though, must have brought
Miriam an unwelcome shock. Her mother greeted her at the door
a changed woman. Ashen and withered, she held the knob for support and emitted a sour, feculent scent beneath her cologne. Later
she would tell Miriam about the discharges, and Frank would procure the leading specialist in women's diseases, Dr. A. K. Gardner,
a medical writer for his *Illustrated Newspaper.*

In other ways, too, it wasn't the homecoming they envisioned.
Frank had stopped his wife's support and charged her this time with
adultery—an ill-considered move. And E. G. returned to bankruptcy
and mounting debt and depression. None of them bargained for the
reentry into the business scrum. While they were gone, the postwar
greed grab had become a cutthroat commercial corrida and carnival
of corruption.

Everyone's hands were dirty in the race for riches. The conta-
gion bred at the top spread downward through every order of society.
Cornelius Vanderbilt, the richest man in America, had built a fortune through ruthless railroad takeovers and stock manipulations
and bragged, "What do I care about the law. 'Haint I got the power?"
Financial lords, like "Mephistopheles" Jay Gould and his partner
"Diamond Jim" Fisk, picked the bones of investors, using bribery,
fraud, armed vigilantes, and watered stock to rack up millions. When
they pulled off an Erie Railroad heist with $8 million in fake shares,
they escaped prosecution through a deal with "Boss" Tweed and his
infamous Tammany Ring.

Corruption saturated politics like everything else. William M. "Boss" Tweed, a fireplug of a man—all brawn, big belly, deep-set crafty eyes, and a diamond stickpin—looked and acted like a stage gangster. For over a decade he and his cronies controlled the city through extortion and purchased votes, pocketing millions in kickbacks, overcharges, and larceny. Elected state senator in 1867, he was at the height of his power. His tentacled grip reached everywhere, from Manhattan real estate to the Tenth National Bank, the Erie Railroad, the courts, and the newspapers. He bought the silence of the press with bribes and leaned on editors in exchange for patronage. The extent was unprecedented: "Never in American history had so many publishers and editors sold out to a corrupt administration."

It's hard to gauge Leslie's complicity, apart from his pro-Tweed editorial stance, but corruption was in the cultural drinking water and competition in publishing had grown vicious. When Frank returned to his office in November 1867, he encountered twenty weeklies that used innovative equipment (like the new Bullock press that produced sixty thousand sheets an hour, and cost less than his Hoe) and piratical tactics. It was no time for scruples, to be on the wrong side of an omnipotent city "Boss."

Leslie rose to the challenge. He redoubled output, upgraded infrastructure, increased staff, launched more publications, and tweaked content. He played to the growing taste for entertainment, vicarious adventure, and visuals. With seventy engravers in operation, he splashed illustrations across every story. If readers craved more sensationalism, he would fill their eyeballs with it. For graphic horror, no one matched his sketches of charred corpses and mass hysteria after the "Angola Horror," a derailment near Buffalo on December 18 that plunged a train into a forty-foot gulch, killing forty-nine passengers.

He courted the widest possible audience—women, families, children, German and Spanish readers, churchgoers, social aspirants, and men of base appetites. In a move he would later repent, he defied American prudery and published a male-only risqué paper, *The Last Sensation*, later *The Days' Doings*, which specialized in executions, police reports, violent sports, and off-color tales of strumpets and illicit sex, such as "The Black Bell Boy and the Fair Belle." Mark Twain contributed four articles, among them "An Awful Terrible Medieval Romance," and hoped to become an editor.

A cartoon at the time depicts the frenzied effort to keep all these wheels spinning. Pictured is a hive of editors, artists, and managers at 537 Pearl Street hustling papers to press on a Saturday afternoon. A caricaturist dangles by one hand from the bookcase; the literary editor, John Shea, slams his head on a proof sheet; an editor contemplates an indecipherable hieroglyph, while forty Leslie employees buzz around them.

A new face in the crowd is the ad agent—in the foreground wearing a top hat, frock coat, and shiny knee-high boots. He was the forerunner of the new age of advertising. Every surface in the city— fences, lampposts, house fronts—was blazoned with promotions for shows, corsets, tonics, shipping lines, cigars, hotels, and hot-off-the-press newspapers and magazines. Publishers increasingly depended on advertisements to sell copies and income-generating space to boost profits. J. Walter Thompson was about to become the kingpin of the business, bundling ads, "classifying" them, and offering "full service," including content.

As P. T. Barnum's pupil, Leslie was a veteran publicist. Besides packing the back pages with ads, he drummed up a team of sales agents nationwide, introduced clubs with gift incentives for bulk orders, and out-hyped the competition. He plastered his name in papers and on billboards, ballyhooed his unsurpassed journalism, and even, celebrity style, endorsed Burnett's Cocoaine Hair Cream.

All the while, he pragmatically appeased his base with a please-'em-all editorial policy. He took the safe middle ground and echoed the status quo on the issues of the day, such as poverty, race, women, and the widening wealth gap. Only *Harper's* beat him in circulation. The *Brooklyn Daily Eagle* claimed he now earned a salary of $91,000 a year; his comeback seemed to be working.

Miriam came up against the same pressures and steep competition on the women's magazine front. As if she didn't have enough to contend with—her ill mother, bankrupt husband, and volatile lover—her rivals were gaining on her. Suddenly in the lead were *Godey's Lady's Book* and *Mme. Demorest's Illustrated Monthly*, and the new fashion weekly, *Harper's Bazar*, edited by the brilliant Mary Louise Booth. Mme. Demorest, regarded as the "reigning monarch of New York fashion," operated a factory on Fourteenth Street to manufacture patterns from her *Monthly*, which she distributed via catalogues and a fleet of agents throughout the country. The family-centered *Chimney Corner* demanded attention, too. The months away had set her back; she needed to work fast. The February 1868 issue of her *Frank Leslie's Lady's Magazine* promised "new features," but no significant changes occurred until after the first half of the year.

Her mother was probably the reason. Throughout the winter and spring Susan Follin declined rapidly. Dr. Gardner diagnosed vaginal cancer, a rare malignancy that can cause chronic fecal discharge and excruciating pain in the pelvis and back. It also carried a stigma in Victorian America, signaling either postmenopausal "excitement" (i.e. lust), as Gardner believed, and/or a history of multiple sexual partners. Given Susan's rumored career as a "light woman" and brothel keeper, the charge might well have stuck, and her presence in an already compromised household become inconvenient. Not to mention the sickroom distress: the constant odor of excreta and laudanum, the night watches, and incessant suffering.

Captain Molyneux Bell materialized at this impasse—who knows how. A shawl merchant on Canal Street with a fake military moniker, he possibly cultivated Frank Leslie for promotional purposes. Maybe there was a quid pro quo arrangement, but he tended Susan during her final illness at his home in Carmansville—a village along the Hudson River in what is now the Hamilton Heights neighborhood. The summer of 1868 was the hottest in forty years, and the village, among other advantages, offered a cool refuge above the river near the High Bridge Reservoir. Susan Follin died there on July 25, 1868.

Whether Miriam was at her bedside is another unknown. If not, she boarded the Hudson River Railroad the next day in the stifling heat with E. G. and Frank, disembarked at 152nd Street, and attended a private service at the Captain's residence six blocks south. Why Susan never received a proper funeral, and why she chose to be buried beside a friend, Eliza Hall, instead of her husband, deepens the mystery further. Both Frank and her son-in-law were devoted to her, and later moved her remains to the Leslie/Squier plot in Woodlawn Cemetery.

Her mother's loss must have been a staggering blow. Susan had been Miriam's faithful counselor, friend, champion, and domestic support system. The timing, too, was terrible. That July Frank's legal maneuver against his wife misfired. Newspapers headlined the case from coast to coast. During the drawn-out courtroom drama, Sarah Ann Leslie fed gossipmongers a daily dose of marital horror stories. Frank, she charged, had sold her furniture and dresses and abandoned her and their three children with insufficient funds when he left England in 1848. Later in America, the ill-treatment worsened: he neglected her, reduced support from twenty dollars to twelve dollars to zero, and palmed her off on another man while he had affairs with thirty different women. She possessed proof, she warned, of his infidelity that instant (surely unwelcome news to Miriam).

To make matters worse, Frank had no defense. Under cross-examination, his answers crumbled like dry rot. He returned the dresses, he demurred, and couldn't pay support because his wife neglected him, blackened his character, and committed adultery. Judge Brady ruled against him. Leslie was ordered to pay fifty dollars a week in alimony and legal fees—a sentence he was going to ignore.

None of this sat well with the press. "I am afraid," wrote the *Philadelphia Evening Telegraph*, "his reputation is just a little spoiled [and] once spoiled is like an ironed ribbon, never the same again." Miriam could not have been reassured by these revelations about her intended, nor the concurrent report that Frank Leslie was spotted in Richfield Springs with "Mrs. Gilbert and a pair of fast horses." Harriet Beecher Stowe, she must have heard with alarm, was preparing a book about broken marriages from the wives' standpoint that was to include the Leslie rift.

Frank's finances should have raised a warning flag, too. Even in an age of excess, his spending was reckless. He launched yet another magazine, *The New World* (which failed), threw a wedding blowout for his son in Saratoga, and filed an expensive libel suit against *The Boston Post*. Unpaid city income taxes pended, along with a $50,000 price tag for an indecent picture of "Miss Ellwood on the Skating Rink."

Closer to Miriam's pocketbook, E. G. seemed in a tailspin. Although he cadged a small income from his editorial job, his debts and fantasies of a fortune continued to mount. When the American transcontinental railroad was completed in early 1869 and demolished his Honduran project, he refused to admit it. The ten-day train trip across the country, he declared, was "beyond the limits of human endurance" and posed no threat to the superior HIR route. He expected a windfall any day.

That was the least of his delusions. Despite his dimmed prospects and financial embarrassments, he envisioned a lucrative governmental post and wrote an open letter to President Grant recommending himself as consul to Cuba. His insider friend in Washington, Admiral David Dixon Porter, got a big kick out of that one. For starters, he chided, you need to fork over a thousand dollars; and don't complain, "you old sinner, you'd do the same thing if you were president."

E. G. settled instead for chargé d'affaires to Honduras, an honorific title unrecognized in America. His precarious mental footing appeared to be slipping. After his brother's accidental death on the Erie Railroad in November (a job he'd procured for him), E. G.'s health and handwriting deteriorated, and his letters spoke of imminent collapse and doom. His behavior grew erratic. He started staying out all night, playing poker, "running after other people's wives," and taking to drink.

MIRIAM, ACCORDING TO E. G., bore up nobly. "The changes in the house," he wrote, "have kept Minnie so occupied that she has not dwelt so much on her mother's death as I feared. No woman ever worked harder than she does, but it took her mother to manage the details of the household." He didn't underestimate the hardship. Ninety-five percent of working American women also took full responsibility for the home throughout the nineteenth century, most without protest. Miriam, though the avatar of domestic industry in her magazines, loathed housework. For practical purposes, she published *Mrs. Beeton's Book of Household Management* and endless recipes for polishes, bleaches, and stews, but she detested the drudgery of "domestic cares," and thought a woman justified in marrying for money to escape it. Maybe memories of her mother's tireless servitude were still fresh.

The unglamorous labor of maintaining the Thirty-ninth Street townhouse must have been torture. There was a merciless round of toil: daily food purchases and preparation, account books, and soul-numbing minutiae—laundry to sort, wicks to trim, ashes to dump, and cockroaches to poison with chloride of lime and sweetened water. Whether to E. G.'s liking or not, Miriam hung up her apron and looked after herself instead of the house. She hired a housekeeper, Miss McKinley, to handle domestic responsibilities; acquired a support dog, Follette (a little Follin?); and returned to her office on Pearl Street.

Some would say she exchanged one grind for another. To run two monthlies demanded heroic stamina and managerial industry and vision. She had to give each magazine a distinct identity, capture a strong demographic, attract top contributors, vet submissions, monitor staff, balance books, meet deadlines, and handle the nuts and bolts—copyedits and paper purchases. For a nineteenth-century businesswoman, she logged long hours—nine to four, without a lunch break.

But she displayed a knack for the work. She enriched the *Chimney Corner* with stronger visuals and "suitable nourishment" for the family circle, boosting circulation to a yearly eighty-five thousand, higher than Frank's *Illustrated Newspaper*.

Her best effort, though, went into the *Lady's Magazine*, her fashion publication where the competition was fierce. She brightened the layout with colored foldouts of animated models to eclipse customary stiff pastel engravings and added "extensive patterns" to undercut Mme. Demorest's monopoly. Then she glommed on to her target audience—the postbellum professional classes and new rich who strove for respectability and sought to dress the part and "pass."

The *Lady's Magazine* gentrified accordingly. Issues contained biographies of aristocratic notables, cultural snippets, effete poetry, and romantic stories steeped in titled heroes, noble deeds, and edifying sentiments. Miriam engaged popular society writer, Etta W. Pierce, who supplied silk-stocking historical fiction, such as *A Mad Passion*, featuring *ancien régime* belles and chivalric beaux.

In the fashion department, she usurped the role of arbiter. Dethroning Mme. Demorest, she claimed ultimate authority in the style world. Like the future Anna Wintour, she positioned herself as taste maven and icon and paraded couture creations at public events, often donated by the designers she promoted. She made it clear she had access, as no other editor, to the inner sanctums of elite couturiers and knew what a lady should and should not wear. Faux pas abounded. A novice could slip up in a host of ways: wear, for example, a "ridiculous" balloon crinoline or "long, draggling" skirts, and render herself "utterly absurd." Miriam walked the uninitiated through this sartorial thicket. An evangelist of postbellum consumerism, she impressed on readers the importance of purchasing, "in these days of often-shifting fashions," "a certain number of toilets, fresh and fashionable, as elegant as their means will permit."

A society lady required dozens of ensembles per season, with at least four costume changes a day. This, exclusive of underwear: a lace-trimmed chemise, steel-ribbed corset, a "breast heaver" or "enhancer," a bustle crinolette, and up to five petticoats. Miriam recommended a cashmere *robe de chambre* for morning; a satin-fluted walking dress for shopping; an embroidered visiting toilet for afternoon calls; and a décolleté gown with a *gaze-de soie* overskirt and long train for evenings.

Deviant though she was—a domestic turncoat and tough professional in a man's world—Miriam reminded her female audience of their proper role in refined society. Columns advised women on how to decorate walls, content husbands, nurse the sick, and dry flowers, while poems celebrated mothers and the ideal woman: "small, frail of figure, young; and like a child" with a "rosebud mouth [and] sayings not too wise."

If she were so inclined, a reader could find a discordant note in the fine print. Secreted in squibs and the back pages was a substratum of female irreverence—a cartoon panel, "woman of the future," for example, that pictured a triumphant lawyer, baseball player, and postman, and the definition of a bachelor as "a man who has lost the opportunity of making a woman miserable." For now, though, this was still a trace element, covert and muted.

Miriam's response to the feminist initiative was equally muted. About the "Woman Question," the burning issue of the day, she was silent—ironic in view of her later place in the movement. And in 1869 female activists were hard to ignore. Susan B. Anthony, Elizabeth Cady Stanton, Lucy Stone, and others founded two suffrage associations and were harrying the patriarchy and sowing discord.

Most conspicuous of the lot was spitfire Victoria Woodhull. Under different circumstances, Miriam might have found a kindred spirit; both shared drive, mettle, dramatic flair, and a seamy past, which included prostitution. A full-figured beauty with the features of Pallas Athena, Victoria had seduced Cornelius Vanderbilt, and under his aegis, made a fortune and opened a brokerage house with her sister. She then took up women's rights and made a stir at the first Woman's National Suffrage Convention in 1869, as the "coming woman." Her platform raised the roof; she demanded nothing less than full female emancipation—the vote, domestic liberation, equal job opportunity, federal support services, and sexual fulfillment.

None of Miriam's peers in women's publishing went so far as recognizing Victoria Woodhull, but many sympathized with the crusade. Mary Louise Booth published "noble and dignified portraits" of four suffrage leaders in the June 1869 issue of *Harper's Bazar*, and *Demorest's* editor, Jane Cunningham Croly, launched the Sorosis club to empower and further women of accomplishment. Thirty-eight writers, six editors, twelve poets, two doctors, and four professionals joined, but not Miriam.

She chose the oblique, clandestine route. She knew too well the fate of women without money, and Frank Leslie was her meal ticket. He bankrolled her, kept her in diamonds and furs, and promised to be husband number three. (Booth and Croly both had the luxury of supportive partners.) Leslie's position on the "woman question" was adamantine. A patriarchal diehard, he portrayed women in the *Illustrated* as either idealized or dangerous "types" and lambasted feminist agitators. He despised Sorosis with its "shrill objurgations and symposiums" and reviled Victoria Woodhull. The "modern Amazon," he fumed, was "repugnant to the true representative woman who fills with dignity the position which Providence, as well as custom, assigned to her."

It was in the disguise of the "true representative woman" that Miriam plotted her path to the corridors of power. Frontal assaults weren't working; Elizabeth Cady Stanton's weekly newspaper, *Revolution*, folded, along with her suffrage campaign, and Victoria Woodhull's meteoric career imploded. Followers defected when she championed free love, defended the underclass, and ran for president, forcing her to flee, penniless, to England.

Better, in Miriam's view, to "hasten slowly," conceal the "iron hand" in a "velvet glove," and sidle rather than lean in. No one would guess the perfect "lady" dressed in fashionable splendor was an adroit business executive with a furious appetite for wealth and power. At the end of 1869, her appetite grew. Circulation for the *Lady's Magazine* that year reached a respectable fifty thousand, but the numbers still lagged behind the competition. Miriam wanted a winning edge. Her status-conscious audience was growing more adventurous, seeking inspiration abroad. A record number of afflu-ent Americans steamed to Europe at the turn of the decade in quest of old-world polish and sophistication.

FROM EVERY STANDPOINT, 1870 seemed a good year for a second tour of the continent. Miriam likely sought a fresh take for her magazine and another extramarital holiday; E.G., a Honduran bailout; and Leslie, an escape from an alimony injunction, which he had appealed unsuccessfully.

The voyage began well. They sailed on the RMS *Scotia*, Cunard's showpiece liner, a luxurious paddle steamer that held the record for size and speed and offered only first class accommodations. Instead of languishing below in the "ladies' cabin," Miriam promenaded up and down the deck and "got on famously," reported E. G. He did not say with whom. Accompanying them on this trip was a chap-erone, Mrs. Abbie Wheelock, probably to deflect adultery rumors. E. G. called her a "cricket," as in "merry" or "talkative," but Miriam could hardly have found her a happy addition. A garrulous watchdog was the last thing she needed; Frank's sister, Mrs. Jubber, had been tedious enough before.

But like a debt collector, Mrs. Jubber was back again. As soon as they arrived in Oxford, she appeared at the Mitre Hotel, on hand to record the damning details. Mrs. Squier, she complained, never left her brother alone: She hovered in a cab while he visited his aunt, dismissed Mrs. Wheelock, and spent the day with him in her bed-room. Twice Mrs. Jubber entered the room only to find "Mr. Leslie at the foot of her bed" (fast work on his part) holding a book. At dinner, snarked Mrs. Jubber, Mrs. Squier sat beside her brother each night in such a way that everyone took notice. He had the effrontery to ask her for money to buy Miriam "expensive presents," even before the London binge.

In London they stayed at the Langham "Grand Hotel," the largest, most exclusive hotel in England, with hydraulic lifts, piped water, and a forty-by-one-hundred-foot columned coffee-room overlooking a formal courtyard. A favorite of the royal family and celebrities like Charles Dickens, the Langham hosted afternoon tea, a tradition they inaugurated, and haute cuisine dinners. Mrs. Jubber stalked them there, too. She watched Frank laden with packages for Miriam's approval, which they opened, inspected, and purchased from a fleet of tradesmen. Among these gifts, said Jubber, were diamond and emerald rings valued at £120, and £450 diamond earrings. (A Langham suite cost £21 a night.)

Once, she testified, Mrs. Squier and her brother traveled alone together to see the Selby-Lowndes estate in Buckinghamshire, excluding herself, Mrs. Wheelock, and E. G. She distinctly heard E. G. say, "I should have been very glad to have come, but I was not wanted."

E. G.'s state of affairs in London is difficult to determine. Either he was delusional (a possibility given future developments), or he did, in fact, find investors. Soon after he settled at the Langham, he wrote his surviving brother, Frank: "Honduras [is] an undoubted success," and a few weeks later, "All the money requisite is raised and I shall make enough I hope to make me reasonably comfortable for life." The money, if true, was floated on false promises. He had sold British investors on the illusion that the railroad was a surefire success. The Honduran Interoceanic Railroad, however, was defunct—debt-riddled, with a mere fifty-seven miles of track completed, and destined to soon fall into ruin.

It could have been E. G.'s machinations, the presence of Mrs. Wheelock and Mrs. Jubber, or friction with Frank, but London began to wear on Miriam. She fatigued easily, missed her dog Follette, and was "anxious to see Paris."

Paris, however, was not the same city of light and carnival she remembered from the 1867 Exposition. Visitors felt the tension at once—the sense of impending crisis beneath the fevered gaiety. Prosper Merimée compared that summer to "Mozart's music when the Commendatore is about to appear." Napoleon III, the cynosure of imperial grandeur, was losing his grip and *gloire*. Weakened by chronic pain from an enlarged bladder stone, he had suffered a barrage of international and domestic reverses.

One foreign policy debacle followed another. He surrended the French claim to Mexico, then engaged in an ill-conceived clash with Germany. In a case of chauvinistic hubris, he forbade the Prince of Hohenzollern's candidacy for the Spanish throne and threatened military action. Sabers rattled. At the same time, the long-oppressed Parisian poor rebelled. After an outbreak of riots, strikes, and street protests, Louis Napoleon's hand was forced. He held a plebiscite, which displaced the Bonapartist majority, and declared a "Liberal Republic." But the people weren't appeased so easily.

None of this was immediately apparent at Le Grand Hôtel. This palatial establishment on the Boulevard des Capucines was the apotheosis of Second Empire splendor. Within its gilded corridors and receptions rooms drenched in mirrors, statues, hangings, and tiered chandeliers, Empress Eugenie said she felt "at home." "I could well imagine myself at Compègne [her immense country chateau]," she effused, "or at Fontainebleau."

The entrance seemed designed for a royal procession—a courtyard eighty-two feet long, with three wide gateways surmounted by a four-story glass-and-steel dome. From the travelers' suite, fitted with such luxuries as electric bells and hydrotherapic baths, it was hard to envision a city on the verge of calamity.

Leslie and the Squiers did their best to look the other way. They attended the Grand Prix de Paris at Longchamp Racetrack and sent victory pictures of the "weighing station" to the *Illustrated*. They made the Parisian rounds: the Café Anglais, with Chef Dugléré's larks with cherries; the Bois de Boulogne, where demimondaines like Cora Pearl, her dog dyed blue to match her dress, bowled past; and the boutiques. Miriam replenished her wardrobe at Worth's and Madame Morrison's Millinery and recorded the latest Parisian fad for slim silhouettes and small hats perched on high coiffeurs with "kissing strings" behind.

They surely attended Jacques Offenbach's popular *La Grande-Duchesse de Gérolstein* at the Théâtre des Variétés. In this comic operetta, a spoiled, tyrannical duchess incites a war with Germany for her amusement. During a series of farcical battles (won by inebriating the enemy), the duchess falls in love with two officers, fails to win either. At the finale, she has to settle for her dull, discarded fiancé and recites with pre-Summer-of-Love insouciance: "If you can't have those you love, you must try to love those you can have."

Distracted by the merriment, Parisians forgot Count Bismarck's response to the performance. From his box, he chuckled menacingly, "That's exactly how it is!" If Miriam stopped by the Café de la Paix afterward with the après-theater crowd, she would have heard voices that took Bismarck seriously. Perhaps at the next table, habitués Émile Zola, Édouard Manet, and Guy de Maupassant were sounding off, like the rest of the intelligentsia, about France's unpreparedness and Prussia's burgeoning military ambition.

The brooding atmosphere in Paris, in combination with the fraught ménage, must have finally proved insupportable. Miriam's health foundered, and E. G. feared she was "in a bad way." He was "much concerned about her."

A return to London and the Langham hotel brought no improvement. When E. G. and Frank attended the American Embassy's Fourth of July celebration, a state gala Miriam would have loved, she was conspicuously absent. Tension in the three-cornered household (four if you count Mrs. Wheelock) was escalating. Frank made random side trips to Paris and Cologne and was on poor terms with E. G., who had difficulties of his own.

As the guest of honor at a dinner given by Honduran minister Don Carlos Gutierrez, E. G. plugged his phantom railroad, deriding competing projects and decreeing his interoceanic line "an accomplished fact." No one appeared convinced. By June 28, the US Congress pronounced the effort "hopeless" and ordered an exploratory fleet to "try again." Frank was treating him without consideration, too. E. G. felt abused: "Coming to Europe," he whinged, "is anything but a pleasure when Mr. Leslie is about. He works here [i.e., slave-driving E. G.] four times harder."

Attempts to restore Miriam proved futile as well. Neither a trip to Boulogne nor a second Yorkshire terrier, a "husband" for Follette, helped. By the twenty-first of July she was too sick to write a letter or sit up in bed. She "detest[s] England," E. G. wrote, and, as per current medical advice, took her to Spa, Belgium, for the waters and a change of scene—presumably on his British investors' funds. After two weeks of peat baths, *Enragée* water (a bitter sulfuric potion), and therapeutic walks, she recovered sufficiently to insist on another excursion to Paris. She must not have heard the news.

On July 18, Emperor Napoleon III declared war on Prussia to a chorus of ecstatic *"marchons, marchons"* throughout Paris. In little over a month, France repented. His cheeks rouged to hide his pallor, an ill Louis Napoleon rode out and surrendered to the German high command after an avalanche of defeats that culminated in a double pincer assault at Sedan. "We're in a chamber pot," cried French general Ducrot, "and they'll shit on us."

The shitstorm wasn't over. After Louis Napoleon's exile and the collapse of the Second Empire, the newly constituted Republican government believed the hostilities had ceased. Instead, the Prussian army steadily advanced toward the capital and an unsuspecting populace danced in the streets, celebrating the emperor's downfall.

While Miriam recovered at the Spa springs and strolled the Ardennes Valley, German Uhlan cavalry stormed Versailles and encircled Paris with a "ring of iron." The siege began. Soldiers and

volunteers threw up breastworks, and terrified citizens hoarded provisions and sought escape routes.

Yet "despite the threat of [attack] and lack of safety," wrote E. G.,
"Minnie" persisted in her Paris entreaties. They compromised on
Brussels, a center for Parisian refugees, especially couturiers, where
Frank joined them. Once more, he bought out the store for Miriam,
yards of fancy lace, a fur jacket, and muff bag mounted with ormolu.
In spite of the splurge, she relapsed so seriously E. G. had "no hopes
of getting her across the Atlantic."

THE YEAR AHEAD was off to a bad start. E. G.'s income from
British backers evaporated, and he began stashing Peruvian relics
with his brother, warning him to "say nothing" about his affairs. His
friend Admiral Porter remarked that he seemed to have "gotten into
the hands of *ladrones* [highway robbers]." Frank, meanwhile, came
home to both a libel suit and a summons to pay $8,000 in back
alimony or face jail time.

With her health still fragile and her two providers in jeopardy,
Miriam might well have collapsed under the strain. But she prepared
a soft landing and instructed Miss McKinley to hire a cook and make
the house "as comfortable as she knows how." Then she mobilized
and dusted off and republished her French translation of Morelet's
Travels in Central America. Critics applauded her "pleasant, clear,
crisp style," and Frank seemed sufficiently encouraged to boost her
responsibilities. Miriam's friend Jane G. Austin recalled the scene:
Leslie paced up and down in his "handsome library" and in a flash,
"saw" a new publication for Miriam, sketching out its look, scope,
and purpose with "earnest gravity."

The idea behind *Once a Week: The Young Lady's Own Journal*
was a magazine that would cut into the top-grossing weekly *Harper's
Bazar*. Miriam targeted a similar audience, the female-dominated
parlor circle, and promised "fastidious taste" in fashion and reading matter. She invited reader participation through an amateur

contribution column and futuristically offered a purchasing agency where subscribers could buy the "look" she promoted in her pages. During the spring and summer, though, the weekly didn't gain the hoped-for traction.

Further personal drama could be the explanation. On April 18, 1871, Frank's estranged wife, unappeased by $10,000 in back alimony, opened fire. She charged him with adultery and named the co-respondent, Miriam Florence Squier, as well as the dates and places of their assignations. Under oath, E. G. denied the charge as a "malicious" lie and attack on his "domestic peace" and friendship with Mr. Leslie. Miriam testified in turn: "I am . . . in accord with my husband; and our relations are perfectly harmonious." But people were already talking, and nothing prevented leaks to the press.

Fortunately for Miriam, the press had more dramatic news to cover. When the siege of Paris ended with a "treaty of shame" and Prussian occupation, the working classes and "Red" sympathizers mutinied against the Republican government and set up a rival Commune de Paris. The Commune and its aftermath had a seismic impact on America, altering the political and cultural climate for decades. The revolutionary regime was a living laboratory of egalitarian socialism. The Communal Council leveled the entire social structure: women won equal rights, including the vote, widows gained pensions, and the laboring poor received humane work hours, free soup kitchens, and open admission to concerts, plays, and art galleries.

Three months later, Republican forces led by General MacMahon invaded Paris after weeks of bombardment and went in for the kill. The resistance was fierce—a rampage of slaughter and destruction. Communards tore down the Place Vendôme, shot the Archbishop of Paris, mounted the ramparts, and, joined by a female battalion of Molotov-cocktail-throwing Petroleuses, torched the Tuileries and dozens of public buildings, nearly burning Notre Dame to the ground. In the end, the revolutionaries were savagely put down—tortured and executed during a bloody week in May, with casualties that exceeded twenty-five thousand.

New Yorkers watched in horror. The privileged could see the parallels all too clearly. "Let some such opportunity occur as was presented in Paris," worried the *New York Times*, "and we shall see a sudden storm of communistic revolution even in New York." And those incendiary women raised special alarms—the specter of women released from domestic captivity, wreaking vengeance on men and the ordained social order. Such feminine outrages, scolded Frank Leslie, were enough to even shock the "shrieking sisterhood of America."

Manhattanites had only to step from their doors to see the makings of a similar social upheaval. As the *Illustrated* documented, "thousands upon thousands" of men, women, and children—half the population (an estimated five hundred thousand)—lived in "rags and wretchedness." Forty thousand poor were homeless and the rest were crammed into dark, narrow, fetid tenement houses—126 families to a five-story building.

The Orange Riot on July 12, 1871, seemed a prelude to the apocalypse. During a heavily guarded Irish Protestant Orangeman parade on Eighth Avenue, a crowd of working-class Irish Catholics pelted marchers with insults, bricks, stones, and crockery. Gunshots rang out. Troops fired indiscriminately on the mob, killing over sixty civilians and injuring a hundred or more. To a nervous bourgeoisie, the riot demonstrated the anarchic, disruptive designs of the "dangerous classes" and mirrored the worst outrages of the Commune.

The Riot did Catholic sympathizer Boss Tweed no service. Now on the wrong side of the Establishment, he and his ring came under scrutiny by the *New York Times*, which documented his crimes in a four-page supplement—his system of kickbacks, padded bills, money laundering, creative accounting, and total theft of $25 to $45 million from city taxpayers. His arrest in October, combined with the Commune fallout and exposés of corruption throughout Manhattan and the Grant administration, signaled a tidal shift in public sentiment. The national mood turned conservative: respect for law and order and a hard line toward the underclass that lasted until the end of the century, if not beyond. There was a return to hierarchy and authority and a desire to rid the body politic of crooks, menacing foreigners, uppity women, the undeserving poor, and communist agitators.

At this juncture, Frank Leslie might have found himself in a tight spot. He was a known "friend of [Tweed]" and Grant supporter, and had his hand in devious dealings at the Custom House, illegally importing cheap British paper to America. The lawsuit with his wife still hung fire, with her accusations of adultery unresolved and perhaps in circulation. His solution was flight.

First he settled accounts at home. To silence adultery rumors, he and Miriam threw a fiftieth birthday party for E. G. on June 17 at Indian Harbor near Greenwich, Connecticut. At a festive, widely reported "Rhode Island Clambake," guests drank lager "à la Peru" and "clams à la Serpent Symbol" in honor of his books and toasted the "Squier of Chivalry." The charade probably fooled no one. Afterward, Leslie planted a promotional piece in newspapers hailing Miriam as "the great arbiter and authority in the *mode*," and sailed abroad. For three months he traveled incognito through Europe.

During his absence, Miriam had her work cut out for her. There were two monthlies and a weekly to update and see to press—the *Chimney Corner, Lady's Magazine*, and *Once a Week*. Trading on the new conservative tenor, she expanded domestic coverage and catered to the bourgeois desire to rise above the rabble and repel the forces of chaos. Now children's fashions and verses like "Grandma's Birthday" predominated, along with gentility lessons and features that fed the growing vogue for the professionalization of housewifery.

The greater challenge, though, was how to rejuvenate *Once a Week*. This time Miriam zeroed in on daughters of the well-to-do, young women eager to upclass, spend, and make prestigious marriages. She renamed the magazine *Frank Leslie's Lady's Journal Devoted to Fashion and Choice Literature* and assured her charges they would find all they needed to navigate "the high state of culture to which our society has advanced."

Her ingenue learned to walk with the "gait and carriage" of Marie Antoinette, host a reception at home "decently and in order," and sit out the rowdy German (an unrefined dance). In the fiction pages, she read of titled husbands and moated granges. "This is our future home, dear," says one hero, as he ushers "his betrothed, a beautiful girl of eighteen, into the hall of his ancestral castle." And the "Gossip" column kept a hopeful debutante abreast of ways to enter the hallowed ranks—charity benefits, literary receptions, art exhibitions, and news of available noblemen.

Proper dress was paramount; clothes could make or break you in the status-sphere. And since the Franco-Prussian War, fashion had been thrown into confusion; without Eugenie's court, taste-makers turned to a hodgepodge of sources for inspiration—theater, literature, and painting—and heaped on trimmings and novelties with chaotic abandon. At the same time, conduct books warned of classless extravagance and finery. An ambitious young woman needed guidance. She had massive wardrobe requirements; nearly sixty gowns a year, plus fans, gloves, trimmed bonnets, wraps, parasols, and chatelaine bags, at an annual cost of $10,000 to $30,000.

With the *Journal's* instruction, a reader could make the right choices and be assured of "a niceness of discrimination and refinement of taste only equaled in the court salons of Europe." "A lady," pronounced Miriam, "seldom makes mistakes." Deftly shifting the fashion capital, she began each issue with "What New Yorkers are Wearing" and sorted through the clutter of styles. A $1,500 reversible India shawl, for example, was smart and *comme il faut* without being flashy.

The magazine's larger message was deliberately ambivalent, designed to cast the widest net. At one level, the *Journal* drilled young ladies in conventional femininity and told them to embrace the "separate sphere" of home or the "social structure would be destroyed." "Household receipts," childcare directives, and hints for the hearth and happy marriages filled each issue.

On another level, these same daughters could find a subversive countercurrent; they belonged to a generation on the cusp of change. Beneath the sanctioned angel in the house ideal, the "new woman" was on the ascent. In 1871, a third of New York City workers were women, many of whom filled the professions, while another contingent, often from the upper class, supported suffrage and made serious money on their own. Like whaling heiress Hetty Green, who played the stock market to become the "richest woman in America."

Increasingly, women's magazines served as a virtual forum, a safe space to air dissenting views. Exploiting this to the full, the *Journal* compared the American Girl to an "oak in an iron-bound flower-pot"—denied maturity, education, self-development, and an independent existence. Vanguard heroines were profiled: the inventor of a needle-gun carriage; a Sandusky, Ohio, surgeon; and Miss Ida Lewis, who refused to take her husband's name.

Opinion pieces began to take men to task. Too often men create heartbreak and misery and make dissolute husbands. "How few marriages prove to be happy marriages," wrote Miriam, and how many women drag out a life of "hidden grief" with a "broken reed to lean on." Every woman, she instructed, must brace herself for the worst, cultivate "masculine occupations," and "be ready to stand alone."

BY SUMMER 1872, Miriam was ready. E. G. had become a certifiable "broken reed." Perhaps in a renewed syphilitic flare-up, he suffered skin eruptions, sleeplessness, debility, and such neuralgia that he could barely stand up to deliver the annual American Club address. He was morbidly depressed and predicted his early death.

In contrast, Frank's circumstances seemed improved. He trimmed his sail to the prevailing wind, joined the Reform Republicans, and condemned corruption in the Tweed and Grant administrations. With self-righteous wrath, he berated banksters and profiteers in the *Illustrated*, effectively clearing his name—for the time being. He cultivated powerful wire-pullers, Leonard Jerome and August Belmont, at Long Branch, New Jersey, and squared his debt to his wife to end the long court battle. For $28,000 he secured a divorce and was free to remarry at last.

All that remained for Miriam was to dispose of E. G. If abuse were grounds, divorce would have been easy. E. G. was drinking heavily, trawling disreputable haunts, and collecting pistols. One terrifying night he brandished firearms in the room and "threatened to hurt somebody"—Miriam, Frank, and himself. After that, they separated—he to a Twenty-seventh Street apartment, she to 41 West Twenty-fourth Street—and the Murray Hill house was sold. Separation, however, counted for little in New York State; the law demanded clear proof of adultery. Miriam was not to be deterred.

On a raw April night, with bitter gusts whipping off the East River, three men arrived by horsecar at Thirty-fourth Street and Fourth Avenue. Matt Morgan and Dewitt Clinton Hitchcock, artists from the *Illustrated*, led the way, followed by E. G. He'd recognized Dewitt, his old Central American sidekick, but forgotten his failure to credit his engravings in *Peru*, which had sabotaged Hitchcock's career. He should have grown suspicious when they swung southwest toward Sixth Avenue and the Twenties: the Tenderloin. The neighborhood was infamous—Ladies' Mile by day, where Mrs. Astor shopped, and a gentleman's playground by night.

But E. G. had been promised a "grand dinner," and after his domestic trials, he must have welcomed a reprieve. How the evening transpired can be pieced together from court records and contemporary accounts. The artists turned on Twenty-seventh Street, a block with twenty-three assignation houses, some high end. Prostitution had become big business since the war; bribed police winked, cash flowed, and successful madams could net as much as $200 a night and retire in luxury. An estimated twenty thousand women, one in twenty-four, worked either in the city's five hundred brothels or on the streets.

The men stopped in front of a three-story brownstone, one of the toniest "temples of Venus." A rouged matron in a black gown with a filigree pearl and sapphire cross around her neck greeted them at the door. She was Mrs. Lizzie A. Rice, a grande dame of the business. She ushered them into the parlor, a maroon-and-gilt paneled room furnished in the height of elegance. Oil paintings of gods and goddesses lined the walls, canopied brocade curtains pooled on the carpet, and tufted sofas and settees surrounded a center table filled with a champagne cooler, waxed flowers in a glass dome, a faun statuette, a stereoscope, and a tasseled fan. In a corner stood a shawl-draped piano, and on the mantelpiece beneath a pier glass mirror perched a stuffed peacock.

The "lady boarders" entered: Gypsy and Indiana. Both were dressed in evening toilettes of shot silk with court trains and gathered flounces and might have been mistaken for Fifth Avenue debutantes were it not for their bare-it-all *en coeur* bodices. Or the reception afterward. They popped champagne bottles and tucked the corks in their cleavages and entertained them with naughty pictures in the stereoscope and a Spanish waltz at the piano: "There was a young farmer who sat on a rick/ranting and raving and waving his . . ."

The dinner was as "grand" as E. G. could have wished—an "elaborate supper" served on chased silver: soup, sturgeon, *boeuf aux champignons*, canvasback, salad, and Charlotte Russe. Gypsy and Indiana sat on either side of E. G. and refilled his glass with wine and Roman Punch (a strong concoction of brandy, rum, and lemon ice) between courses. After bonbons and Madeira, Gypsy tugged his waistband and led him upstairs, with Indiana close behind.

Thirty minutes later, Matt and Dewitt entered the room with their sketchbooks and set to work. They drew E. G. nude in a chair with Gypsy naked on his lap and Indiana sprawled at their feet. The artists testified that he boasted he'd slept with both girls, and, added Dewitt, many "others in New York's houses of prostitution."

In three weeks, the law firm of Hilton, Campbell & Bell threw the bolt. E. G. received a letter from Douglas Campbell assuring him that the incident would be kept from the press—Frank Leslie's *Days' Doings*—if he agreed to certain conditions: the adultery charge and a swift divorce. "Mrs. Squier tells me," wrote Campbell, "that this proceeding is to be friendly [if] you consent to it under the circumstances."

E. G. did not take this with good grace. Humiliated and livid, he refused to either meet her lawyers or answer the court summons and laid down "circumstances" of his own. He had "surrendered every consideration of pride and manhood" and would not permit his name to be besmirched in the city by this "apparent disgrace." The affair, he charged, was "rotten to the core," and if by some chance "he were to be disturbed" by the proceeding, he would take his revenge. "My mouth shall be opened," he threatened, "and your client [will know] what all this means."

On May 31, 1873, Justice William R. Curtis decreed the Squier marriage of fifteen years dissolved. E. G., the guilty party, was forbidden to remarry until his wife's death. Miriam was under no such obligations; she was at liberty. She shrugged off E. G.'s demented threat and must have congratulated herself on a job well done—too soon, it would turn out. E. G.'s humiliation had struck deep. And marriage to Frank would hold its own unpleasant surprises.

CHAPTER FOUR

"THE GRAND SEIGNEUR OF PUBLISHERS' ROW"
1873–78

WITH THE LAST obstacle removed—an inconvenient E. G. out of the way—nothing stood between Miriam and her goal, marriage to the American "newspaper prince." Frank Leslie would give her the position, clout, and secure income she had so long desired. The wedding might be tomorrow, as far as the courts were concerned. But it would take a full year—an *annus horribilis*.

The law wasn't finished with Leslie yet. He faced imprisonment once more, and this time he should have been scared. The conservative clamp-down after the corruption scandals and Paris Commune excesses had bred a climate of severe prudery. A stable society depended on a clean sweep of the lower appetites—sexual indecency in particular. At the forefront of the crusade were such groups as the Salvation Army and the Young Men's Christian Association, and one man, Anthony Comstock.

Comstock, the purity warlord, conducted a forty-one-year terror campaign in America, hunting filth mongers and profligates like "rats without mercy." He began his career as a Manhattan dry goods clerk and was the image of a stodgy bean counter—corpulent and balding with a smug prison warden's face bracketed by mutton-chop whiskers. Incensed by the shenanigans of his fellow clerks, he appealed to the YMCA to combat the scourge of dissipation and depravity in the city. He impressed the board, among them J. P. Morgan, and received a stipend, secretary, and their support. Together they formed a Society for the Suppression of Vice, and in early 1873 pushed the "Comstock Law" through the US Congress, banning "obscene, lewd, or lascivious material" in the mail or in print. Congress appointed him Post Office Agent, and by the end of the year Comstock had confiscated 130,000 pounds of "vile books," 194,000 "bad pictures," 55,000 lewd playing cards, 3,150 boxes of powders, and 60,300 "rubber devices," and reported fifty-five arrests and twenty convictions.

One of these arrests was Frank Leslie. Unknown to Leslie, Comstock had him in his crosshairs for months. Finally in mid-January 1873, Comstock gloated, "At last, at last! At last action is commenced against this terrible curse." The "curse" was Leslie's highly spiced *Days' Doings*, packed with portrayals of wanton women and ads for indecent products and "homosexual" literature. Comstock produced incriminating tearsheets and three book advertisements: *The Secrets of Affection, The Spice of Life*, and *Scenes Among Nuns*. Leslie was convicted, fined $500, and sentenced to ten years in prison. The purity brigade exulted. The women of the Moral Education Society, among others, applauded the "arrest [of] Mr. Frank Leslie who publishes and circulates . . . the most pernicious kind of literature."

In the end, Leslie worked insider connections with city power-brokers, and New York District Attorney Benjamin K. Phelps dropped the charges—to Comstock's wrath. In his notebook, he scrawled, "Fixed in Dist. Attys office," and vowed to hound Leslie. From now on, Frank had to watch his back. Comstock's campaign accelerated at an alarming pace. Armed with warrants and revolvers, he tracked down "smut" and smut dealers with relentless fury, confiscating an additional 160 tons of obscene literature, including "classical traps" like Rabelais and Boccaccio, and convicting 1,260 malefactors, enough to fill sixty-one railroad coaches.

WORSE WAS IN store for the country than Comstock. On September 19, 1873, the Stock Market crashed, instantly driving over five thousand businesses and eighty-nine railroads into bankruptcy and putting three million people out of work. "The epidemic of fraud" had come home to roost. Jay Cooke's financial skullduggery—overextended ventures, sales of nonexistent railroad stocks, and $300,000 in unpaid debt—was the immediate cause. Unable to get loans in a tightened money market, the investment house Jay Cooke & Co. closed, taking heavily leveraged banks and speculators with it, precipitating a depression that lasted for at least six years. Building construction ceased, wages fell, and corporate profits vanished. One broker called the catastrophe the "worst disaster since the Black Death." A "mad terror" gripped the populace.

Everyone except Frank Leslie. Either blinded by defensive optimism or delusions of omnipotence, he failed to grasp the full impact of the crash: "The storm, which has lately passed over Wall Street," he decreed, "will not affect the material interest of the [nation]," or "legitimate business[es] such as buying for investment [by] a single dollar." He forgot the ripple effect of financial panics; how loans dry up, debts come due, and real estate values plunge.

Instead, he continued as before, playing the big spender and "Grand Seigneur of Publishers' Row." He purchased a state-of-the-art press, the Campbell Perfector, brought out three more publications, and siphoned income from his still profitable publishing company. He transformed his ninety-two-acre property in Saratoga into a German nobleman's estate. With architect Gilbert B. Croft, he constructed a turreted mansion with a studio tower, guest cottages, conservatories, stables, and a park landscaped with waterfalls, fountains, rivulets, arbors, and a grandstand on the shores of Lake Lonely.

Miriam was too shrewd a businesswoman not to have seen Frank's prodigality and the perils ahead. But what were her options? She had thrown the die. Frank paid her way, and an unattached divorcée was ostracized, condemned, and forced to shift for herself in a tanked economy. Miriam at thirty-eight must have rationalized, resigned herself, and decided to seize the day and the available spoils.

They were married July 13, 1874, at fashionable St. Thomas Church on Fifth Avenue. Miriam later recalled Frank's stately presence beside her at the altar as both "best man" and ideal groom— "ambitious, enterprising," and "brave as a lion." To be sure, she conceded, he was "not handsome"—fifty-three, stout, and white-bearded—but he was still the titan of publishing, and to all appearances, a pillar of respectability and prosperity.

They moved to 511 Fifth Avenue, on the corner of Forty-third Street, the old home of Boss Tweed (now imprisoned in the Tombs), where they lived in style. They refurbished the handsome brownstone with period furniture and rich hangings and dined each night with or without company, in their "choicest toilets," he in frock coat, vest, and wing-collared shirt, she in low-cut evening gowns. They embarked on a "round of gayeties and extravagance"—Central Park promenades drawn by gaited horses, performances at Wallack's Theater from a private stall, and six-course dinners at Delmonico's, with Miriam appareled in jewels and dresses of velvet and Venetian rose point.

In the unlikely event that they thought of E. G., he was quickly forgotten, confined since the wedding in Sanford Hall Lunatic Asylum in Flushing, New York. Newspapers attributed his breakdown to Miriam's desertion and remarriage, but end-stage syphilitic dementia might have been the cause. The newlyweds had no reason to expect trouble from that quarter and, at any rate, were preoccupied.

Although engaged in a demanding profession with career fulfillment and recognition, Miriam nurtured a higher ambition—to rise in the world and join the gratin. She wanted to conquer Society, perhaps for glory, perhaps for unsettled scores against New Orleans and the class humiliations of her past. And wherever she turned, the world was being stung by the "social bee."

The stampede for status was at full tilt in the mid-seventies. The newly-minted postwar millionaires were rapidly displacing the staid Knickerbocker elites and fashioning a hedonistic, glamorous social set that fed the fantasies of the entire nation. Society swells, the equivalent of film stars, provided the romance of the Gilded Age and inspired thousands with gentrification dreams. "All or most of us," Miriam noted, "cling to society."

And it seemed, at first, as though enough money was sufficient. August Belmont, a poor Jewish orphan from Frankfurt, breached high society through a politic marriage and Wall Street fortune and entertained like a maharajah, serving dinners for two hundred guests on gold plates at his Fifth Avenue mansion. Ladies once found a platinum bracelet in their napkins. Another upstart, Edward Luckemeyer, an export-import merchant, elbowed in through a single dinner. In 1873 seventy-two guests arrived at Delmonico's to find a thirty-foot lake filled with four swans and the room transformed into a sylvan grove hung with songbirds in gold cages. Marietta Stevens, a former grocer's daughter and chambermaid, stormed the inner circle by sinking millions into décor and holding champagne Sunday musicales.

With Leslie's stature as international opinion maker, his contacts, and apparent wealth, Miriam must have believed they too might scale Society. After all, she tutored aspirationals in *bon ton* for a living in her publications and seemed the perfect gentlewoman. Lola Montez had taught her to play grandees onstage, and who were these parvenus but amateurs aping aristocrats?

They increased expenditures. "More money was spent on grand entertainments, and more diamonds were bought." Wherever they "obtain[ed] admittance," they went—charity benefits, Steinway Hall readings, Academy of Design exhibits, open-invitation dinner dances, and a Leiderkranz masquerade ball.

But Miriam was naïve to think she could break into the beau monde through a display of class and cash. As early as 1872, Society became a closed shop. The moneyed elect decided that the invasion of rich nobodies had gone too far. Ward McCallister, a snob from Savannah with a hamster-like countenance and large imperial mustache, was the self-appointed architect and gatekeeper of this new social citadel. He found the perfect chatelaine for his domain in Caroline Schermerhorn Astor. Mrs. Astor seemed strikingly unsuited to the role—a dull, plain woman with a thick snub nose—but she possessed a massive fortune and a ruthless will to rule. Her husband left her with time and spite to spare, living on his yacht, *Ambassadress*, all year with actors, bons vivants, and paramours. With her mentor and major domo McAllister, they created an A-list of the well-heeled and wellborn and purged undesirables—the divorced, unpedigreed, or anyone who had appeared on the stage. Three strikes, for starters, against Miriam.

McAllister's scheme was a masterpiece of power by exclusion. He chose twenty-five men of breeding, wealth, and standing called the "Patriarchs," each of whom agreed to give two balls a season with the privilege of inviting four ladies and five gentlemen and several "distinguished strangers." Social strivers clambered for invitations. "We knew," snooted McAllister, "that the whole secret of the success of these Patriarch Balls lay in making them select."

The third Monday in January, though, was the most coveted, exclusive event of the year: Mrs. Astor's annual ball. She received the chosen few, the four hundred who fit into her ballroom, caparisoned like a Byzantine empress beneath a life-size portrait of herself. She wore a diamond tiara on top of a tall black wig and a pearl-encrusted dress festooned with broaches, bracelets, triple ropes of diamonds, and a diamond stomacher that belonged to Marie Antoinette. Inside the ballroom, she presided over the dance on "the throne" with her court train. Not to be picked for the court was a slight (Mrs. John Drexel sobbed and rushed from the room); to be left off her list, social death.

Finally Miriam and Frank could deceive themselves no longer; "the doors of New York Society [never mind Mrs. Astor's] were not open to them." The "high-toned" met them in the street and cut them dead, a practice perfected by McAllister, who passed the wrong types with a cold stare, annihilating their identities. Throughout, the Leslies "went about with brazen faces," but the snub stung. Miriam would harbor the grudge for the rest of her life and resolve to snub back, to avenge the "slights and covert sneers and taunts" of "these haughty ladies."

FOR THE MOMENT, she sought a more hospitable arena. By 1874, Saratoga Springs had grown déclassé, eclipsed by gated Newport and frequented by arriviste tycoons who installed "secretaries" in hotel cottages for illicit affairs. Men loosened up in Saratoga—gambled, raced horses, and swam nude in bath houses where they drank mint juleps on cork trays—while women could be as showy, as spend-thrift, and as flirtatious as they pleased. And it was still a magnet for people worth knowing: the Vanderbilts, Goulds, politicians, British sportsmen, and popular celebrities. Leslie fast-tracked construction on his Lake Lonely property and opened the coffers. Miriam would have her social stage and carte blanche to dress the set.

In July as they clattered downtown to Grand Central Depot in a carriage piled high with Saratoga trunks, they couldn't avoid see-ing casualties of the crash—scenes they encountered every day to and from Publishers' Row. The city was a disaster zone. Lines of hunched, ragged paupers snaked around church soup kitchens, and approximately thirty thousand tramps roamed the city, begging or selling scrap coal and rags. But neither Miriam nor Frank probably gave a second glance to the sunken-faced man who rapped at their cab window with shoestrings for sale in a basket.

Few felt sympathy for the destitute in the aftermath of the depression. The prevailing Social Darwinian view dictated that the "suffering poor" had brought misery on themselves through idleness

and depravity and should be warehoused in reformatories and work-
houses or left to tough it out. The pauper/tramp, argued Leslie, "is a
dangerous element in society" and ought to be dealt with accordingly
through "corporal punishment" if necessary. Frank's own coachman
turned up at St. John's Guild petitioning for food and clothing. The
Leslies, like most of the privileged, ignored the human wreckage on
the street and concentrated on the summer ahead.

They fitted out "Interlaken," their Saratoga Springs estate, with
such magnificence that it became a must-see destination for visitors
who viewed the grounds from tour boats. Leslie spared no expense.
He repaved the estate drive until it was "the smoothest, easiest, and
safest road to be found between Maine and Mexico," refenced the
property, installed "one of the largest" stables in New York, and
built a coach house that held landaus, victorias, pony phaetons, and
dog carts. The gem of the collection was a facsimile of the Shah
of Persia's carriage, custom-ordered from Paris. The maroon and
black C-sprung carriage was the last word in opulence, furnished
with gold harnesses, velvet footmen's mounts, and a leather-lined
interior that featured pearl handles, gold-tufted cushions, galloon
trimmings, concealed silver mirror, and gold card case monogramed
"F. L." in diamonds.

The Leslie entertainments were the talk of Saratoga. They
hosted Regatta Week from their boathouse and provided the winning trophy in Miriam's honor, a Tiffany Challenge Cup with an
Egyptian barge helmed by Cleopatra. They purchased a steam yacht,
the *Frank Leslie*, and ferried guests around Lake Lonely during parties. After two seasons, their fêtes gained "world-wide celebrity." A
journalist sent to investigate reported that "the genial editor took
pride in bringing out his champagne on ice for his friends [from]
the best vineyards of La Belle France," while his wife exercised her
"charming manners" on the assembled company with "her immense
black-spirited eyes."

Frank was perhaps unaware of a target of her charming manners and a friend who was helping himself to more than champagne.

Joaquin Miller is a forgotten name today, but he was a nineteenth-century literary celebrity, "the most lionized personality of the day." His dramatic persona accounted for at least half of his renown. A Barnum version of a Wild West frontiersman, he dressed in fantastic cowboy costumes, told desperado tall tales, and trailed starshine. His poems, sprawling, exclamatory verses about heroic men and high passions, epitomized the popular taste of the time. Nicknamed the "Poet of the Sierras" and the "Byron of the Rockies," he was Leslie's top contributor, paid in blank checks. Joaquin was also a ladies' man and rakishly handsome. He had a chiseled face with ice-blue eyes and blond curls that frothed over his collar. When he and Miriam became lovers isn't clear, but the affair seems to have been underway as early as 1875.

Miriam, a self-mythologizer herself, would have appreciated his history. There were many renditions, all highly colored. He claimed to have been born in a covered wagon and brought up in the wild menaced by savage beasts and marauding Indians. In one fracas, Native Americans shot an arrow through his neck; in another, they took him captive and made him chief of the tribe. There he married a Wintu princess who died rescuing him from jail. More preposterous adventures followed, from Nevada bonanzas to Nicaraguan guerilla raids. The great bandit Joaquin Murrieta christened him in Mexico.

The truth was less picturesque. His real name was Cincinnatus Hiner Miller, and his Quaker parents raised him and his four siblings on a small freehold in Liberty, Indiana, before moving to an Oregon fruit farm when he was thirteen. He soon set off for the California gold fields, where he failed, then bummed around the West in various capacities—mining camp cook, horse thief, Pony Express rider, "lawyer," and newspaper writer. At one point, he lived for a year among a tribe of Native Americans in the Great Basin, perhaps in the company of an indigenous woman. No evidence exists of tribal leadership, a martyred bride, or military forays, either south of the border or with Native Americans. At last, he found an identity that stuck—cowboy poet. He assumed a Byronic limp, produced reams of operatic verse, and married poet Minnie Myrtle, the "Sweet Singer of Coquille." After the birth of their third child, he deserted her to seek his literary fortune in San Francisco.

Unsuccessful there, he tried his luck in England. Arrayed in frontier regalia—sombrero, polka dot bandanna, high-heeled boots, and pantaloons strung with silver bells—he toured the country, laying laurel leaves on the graves of British poets and reciting threnodies in a basso twang. He made the desired impression. In London, fascinated literati gathered around. He circulated his self-published *Pacific Poems*, and cultural mandarins proclaimed him an original, a rustic Western bard, and persuaded Longman & Co. to publish *Songs of the Sierras*.

Although the American press panned *Songs*, the British found him and his poetry a piquant novelty and invited him everywhere. He arrived at West End drawing rooms in fancy dress, bowie knives in his belt, and regaled guests with hairbreadth adventures. He performed stunts—swallowed goldfish, recited faux Indian chants on parlor rugs, and once bit a lady's ankle in the throes of poetic ecstasy. "It helps sell the poems, boy," he explained, "and it tickles the duchesses." At the height of his popularity, he was invited into the Savage Club and introduced to Whistler, Prime Minister Gladstone, and Queen Victoria, who supposedly gave him a copy of her poems and a ring with four diamonds that he wore on his little finger. He hired writer Prentice Mulford to ghost a memoir, *Life Amongst the Modocs*, and secured his reputation in England.

Around this time, Frank Leslie "discovered" Joaquin and promoted him in the *Illustrated*. Joaquin always called Leslie his "first, best friend" in America. He must have met Miriam on his trip home in September 1871. In Joaquin's version, she greeted him at the Saratoga railroad station with specific orders: "You go get your mail," she commanded, "and we will meet you on the Grand Union Hotel Piazza. You enter by the north steps and walk the piazza until you find us—probably at the southern end." She proved to be a woman with promotional instincts equal to his own. She prepared a red carpet entrance—a passage down an eight-hundred-foot arcade crowded with guests in rocking chairs who put down their papers and needlework to watch the handsome, spurred-and-booted poet limp past. The attraction between these two limelighters must have been instant.

For the next few years Joaquin avidly courted Miriam. He wrote a 548-page novel, *The One Fair Woman*, with a heroine modeled on her. The Byronic artist/hero, Alphonso Murietta, pursues Annette, the "most matchless and magnificent of women in the world," from England to Italy, strewing rose petals in her path and kissing her hand "in devoutest worship." She is his "destiny"—a dark-lashed dream of perfection—and "the only woman he had ever really loved or now could ever love."

He dedicated the novel to Miriam, and followed it up with a love poem, "Lesley." In seven fulsome stanzas, he hymns his "Queen" whom he sees in a dream dressed in majesty beneath St. Peter's dome, receiving tributes from ten thousand men who genuflect at her shrine. He alone will immortalize her:

> Thou shalt walk the milky-way,
> For I will give your name to song.
> Yea, I am of the kings of thought,
> And thou shalt live when kings are not.

Another woman might have smiled indulgently at such panegyrics and sent Joaquin on his way (as professional beauty Lillie Langtry did), but Miriam could well have been susceptible. Although she had realized her great ambition—a distinguished marriage that conferred rank, respect, and financial freedom—she might have begun to grow restive. She didn't deceive herself about married life. After six months, she believed, disillusion sets in as couples submit to the daily grind and become glorified business partners, friends based on "mutual needs, mutual interest [and] habit." Some women, though, still pine for the "pyrotechnic bouquet" of romantic love, "the great irresistible desire of a woman's heart." They want a "champion knight" and flirtation on the side. Nothing, she must have learned from experience, was more "dangerous," more "alluring," than flirtations among "married persons."

And the swashbuckling Joaquin must have been too big a temptation. He was roughly her age, in his mid-thirties, enamored, undistracted by business cares, and her kind of man: fervent, full of "prairie ozone," virile, lean, and "manly in figure." "The handsome man," she let slip, should never be stout—as in Frank Leslie. By the end of her first year of marriage, Miriam must have become Joaquin's mistress. Considering her sexually lax upbringing and promiscuous past, Miriam probably regarded the liaison, which lasted thirty years, with less angst than other Victorian American women. She was a product of the easy erotic mores of New Orleans; love was a luxury she could afford.

Frank may or may not have suspected anything. He serialized Joaquin's novel about Miriam in the *Illustrated* (retitled *The Pink Countess*, diverting attention to a secondary heroine), and touted Miller as a poet of "titanic fiery energy." He rolled out the welcome mat. Joaquin, who had seen his share of swish entertainment in London, marveled at the "royal splendor" of Frank's dinners for heads of state and visiting celebrities. Prodigal in hospitality, Leslie was operating with a cavalier disregard of expenses.

When he was chosen state commissioner for the upcoming Philadelphia Centennial, his spending soared. He adorned Miriam in $70,000 worth of diamonds for New York Governor Tilden's reception, the man likely responsible for his appointment, and sank thousands into the fair.

THE 1876 CENTENNIAL Exposition, a celebration of the hundredth anniversary of American independence, was conceived on a majestic scale. It was the first international fair in the United States,

designed to trumpet national achievements in technology, democ-
racy, industry, and culture. Grandeur was the theme, a display as big
and splashy as the era itself. The fairground defied the world to rival
America in prosperity, invention, and sheer magnitude.

Eighteen months in construction, the site covered 285 acres
in Philadelphia's Fairmount Park and contained eighty miles of
asphalt walkways that conveyed visitors (by rolling chairs for sixty
cents) to five massive exhibition buildings and 250 pavilions. The
Main Hall, the largest structure in the world, enclosed twenty-one
acres, rose seventy-five feet high, and stretched 1,880 feet, about
the size of the Central Park's Great Lawn. Inside the cathedral-like
nave, hundreds of booths branched off from a central grandstand,
showcasing the latest wares in manufacturing, education, science,
and metallurgy—all for tourist consumption. On the same grounds
stood four equally impressive structures: Agricultural Hall, Hor-
ticultural Hall, Machinery Hall, and Memorial Hall, a granite art
gallery with a 150-foot dome. Sixty thousand exhibitors from thirty-
seven countries contributed to the Exposition, which opened May 10
and closed November 10.

Frank Leslie threw himself into the fair. He built an elaborate
octagonal pavilion beside the lake with ornamental siding, a library
of his publications, and a fretwork tower that flew a large "Frank
Leslie" flag from the top. "Excelsior," his personal motto, was also
the Exposition's, and he was in an "always upward" frame of mind.
He'd added two more publications, the *Popular Monthly* and *Sunday
Magazine*, to his inventory, tripled book production, and was preparing a platter-size souvenir book, *Frank Leslie's Illustrated Historical
Register of the Centennial Exposition*.

Bells rang throughout Philadelphia to signal the grand opening
of the Exposition. After a rainy start, the sky cleared and thousands
streamed past the turnstiles and bronze statues to watch the Philadelphia Cavalry and dignitaries march down Fountain Avenue to
Memorial Hall for the morning ceremony. Admitted onto the platform with the official party, Miriam sat for over three hours through

the anthems, invocations, benedictions, poems, and a short mut-
tered speech by President Grant.

Beside the President stood the Emperor of Brazil, Dom Pedro,
who waved his hat at the end, endearing the crowd and surely catch-
ing Miriam's eye. Tall and handsome with deep-set, penetrating eyes
and a Garibaldi beard, Pedro II was an enlightened, compassionate
ruler and scholar, admired by the likes of Charles Darwin, Victor
Hugo, and Friedrich Nietzsche. His plump Sicilian wife, Teresa,
clung to his arm, but the marriage was pro forma and passionless,
and he sought out women of his intellectual caliber for "discreet
affairs." How far things went with Miriam later on is still a source
of conjecture.

After the ceremony, canons exploded and Dom Pedro and the
President led the procession through the grounds. Ahead of them,
Alfred Goshorn, Director General of the fair, indicated attractions
along the way—the unfinished hand and torch of the Statue of Liberty, the "Freed Slave" sculpture with unshackled, outflung arms,
and Old Abe, the eagle mascot, dismembering a live chicken.

The Leslies followed the retinue to the main event: Machinery
Hall, a shrine to American scientific and innovative genius. Grant
and Pedro II threw the switch on the giant twin Corliss engines,
which moved seventy-five miles of belts and shafts to power eight
thousand machines. The hall thundered and clacked as rows of
machinery leapt into motion, from newspaper presses to looms that
wove customer's names in suspenders to a sugar popcorn maker
and chewing tobacco machine run by four Black gospel singers who
keened a syncopated "Jesus is a rock in a weary land."

The entourage viewed other novelties—the Remington type-
writer, Alexander Bell's telephone, and an internal combustion
engine—before heading to the Women's Pavilion. The first of its
kind, this exhibit promoted female equality and independence and
displayed innovative products by women. But none of the eighty
patented inventions—a self-heating iron, dishwasher, and glove and
stocking darner—were calculated to interest Miriam. Never mind

the dress reform brochures. She must have been conspicuous there, though, as Frank's wife and editor and been presented to Empress Teresa after she pulled the gold cord to start the engine that ran the looms, spinning frames, and presses. At their introduction, Miriam probably first brought up the subject of Saratoga, extending Leslie hospitality in Italian and Portuguese.

The Brazilian emperor and empress visited Saratoga in mid-June during a Philadelphia heat wave with ten days of hundred-degree temperatures. They arrived by a special Pullman Palace Car and spent "a right jolly time," reported the press, at Interlaken, sailing around the lake in Frank's "pretty little steam yacht." The royal couple doubtless attended one of Leslie's parties. Since Joaquin Miller was in residence in Saratoga that summer, he would have been there in performance mode, reciting his latest poem, "Song of the Centennial." Bedizened in chaps, fringes, and Western gear, he stood on the banks of Lake Lonely and declaimed, "Hark ho!, All is well," and hymned American's virtues through the voices of the common man—an orator, "Indian," miner, ranger, and "Negro" idling on a wharf who was "Gwine to dat Centeni-aw." Later, Dom Pedro thanked "Madame who speaks so fluently all languages," enclosing two sentimental photographs, and Carlos Gomes's "Centennial Hymn," perhaps in response to Joaquin's effort. "Good taste," the Emperor confided afterward, "is what is almost always lacking [in America]."

But more was lacking than good taste in 1876; all was emphatically not well. The Centennial celebration was an elaborate effort to reject the reality of the depression and fissured state of the country. The working class of Joaquin Miller's paean was unable to earn a living wage despite brutal hours and at loggerheads with the Establishment. The depression had deepened, and foreign visitors to the fair were appalled by the poverty they witnessed, comparing laborers to "slaves and drudges of Capital." The crackdown on the poor wasn't working. Homelessness reached one in five in New York City; hospitals ran out of beds; prostitutes spilled into respectable neighborhoods (even to the gates of the Exposition); tramps multiplied; and prisons overflowed in a spate of rape, robbery, and murder.

Violence pervaded society, from criminal gangs in Manhattan's Eighth Ward to the lawless badlands of the West. Blacks were increasing targets of white terrorism in the South—up to five hundred acts of violence in Louisiana alone—while the government watched with complacent indifference. African Americans must have regarded "The Freed Slave," the incomplete Statue of Liberty, and gospel dirge with bitter irony. US Armed Forces, meanwhile, like the eagle "Old Abe," were annihilating Native Americans with genocidal ferocity in the Indian Wars throughout Western territories.

Nor could the pious benedictions of poets and clerics obscure the canker of corruption that still infested the country. In spite of reform committees, civic turpitude ran rampant. Manhattan police took bribes from criminals and shared the spoils; straw judges proliferated; and corrupt elected officials like William H. Barnum, who bought a Connecticut senate seat for $20,000, were the new normal. The White House wasn't exempt. Scandals honeycombed the Grant administration: the president's private secretary colluded in a Whiskey Ring to defraud the Treasury of $3 million; War Secretary Belknap ran an extortionist Trading Post Ring; and the secretary of the interior, attorney general, and secretary of the Navy were charged with bribery.

Given this state of affairs in an election year, Tweed-ringbreaker and reformer Samuel J. Tilden was the odds-on favorite for president, nearly certain to beat the Republican candidate, Rutherford B. Hayes. New York Governor Tilden was without obvious charisma—a terse, clean-shaven workaholic of monkish habits whose left eye and lip drooped from a stroke. Frank Leslie counted among his chief supporters; he endorsed him in editorials, gave him extensive coverage, and publicized his image (pleasingly retouched) on the frontispiece of the *Illustrated*.

On September 21, New York Day at the Exposition, he and Miriam figured prominently with Tilden on the grand piazza. Over one hundred thousand turned out, the largest attendance in a single day, for a full-dress parade and Tilden's speech and reception. Pictured in the crush of well-wishers is Miriam dressed in a dark silk visiting costume with a triple-shirred hem and a matching ostrich-trimmed tricorn bonnet. As intended, she was noticed. "This lady," wrote a *Cincinnati Enquirer* correspondent, "is a sagacious witty blonde" with a "very gracious power to entertain statesmen." Her hair, he continued, "is a rare Titian's red, actual gold" (perhaps due to Atmospheric Liquid Hair Dye, introduced at the fair); her eyes recall the "spirit of Catherine the Great"; and her form is "not only elegant, but sufficient," "more than a full bushel," i.e., the preferred Junoesque build. Miriam's stock was rising.

At the closing ceremonies, VIPs sang the praises of the Centennial and America. Despite the growing stress fractures throughout the country, choirs sang doxologies and Te Deums, and President Grant struck the hammer that switched off the Corliss engine. The Centennial, he reflected, had "gone off very well"; the nation was stable, peaceful, and a source of "pride." Frank Leslie must have felt euphoric that day. He had risen to new heights of distinction, had lucrative projects in the works—the illustrated *Exposition* book, and a scheme to auction ten thousand unsold items to subscribers—and had every expectation of a just reward from Tilden. Editors routinely received direct payment or preferment from candidates they endorsed, a policy Leslie defended. Politically ambitious, he counted on a plumb governmental post, perhaps in the patent office.

Although Tilden won 184 of the 185 electoral votes needed to win the presidency (versus Hayes's 165), Republican operatives disputed the election results in several states and plunged the country into a pitched battleground. A campaign that promised to be a shoo-in for Tilden turned into a slugfest. The conflict centered on three Southern states with two different sets of returns, which touched off a bribery blitz and deadlock that was finally settled February 27 by a committee in favor of Hayes—not, however, without a full-scale constitutional crisis and the threat of a "horrible civil war." Marines mobilized, mobs cried "Tilden or blood," and generals on both sides volunteered to lead insurrections. The losers in the end were the poor, whose worsened misery was unaddressed by either candidate, and the Southern Black population—sold out to white supremacist rule in the devil's bargain to elect Hayes.

By the end of the year, frightened Americans felt that the whole edifice of the country was collapsing, symbolized by the "Ashtabula Horror." On a night of blinding snow, the Lake Shore Pacific Express crossed the Ashtabula, Ohio, iron truss bridge, which cracked midway, plunging the train sixty-nine feet into the ravine and killing eighty passengers. The senior civil engineer shot himself two days later; the bridge had been built by a financier on unsound principles. It seemed to augur the fate of the nation.

AS 1877 DAWNED, Frank Leslie should have started to worry. He lost a libel lawsuit, which cost him $4,500, faced a court injunction for failure to pay carriage import duties of $6,000, and overreached with his *Historical Register.* The book didn't sell, and the ploy of auctioning off Exposition goods ran aground, triggering a barrage of lawsuits. But he remained upbeat, sure of a palmy, prosperous future. The national "fit of blues" was over, he announced, and "the foundations of our prosperity are unimpaired": banks were flush, the "mass of people" comfortable, and the railroads on track and in "no danger of bankruptcy."

Riding high, he embarked on his most extravagant undertaking to date—a two-month luxury train trip to California and back with Miriam, friends, and staff. On a Tuesday night in April the group assembled in the sepia glow of gas lamps at Grand Central Depot beneath the soaring 112-foot iron-truss ceiling—bells clanging, boilermen hallooing. In the company were Mr. and Mrs. C. B. Hackley; three young artists, Miss G. H. Davis, Walter Yeager, and Harry Ogden; a photographer, W. B. Austin; W. K. Rice, son of the Massachusetts Governor; and a (clearly nervous) business manager.

They were soon joined on the platform by close to a hundred well-wishers with food hampers and champagne who cheered as the "Frank Leslie," a bespoke Wagner Drawing Room Car, chuffed out of the station to a salute of exploding signal torpedoes. Onboard they found a hotel suite on wheels, with a kitchen, dining car, parlor car, and sleeping compartments furnished with soft beds, pillows, "snowy linen," and silk-tasseled shades on the windows. All this, gratis from the railroad in exchange for publicity.

Contrary to Frank's prognosis, the industry was in grave difficulties and needed all the PR they could get. During the winter and spring of 1877, 7,225 miles of rail were in foreclosure and the five main lines were engaged in a ruinous rate war. Rail stocks sank lower and lower. Management hoarded dollars and cut wages and expenses, leaving trainmen starving and desperate. "Anarchy," stated the New Year's edition of *Railway World*, "prevails in the conflict of the roads."

That night and throughout the expedition, Miriam drew her silk shade and curtained off the railroad tribulations and the gathering storm of 1877. She had put poverty behind her; she was Mrs. Frank Leslie—a "stately and self-sufficient woman," mistress of Interlaken and dean of fashion and the press. She would enjoy her "pleasure trip." She sank into her plush couch, lulled into a "sweet sleep" beside her Yorkshire terrier, Follette.

During the journey Miriam recorded her impressions like a liege lady on a tour of the provinces. Chicago was déclassé. Although the city furnished a respite from "per-air-ry country" with its posh Grand Pacific Hotel, the Art Academy rather "languish[ed]," and household dwellings displayed the "crudity of youth." Chicago mogul George Pullman, however, sent them off in state. A survivor of the panic with seven hundred cars in operation, he gave the Leslies his $35,000 "Hotel Car" to transport them to California.

This leg of the trip was less disappointing. The train resembled a rolling petit palace with a talented chef of "ebon color" (freedmen worked for Pullman for a pittance) and scenery that elicited a string of superlatives. The Ute Pass, with its "heaven-piercing" crags, rivaled the Alps and the Andes; the Garden of the Gods evoked visions of a Pharaonic processions; and the buttes, precipices, and turreted rocks of the Uinta Mountains seemed the handiwork of a lost race of Titans. As they left Cheyenne, where broncos in flaring blue capes caracoled through the street, the conductor told of fiendish Indians who scalped his nephews and left them for dead.

For these Indians, Mrs. Leslie had no mercy like most of racist America. The "dirty and squalid" Native women, she railed, pestered them for money at every whistle-stop while "equally dirty and more dangerous" "braves" stood aside. She either didn't know or didn't care about the Native Americans' fate that spring. Throughout the West, they were being liquidated by starvation and indiscriminate slaughter in a four-front war to seize possession of their land and resources. In April and May, the Sioux and Cheyenne tribes of the Dakotas fell to federal forces—double-crossed and outgunned. "All we wanted was peace and to be left alone," said Chief Crazy Horse before two soldiers bayoneted him to death. The American government, however, wanted gold in the Black Hills and the open lands further west, and peace wasn't on the agenda. The rallying cry was "the only good Indian is a dead Indian." Miriam wasn't alone.

Besides Native Americans, Miriam found another source of censure in Utah. At the Salt Lake Mormon settlement, she inspected the "evil of polygamy," questioned plural wives on rivalries, and advanced on patriarch Brigham Young in his private office. He was a "magnetic" presence, Miriam discovered, well-built, with a ruddy complexion, "full mouth," and low, engaging voice. When he attempted small talk, she interrupted: "Do you suppose, Mr. President, that I came [here] to hear that it was a fine day?"

"I'm sure not," replied Young, "for it must be fine weather wherever you are."

She pressed on: "What religion can make a woman happy in seeing the husband whom she loves devoted to another. Any woman, I should think, would spend all her strength to attract and retain his love, admiration and attention. Isn't it so, Mr. President?"

He cast her an appraising glance and riposted (never imagining plural husbands): "You look like just the woman to do that sort of thing."

From Utah, the Pullman Hotel Car chugged across the Great American Desert at twenty miles an hour, past alkaline flats (a business opportunity "going to waste," snipped Miriam), through the Sierras to California. San Francisco was the "Eldorado" of the journey. They stayed at the Palace Hotel, a wonder of the West, with a glass-domed inner courtyard seven stories high, encircled by tiers of balconies that held tropical plants and flowers, birdcages, and sofas and easy chairs. On their arrival, the hotel treated them like visiting royalty, illuminating the courtyard, serenading them with a brass band, and escorting them to the imperial suite on the top floor.

The "Pacific Club Set," California's big money men, paid their respects. It was best not to examine the business practices of these merchant princes too closely; they had gouged fortunes from railroad monopolies, mines, and bank failures through dark deeds of every stripe. Miriam, though, parroting the upper crust, thought them heroes, Napoleons of commerce. Profiteer William Sharon won her special regard, both for his smooth charm and Belmont estate, built with his "colossal fortune" on fourteen manicured acres. Guests, she wrote, proceeded down a glass piazza to a curved staircase leading to a mezzanine gallery surrounded by six Parisian Opera House boxes that held guestrooms complete with marble basins and hand showers. Which was nothing compared to the mirrored Versailles ballroom and dining room that seated 110.

Leland Stanford's dinner party was another high point. Thirty guests sat down in a palatial gallery with everything "wealth could provide," attended by a stately hostess in crimson velvet, embellished with diamonds and opals. Two other San Francisco magnates befriended them—William Coleman, owner of the San Rafael Valley, and the "genial" mayor, Andrew J. Bryant, who escorted them through government office buildings and handsome housing developments in his carriage and four-in-hand. Both would soon gain notoriety as instigators of race riots in a less salubrious part of town.

Before she left, Miriam insisted on seeing the seamier side of San Francisco. She visited the nefarious Barbary Coast, haunted by the "vilest class of poor whites," and the County Jail where "bold and loathsome" inmates surveyed her with "horrible eyes." In Chinatown she enlisted the protection of a detective to lead her with lighted candles through the twisted, dark alleyways. She watched pigtailed men burn offerings to "grotesque" tinseled gods in a dingy joss house; she toured a Chinese theater, an opium den, and a brothel crowded with women wearing coiled coiffeurs and "mechanical smiles beneath heavy make-up." "The poor creatures," she lamented (perhaps with a stab of memory), were "bred to evil" by money-hungry parents. In a rare display of underclass sympathy on her journey, she espoused liberal treatment of the Chinese, despite their "squalid and odorous mode of existence." Her sentiments would be unheeded. Two months after they left San Francisco, a white mob, led by Coleman and Bryant, stormed Chinatown, killing four and burning $100,000 in homes and businesses for three days.

On the return trip, the Leslie party swung through Redwood country and Yosemite, then south to Los Angeles. En route Miriam encountered newlyweds of her acquaintance "born to millions," and spent a memorable night cooped up in a three-room general store during a rainstorm. She felt like Marie Antoinette at the grocer's; one bed for sixteen travelers, canned oysters and peaches to eat, and once a squalling child thrust into her arms. If there was anything Miriam abhorred (perhaps related to her 1858 Swiss "pregnancy"), it was children, second only to the night she spent there on a kitchen table with a bag of salt for a pillow.

Still smarting from her general store mishap, Miriam made a final stop at Virginia City, Nevada—an ill-fated choice, it would turn out. Virginia City was a mining town that had arisen in the wake of the Comstock silver lode and boasted a roughneck population of scofflaws and barflies, which once included cub reporter Mark Twain. While Frank and others descended 1,600 feet into the Bonanza Mine to examine shafts, pumps, and ore crushers, Miriam canvassed the town. The place, she griped, was "dreary, desolate," and "godforsaken," overrun with brazen, bad women and debauched men. Nothing in sight but gambling and drinking saloons in the "lawless little city." She would find she had gone too far.

That was the least of her concerns when they returned to New York on the seventh of June. Frank Leslie stepped out of his bespoke Pullman Car into financial ruin. It was time to pick up the tab. He hadn't counted the costs of his orgiastic expenditures, and his creditors descended. He lost his publishing house and other assets to Isaac W. England, publisher of the *New York Sun*, and five trustees who took control of his business and finances. He was permitted to remain on the job at a salary and given three years to repay. It had all avalanched: devalued real estate investments, industry outlays (a $70,000 press), a publication glut, circulation declines, and his extravagances, from California overruns to Saratoga purchases and Miriam's jewels. He also hadn't seen the end of his Centennial *Historical Register* morass; he came back to find his Philadelphia agents had fleeced him of $2,800 and failed to deliver his merchandise, which embroiled him in an expensive, lengthy lawsuit.

Another bankruptcy should have broken Miriam; some perverse hand of fate had dealt her a string of financial incompetents, from her father and brothers to E. G. and now Frank, the mogul with money to burn. The usual recourse for women in such crises (hers in the past) was the sickbed. But she was forty-one and wise in the ways of resilience, survival, and power. She kept the Saratoga house in her name shielded from creditors, gathered her travel notes, and worked them into *California: A Pleasure Trip from Gotham to the Golden Gate*. The book appeared in December to warm reviews. Critics quibbled over the empurpled prose and incessant "homage to Mrs. Leslie" but praised its sprightly narrative and "happy faculty of description." There's evidence novelist Jane G. Austin wrote the account from "very poor notes of Mrs. Leslie's," but Miriam was in understandable duress that summer and fall.

As was the country at large; whoever wrote *California* wrote it amid a 6.5 culturequake. In July, railroad workers went on strike against management, sparking the deadliest labor insurrection in American history. Throughout the Leslies' transcontinental train trip, tension had been mounting. The troubled lines slashed wages another 10 percent, reducing brakemen's wages to as low as one dollar for a twelve-hour day on the railroad's most dangerous job.

The "Great Strike" began in Martinsburg, West Virginia, on July 18. In response to a third 10 percent cut, B&O employees uncoupled engines and refused to return to work. The militia intervened, violence erupted, and strikes spread to eleven states in rising shock waves for the next two weeks. In Pittsburgh, militiamen bayoneted and killed forty rioting strikers, resulting in the destruction of $5 million in cars, locomotives, and property; in Reading, state troops "massacred" sixteen people; in Chicago, police and vigilantes gunned down eighteen of the five thousand of the Grand Army of Starvation; in St. Louis, three thousand federal troops and five thousand special police shot at least eighteen Workingman's strikers.

All told, the insurrection resulted in 117 deaths, hundreds wounded, thousands fired and blacklisted, and a legacy of class division, military action, and industry dominance that lasted into the next century. Flare-ups in mining country continued through the fall, then sputtered out. The social and political elite were left terrified of rabid Communists—1871 Paris all over again—and the working class were abandoned to their lot. Frank Leslie, perhaps chastened by his own losing battle with the business establishment, broke rank with the rest of the conservative press. Though he decried "Reds" and "roughs," he called for "kindlier treatment of employes [sic] by capitalists and corporations."

* * *

LIKE A CORNEILLE tragedienne, Miriam drew herself up and set her face against the world. Somehow she wheedled travel expenses from the *Illustrated* and in February 1878 sailed south with author Jane G. Austin, "sister of [her] heart," and staff artist Walter Yeager. Absent were Leslie, battling for his empire at home, and her *cavalier servente*, Joaquin Miller, pursuing an engagement to Abigail Leland, daughter of the owner of the Saratoga Union Hotel. Miriam boarded *The City of Macon* during a cold snap so severe armies of pickaxes had to hack a path through the snow and ice to Pier 47. Pleasure, though, wasn't the purpose of the trip, at least not entirely; she would write "Scenes from Sun-Lands," for publication and a hoped-for profit.

Again she assumed the persona of a Society doyenne, bidding her husband, "the lord of [her] destiny," a lofty farewell as the steamer cast off. At their first layover in Savannah, she found nothing up to her standards. Both the hack carriage and the hotel were subpar, the tea inedible, and the bitter weather, not as advertised. Yet the narrative improves in quality. The sightseeing accounts, both in Savannah and later, are less overwritten, more precise, even poetic. The Spanish moss on live oaks at a Georgia cemetery droops "in deep festoons, or long pennants, or waving masses like tattered banners in an old cathedral."

Once in Nassau, Miriam left no landmark or curiosity unexplored. She descended into a dungeon at Fort Charlotte, trooped through churches, barracks, official residences, and market stalls; boarded a skiff for an underwater view of coral reefs; and coached out to Grant's Town, a settlement for freed African slaves. Each stop tailored to her readers' genteel fantasies of Southern travel. They, too, would like to stay in the Royal Victoria with its large airy bedrooms that opened onto verandas, buy costly conch pearls on Bay Street, and attend the governor's party for the "elite of island society."

Miriam led a tightly chaperoned expedition through Cuba. She landed in Havana at the height of Carnival. Decorated open carriages, *volantes*, whirled though town filled with masked, high-combed señoritas; revelers danced the *danza criolla* in blackface disguise and at midnight smashed the piñata, releasing a shower of sugarplums.

But the country was a time bomb. Cuba had just ended the Ten Years' War of independence from Spain, a conflict of unsurpassed butchery. Rebel forces were regrouping in the hills for a final putsch, the Little War of 1879 to 1880. For now, Spanish General Arsenio Martínez Campos ruled with an iron hand. Slavery and paternalistic dominion prevailed, sustained by a strong military presence.

From Miriam's Cook's tour perspective, colonial rule seemed a civic paragon. New York could never be "as picturesque and genial as Havana," or as compassionate, she professed. Here people treated the less fortunate with greater kindness, "purely for the love of God and his children." Her observations, though, belied her words. After inspections of model schools, hospitals, and factories, she witnessed nightwatchmen armed with staves patrolling the streets each evening.

Harder to reconcile with her charitable claims was her visit to a sugar plantation. At Las Cañas, Don Frederico and his elegant wife Doña Teresa oversaw an industrial complex of eight hundred enslaved Blacks and Chinese laborers who were "kept closely at work" from 5:00 A.M. to 9:00 P.M. Miriam observed children tossing cane stalks onto iron rollers, half-naked men feeding boilers, and women hacking underbrush with "heavy knives and their own horny fingers." A "negress" ladled rations of yams and corn in the communal kitchen while "piccaninnies" capered for handouts from the "mistress." If "all slaves [were] as happy as those of Las Cañas," she stated straight-faced, "we might consider emancipation a huge mistake."

But as she dined on "first-class Cuban fare," served by "quietly trained servants" in the Las Cañas dining hall, she couldn't miss the sandbag barricades outside and fortifications pierced with loopholes for musketry. Unnecessary safeguards against insurrection, Doña Teresa assured her. All the while sentries cried: "*Alerta!*" (are you on guard?) "*Alerta, estoy!*" (I am on guard!).

A return circuit through Havana should have demolished any remaining illusion of Cuban compassion. Boys in segregated reform schools were forced to rise at 4:00 A.M. and roll cigars; cemeteries shoved the poor three deep in unmarked graves; and the penitentiary made indigent prisoners consume rank cod and sleep on floors without pillows. "A prison," Miriam remonstrated (forgetting E. G.'s Liverpool sojourn and her husband's close call), "is a place of punishment and not of luxury."

The lunatic asylum would have made madmen wish they were in jail. A fearsome "negress" who had clawed her face raw gnashed her teeth and shook her bars as Miriam filed past, followed by a succession of female psychotics produced to entertain the guests. The "milder maniacs" sewed straitjackets. The men's annex was drearier still—cells that gave onto a dark stone courtyard with grotesque, pleading patients locked up inside. One thought he was a horse, some were violent.

An incarcerated E. G. in Sanford Hall must have been the last thing on Miriam's mind. She spent the final days in Havana on carefree rambles through the Aqueduct and country drives flanked by *cabelleros*. Then she and her companions embarked for New York City, torn between "leaving the land of our love and joy [and] returning to the land of our belongings." Had she guessed what awaited her from E. G.'s Long Island asylum she would have stayed in Cuba.

CHAPTER FIVE

"A BITTER PILL"
1878–81

WHEN MIRIAM BOARDED *The City of Macon* for her Caribbean tour, she called Frank Leslie the "lord of [her] destiny." That was February 1878. Two months later, he must have seemed her evil genius. Instead of sorting out his chaotic business affairs in her absence, he'd become ensnarled in further difficulties.

The terrible moment in January was still fresh. They had been reclining in the parlor car on the night Express to New York after luncheon with President and Mrs. Hayes at the White House—a welcome morale boost for the bankrupt, financially disgraced Frank. Miriam had drawn her cloak across her reception dress—likely the *Journal*-featured olive brown sheath with rows of silver buttons down the front and triple plaited flounces behind. The day had gone well. She had shown Ohio-bred Mrs. Hayes, "Lemonade Lucy" in her black ready-made, how a first lady of fashion dressed.

They had just dozed off when the train hurtled to a stop in Philadelphia and a swarm of men erupted into the car. The burly one with the sheriff's badge seized Leslie by the sleeve and told him he was under arrest. After "quite a scuffle," proclaimed the papers, the constables hustled Frank Leslie and his "very pale" wife into a paddy wagon. A hapless search for his $5,000 bail ensued, with calls to Daniel Dougherty and George Child at Twenty-second and Walnut Street. But neither was home, and at midnight Frank deposited Miriam at Philadelphia's Continental Hotel and continued his circuit in the wagon until dawn without success. That afternoon he was charged with libel in a suit he thought he'd settled.

The dispute involved a contest over unsent Centennial merchandise and poor sales of the *Historical Register*, which Leslie's agent, W. W. Weigley, and his salesmen had managed while he was in California. Among his other reverses, Frank returned to find they'd bungled the job. Not only were they in debt for unsold copies of the *Register*, but they also failed to deliver 2,800 fair items to book subscribers who'd paid an extra dollar in a lottery draw. To compound matters, Weigley fined Leslie $2,800 and distributed a circular to customers blaming him for the unsent goods.

Leslie should have been smarter than to tangle with a lawyer like Weigley. But in August 1877, Leslie served him an arrest warrant for libel and $10,000 damages and informed the *New York Tribune* he could sue Weigley for embezzlement if he wished. The feud seemed to have ended there, with a verdict for Frank. Then this: Weigley mounted a libel countersuit that would crawl through the courts for over a year and cost Leslie more than he bargained for.

As if his memory of legal skirmishes deserted him, Leslie sued his eldest son, Henry, in April 1878 for appropriating his name and brand on rival publications. The trial, however, didn't go as planned. Defense lawyers unearthed damaging evidence against Leslie— inconsistent directives and underhanded ploys, such as a forged restraining order—and Judge Daly ruled in Henry's favor.

At work Frank fared no better. He was in the humiliated role of salaried employee in his own company, reminded daily of his imprudences and $400,000 debt by his manager, Isaac W. England, and board of five trustees. They twisted the knife: He hadn't paid his employees, owed $500 damages in undervalued paper imports, and must forfeit 80 percent of company profits to creditors until 1881.

They demoted him to general manager of the artistic branch and moved operations to cheaper quarters on Park Place.

Miriam hadn't reckoned on this diminished version of Frank Leslie. Bankruptcy was hard enough—yet another inept male provider—but the aftermath, with its attendant mortifications, must have soured her homecoming. Not to mention the cultural turn of affairs. The forces of temperance and moral purity were on the march and increasing in influence and rapacity across the country. In New York City the Society for the Prevention of Crime was arresting Sabbath-violating saloon keepers and rounding up and jailing prostitutes throughout the spring. Anti-vice czar Anthony Comstock, Frank's old nemesis, had just apprehended the long-tolerated abortionist Madam Restell at her Fifth Avenue home, after which the "wickedest woman in New York" slit her throat in the bathtub. Next up, Miriam feared, was her husband, whose *New York Illustrated Times*, a thinly disguised version of the scabrous *Days' Doings*, wouldn't have escaped Comstock's spy ring.

All of which paled beside the trouble in store. There were no warning signs, unless Miriam, with Bayou-bred superstition, consulted the stars. If she'd read "Important Astrological Events," in the April 27 *Illustrated*, she'd have been alerted to a total solar eclipse on July 29, which heralded the Day of Judgment, and a rare transit of Mercury on May 6, which brought hidden truths to light. Even so, she couldn't have expected menace from this quarter.

Throughout *California: A Pleasure Trip*, she'd been a model of discretion and commended every stop along the way, except the "desolate," "wicked" Virginia City, Nevada, which Frank's reporters remedied with praises of the "remarkably enterprising city."

Miriam had forgotten to account for her ex-husband, E. G., and his threat during their acrimonious divorce: "There is but one chance in a hundred," he warned, that he would speak; however, "if disturbed in some fashion, his mouth [would be] opened." Like others, she assumed he was non compos and confined to Sanford Hall Sanitarium out of harm's way. But he wasn't. He was "disturbed," and the bankrupt Leslies and Miriam's airs were insupportable. Unsuspected by anyone, E. G. had Nevada connections to aid him, and he sought revenge. And Virginia City wasn't appeased; they remembered the highfalutin New York lady who called their town a "god-forsaken" haunt of gamblers, drunks, deadbeats, and "audacious" bawds.

Rollin Daggett, the editor of *The Virginia City Territorial Enterprise*, a weekly with the widest circulation west of the Mississippi, "dearly loved a fight" and found his ammunition. His friend E. G. had been released from the hospital and was ensconced with his brother and family in Brooklyn. Squier had come to that "one chance in a hundred" and wanted to talk.

On July 14 the story broke, a twenty-three page *Territorial Extra* entitled "A Full Account of Frank Leslie and Wife," with a pseudo-anonymous introduction by E. G. Squier. The author stated he had known Mrs. Leslie for over twenty years, lived with both for eighteen, and suffered grievous wrongs at their hands. They were a pair of arrant reprobates who had "set aside all the laws of God and man" and feared neither. Every word of the account, he attested, could be "fully proven."

The whole unsavory story spilled out for the world to see. The swells Miriam had been at such pains to impress—the Leland Stanfords and Manhattan "firsts"—could open their *Territorials* and pore over Mrs. Leslie's "Life Drama of Crime and Licentiousness." The high-bred publisher's wife and bastion of propriety, was, in fact, a fraud. Born out of wedlock to a quasi-madam and wastrel father, she spent a depraved youth as a "well-known" girl about town who traded sex for diamonds and coerced a jewelry clerk, David Peacock, into a shotgun marriage. Nothing was spared: the sordid annulment, stage adventure with Lola Montez, affair with the Tennessee congressman, and threesome with E. G. and Leslie. She led Squier to "a dog's life," ranted the author, and "like husbands in such cases, [he] took to drink." She then contrived a nefarious plot to entrap and divorce E. G. and marry Mr. Leslie, after which the pair ran through a fortune in riotous debauch. "Was there ever such a couple as this man and woman found?" concluded the exposé. "Verily they will yet meet their reward."

After his tell-all catharsis, E. G.'s health improved. "On the whole," he wrote his parents in September 1878, he was now a "very good case." But the *Extra*'s effect on Frank Leslie was the reverse. Apoplectic with rage, he directed envoys to buy up every copy and hired a detective, I. C. Nettleship, to track down the perpetrator, suspecting everyone but the source. He was equally obtuse about Miriam. Uxorious and gullible, he was unaware of her checkered past and swallowed her explanation that "she and Mrs. Peacock were two distinct persons" without question.

Beneath the expedients and damage control, though, Miriam was surely gut-punched. Her carefully crafted persona lay in rubble at her feet in full public view. She nonetheless kept her countenance. With regal sangfroid she brought her *Lady's Magazine* to new heights of genteel authority and moral sanctity. Fashion edicts came down like papal bulls: slim, long-waisted gowns should be worn "either short to show feet and ankles," or "quite trained," she commanded; "semi-long" is "no style at all." Women in the *Magazine* were pedestaled and haloed—images of "guardian angels," invalids, nurses, mothers at prayer, and libeled wives whose husbands failed to believe them and came to grief. A true man, she preached, keeps the faith, supports his wife in his "manly arms," and "dares not distress her." If false rumors assail her, she must "bear and forebear" and disregard those who cannot "mind their own business." A victim of such calumny deserved "practical sympathy" and guidance through her "darkest days" to a "happy and peaceful ending."

Miriam might well have thought she could bury the scandal and ordain a happy ending with sufficient splendor. She and Frank summered in Interlaken on credit as if nothing had happened. On August 18 they threw a lavish gala at their sixty-two-acre Saratoga estate. Judge Fitch, Governor McKnight, and a party of thirty cruised on the *Frank Leslie* across Lake Lonely to White Sulphur pleasure grounds, where guests dined, watched a partial eclipse of the moon, and drank champagne until midnight.

AT FIRST THE new year promised well. The dreaded media feeding frenzy over the *Extra* story failed to materialize, aided in part by journalistic favors and Miriam's maneuvers. There were also bigger stories than hers in the churn. Eighteen seventy-nine marked a watershed in American history. In January, the long depression ended and ushered in an era of big business rule and heightened class inequality and conflict. With financial recovery, the wealthy elites became the nation's governing class. This was a period of hard money, income tax exemption, lowered interest rates, 10 percent stock margins, and breakneck industrial expansion and incorporation—the heyday of the kings of capital. A "Great Merger Wave" swept the country; small companies fell like dominoes to behemoths like National Bell Telephone, Standard Oil, and Union Pacific Railroad. What industry barons wanted, they got: complete autonomy and conservative, pro-business government, an oligarchy in all but name.

America had always been the land of get-rich dreams, but the rise of post-depression fortunes spawned a fanatical cult of wealth. Money was the holy of holies, and the rich received the adulation of divinities. Like media celebrities today, they incarnated transcendent glamour to the masses, who obsessed over their clothes, possessions, travels, and prodigal festivities and strove to emulate them. The first "society" magazine, *American Queen*, debuted in 1879, accompanied by a burgeoning journalistic industry devoted to the social rich.

The scale of ostentation was unparalleled in America. William Henry Vanderbilt's double mansion under construction that year rivaled a Medici palazzo. Spanning the whole Fifty-first Street block of Fifth Avenue, the estate comprised two massive Italianate buildings crowned by a perforated stone balustrade and faced with architraves, pilasters, and decorative panels. The interior was the star attraction—fifty-six rooms of Nubian marble pillars, antique tapestries, gold-leaf doors, gilded friezes, ormolu and mother-of-pearl inlays, Chinese silks, and hand-painted murals. A four-story entrance hall lit by nine stained-glass skylights greeted visitors, and a 140-foot art gallery held Vanderbilt's private collection of two hundred paintings. It took six hundred workers and sixty European sculptors two years to complete and cost more than any private residence in the country. His twin palace, he said, represented "the new impulse felt in American life."

The impulse was squanderlust. He and the new wealthy blew fabulous sums on houses, horses, goods, and amusements, gourmandizing at the Kitten Club on fourteen courses washed down with vintage claret. At private banquet halls, footmen in knee breeches and powdered wigs served 150 at seated dinners on gold plates. Home ballrooms hosted operatic evenings where guests in court trains and bird-of-paradise aigrettes quadrilled and feasted on champagne, truffle pâté, and plovers' eggs. Formerly modest weddings became state ceremonies. At the sumptuous marriage of her third daughter, Mrs. Astor appeared at Trinity Church cuirassed in diamonds—diamond rosebuds scattered through her hair, pins and diamonds across her chest, rouleaus of diamond bracelets on each arm, and a pair of solitaire earrings.

Besides celebrity and consumption, the monied grandees sought aristocratic rank and distinction. They raided European chateaux of ancestral trappings, tonied up their names (like the Astors, who dropped "Backhouse," i.e. privy), spoke with broad a's, rode to hounds, installed cricket pads, served high tea, enforced formal etiquette, and adopted family crests that could be selected from stationers' books. They believed in their divinely-appointed status, their fixed preeminence in the social hierarchy.

However, without inherited titles, the ranks could be porous; hence the tight border controls among the rich elites—pedigree inquests, etiquette tripwires, and class markers such as the wrong accent or money. Asked why she excluded the department store mogul A. T. Stewart and his wife from her parties, Mrs. Astor replied: "I buy my carpets from them, but then is that any reason to invite them to walk on them?" Her "astorimperious" manner was widely copied by the gratin.

If the tiny percentage of the wealthy (2 percent owned more than a third of the country) were thriving, the rest of the country was barely scraping by. Wages shrank and costs rose. There was a yawning gulf between the "House of Have" and the "House of Want," inveighed economic reformer Henry George in his 1879 *Progress and Poverty*. The average worker, who made $2.32 a day, found the price of coffee up from $2.35 to $3.77 a pound, and the rent for a four-room tenement doubled to $37.80 a week. The same year, Walt Whitman saw a roving band of tramps in New Jersey and warned of "grim and spectral dangers" in a nation where "poor, desperate" men confronted an "anti-democratic, diseas[ed]" state. Had Whitman been well enough to leave his brother's house in Camden and witness the poor man's Manhattan, he would have sounded a shriller alarm.

Three-fourths of the city of over a million lived either in shantytowns on the periphery or in cramped Astor-owned tenements. These warrens, despite the "improved" dumbbell model, abutted noisy, garbage-heaped airshafts, lacked light and sanitation, and were breeding grounds for disease. Still, demand was high. The immigrant tide was swelling—twenty-two thousand more than the previous year—and depositing an indigent population of largely unskilled workers from Southern and Eastern Europe, all scrambling for scraps from the American table.

Except for the affluent minority, everyone was feeling the pinch. Over twenty thousand impoverished African Americans, "Exodusters," fled the Jim Crow South to Kansas and St. Louis, where hundreds fell into destitution. Laborers throughout the country struggled to make ends meet and formed protest organizations, such as the Greenbackers and Knights of Labor, to lobby for a living wage and improved conditions. Anyone who cared to listen could hear the subterranean rumble of future labor conflict and violence.

The plutocracy wasn't listening. Big money controlled government policy and the mainstream press, and their position prevailed: unilateral hostility to workers, minorities, swarthy immigrants, and the great unwashed. Even equilibrist Frank Leslie tipped his hat to them: the "Party of Discontent," declared the *Illustrated*, should pipe down and count their blessings.

On this score Miriam was foursquare establishment. Like the classic parvenu with a disordered, impecunious past, she leagued with the patriciate. She also must have thought herself one of nature's aristocrats and coveted what had been denied her in her youth—luxury, privilege, social acceptance, and the armor of class.

In light of Frank's legal and financial imbroglios and the *Territorial* exposé, she took special pains to curry favor with the upper class. For the rest of the year, she stepped up efforts to please Society, promoting fashions with "very frighten[ing]" price tags—couture reception costumes of satin and "shimmering silks"—and featuring stories and serialized novels about high-born heroines and heiresses. Doubling down on her elite sympathies, Miriam syndicated an essay in praise of the Chicago and Northwestern Railway monopoly and published a white-glove tour of the Nassau pineapple trade replete with obeisant escorts and capering, swindling "darkeys."

Frank's affairs, meanwhile, began to look up. In March, he negotiated a secret "compromise agreement" with four creditors in which he agreed to pay 50 percent (instead of the original 80 percent) of the remaining $320,000 debt in return for restoration of his property at the end of 1881. A court challenge ensued, but by mid-March, Leslie struck a deal and paid $151,000 upfront. The arrangement contained hitches, such as the creditors' right to approve purchases, fire staff, add or drop publications, and retain copyrights, while Frank remained on salary and responsible for liabilities and rent. Nevertheless, it was a toehold on solvency.

This should have boded better times. But weeks later, his bête noire, Weigley, relaunched his countersuit. All it took was two days in court. Weigley's lawyer opened with a string of denials: the

Philadelphia agents had not contracted debts, failed to deliver merchandise, or requested money from Leslie. In fact, they'd tried to compromise with him. Frank's letters to subscribers were entered into evidence, which slandered Weigley "for obtaining money under false pretenses." Then he delivered the kill shot. Leslie's son, Alfred, took the stand and swore his father approved the agents' work and creamed off profits from the World's Fair deal. He concluded by prompting Weigley to ask Leslie "if he believed in God."

"Mr. Leslie," reported the papers, "was so astounded by his son's testimony that he refused to allow his counsel to cross-examine him." The judge delivered a double humiliation—a guilty verdict and an order to apologize publicly. The May 3 edition of the *Illustrated* ran a formal retraction: Frank declared that "he fully vindicated Weigley and had done him an injustice."

A tense summer followed. Leslie seems to have spent the months in Saratoga nursing his accumulated wounds—the legal defeat, his son's betrayal, and workplace indignities—and building up a head of steam. He spent money he didn't have. At Interlaken, he entertained a "cottage full of guests," hosted the intercollegiate boat races, cruised on his "fine yacht," and indulged in "other items of expense." He replenished Miriam's wardrobe so that she was "one of the most exquisitely dressed ladies to be met with." Heedless of the bad press generated by his "princely" extravagances, he junketed off to Long Branch, where they paraded through town in a "stately barouche drawn by two noble animals holding their heads proudly high."

They returned to Saratoga in August to two freak accidents. First, their French maid set herself on fire lighting a kerosene lamp and died "in agony" eighteen hours later. Three weeks later, the elevator cables in Frank's office building snapped, plunging the car five stories and seriously injuring an employee, John McCabe.

By the fall Frank's festering grievances got the better of him. He resumed his failed lawsuit against Henry for the theft of his name. It was an injudicious step. Precedents backed Henry's side:

two people could legally use the same name in business except in extreme cases of intent to deceive or commit fraud. And public opinion was pitted against him. Frank's personal history, protested the papers, was tarnished enough with legal scandals and indecent "family matters," including a divorce to marry a woman of unusual "personal attractions." "His action against his own flesh and blood," railed one reporter, was "worse than death itself . . . This city ought to be large enough to afford a good living to both father and son without his shameful quarrel."

In the courtroom, Henry came re-armed with affidavits from his mother, wife, and schoolfellows proving his right to be called to "Frank Leslie, Jr." Leslie's lawyer, William Fullerton, fired back that the son had both debased the trademark through his poor character and publications and inflicted financial injury on his father. He charged the accused with "intentional deception," as well, and exhibited receipts from clubs, hotels, bills, and licenses marked "Henry Leslie." The evidence mounted; the case began to lean Frank's way. But not soon enough.

TOWARD THE MIDDLE of December, court reporters noticed that Frank Leslie no longer attended the hearings. One morning he discovered that his collar seemed too tight. "Put your finger here on my throat," he asked Miriam, "and see if there is not some kind of swelling there." She felt nothing. Two days later, he repeated the request. This time she detected a small nodule, which she attributed to a cold, and let his collar out with a loop. She thought no more about it, she told reporters, until she called a doctor to the house for her dyspepsia. On the way out, he examined Leslie and prescribed Pond's Extract, a witch hazel/alcohol nostrum for everything from nosebleeds to boils.

Over Christmas, though, he had trouble swallowing and called in a team of eminent doctors. Afterward they took Miriam aside and delivered the diagnosis: throat cancer, with an inoperable tumor on the jugular vein that would kill him within the week. He would suffer, they warned. Concealing the prognosis from Frank, Miriam hired an itinerant faith healer who furnished an opiate-laced "Elixir of Life" that dulled the pain. She spoon-fed him beef tea, soft-boiled eggs, and raw oysters.

To no avail. On New Year's Eve, Frank felt his throat close up and appealed to Miriam. In her version, she knelt down and told him the worst, which he took like a "strong man." He drew her to his side, and said: "Go down to my office, take charge of it, and sit in my place till my debts are paid." The elixir must have gone to his head—the thought of a woman at the head of a publishing empire in a male preserve was preposterous. In the same breath, he summoned lawyers to sort out his "tangled affairs" and rewrite his will. Although Miriam insisted she tried to restrain him, he disinherited his sons and left everything, including his name and trademark, to his wife. And credulous to the end, he instructed his lawyers to deny slanderous reports about Miriam's past. "There is no truth in them," he trailed off, muttering that "she made a great sacrifice when she consented to marry me."

By Tuesday, January 6, it was a question of hours. Overtaken by slow suffocation, Frank lapsed in and out of consciousness and could only speak in a whisper. Friends and colleagues gathered for formal farewells. His last recorded moments were a model of an ideal Victorian death. Though moribund, he remained "bright, cheerful, affectionate" and spoke of no regrets, except for his "dear darling" and for the unavenged crimes of certain persons who'd killed him. News of unavenged crimes must have alerted his sons, who rushed to his deathbed in hopes of a reconciliation and a place in his will. Whether or not Miriam turned them away became a matter of dispute, but Frank never made his peace with them.

January 10 brought a marked improvement. He miraculously got up, dressed, and ate a hearty breakfast. Encouraged by his rally, Miriam returned to her office, where she worked on the April edition of the *Lady's Journal*. Around noon she received a telegram to come home at once, and found him semi-conscious on the divan. As she recalled it, he opened his eyes, said, "You are beautiful and I love you," and died. The cause was likely a stroke or massive hemorrhage due to the cancer's invasion of the jugular. Miriam, however, gave the press a different account. In the obituary she dictated to the *New York Times*, she blamed the "vexation" of his lawsuit with his eldest son and cited "complicated diseases" rather than cancer, which signaled punishment for carnal sins such as sexual misconduct and bankruptcy.

"ONLY THE RICH," noted a Gilded Age reporter, "can afford to die in [New York City]." Funerals were exorbitant—the price of a "comfortable dwelling" or forty buggies—and cost more than weddings. Frank chose an inconvenient time to die. Miriam was at the end of her resources, with assets drained by summer outlays and debts to Frank's creditors, lawyers, and doctors. Leslie's reputation, though, was at stake, tainted by marital delinquency, bankruptcy, courtroom scandals, atheistic rumors, and a shameful death. A grand exit was essential. Late nineteenth-century funerals reflected the stature of the deceased and this one would be an imperial send-off.

Tuesday, January 13, should have been a beautiful day for a funeral. Albany forecasters predicted perfect weather, with temperatures closer to April than January. Preparations were in place. At 511 Fifth Avenue, mirrors had been covered in crepe, clocks stopped, blinds drawn, and black-bordered invitations hand-delivered. Overnight, though, an arctic front ripped through the Catskills and barreled into Manhattan, clocking thirty-mile-per-hour winds and blanketing the city with snow. Whiptail gusts hurled foot-high drifts against door fronts, shrouded stoops, and spattered the Leslies' black-ribboned bell knob with gouts of snow.

Fifth Avenue was at a standstill, the funeral procession ruined. A phalanx of employees and pallbearers was supposed to have borne the coffin on foot to the Church of the Divine Paternity two blocks away, but a whiteout blinded the path. When the horse-drawn hearse finally heaved through the snow to Forty-fifth Street, the church was filled, despite the storm, with almost three hundred employees and assembled delegates from publishing, politics, business, and entertainment.

One of them, showman P. T. Barnum, a member of the congregation and Frank's first American patron, might have suggested the Divine Paternity, a church designed to receive and redeem Leslie, who claimed "not to be a Christian." The liberal Universalists believed in a non-doctrinal god, good works, tolerance, and universal salvation, regardless of creed. A further bonus was the rector, Dr. Edwin Hubbell Chapin, a renowned author, social reformer, and preacher who drew overflow crowds to his 1,800-seat church each Sunday.

By 10:50 A.M. the service was underway. Dr. Chapin, a familiar figure with his spade beard and wire spectacles, stood readied at the narthex in his surplice and stole. Even with Barnum's aid, Miriam was lucky to engage him. In the final stages of progressive muscular atrophy, he would not last the year and supported himself on a silver-tipped cane.

Not every eye was on him, however. The widow in the front pew was a conspicuous presence. She sat beside Frank's reclusive brother, William, dressed in a resplendent black gown with a weeping veil that fell below her waist. Behind her thick veil, she must have concealed a welter of emotions. There had to have been grief. She'd lost her powerbase, an industry magnate who treated her as an equal, a nineteenth-century anomaly, and promoted her talent and brains. He'd supplied protection, status, and luxuries. Gone was the high life at home and abroad with her "cheerful, convivial host and companion." Guilt, too, might have welled up—her serial falsehoods and infidelity.

But Miriam must have felt a payload of anger as well. Frank, her rock and sole provider, left her to confront her worst fear, a return to the degradation and helplessness of her youth and the bone-grinding fight for survival. She seemed cursed with male failures who left her to pick up the pieces alone. The pieces now were radioactive. Predators lay in wait in the congregation—creditors, press hounds, and her stepsons, Henry in the rear and Alfred Leslie and his family in the pew directly across from her.

On cue, the organ struck an F-sharp, and a trio sang "Nearer My God to Thee." The processional began—Dr. Chapin with ten pallbearers in white sashes and floral rosettes, followed by six of Leslie's oldest employees, who bore the coffin on their shoulders. At the chancel, the bier sheet was removed and the casket opened. Embalming had just come into fashion, and the preparation of the departed required "the utmost care."

The fifty-nine-year-old publisher seemed in a serene sleep after a state banquet. He wore evening clothes, gold studs, and Moroccan pumps with silver buckles and rested in a satin-quilted coffin on a floral pillow donated by his staff, with "F. L." worked in forget-me-nots. Across his chest he held two palm fronds, the symbol of Christ's entry into Jerusalem.

The music stopped, and Dr. Chapin shuffled to the lectern and read from the Scriptures. Soprano Florence Rice-Knox, a veteran of Society salons, sang Mendelssohn's "O Rest in the Lord," after which Chapin delivered a short eulogy, praising Frank Leslie's achievements and moral stature—his benevolence, kindness, energy, and perseverance. At this point, the choir broke into "Jesus Lover of My Soul" while the congregation filed up the north aisle to view the remains.

The family came last. There was a scene. Never, wrote one reporter, had he witnessed a "more painful illustration of a house divided." First, the estranged Alfred, his wife, and two boys strode defiantly to the bier. Then a commotion erupted at the back of the church. Frank's son Henry burst into violent sobs and collapsed in the arms of a "gentleman friend" who bore him lurching down the nave. At the sight of his father's body, he "fell upon the pallid face with a moan" until the ushers bore him away "trembling like a leaf and looking back with drenched eyes and unutterable anguish."

Perhaps he was overcome with remorse—or perhaps he'd heard the morning news that he'd lost the case against his father and the right to his name. Finally, Miriam rose, drew back her veil, and kissed Frank's mouth and folded hands before sweeping past the Leslie clan on the way out. She was wrong if she thought she'd seen the last of them.

As she waited at the church door for the next stage of the funeral, the graveside service, she might have had another awkward encounter. Among the mourners was her sometime lover, the "Byron of the Rockies," Joaquin Miller, outfitted for the occasion in a bearskin cape. Anyone might have seen the telltale look between them and his hand on the small of her back.

Soon carriages queued up and carried guests down snow-heaped streets to Grand Central Depot, where they boarded four private trains for Woodlawn Cemetery. There another hearse waited, with Frank's body transferred to an "ice coffin," which contained a see-through pane for the departed to view the rites. Only the best. The lot alone cost at least $600 (twice an average annual salary), exclusive of porters and gravediggers, and the Westminster Presbyterian Church pastor didn't come cheap. Yet it was no time to skimp. Covering every doctrinal base, he read the Episcopal Burial of the Dead at the graveside: "The Lord make his face to shine upon him and be gracious unto him, the Lord lift up his countenance upon him and give him peace. Amen." Later, Miriam erected an expensive tombstone, which she inscribed with an epitaph of 150 words, among them: "He never caused any other grief than his own death."

NOTHING COULD HAVE been less true. The grief he bequeathed Miriam beyond the grave surpassed all that had gone before. But she never let on. Back at work, her future in jeopardy, she milked the prestige of widowhood and pitched into Frank's rehabilitation. She garlanded Leslie's office with black draperies, wreaths, and yew boughs, and enshrined the room as he left it—his coat draped on the chair and his pen and paper readied at the desk. She placed his image on the cover of the *Popular Monthly*, eulogizing him in a six-page spread as a "genius" and giant among men. She vowed never to dance or wear colors again.

The reckoning came three days after the funeral. Frank's will was unsealed, and the sons learned their fate: their disinheritance and bestowal of the entire estate to his wife. "Mrs. Leslie," pronounced the press, "will become a very rich woman from the will of her late husband." Perhaps the Leslie brothers believed it; instead, she inherited a bucket of fishhooks—mountainous debts and indenture to a board of predatory creditors. Then a diabolical lawsuit. Two weeks after the disclosure, Henry and Frank Leslie contested the will in court, alleging parental insanity, fraud, and Miriam's occult influence over their father, not inconceivable in a culture where a Manhattan woman was arrested as a witch the year before.

During the same month, she was forced out of her Fifth Avenue home. After twenty years of cosseted living in comfortable houses and posh hotels, Miriam found herself reduced to a garret. Her one-room attic apartment on the "featureless wasteland" of 13 West Fiftieth Street lacked a carpet, "fire in the grate," or window, except a fanlight so high she had to stand on a chair to see the sky. She knew, she said, "what it was to be cold and hungry."

She also knew abject squalor. Instead of a "private cabinet," she had to use a chamber pot and empty it each morning between five and seven in reeking, doorless WCs in the basement, which drained into the street sewers. Not until 1881 did a sanitation department grapple with the city filth. Just to walk from Fifth to Sixth Avenue, Miriam navigated a walkway gullied with horse urine and strewn with ash, animal waste, and vegetable scraps, her skirts powdered with dried manure.

This was the route Miriam took to the train for eleven months to contest her stepsons' lawsuit. The Sixth Avenue Elevated was a harsh letdown from her "stately barouche." Despite the vaunted conveniences—smooth double-track steel rails and pastel green cars

with spring-cushioned seats, plate-glass windows, and rep blinds—
travel on the El demanded strong nerves. Well into old age, Miriam
remembered the wretchedness of those twenty-eight-minute com-
mutes to City Hall.

When she traveled during rush hour, platforms were "black
with struggling crowds" who shoved onboard only to find standing
room—"sometimes hardly that." Conductors were brusque and the
packed passengers supplied "a rich harvest for pickpockets and a
free field for bullies and ruffians." Male commuters, Miriam carped,
behaved like swine. They refused seats to women despite the painful "constrictions of female dress" and refused them the respect
they "would pay to a well-dressed woman of leisure and wealth." She
described one "terrifying" run-in with four "ruffians" who "hustl[ed]
and annoy[ed] a lady."

ONCE IN THE courtroom she encountered worse "ruffians." The
brothers produced three lawyers to Miriam's one—alley fighters
with the force of social convention behind them. Playing into Gilded
Age prudery and gender prejudice, they promised "to lay bare" Mrs.
Leslie's "whole bad history," a "history black with evil doings," and
demonstrate her demonic influence over her husband. Everything
was stacked against her; she stood to lose her reputation, stake in
the publishing house, and Frank's remaining resources. At forty-
three she would be a social pariah, a ruined woman with nothing
of her own.

During the first half of the trial, the prosecution mounted a
slash-and-burn offensive. A procession of coachmen, tradesmen,
work colleagues, and family members testified to Mrs. Leslie's
"unhappy influence over her husband." "She completely fascinated
Mr. Leslie," they charged, and "controlled his acts" through her
"great personal charms." The court was all too familiar with this
breed of female, the femme fatale whose diablerie robbed men of
reason and willpower.

Under her seductive sway, pursued lawyers, Mr. Leslie engaged in ruinous over-expenditures—real estate, entertainment, jewels, unprofitable publications—and deferred to her business judgment, hence his "financial troubles" and bankruptcy. Most viciously, she set father against son. The instances were legion: her threats to the "children of his loins" at work, and her repeated refusals to admit his flesh and blood to the deathbed. Such iniquity was to be expected of a woman who abandoned domestic life for the workplace—a medical aberration, a virago, and "cesspool of the combined forces of [evil]."

Her brazen adultery, her "improper intimacy with Frank as Mrs. Squier," befit her dissolute character. Stephen J. Cox, a company engraver, stated that he saw her and Mr. Leslie "making up" on the train; a second coachman discovered Mrs. Squier in a wrapper in Frank's dressing room; and innkeepers from Greenwich to Long Branch certified that the pair occupied adjoining rooms during their summer visits.

Alfred Leslie drove the dagger home. He unveiled a floorplan of the Thirty-ninth Street house, which depicted connecting bedrooms on the second floor and the hall alcove where E. G. bunked. He said Miriam told his wife "that she hadn't slept with [Mr. Squier] for years," and recounted two scenes he witnessed firsthand. Once he saw something in the library "too delicate to state"; and on another occasion, he caught the two at the Parker House—his father in his "nightgown" with Mrs. Squier's clothes strewn on the sofa. As if his testimony weren't incriminating enough, the court subpoenaed Mrs. Jubber, Frank's British sister, who itemized the affair in graphic detail, from shared hotel rooms to unseemly conjugal intimacies. "Their conduct," she attested, "was such as one would expect between a man and a wife."

The case seemed locked up. Miriam had been incontestably routed, proven guilty of depravity, adultery, malign power over her husband, and cruelty toward his rightful heirs. And the law was partial to offspring in will disputes.

The trial wasn't over, though. Miriam came prepared for her day in court. She believed in women's superior strength under attack, their "subtlety [and] the unexpectedness of [their] maneuvers," and put her theory into practice. A past mistress of self-presentation, she appeared before the magistrate in the guise of "a tearful modern Niobe" clothed in "splendid mourning," "weeping for what another woman's children would wrest from her—a picture of pathetic despair." To shore up her respectability, she surrounded herself with a praetorian guard of genteel lady friends.

As the session resumed, she demonstrated her "female advantage" to the full—tactical cunning and the "wise intelligence and quickness of the serpent." Throughout the hearing, she plied her lawyer, William Fullerton (Frank's faithful counsel), with "frequent suggestions" and handled the defense like a "veritable Portia." She avoided the witness stand, where she would have been demolished, and executed a shrewd, theatrically inspired counterattack.

First, she sicced Fullerton on the sons. When he was finished with them, they could have walked out of a pulp melodrama, villainous specimens of filial greed and treachery. Under cross-examination, the rattled Alfred admitted to Fullerton's charges that he knowingly published rival papers without his father's approval, stole subscription lists, bore witness against Frank in Philadelphia, and aided and abetted bankruptcy creditors. Why? Thundered Fullerton, "To succeed to his business."

Henry received the same keelhauling. He, too, confessed to a battery of crimes against his father, such as purloining subscribers, conspiring against him after his bankruptcy, and scheming to appropriate his trademark name. Further offenses were enumerated: embezzlement, deadheading (free trips for journalistic favors), and marital brutality. At Bergen Point, hotel guests watched Henry whip his wife "until she was insensible." Both sons, inveighed Fullerton, were perfidious hypocrites who feigned affection for Miriam while plotting to displace her and seize the publishing empire for themselves.

The defense barged on. A surprise witness mounted the box on September 10. Mrs. Emily A. Pierce identified herself as a Denver resident who'd befriended Mr. and Mrs. Leslie during their 1877 California expedition. An unknown entity, she could have been any-one from Denver's rough-and-ready population of anomalous female floaters, possibly an actress.

On the stand, she appeared an evident lady. In clipped, school-mistress English, she told the judge she'd been Mr. Leslie's "confi-dante" for over a year in everything that "nearly and dearly concerned his domestic and business interest." During their regular "Sunday conversations," he unburdened himself and called Alfred a perfect "scoundrel," and Henry a "brute." She remembered his words ver-batim: They "have humbled my pride; they have broken my heart and they shall not profit from my death. I have remade my will, Mrs. Pierce, and that will is ironclad."

She next recited a reprisal of Frank's last days, with Miriam cast as the sainted stepmother and the sons as blackguards. The opposition objected: Hadn't this been scripted for her by Mrs. Leslie? But the motion was overruled and Mrs. Pierce continued. She began with the moment Frank learned his diagnosis. While Miriam wept "violently," he declaimed: "I do not ask you to cherish my memory, my darling, for I know you will do that; I ask you to vindicate it." Presumably to spare his wife's fragile feminine nerves, he took Mrs. Pierce aside and dictated a business prospectus for Miriam, which Pierce recorded on two sheets of paper with her self-supplying Mac-Kinnon pen.

For a coup de theatre Mrs. Pierce depicted the death scene, dur-ing which Miriam rose to angelic heights. She disobeyed her hus-band's dying wish to debar Alfred and pleaded with him when his son arrived: "Do not ask me to send him away when he is standing at the door in penitence and tears," she said. "For the sake of your wife whom you love, let him come in and give him your hand." Due to her entreaties, Frank relented, but the interview did not go well. Afterward, Mr. Leslie blazed out: "I forbid you to let Alfred Leslie enter this room again." Although Alfred sneaked in a second time and nearly killed his father with rage, Miriam forbore. She continued to speak "very kindly of Mr. Leslie's son." She even countenanced the traitorous Henry. At his appearance on the eve of Frank's death, she tried to effect a reconciliation, which her husband refused point-blank. His last words, spoken in Mrs. Pierce's presence, were "Keep those young men out."

To nineteenth-century Victorian Americans, final wishes of the dead were sacrosanct and carried a God-ordained directive. That, combined with Fullerton's magisterial rebuttal, sealed the will dispute. The December 18 edition of the *Illustrated* headlined the news: "Frank Leslie's Will Sustained."

MIRIAM HAD BEEN overmatched, outspent, and outgunned and had won. But it was a barbed victory. Despite the Pierce make-over, her image had been dismantled and irreparably damaged on public record, free for her enemies to use at their pleasure—and they would. Nor did Frank Leslie's reputation survive unscathed. During the testimony, witnesses noted his penchant for profanity, hypochondria, and strong drink and cited two incidents of drunken belligerence. They summed up his business philosophy: "Pirate all you can."

The character assassination was the least of it. Miriam inherited an estate in colossal disarray. The publishing house was on its beam ends—crippled by unprofitable publications and poor guidance and saddled with unpaid loans. By the end of the trial, Frank's assignee, Isaac W. England, had shaved Frank's debt from $151,000 to $98,000, which the five trustees seized as a buyout opportunity. With the blessing of the Court of Common Pleas, they demanded half the payment, $50,000, from Miriam within ten days, or forfeit the company lock, stock, and barrel. They had her in their grip. "She had no ready money, nothing to mortgage," and a mound of outstanding bills, not least for the funeral. At first the creditors soft-pedaled and offered to buy her off with a $20,000 payment and an all-expense trip abroad for an indefinite period. She refused. "No," she flashed, "I am Frank Leslie's widow, and will carry out [his] instructions to the letter whatever happens." Brave words.

She spent the winter, the coldest on record, in her unheated garret, "suffering from the very necessities of life." A series of mammoth snowstorms pummeled the city, temperatures hovered in the teens for months, and contagious diseases, like scarlet fever and diphtheria, raged unchecked. She recalled withstanding the ordeal with noble fortitude. "If poverty [comes], it is woman's courage that meets it," she reminisced; she "reigns a queen" despite those "who cannot comprehend her or her royalty." But there must have been predawn hours on her cold "hard bed" when fear clutched her throat and palsied her nerve.

By spring the creditors decided to crush Miriam "with a single blow." On May 13 Alexander Rice, John Hall, Edward Goodwin, William Wilson, and William Parsons invited her to the boardroom and handed her an ultimatum. She had little over a week. She "knew of nobody" who would help, and in a dark hour cried, "Oh! If I could only find a woman with $50,000 to lend," which gave the men a good laugh. She later winced at the memory: "The man's sneer [can] beat courage with blows of a fist or the stinging cuts of a whip." She felt like "running away." Reverend Charles Deems, pastor of the Church of the Strangers (destined to play another pivotal role in her life), prayed for her.

His prayers were heard. A young artist at the firm, Charles Beecher Bunnell, a future science fiction illustrator, learned of Mrs. Leslie's plight and mentioned it to his Brooklyn neighbor, Eliza Jane Smith. Mrs. Smith, a former housemaid, was the widow of millionaire Thomas K. Smith, who'd made a fortune in the Civil War selling shoddy clothing to the government. Moved by Bunnell's account, she wrote a check for the full amount at the eleventh hour on the condition that Miriam leave her jewelry as security and repay her in 10 percent installments, starting November first.

The same day Miriam paid off the creditors and on June 4 assumed control of Frank Leslie Publishing. But her problems had just begun. She braced for battle by legally changing her name to "Frank Leslie." There must be no doubt about her claim to the company and her authority in a misogynistic male-dominated industry. A woman at the head of a business empire was unheard-of and profoundly threatening. Women, by definition, were lesser men with smaller brains, who couldn't reason or rule and emasculated the male workforce. Miriam now commanded hundreds of male employees, several of whom had testified against her during the will dispute.

On the business front, the situation was desperate. After she liquidated the remaining debt, she encountered twelve languishing publications—six weeklies and six monthlies—at one of the unluckiest times in journalism. Devotee Joaquin Miller romanticized her resumption of the firm: "Mrs. Leslie," he rhapsodized, "went straight to the dead man's office, directing and controlling every detail of the most wonderful publishing house in the world like a Napoleon." But he was conveniently absent in England at the time, or he would have found the house in a shambles and his Napoleon at bay. The print culture conspired against her, too.

The year 1880 was a turning point in American journalism and Frank Leslie had been asleep at the wheel. New periodicals flooded the market (and would multiply by four and a half times in the next five years) and weeklies were increasingly supplanted by illustrated sensationalistic dailies. Costs had risen for serialized novels, and technology had transformed the industry through telephones, typewriters, faster presses, and revolutionary illustration techniques.

The Leslie method was no longer cutting-edge. Rival magazines boasted novel engravings that worked directly from photographs reproduced on wood, rendering pictures with greater texture, verisimilitude, and atmosphere. *Scribner's Monthly* offered prizes for beginners in this "New School of Wood Engraving" and hired inventor Theodore L. De Vinne, who pioneered cylindrical printing on pressboard that further refined illustrations. *Scribner's* reader-ship skyrocketed. The halftone process—images filtered through dot grids onto metal plates—was also gaining ground and creating unmatched smooth-line tonal effects.

Miriam took her bearings and the helm. Ignoring Frank's last wishes, she discarded his business plan, which stipulated that Andrew Armstrong, a Scribner publisher, run the firm as a stock company. Instead, she took full control and left nothing to chance. She monitored every facet of the company, from balance sheets to make-up and distribution, and logged twelve-hour days from 8:00 A.M. to 8:00 P.M. Still business flagged.

By her own admission, she was "inexperienced in business affairs [and] unused to exercising authority." Even the weather refused to cooperate. Rainstorms battered the city for three weeks in June, flooding basements, disgorging sewage, and gully-washing sidewalks. Miriam walked down a debris-choked flume of mud in soaked skirts to and from work each day. Then on the twenty-eighth an unprecedented heat wave arrived. To breathe was like being struck in the face with "a draught from the heated depths of a mine," reported the *New York Times*.

"It was a bitter pill," she said, "but I downed it." She persevered. She waged a successful campaign to win the "respect and sympathy" of the staff and made an aggressive bid for subscribers. In a June 18 "Business Statement," she promised readers that "neither labor nor expenditure [would] be spared to keep them abreast of the demands of the times" and latest developments. But delivering on her prom-ise was another matter. As luck would have it, the early summer of 1881 was an empty stretch of slow news days, and Miriam had 125 double-columned pages of the *Popular Monthly* to fill, besides weekly editions of the *Illustrated* and ten additional magazines.

She made the most of the thin pickings; she padded, bright-ened layout, and ginned up available stories. The only news from the White House, which President Garfield had occupied for nearly four months, was a fight over the spoils system with party boss Roscoe

Conkling. She covered Conkling's resignation and Garfield's victory for Civil Service reform until interest faded.

Now Congress was recessing. When the Canadian steamship *Victoria* went down and killed 250 onboard, she sensationalized the wreck with front page coverage and lurid illustrations of flailing victims and mangled bodies. For the most part, though, it was a question of fillers—the umbrella ant of Brazil, Japanese children, tours of Luray cavern and Nantucket, and a Ladies Sewing Circle lawsuit against the church. She worked the winning Leslie formula, avoiding flammable topics (such as labor unrest) and providing an eye-friendly mix of cultural nuggets, sentimental fiction, recipes, spicy curiosities, and "Fun" pages.

Still readership dwindled and revenue declined. To offset sagging sales, Miriam increased ads to forty per issue, introduced a promotional contest for the best holiday cover design, and put the Interlaken estate on the market—in vain. By Friday, July 1, the company was bleeding red ink, and vultures were circling. She had four months left to pay the first installment of her $50,000 loan. Looking back, she said, it was a "shipwreck." Then Saturday arrived, and in an instant, the wind changed.

Miriam Leslie, pictured wearing the medallion of the Venezuelan Order of the Bust of Bolivar. First published in the *Los Angeles Herald*, February 13, 1892.

Granger Historical Picture Archives

Miriam Florence Follin as "Aspasia of the South."
First published in *Book News*, April 1893.

The French Market in New Orleans on a Sunday morning, 1883. Illustration
from *Frank Leslie's Illustrated Newspaper*, March 31, 1883, p. 95.

World-renowned courtesan and mentor to Miriam, Lola Montez

Courtesy of the Metropolitan Museum of Art. Gift of I. N. Phelps Stokes,
Edward S. Hawes, Alice Mary Hawes, and Marion Augusta Hawes, 1937.

"Minnie Montez" (second from left) with Lola, crossing the Hudson in the 1857 "great
inundation." Illustration from *Frank Leslie's Illustrated Newspaper*, March 7, 1857.

Photograph from *Purple Passage* by Madeleine B. Stern
(University of Oklahoma Press, 1953), photo insert, p. 70

Miriam as a young woman of the town

Miriam's second husband, anthropologist Ephraim G. Squier
Smithsonian Institution Archives

Mr. and Mrs. E. G. Squier

Photograph from *Purple Passage* by Madeleine B. Stern
(University of Oklahoma Press, 1953), photo insert, p. 70

Miriam Squier, fashion plate, 1870

Photograph by Charles L. Wrenn, from *Purple Passage* by Madeleine B. Stern
(University of Oklahoma Press, 1953), photo insert, p. 70

Mrs. Squier (third from left), belle of Lincoln's inauguration ball. Published in
Frank Leslie's Illustrated Newspaper, March 23, 1861, p. 285.

Library of Congress, Prints and Photographs Division

Frank Leslie, the "grand seigneur of Publishers' Row"

Cartoon of the busy Leslie office, by Edward Jump, 1868

Mrs. E. G. Squier, "editress" of *Frank Leslie's Lady's Magazine*

Photograph from *Purple Passage* by Madeleine B. Stern
(University of Oklahoma Press, 1953), photo insert, p. 150

Frank Leslie's Lady's Magazine,
November 1869 issue, cover

Courtesy of the author

Frank Leslie's Lady's Journal,
December 13, 1873, cover

Courtesy of the author

Joaquin Miller, "Byron of the Rockies"

Photograph by Matthew Brady. Brady-Handy
Photograph Collection, Library of Congress,
Prints and Photographs Division.

Poet and fiancé Marquis
de Leuville, 1874

Courtesy of Dick Weindling
and Marianne Colloms

Fourth husband, Willie Wilde

Photograph from Alchreton, Free Social
Encyclopedia for the World. Public domain.

Admirer Prince Guy de Lusigan

Portrait by Diogène Maillart, 1898.
Wikimedia Commons.

Mrs. Leslie's private office. Illustration printed in *Frank Leslie's Popular Monthly*, August 1883, p. 132.

Courtesy of the author

Miriam as "Frank Leslie," at the helm of the publishing company, 1880

Originally appeared in *New York, the Metropolis: Its Noted Business and Professional Men* by John Franklin Sprague, digitized by the Internet Book Archive. Public domain.

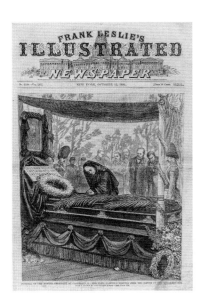

The editorial room at Frank Leslie Publishing. Illustration printed in *Frank Leslie's Popular Monthly*, August 1883, p. 136.

Courtesy of the author

President Garfield's funeral coverage, the coup that saved the publishing company. *Frank Leslie's Illustrated Newspaper*, October 15, 1881.

Courtesy of the author

Oscar Wilde in America

Photograph by Napoleon Sarony. Billy Rose Theatre Division, the New York Public Library Digital Collections.

Mrs. Leslie, "World-Famous Publisher"

Photograph by Culver, from Lynne Vincent Cheney, "Mrs. Frank Leslie's Illustrated Newspaper," *American Heritage*, October 1975, p. 45

The celebrated Thursday salon. Mrs. Leslie is second woman from the left, holding her Yorkshire terrier.

Photograph by Brown Brothers, from Lynne Vincent Cheney, "Mrs. Frank Leslie's Illustrated Newspaper," *American Heritage*, October 1975, p. 47

High society gatekeeper
Ward McAllister

Photograph by Brown Brothers.
Courtesy of Boston Public Library,
Leslie Jones Collection.

Caroline Schermerhorn Astor,
first social queen

Wikimedia Commons

Mrs. Alva Vanderbilt (later Mrs. O.H.P.
Belmont), second social queen

National Photo Company Collection,
Library of Congress

Marion "Mamie" Graves Anthon Fish,
third social queen

Wikimedia Commons

A later portrait of Miriam, perhaps for her engagement to Don Teodoro

Miriam's last love and fiancé, Don Teodoro Martel y Fernández de Córdoba

Frank Leslie Publishing building on Fifth Avenue and Sixteenth Street, 1893

Originally published in *King's Handbook of New York City*, 1893 by Moses King, digitized by Harvard University. Public domain.

The press room at Frank Leslie Publishing. Illustration printed in *Frank Leslie's Popular Monthly*, August 1883, p. 141.

Courtesy of the author

The electrotyping department at Frank Leslie Publishing.
Illustration printed in *Frank Leslie's Popular Monthly*, August 1883, p. 140.

Courtesy of the author

Miriam's parlor at the Sherry Hotel, 1899
Courtesy of the Museum of the City of New York

Frederick L. Colver, the adman
who bought out Mrs. Leslie

Originally printed in *Printers' Ink*,
vol. 52, 1905, p. 36. Public domain.

MRS. FRANK LESLIE A MULATTO, HE SAYS

Relative of First Husband, Contesting Will, Avers That Her Mother Was a Negress.

HER FAMILY HISTORY VAGUE

Executors Report Estate to be Valued at $1,748,550, Besides Six Parcels of Real Estate.

Bombshell mixed-race allegation against
Miriam Leslie in dispute over her will,
New York Times, April 18, 1915, p. 18

Public domain

Carrie Chapman Catt, legatee of Miriam's fortune
and president of the American Woman Suffrage Association

The Leslie Woman Suffrage Commission,
pictured in *The Woman's Journal*, May 26, 1917

CHAPTER SIX

"QUEEN OF PARK PLACE"
1881–83

SATURDAY, JULY 2, 1881, promised to be another dull day at Frank Leslie headquarters, during a midsummer slump of non-descript news stories. Miriam must have surveyed the slushpile of dispatches on her desk with growing desperation. The clock was ticking. Bulletins from abroad provided nothing new. The same con-flicts simmered without incident—continued Tunisian resistance to the French, Irish tenant squabbles with the British, and more nihilist threats against the Russian czar. At home, another dry stretch. Work-ers continued half-hearted strikes against management in Brooklyn, a steel magnate's son tried and failed to commit suicide on a New Jersey ferry, Pastor Heinrich of Long Island denied an adultery liai-son with Mrs. Crippendorf, and in the capital, President Garfield was about to leave on his first vacation since he'd taken office.

At forty-nine Ohioan James Garfield was the third youngest president in American history and had come to office by a fluke. During a locked Republican convention, he was elected as the default candidate—one of the "Half Breeds" opposed to the spoils system, government jobs in exchange for political favors. He had just won a bitter struggle in the White House over spoils kingpin Roscoe

Conkling of the Stalwart faction, and he could congratulate himself. As he told Secretary of State James Blaine in the carriage on the way to the Limited Express to New York, he believed he had "passed the danger-point of his administration, that leaders of the party had begun to understand and agree with the purposes of his government." He was in high spirits; he'd performed handstands and sung snatches of Gilbert and Sullivan songs for his children before he left to join his wife at Long Branch for a ten-day holiday.

At the Baltimore and Potomac Railroad Sixth Street Station, a man in a shabby suit with a "queer, wild look in his eyes" prowled inside. When Garfield arrived to catch the 9:36 A.M. Express, he and Blaine strode together through the ladies' waiting room. Suddenly shots like firecracker reports rang out through the station. The President threw up his arms, cried, "My God what is this," staggered, and fell. Charles Guiteau, a disappointed office seeker, had haunted Washington for months and waited for his chance, firing twice at Garfield with a high-caliber bulldog revolver, hitting him in the arm and back, and knocking him to the floor. As the police escorted Guiteau away, he cried, "I did it and want to be arrested. I am a Stalwart of the Stalwarts! Arthur [Garfield's vice president] is President now!" At first, Guiteau seemed to have attained his goal. Garfield lay insensate in a pool of blood, surrounded by a clutch of alarmed doctors.

By 9:45 A.M., Miriam got word of the shooting. "I knew," she reflected later, "what my husband would have done under the circumstances." Within an hour, she dispatched two artists by train to Washington. They returned on the midnight Express Saturday with a portfolio of sketches and worked all day Sunday, sustained by Miriam's champagne and sandwiches. For two days, she never left the building. On Monday, a fully illustrated edition of the weekly *Newspaper* hit the stands—an unparalleled feat of publishing.

She wasn't the first to get the story; every paper in America posted "Extras" by Saturday afternoon. But she was the first to provide a pictorial record of the event. A century ahead of tabloid journalism, she grasped what readers wanted—up-close visual participation in events and vicarious intimacy with public figures. In a journalistic breakthrough, she breached presidential privacy barriers and portrayed the inside of Garfield's sickroom, accompanied by a running commentary of his symptoms, vital signs, doctors' prognoses, and his wife's whispered confidences and sobs at the door. As he lay dying over the next two months, *Frank Leslie's* produced eleven cover engravings to *Harper's* six, and more graphic illustrations and more intimate coverage than the competition.

Miriam also sent reporters into Charles Guiteau's jail cell and monitored his day-to-day behavior. Guiteau made excellent copy. He mugged for artists (he covered his head with a blanket if guards appeared) and begged for caricature, with an off-kilter face with wide-set sunken eyes, a hooked nose, jug ears, and a "startling" *en brosse* haircut. He talked a blue streak, raging that God instructed him to kill Garfield in revenge for his thwarted diplomatic ambitions. After all, he was supremely qualified as a "lawyer, a theologian, and a politician."

In fact, he was none of the above. A serial loser, the forty-year-old assassin had failed at everything he attempted. He'd flunked out of a free love commune where women nicknamed him "Charles Getout," blown a quasi-legal career, and served jail time amid hardscrabble years on the evangelical and political trails. His grandiosity, though, knew no bounds. He basked in his moment of glory and bragged to reporters of his exploit. Once he raved that the doctors—not he—killed the President.

A madman's rant, but prophetic. The president's ten doctors, led by the autocratic Dr. Bliss, discredited Lister's antisepsis discovery and probed the wound repeatedly with unsterile fingers, which created a bacterial infection that proved fatal. Throughout the long, unusually hot summer, Miriam rode herd on the story. She ran attacks on the spoils system and profiled Garfield as a bootstrap American hero, a poor frontier boy who became a school president at twenty-six, a Civil War general, and a congressman for seventeen years. She procured a bedside seat at his final struggle, where reporters recorded his tortured cries "for a drink of water," and artists drew explicit sketches of his ravaged features.

When he died on September 19, Miriam achieved her masterstroke. Although the *Illustrated Newspaper* had already gone to press that Monday, she destroyed the edition and printed a second issue filled with fresh engravings of the President's final hours at Elberon, New Jersey, on a gurney beside the sea. Her gamble paid off. The Wednesday number reached all-time highs. She followed this with another bold move. Despite warnings from the president of the American News Company that it couldn't be done, she delivered thirty thousand papers to Cleveland for Garfield's burial with coverage of the Washington state ceremony. The crowds on September 26 surpassed those at Lincoln's funeral, and the papers sold out. By October, she'd raised circulation from thirty-three thousand to two hundred thousand and posted a profit. In early fall, she repaid Mrs. Smith's loan of $50,000 with interest, and then, as she told it, went "home and [fell] on the floor, completely exhausted."

WHEN SHE GOT up, she found an unimagined prospect before her. Overnight her feat transformed her into the "Queen of Park Place." She was suddenly a force on Publishers' Row, head of an empire that led the pack with a "complete pictorial history of the [Garfield] affair" and was poised for takeoff. At work she powered up, fashioning her persona for maximum force and effectiveness. In an artful Trojan horse maneuver, she re-amped her femininity and adopted the guise of the porcelain Southern belle who directed affairs from her "bijou sanctuary" in a "musical" contralto. Businessmen found her at her oak desk in a ruffled organdy apron over a tight black gown with a raven quill in hand, her "hair parted with delightful insouciance at the side." Caught off guard, they were disarmed and brought to heel.

Beneath her soft feminine façade, Miriam ran the company like a field marshal. Her command was absolute; her control, panoptic. A contemporary print baron said he knew no one "who was so thoroughly acquainted with every detail of the business." Nothing escaped her watchful eye. Nine department heads reported to her each day, and between vetting editorials and story submissions, she proofed manuscripts, approved makeup, signed all contracts, checks, and money orders, and oversaw four hundred employees. By the end of 1881, she could boast of the lead that Frank Leslie's "enjoyed in the illustrated journalism of the country."

With her position solidified, she began a stem-to-stern company makeover. While tracking the Guiteau trial and execution through June, she started a massive modernization of 53–57 Park Place. She brought the production department up to speed with new technology, including house-patented curved electro-plates; introduced higher grade newsprint; increased type size; decreased letterpress columns; and pared down publications. Over five years, she reduced Leslie's six weeklies and six monthlies to three weeklies and four monthlies, and dropped the risqué *New York Illustrated Times*, a soft target for Anthony Comstock's purity police. She worked in overdrive. "It was a gigantic undertaking," she said, "and I threw myself into it so completely that I thought by day and dreamed by night of nothing else." Determined to "make her mark" or "die in the attempt," she became, for a time, "no longer a woman but an embodied idea."

Miriam, however, wasn't likely to forget she was a woman for long. Soon after her Garfield coup, a "fine-looking Englishman" arrived in New York to remind her. He was the toast of the ladies and a lord in the bargain. On tour to promote his poetry collection, *Entre-Nous*, the Marquis de Leuville made a dramatic impression. Tall and handsome with shoulder-length black curls and a flaring mustache, he dressed for display in loud velvet coats, bedizened with silk scarves, mosaic jewelry, and gold chains. He wore large rings and high-heeled boots with lifts that accentuated a limp—caused, he said, by a wound from a duel.

A titled Euro-version of Joaquin Miller, he was a gentleman of the chivalric school who espoused courtly love and worship of the fair sex, an exemplar of Miriam's "ideal champion knight of the nineteenth century." Her friend, writer Mary Elizabeth Braddon, portrayed him as a "dangerously attractive" "Don Juan" in an 1882 novel, *Mount Royal*.

As soon as he met Miriam he gave her the full troubadour treatment. When he saw her descend from a carriage at a friend's reception—first her "dainty little foot," then her "charming" being, all "done up in crape"—he was "infatuated at first sight." He paced the parlor "with utmost impatience" until they were introduced and courted her *con furioso* thereafter.

Miriam at this point might have welcomed a royal rush. She was overworked, bone-tired, and relished the "diversion" of male companionship. She also yearned, despite her cynicism about female erotic dependency and love's "soap bubble," for "manly protection" and romantic love. Intensity, she also thought, was "the most attractive trait a man could possibly possess," second only to flattery. And the Marquis pulled out the stops. She was a goddess to be propitiated, worshiped "on bended knee," and pampered. He carried her dog on walks, and when her wedding ring fell off at the opera, he placed his crested signet ring on her finger and told her to wear it instead. He was with her at Saratoga in early September and so attentive that gossips predicted she would soon cease to be a widow.

The Marquis's first siege on her affections, though, was premature. He would have to wait a full year before resuming his campaign. Miriam had more pressing matters at hand—the company overhaul to manage and profit margins to maintain after the Garfield bump. She depended on a mid-level audience that was increasingly at odds. Her base, a mercurial mix of workers and upwardly mobile bourgeois, was growing more polarized about the defining issues of the day—poverty, immigration, race, class, labor and capital, and women's rights. To appease both groups required a balancing act, rendered trickier by the upheavals of 1882.

* * *

JANUARY 1882 BROUGHT with it another economic recession, which ignited tensions that had smoldered underground since the end of the long depression three years before. This crisis, triggered by runaway railroad wars and mismanagement, dried up construction, trade, and money supply and levied deep wage cuts on laborers. Strikes ticked up and union membership in the anti-capitalist Knights of Labor swelled to over a hundred thousand nationwide. Battle lines hardened.

Miriam couldn't afford to lose readers, especially with competition from the flood of popular dailies. In a diplomatic sleight of hand, she lowered the volume and soothed labor grievances, acknowledging the "evils" of monopolistic industries and the rights of labor. When Cumberland miners walked out in June, the *Illustrated Newspaper* equivocated, pairing an anti-strike editorial with a front-page image of a peaceful shutdown in the Maryland town. Coverage of the first Labor Day Parade in September was positive: the New York City pageant was orderly and sober and "in every way credible to those engaged in it."

At the same time, the paper was careful to placate conservatives. While condemning the "oppression of working men" to enrich millionaires, issues featured stories designed to assuage the privileged. Editorials praised American prosperity, British colonial expansion, and anti-tax legislation, and laced into the immigrant invasion—the new tide of southern Italian laborers and "squalid, filthy" Russian Jews. Society took pride of place, with items devoted to the rituals and daily minutiae of the fashionable world.

For uncut elitism, readers could turn to *Frank Leslie's Popular Monthly*. Marketed to white-collar professionals who paid twenty-five cents a copy (versus ten cents for the weekly *Illustrated*), the magazine didn't require the same difficult balance. Miriam could relax appeasement efforts and air her patrician sympathies. In February she launched "The Editor's Opera Glass," a vehicle designed to celebrate the "great wheel of social brilliancy."

She talked up Delmonico's balls, cotillion dinners, ladies' coaching parties, lawn tennis competitions, and stylish charities, such as a benefit for the Decorative Art Society in which the Four Hundred donated a trove of antique fans. Mirroring elite tastes, she congratulated President Arthur on his gentrification of the White House and Vanderbilt on his "sumptuous" palace produced by his "Aladdin's lamp."

"Wealth and material progress," she pronounced, "are the topics to which we cling." Except when she didn't. Within her veneration of the gratin lurked a buried hostility toward high society that seeped into her columns. On the subject of the social exclusion of actresses, she flared up: "Where, now, are the old edicts against the play?" she demanded. "From what club or social gathering [are they] barred?" The answer was obvious: from the best clubs and from Mrs. Astor's guest list, where even a brief stage career, like Miriam's, was a death knell.

In May, she pilloried Society's most select institution, the Patriarch's Ball. The "fastidious" social ladies, she scoffed, have decided to form an even more restrictive "Lady Patriarch's Ball." "As if Lady Patriarchs were nice! Why don't they give really exclusive balls called 'Aspasias' "—a nom de guerre for courtesans. She ended with a veiled threat: "It is the uninvited guest who remains master of the situation"—doubtless a reminder of her influence in the press. She chided further that if "clever society women" entered Columbia College, they'd be able to write the "long-expected" American novel, given their intimate knowledge of the monde. Paradoxically, she wanted nothing more than that knowledge herself and acceptance in the monde. Perhaps the conflict proved too great a strain; she dropped "The Editor's Opera Glass" after eight months.

A MAN WHO also understood that conflict came to America at just that moment. Some sources attribute Oscar Wilde's 1882 lecture tour to Miriam's suggestion, although they couldn't have met until now. He was twenty-seven, a fellow showman, and they got on at once, becoming fast friends. One of his first calls in New York was to Mrs. Leslie's home, where he "poured out his soul," possibly about his dubious acceptance by Americans, adding that "to be in society is merely a bore [but] to be outside is a tragedy."

As it turned out, his yearlong tour through the states was closer to a farce. The object of the lectures was to feature Wilde as the model for Reginald Bunthorne, the caricatured Aesthetic fop of Gilbert and Sullivan's *Patience*, which was playing at the Standard Theater. Wilde needed the money and liked the spotlight—or thought he did. When the *Arizona* docked in January, he greeted the press dressed like his counterpart in a Byronic tie, frogged bottle-green fur coat, and a seal smoking cap over a long wavy bob. Affecting an Aesthetic pose, he slouched against the railing and fielded a drumfire of questions from reporters: "Did he fry his eggs on both sides?" Bathe in "triple essence of verbena?" "Trim his nails in the style of the Empress of Japan?" On cue, he told the customs officer (who'd opened his bags to see if he slept in lace nightgowns) he "had nothing to declare but his genius."

By the time he checked into his suite at the Grand Hotel on Broadway, he'd soured on "decivilized" Americans and begun to suspect the real purpose of the tour: a Barnum roadshow. In the beginning it seemed otherwise. The cultural lights of Manhattan feted him like a "petit roi," and the literary set, including the Marquis de Leuville and Joaquin Miller, paid tribute. Joaquin embraced him as a soulmate and hustled tickets for his opening night. He needn't have bothered. On January 9 the house was packed at Chickering Hall with an overflow crowd.

Promptly at eight he walked onstage in a purple dress coat with a diamond-studded vest, velvet knee breeches, silk stockings, and pumps with grosgrain bows. For two hours he expounded on Aesthetic ideals in an Oxonian singsong: the revolt against Victorian mores and materialism and the devotion to art, ritual, and beauty. A poem, he said, had no morals; it was "either well or badly written."

He compared artists to Greek gods and cracked that Gilbert and Sullivan's satire was the tribute mediocrity paid to genius. The audience fidgeted; most were bored. Colonel Morse, his manager, billed Wilde's debut as a success, and Miriam's *Illustrated Newspaper* called the performance a "palpable hit." But the lecture fell flat, pronounced "odious" and "painful" by the mainstream press.

The night augured what lay in store. In one city after another, his act flopped and drew ridicule and parody. Audiences at Harvard and Rochester heckled him, *Harper's Weekly* lampooned him as a sunflower-worshipping "aesthetic monkey," and the *Washington Post* compared him to the "Wild Man of Borneo." Vaudeville comedians and minstrels burlesqued him, venders hawked his caricatures, and families in parlors sang around the piano: "Oscar dear, Oscar dear/How utterly, flutterly utter you are;/Oscar dear, Oscar dear/I think you're awfully wild, ta da!" Insinuations of his homosexuality, then still under wraps, grew vocal. A *Nation* critic denounced his "unmanly manhood," and journalists piled on, attacking his "womanly" physique and "effeminate gestures." He toyed with his handkerchief like a "bashful maiden." Wilde put a brave face on things, parried slights with epigrams, feigned triumphs, and boasted that he was "indestructible." In private, he drank.

Throughout his 140 lectures across the country from Albany to Dubuque to Leadville, Nevada, Miriam did what she could to rally his spirits. She plugged his tour and vilified "long-eared" vulgarians who called him a "fool," reminding boors that he'd been "pedestaled by society" and lionized at Newport. Which was stretching it. The *ton* didn't recognize him and only invited him to Newport for the weekend as unofficial hired entertainment. Finally, box-office receipts petered out, and the venture was declared a "fiasco."

The morning Wilde left for England on December 30, Miriam was at Pier 40 to see him off. The Cunard liner, *Bothnia*, loomed up in drypoint against the predawn charcoal haze of the Hudson River. It was 6:30 A.M.—cold, dark, with the dock in a tumult of departure—and no one wanted to be there. For Miriam it meant the sacrifice of beauty sleep and her strict morning workout; for Oscar, a bitter denouement to a disastrous tour. Miriam said she barely recognized him: He looked for all the world "like a nineteenth century gentleman, quiet in dress and reserved in manner." He'd decided, he told her, to drop his "masquerade" and "affectations of manner and speech" and "give up his knee breeches." His "mission to [these] barbaric shores had been substantially a failure." America, though, wasn't an entire loss. He'd acquired hide, some money, street wisdom, anecdotes, and influential allies like Mrs. Leslie. As they parted, he insisted Miriam visit his mother's London salon (with consequences he couldn't have guessed) and quipped from the gangplank: "I'm going home to cut [my] hair."

MIRIAM DIDN'T TAKE him up on it for six months, but Jane Wilde's soirées seem to have left a strong impression. Neither rich nor patrician, Jane had won acceptance by Society through her lively receptions that attracted the cultural elite of London. For Miriam, social New York remained impregnable; during the 1882 Season she attended only one of several hundred weddings and entertainments listed in Charles Crandall's *Annual Record*. Five days after Oscar sailed, she responded with his mother's strategy and hosted the first of her Thursday receptions to coincide with the exclusive Thursday Evening Club.

Joaquin Miller described the first night: "We [were] ushered into a dazzling scene" where "my Lady Leslie," a "beautiful little woman with a girlish face and with her large eyes full of childish wonder, [took] the homage of all hearts." His buildup and Miriam's social finesse succeeded. By the end of the month, the *National Republican* pronounced her evenings "one of the features of fashionable society." Even if the inner sanctum continued to be off-bounds, her social profile rose and led to a reception in her honor given by stylish author Harriet Spofford and her husband at the Washington Riggs House.

Business now flourished. At work she found her feet. Thanks to hard work, management acumen, and bold vision, Frank Leslie's was netting $100,000 a year. An advertising-age pioneer, she issued a special feature in the *Popular Monthly* to showcase "the most extensive publishing house of illustrated literature" with her portrait in a Mary Stuart bonnet on the front.

She was the "presiding genius of the entire establishment." From her private office, she reigned supreme, monitoring editorials, illustrations, sixteen presses, and business details while gracefully receiving a stream of callers and salesmen. Both "ladylike" and a "thorough woman of business," she was adored by her employees who vied for her "personal approval" and regarded her with the "greatest respect and loyalty." "They all touch their hats to me," she declared, "and I believe they would die for me."

She was soon put to the test. When a strike erupted at the company (amid a rash of labor revolts that year), she marched upstairs and entered the room just as workers threatened to throw the foreman out the window. "I am ashamed of you," she chastised, "to treat an engraver's widow this way. You owe me some allegiance." They obediently disbanded and worked all night to make up lost labor.

In two years, she'd become the acknowledged "Empress of Journalism" who had gone where no American woman had ventured before. She had outsmarted the system and made it in a man's world. The national press, to which she had privileged access, idolized her. She was "young and very beautiful," "a planet star among women in public life." Secure in her power seat, she could afford risks at the *Illustrated*. She could espouse women's causes and court controversy with a column, "Problems of the Time," which published essays by gadflies like socialist Henry George. She had arrived and gotten what she schemed and labored for—success, riches, fame, and dominion at the workplace.

But she wanted more—the ever-elusive imprimatur of proper New York society. And in February there was a promising thaw in the social stratosphere. Alva Vanderbilt, a parvenu from a déclassé

Southern background, was married to multimillionaire William K. Vanderbilt and shunned by the Astor set. Alva, an ambitious striver with the face of an "intelligent Pekinese" and mettle of a railroad baron, did not take kindly to exclusion.

Drawing on her husband's bottomless funds, she commissioned the most lavish mansion in America, a Fifth Avenue limestone chateau with flying buttresses, rococo dormers, and a tourelle decorated with fleurs-de-lis. The interior was on a Babylonian scale—apartments stuffed with Boucher tapestries, Boulle cabinets, Renaissance mantelpieces and marbles, and paintings looted from European castles. Still, Mrs. Astor held aloof.

Undaunted, Alva planned a costume ball to inaugurate her home and invited the world—1,200 guests drawn from the Four Hundred and wealthy arrivistes. In a further afront to aristocratic convention, she enlisted the press to publicize the event. With one stroke, she launched a new era in high society where position and prestige depended on net worth, surface grandeur, and personal publicity. The ice was cracking.

Which might explain why Miriam chose February—the same month invitations went out—to stage a tour through the South to regild her image. With cooperative journalists along, she could fashion herself as a high-born gentlewoman of old Louisiana. She took with her a status accessory, author Jane G. Austin of Plymouth descent, and two artists to document her pilgrimage. The "famous editress," announced the dailies, would be traveling with her entourage in a custom-fitted Pullman car through Richmond and Charleston before arriving in New Orleans February 25.

At her suite in the Charles Hotel, she invited reporters to share her reminiscences. She had come "home," she said, where she'd been born in a Vieux Carré mansion, then raised until she was twelve on Dauphine Street and a plantation. Fast-forwarding to her marriage with Frank Leslie, she rehearsed the story of the "Southern lady who had cultivated literature from her girlhood," surmounted the odds, and gained control of the great Leslie publishing house. Throughout

Mardi Gras week, she cemented her patrician bayou background, taking sentimental journeys to landmarks and entertaining local dignitaries and socialites with antebellum stories. Although no family or friends were in evidence, she received a hometown hero's welcome. Reporters hailed her youthful "pretty-looking appearance" (except one who noted her "dark features in the Creole mold") and praised the exquisite "*drap d'été* traveling dress" she wore as she departed on a Louisville and Nashville "club on wheels."

On the return trip, she stopped in Mobile where she visited her aunt Mrs. Gorham Davenport and the graves of her re-gentrified grandmother and father. To interviewers, she promised to write a book about her trip, *Scenes in Southlands*. But she never got around to it; she had other priorities and distractions in the coming year.

When she and her retinue reached New York, Society was in a fever of anticipation over the Vanderbilt ball. During Lent, invited guests had employed fleets of creative consultants, dressmakers, and dance masters to instruct participants in the intricately choreographed figures Alva had planned. One of the highlights was to be the Star Quadrille, performed by debutantes in yellow, blue, mauve, and white tulle with electric stars in their hair. Carrie, Mrs. Astor's daughter, had worked especially hard on her steps.

By a strange oversight, however, her invitation never arrived. As the day approached, inquiries followed. Alva replied that since neither she nor the Vanderbilts had been formally received by Mrs. Astor, it was impossible to invite her daughter. Within an hour, a servant arrived in Astor livery and delivered her card to Alva's door. The Knickerbockery was dethroned, forced to hand over the keys of the kingdom to the new rich social order.

To drive it home, Alva invited the entire press corps on the premises to record the "ball of the decade." The Frank Leslie crew was among them. By eight P.M. on Monday, March 26, police had cordoned off hundreds of spectators at 660 Fifth Avenue clamoring to catch a glimpse of the gentry in their finery. At ten, carriages began to roll in. To the cheers of the crowd, a procession of fantastically garbed personages stepped onto the red carpet, rigged out as fairies, nuns, pirates, gypsies, exotic birds, historic celebrities, the four seasons, and *ancien régime* nobles.

Powdered footmen in knee breeches and maroon surcoats ushered guests through a white marble doorway to the entrance—a tapestried grand hall embowered with orchid chains, ferns, and six thousand roses at two dollars apiece. Ladies retired to a state bedroom up the fifty-foot staircase to freshen up before descending to greet Alva, stationed beside a portrait of herself, dressed as a Venetian princess in a peacock diadem and gold-figured satin gown with Catherine the Great's pearls looped around her neck.

At 11:30 a trumpet fanfare announced the quadrilles. A hundred costumed dancers assembled on the staircase and filed into the dining room, where they jetéd and chasséd through six square dances based on storybook themes from the "Star" to the "Hobby Horse," executed astride life-size wooden horses. Afterward, the floor opened for general dancing in the block-long vaulted gymnasium that had been converted into a tropical forest. On the sidelines, Frank Leslie's artists sketched the only on-the-spot illustrations of the ball. In the throng, Cornelius Vanderbilt as Louis XVI might be seen waltzing with his wife, "Electric Light"; Mr. Hewitt as King Lear galloping with Mrs. Neilson, the "Queen of Sheba"; or Mr. Cutting as Romeo polkaing with Miss Work, "Joan of Arc." A little past one, the party sat down to an eight-course Delmonico's dinner, followed by more dancing until six in the morning, when Alva closed the ball with a Virginia Reel.

The affair cost about $8 million in today's money, with a million spent on champagne alone—a record in conspicuous consumption. Some newspaper critics grumbled and warned of working-class rage. Times were hard, with rising unemployment and stagnant wages. But most Americans believed in the prosperity gospel—the innate superiority of the very rich and their God-given right to monopolize revenue and splurge. The spoils belonged to nature's noblemen with unknown grandfathers who were claiming their place in the social hierarchy. After the ball, Mrs. Astor delivered her formal concession speech: "We have no right to exclude those whom the growth of this great country has brought forward, provided they are not vulgar in speech and in appearance. The time has come for the Vanderbilts." Miriam might have taken this at face value; why with sufficient sheen shouldn't her time come, too?

IN APRIL 1883, Miriam booked a passage to England and the continent. Besides business interests—writers' contracts, purchases, newsgathering, and shoptalk with colleagues—she saw social opportunity. For aspirationals, Europe was becoming a royal road to acceptance at home. Barriers were fewer, and the aristocracy was hospitable to wealthy, well-dressed American women. The class instability and attendant exclusivity of New York society didn't obtain in the fixed, impenetrable hierarchy of the Old World. And there were advantages in cultivating the newcomers. For the last ten years, the peerage had seen coffers drained by the effects of the long depression and found marriages to American heiresses a godsend.

When Miriam left for England that spring, twenty "dollar princesses" had already married titled British husbands and gained entry into Manhattan's first rank. (Between 1875 and 1905 there would be 454 transatlantic marriages.) Jennie Jerome was the bellwether belle, a daughter of rich "unacceptables" who wed Lord Randolph Churchill, the second son of the Duke of Marlborough, in 1874. Southern women with their practiced charms had done particularly well: Consuelo Yznaga of Natchez, Mississippi, in a union with the eighth Duke of Manchester; Georgian Mary King, with the Marquess of Anglesey; and South Carolinian Kate Howell, with the eighth Earl of Egmont.

Moreover, the British moral climate was less exacting; casual promiscuity carried no penalty as long as you didn't flaunt it. Playboy Prince Edward established a vogue for lax sexuality and the cultivation of amusing, louche women. Miriam had professional contacts to aid her, as well as Jane Wilde's introductions—not to mention a London suitor ready to make her a marquise tomorrow. Before she left, she leaked the rumor that her marriage to the Marquis was the real purpose of the trip.

She sailed on the S. S. *Furnessia*, an ultramodern luxury liner, with a satinwood music room, a steam-heated dining saloon, and a magnificent stateroom that contained a Parisian electro-plated bedstead. It was the *vie de luxe* she loved. As usual, she kept on top of business, but she could rest assured that the company was in safe hands, with a well-drilled staff and *Illustrated Newspaper* editor James E. Sullivan at the controls.

She could trust them to cover and build up the big stories in her absence, such as the May 24 debut of the Brooklyn Bridge, the largest suspension bridge in the world. The opening festivities attracted fifty thousand spectators and included a presidential visit, brass bands, fireworks, and a fleet of ships, all seen in a dramatic crane shot by Leslie artists high in the cables. Six days later, the same artists were there to depict a stampede, during which twelve people were trampled to death after a report that the bridge was collapsing.

When she reached Liverpool, the Marquis de Leuville was surely on the dock to greet Miriam. If he wasn't, he should have been. He had a nasty piece of gossip to quell. Lately papers had spread reports that he was neither a marquis nor a de Leuville, and was already married to the granddaughter of Madame Tussaud, founder of the waxworks museum. The press was hot on his trail.

The Marquis, in fact, was the son of middle-class London landscape painters, and his real name was William (Billy) Redivivus Oliver. After his father died when he was twelve, his mother remarried John Sedgwick, a solicitor, who sent Billy on grand tours at sixteen and nineteen. These tours only served to excite the boy's overactive imagination. He brought back fantastic tales from his travels; he'd fought with Garibaldi in the War of Independence, driven a four-in-hand to the top of Mt. Cenis (where Hannibal crossed the Alps), and slept with the queen of Naples. Once he claimed he'd been abducted by brigands who held three guns to his head and threatened to blow his brains out unless he forked over 250 gold *scudi*. He made the mistake of writing the *London Times* about it, which prompted a full-blown investigation that exposed the lie. Billy was forced to flee Rome for his life.

When he reached twenty-one, he came into a small inheritance from his father and joined the Kaffirs, a London theatrical group. He then adopted the name Marquis de Leuville, based on fictitious descent from the French Marquis, Louis Olivier, whose line died out in 1663. He fashioned himself as a modern-day knight errant and took up firearms, poetry, and romancing women. In 1868, he met the Tussaud Wax Museum heiress, Louisa Kenny, thirty-one, childless, and unhappily married to a bland civil servant.

She'd modeled wax since infancy but lacked skill or interest in the family business and wanted out. As soon as she received her share of the Museum fortune—£46,000 ($3 million in today's money)—she left Tussaud's and ran off with de Leuville. The elopement scandalized London; it was blasphemy for a woman, a Catholic no less, to desert her husband and live openly with her paramour. The Marquis acquired a nickname he found difficult to shake off, "Young Waxworks."

The two escaped to France and Italy, where they lived in grandeur under a variety of aliases, creating a sensation through the magnificence of their lifestyle and equipage. With Louisa's encouragement, he published two poetry collections, *Love and Chivalry* (1877) and *Entre-Nous* (1879), both dismissed by critics as "muddled" and "mere tinsel." In 1879, they returned to London, registered as Marquis and Marquise de Leuville, and installed themselves in a mansion on Regent's Park.

Society snubbed them and soon de Leuville found he'd used up his inheritance. By then, the relationship had fizzled, and he was forced to depend on recitals at Spiritualist lodges. Finally, Louisa agreed to settle an annuity on him in exchange for the title, Marquise de Leuville. His annuity was running out and America beckoned.

He subtracted ten years from his age (to thirty), padded his résumé with faux titles such as "French mayor," refreshed his wardrobe, "penciled his eyebrows," and set sail for New York in 1881.

Miriam was no fool and had to have seen through him—at least partially. But he must have suited her purposes. As she admitted, she was "very fond of [her] beaux" and the romantic perquisites and liked the publicity that boosted her image as a young desirable woman. The summer of 1883, she was unaware of his pedigree. Few at the time doubted his claims; even professional cynic Oscar Wilde vouched that "his title [was] undoubtedly genuine and all right."

During her two months abroad, they were a recognized couple. In London Miriam received a welcome to write home about. "Many people of social and literary prominence," noted the papers, paid her "special courtesies." Richard Monckton Milnes, Lord Houghton, a cultural luminary and patron of poets (once sponsoring Joaquin Miller), gave a luncheon in her honor and opened doors. Among others, bestselling author Lady Brassey entertained her, the venerable Robert Browning paid his regards, and the owner of the *London Illustrated News* escorted her to headquarters and treated her as an industry magnate.

The highlight of the trip, though, was Miriam's encounter with Jane Wilde, a commanding personality destined to become her "nearest woman friend" and exert an unforeseen influence in her life. They shared much in common. Jane grew up in an unconventional, female-dominated household in Dublin with a mother who encouraged her unladylike self-regard and braininess. By eighteen, Jane Elgee knew ten European languages and boasted of her genius and "wild, ambitious nature." She adopted a pen name, "Speranza" (based on a spurious relation to Dante), and wrote translations, poems, essays, and fiery screeds in favor of women's rights and Irish nationalism.

She also had tremendous presence. She wore resplendent costumes of her own design, stage-managed her settings and soirées, and fabulized herself, arranging her age and persona for dramatic

effect. Flamboyant free spirit as she was, though, she yearned paradoxically for true love and a man to "worship" and "fulfill her being."
Which led her into even deeper romantic waters than Miriam.

The man she married in 1851, an eminent ear and eye surgeon,
William Wilde, looked impressive on paper until you looked closer.
He suffered debilitating bouts of depression, fathered three illegitimate children, and had a reputation with women, which came to a
head thirteen years into their marriage when he was knighted for
medical distinction. Mary Travers, a longtime patient and probable
lover, sued Jane for a libelous attack on her wanton behavior with Dr.
Wilde and others. Jane took the stand in her own defense in a widely
publicized trial and the Wildes got off lightly. But Sir William's reputation never recovered, and when he died in 1876, she found he'd
depleted the bank account and left her impoverished.

She uprooted the family and moved to London with her sons,
Willie and Oscar, to live by her pen. She managed to become an
established author and opened a Saturday salon on the French model
that attracted an eclectic mix of cognoscenti. From five to seven, her
cramped rooms were packed with writers—beginners like George
Bernard Shaw and W. B. Yeats—actors, painters, playwrights, and
a mélange of politicians, journalists, clergymen, intellectuals, and
peers of the realm.

By the summer of 1883, Jane had moved to smaller Mayfair
quarters, and the tea at her "crushes" was growing thinner. Money
was tight; rents from her Irish property dried up; her feckless son,
Willie, contributed nothing to household expenses; and Oscar
returned home empty-handed, having burned through his American earnings on Left Bank dissipations. The situation called for
strong measures—the sale of her library, or at best advantageous
marriages for her sons. Mrs. Leslie's visit was well-timed.

On the appointed Saturday, Miriam must have thought she and
the Marquis had the wrong address. Such a modest, insignificant
house with a large tavern on the corner couldn't be where Lady Wilde
held her celebrated salon. Yet the number was plain: 134 Park Street.

The surprises had only begun. When she rapped on the knocker, a saucy Irish maid, instead of a butler, greeted them, and led them into a dark parlor lit by red-shaded candles. Curtain-draped mirrors covered the walls of a room cluttered with books on the floor and crammed with a welter of humanity: corduroy-coated artists, bespangled actresses, aesthetes in "reform" dresses, and dignitaries in cutaways and monocles—all talking in a babble of English and American accents and Irish brogues.

Oscar Wilde emerged from the shadowy depths of the room to receive them, togged out in tight "decadent" French trousers, his hair cut short in Neronian curls. He gestured toward a towering figure advancing toward them. Jane Wilde was enormous—close to six feet—and she played it up, swishing through the crowd in a voluminous antique purple brocade gown surmounted by a high headdress with long tulle streamers tipped with scarlet bows. Even in the half-light she looked raddled and sixty-two despite a thick coat of powder and paint.

The rapport was instant. Not only did Miriam incarnate the *femme forte* Jane admired, she was dramatically chic in a way she appreciated, donned in an à la mode black silk dress with a high-rumped bustle in back. How long they spoke isn't recorded, but they surely touched on kindred concerns—philistine boors, marital drawbacks, and women's rights. Jane would have segued into her favorite spiel: women were "bonded slaves," their intellect, energy, and talent stunted by barbaric custom.

The talk rattled on. Afterward, Miriam called Lady Wilde "the grandest woman in the world," and Jane in turn called her "the most important and successful journalist in the states." She continued: "With her many gifts, her brilliant powers of conversation in all the leading tongues of Europe . . . her splendid residence and immense income, [she] may be considered the leader and head of the intellectual circles of the city."

Miriam's immense income might not have been far from Jane's thoughts when she brought a large man forward. At first glance,

Willie, the elder brother, might be taken for a Fleet Street version of Oscar in a sack suit with a Verdi beard and heavy-lidded eyes beneath high-arched, ironic brows. Jane said, "Mrs. Leslie, I want to introduce you to your future husband." Miriam surely laughed it off; Willie was thirty-one, sixteen years her junior, and although she didn't know it then, a ne'er-do-well who trifled away his talents on penny journalism, lowborn companions, party charm, and drink. He must have cased out Miriam and laid on the praise and blarney.

With no success—for the time being. Chances are Miriam ignored him and followed his mother through the semi-darkness toward a corner table, where Jane seated herself and poured overdrawn tea into faded cups. Oscar would have assumed his accustomed place next to her, leaning against the chimney piece as a pastille of laurel leaves and wood violet smoldered on the mantle. It was the moment for recitations. Perhaps he read from his just-finished play, *The Duchess of Padua:* "What Beatrice," raves the doomed hero, "have I not/stood face to face with beauty; that is enough/for one man's life." Perhaps de Leuville rose next and recited his poem, "A Cry of Love," his gaze fixed on Miriam: "When I wake with tears I know/I cannot, cannot let thee go!"

The love aria didn't last. By the end of June, Miriam and the Marquis quarreled and parted ways. The dispute, according to rumor, involved money: "the sum the lordship insisted on having settled on himself," said insiders, was "altogether beyond the desires and wishes of Mrs. Leslie." De Leuville should have known better. Miriam was a sharp financier who safeguarded her wealth and was too familiar with the mercenary underside of the mating game to countenance it in a man. She wasted no time in summoning reporters and setting the record straight. "When a woman is making $150,000 a year," she sniped, "there is no earthly reason why she should marry a man to help her squander it."

How the Marquis took this can only be surmised, but he wasn't easily beaten. He laid low and remobilized while Miriam set off for Paris with a London acquaintance, Annie Brassey. Lady Brassey, a baroness through marriage, was as much a maverick as Miriam, a pioneer photographer and adventurer who wrote travel books, one of which, *A Voyage in the Sunbeam,* described an eleven-month cruise around the world with forty friends, including five children, two dogs, three birds, and a pet pig. Like Miriam, she must have been eager to see the latest sensation—Paris nouveau.

IN 1883, THE Belle Epoque, the "Beautiful Age"—the celebratory, creative years before World War I—was in full swing. In reality, it was far less beautiful than Parisians remembered after the War. Seventy-two percent of the population, the poor, lived in quasi-medieval squalor on the far eastern and northern rim of the city, where they'd been pushed by urban redevelopment. Sex trafficking of penniless girls flourished. And beneath the surface glitter ran darker currents—the growth of venereal disease and drug addiction, anti-Semitism, rapacious colonialism, political corruption, widespread pessimism, and the sense of moral and cultural decay.

Belle Epoque Paris, however, was the epicenter of carnival freedom, pleasure, and culture for over two decades—the recognized "capital of the nineteenth-century." Here Miriam was in her element, and she would make Paris her second home for the rest of her life. As soon as she and Lady Brassey stepped into a *voiture de remise* at the Gare Saint-Lazare and spun down the shimmering Avenue de l'Ópera thronged with fiacres and pedestrians and merrymakers, they could feel the electrostatic charge of the city.

Since Miriam's last visit before the 1871 Franco-Prussian War, Paris had risen from the ashes and become a gleaming metropolis of stately white buildings, wide tree-lined thoroughfares, and promenades where the public strolled at their leisure, sipped coffee in cafés, and sampled amusements—theaters, music halls, circuses, panoramas, and concerts. The mood was "anything goes." "On the boulevards," said one regular, "one can say everything, hear and imagine everything."

Luxury stores along the boulevards, like the electrically lit Printemps department store, proliferated and promoted guilt-free consumption. Privileged *femmes du monde* thought nothing of spending 40,000 francs a year (more than $100,000 today) on high-end apparel—gold threaded couturier frocks, hand-embroidered lace unmentionables, and fascinators sprigged with real butterflies. Miriam indulged. As she explained, she deserved a reward for her triumph and treated herself in Paris to a "great pair of diamonds." "The diamonds are perfect matches," she boasted, "twenty-seven carats in weight and are nearly as large as nickels." She paid $25,000 and wore them in broad daylight, an anathema in Mrs. Astor's New York.

But Mrs. Astor's style book didn't play in Paris; splendor and spectacle rather than social status determined fashion, and the trendsetters were women "one does not know"—courtesans of the sort Miriam profiled in her translation of Dumas's *Demi-Monde*. These notorious *grandes horizontales* inundated the city. Miriam and Lady Brassey couldn't have missed them on the avenues in satin-upholstered phaetons drawn by cockaded stallions, their faces painted with rouge and kohl, their lustrous costumes foaming with antique lace. Often veterans of the theater, they understood réclame: they carried props like revolvers and tame bears; slept in gold throne beds on raised daises; took heraldic names, and wore jewels the size of macarons. In contrast to the respectable subjugated female population, courtesans were independent women of means and command. If they were lucky, they chose men, set the terms, and grew rich. They were Belle Epoque royalty—the idol of couturiers, artists, and popular culture.

It's likely Miriam attended a hit play about one of these notorious demimondaines that ran at the Ambigu Theater in July. *Nana*, based on Zola's novel, tells the cautionary tale of an "all-conquering" amoral blonde courtesan who devours men with her sexual charms and pays for it with a gruesome, disfiguring death. Miriam must have waved off the noir melodrama; sexual charms had paved her path to power at no cost.

She would have learned the limits of her power in Paris, however. There were places she couldn't go après-theater—along the Boulevard St. Martin at night, for instance—without a male escort. Nor could she lunch at a "high class restaurant," such as Foyot's, where Oscar Wilde dined, or secure orchestra seats at the Comédie Française as a single woman. Select private salons, even the less picky ones like Princess Mathilde's, were difficult to enter without a man to accompany her.

The Marquis would be useful. Around the second week in July he resurfaced in Paris, apparently reconciled with Miriam. Lady Brassey seems to have departed and left the field to the lovers. With de Leuville on her arm, Miriam could circulate at ease—view the Beaux Arts salon inconspicuously, if she pleased, and visit off-bounds night spots such as the Mabille dance hall where "nymphs of the pavé" can-canned until dawn. She could buy indecent *faits divers* (hyper-sensationalistic papers that were the rage) at kiosks and tour the "living newspaper," the Musée Grévin, inspired by Tussaud's Wax Museum. Given the associations, the Marquis might have waited this one out and let Miriam explore this palace to popular taste by herself, with its ever-changing tableaux of current scandals, battles, and deathbed scenes.

To crown their Parisian holiday, de Leuville organized a fête for Miriam—a rash decision. He produced a "grand déjeuner" to honor the Pope's Domestic Prelate, Monsignor Thomas Capel, on the eve of his departure for America, thinking Miriam would be impressed by this esteemed "Apostle to the Genteel." He forgot to account for her distaste for his Catholicism or the Monsignor's reputation. Unsuspected by Miriam, the great prelate was in disgrace, exiled to America for bankrupting the university in his charge and committing "criminal intercourse" with Mrs. Bellew, her maid, and others.

After the luncheon, she published a tribute to Capel in the *Illustrated Newspaper,* which must have caused her some embarrassment. Three days later, she distributed a release that Mrs. Frank Leslie did not "intend to wed the Marquis de Leuville." To compound his blunder, the Marquis lost control of their Victoria and collided with another carriage on the Bois de Boulogne in a newsworthy traffic accident.

The romance was off once more and Miriam completed her European journey to Madrid alone. That was late summer, and de Leuville hadn't given up. A seasoned Lothario, he knew "deeds of prowess [were] dear to the female heart" and found his opportunity in October. Somewhere on the spa circuit, he encountered Count Almensegg, a habitué of German baths, who seems to have made a disparaging remark about Mrs. Leslie. The Marquis demanded a duel. They met with their seconds on the Belgian border where de Leuville gave a bravura display of his marksmanship and wounded the Count in the arm. The story, "A Duel About Mrs. Leslie," made headlines across America, attributing the earlier breakup to the Marquis's Catholicism. After the confrontation in Belgium there was no more talk of irreconcilable religious differences or a broken engagement. They were a couple again—until they weren't.

CHAPTER SEVEN

"CHEATED BY SENTIMENT"
1884–89

THE VICTORIA HOTEL was an "architectural wonder" of New York City that covered the entire block of Twenty-seventh Street between Fifth Avenue and Broadway. Sunday sightseers drove carriages into town just to see it. Clad in marble-paneled brick and faced with stone dormers, the Victoria rose eight stories topped by a mansard tower for servants. With its lavish accommodations and staff interpreter who spoke five languages, the hotel attracted an elite foreign clientele, such as Swedish opera diva Christine Nilsson. If money was no object, private residents could lease an apartment on a long-term basis, suites furnished with antiques and velvet baldachins, fit for royalty—or a marquise.

At the start of 1884, Miriam took one of these suites, fully intending to marry the Marquis de Leuville. In March, she announced her engagement to the press. She worked the match for all it was worth. Newspapers throughout the country broadcast the alliance of "the most remarkable woman living" with the European nobleman. According to reports, he possessed an independent fortune and eight-hundred-year pedigree and was "desirous of figuring in local society." Both gave exclusives; Miriam invited the *Boston*

Globe to her yellow-damasked sitting room to meet her distinguished fiancé, a writer, painter, and marksman who could shoot his initials in a board at twenty paces. As for herself, she was not only "one of the best businesswomen of the world," she was a beautiful "little lady" with refined tastes and "long, slender aristocratic hands."

De Leuville's private interviews circulated throughout the country. Now engaged in a translation of Horace's Sapphic odes, he displayed his celebrated poetry books, watercolors, and collections of Saharan souvenirs and Hungarian pistols. At thirty feet he could cut a toothpick. His secret: an "athletic aesthetic" system by which he kept himself in shape with a regimen of three-and-a-half pounds of raw beefsteak and a glass of whiskey. Only a rare dissenting voice questioned the Marquis. If the press is to be believed, de Leuville was taken at his word, as a nobleman of ancient lineage with palatial estates in England, Paris, and Rome. The marriage would take place, Miriam declared, in a few months, followed by trips to California and New Orleans.

But months went by without a wedding. In June Miriam hedged about the date and stated that the Marquis was to have no part in the Frank Leslie business operation. There was, in any case, no hurry. She was basking in her aristocratic alliance and applause. She received the prestigious "Order of the Bust of Bolivar the Liberator" from Venezuela for "services rendered to humanity, progress, and civilization," and wore the gold medallion set in star-rays of brilliants on her breast. She brushed off the Astor set. She was "indifferent to New York society, preferring titled friends abroad, of whom she [had] many." She would be a marquise, one of the "crested nobility."

She was also indifferent to a more sinister class issue that was brewing, the conflict of the decade. Workers were restive. The Panic of 1884, caused by fast-and-loose loan policies and speculation, disrupted industry and let labor bear the burden as usual. Wages declined, unemployment rose, and strikes spread. Mrs. Leslie responded along party lines; capital had the "muscle" and law behind it, and the "riffraff and scum" should be rounded up and removed.

At the same time, a taste war erupted on the cultural front. A new radical group of Realists took up arms against the genteel tradition in arts and letters. Apostates like William Dean Howells called for literature rooted in observed reality and ordinary experience and repudiated the neoromantic school of escapist melodrama. Miriam leapt to the defense of the genteel camp, with its not-so-secret agenda of preserving the elitist, conservative status quo. Readers required romantic inspiration and relief from serious work.

In her publications she made sure they got it, cranking up neoromantic content. The Leslie company, she proclaimed, ran "like clockwork." What she neglected was an encroaching journalistic revolution. In 1883 a newcomer opened shop on Publishers' Row and rocked the newspaper world. Joseph Pulitzer, a driven Hungarian entrepreneur, bought the daily *New York World* from Jay Gould and in a matter of months, drove circulation from fifteen thousand to sixty thousand.

His innovations transformed the industry. Stealing a page from the Leslie book, he courted a mass audience with sensational, topical, profusely illustrated stories. Instead of once a week, readers got graphic cuts of breaking news the same day. And the *World* was cheap, with bold heads and short vivid sentences. Other dailies followed suit and began to eat into the weekly *Illustrated*'s circulation and profits. Technology, too, was forging ahead with the recent invention of linotype and faster, more efficient machinery.

Miriam would pay attention, but not yet. She and the Marquis spent July until early fall at a Long Branch resort lodged in three expensive apartments. They kept a coachman and two high-stepping bays and led the balls at Ocean House. They were the cynosure of the social columns, she in her "pure-water diamonds," he groomed to a fare-thee-well with the aid of a French valet.

All of which went to the Marquis's head. At one of his first interviews that fall, he cited the offices he held in European cultural institutions—none true. Most New Yorkers either believed him or blew him off. But not General Daniel Sickles. A Civil War veteran of sixty-five, Sickles lost a leg at Gettysburg and had a colorful history of his own, having gunned down his wife's lover in 1859 and successfully pleaded insanity to escape a murder charge. The Marquis, for mysterious reasons, irked Sickles, who made indiscreet remarks about de Leuville's bona fides.

By a perverse twist of fate, Sickles and the engaged couple attended the Academy of Music on the same night. After the first act of *Faust*, the Marquis confronted Sickles in the lobby and accused him of circulating "false stories" about his title and mercenary marital designs. Sickles took it in good humor and stumped off on his crutches. But at the end of the second act, the Marquis repeated the accusation, this time fingering a pistol in his dress pantaloons as he spoke. A crowd gathered, and Colonel Mapelson rushed between the two and separated them. "He had fully made up his mind to shoot him," said bystanders. The encounter's effect was the opposite of what the Marquis intended; he found his credentials under attack, and his grand gesture a source of ridicule. Sickles, the evening's "hero," "whistled merrily" as he replayed the Marquis's high-flown claims and assault.

The affray was Joseph Pulitzer's kind of story. He sent over an investigative journalist to scope out de Leuville. The Marquis appeared in gold bracelets and a flowing white silk scarf and gestured toward an open trunk filled with red-bound volumes and scrolls of parchment. In them, he said, was proof positive of his pedigree. If his title was genuine, queried the reporter, why wasn't he among the foreign nobility listed in *Burke's Peerage*? "Simply a matter of taste," replied the Marquis; he preferred not to be included. He then brandished a sheaf of faded documents and charts and huffed that no one had questioned his title before.

Did he mind tracing his lineage for the last hundred years?

De Leuville did mind. He leaned his arm on a "pile of heirlooms" and retorted that this was the "wrong way" to go about a genealogy; one began with the "founder of the house." An unconvinced *World* reporter repeated his request. "Call tomorrow," said the

Marquis, and he would provide a table and history of his family—nobles "who bled for their king."

Tomorrow never came. Mrs. Leslie said she knew nothing of the affair, except that the "nobleman was not in town." Soon word came that he'd sued the *World* for damages and sailed for Liverpool, informing the press he'd come into a $40,000 inheritance. The legacy, in fact, was £100, and he was a standing joke in Manhattan, lampooned as an "outlandish" imposter and fortune hunter.

MIRIAM PROMPTLY ANNOUNCED she was "too busy to get married." The Marquis de Leuville was history. As she put it, "a man who is the jest and butt of other men will perhaps arouse in women's breasts a certain tolerating acceptance, half-pity, half-amusement, but he will never command more." Nevertheless, the denouement hurt. She was "prostrated," diagnosed with incipient pneumonia and in need of rest. More immediately, she needed to restore her public face. She could hear the voice of mockery rising around her. Joining the chorus of contempt for her "Young Waxworks" and his forty-something "pigeon" were two popular novels, *The Rise of Silas Lapham* and *Huckleberry Finn*, which satirized aristocratic pretenders and the dupes who bought into them.

Unlike other women who had to swallow their bile, Miriam recruited the press. She could shine as brightly without the Marquis and his title. In business, said interviewers, she was a phenomenon; in appearance, the "acme of beauty" with perfect carriage and features. "Her face," raved one columnist, "is her fortune." She endorsed Liebig's "Cosmetic Glycerine" and told the *Boston Globe* she had the "smallest foot of any lady in America," a quote published everywhere. She was still on the market, at her peak.

The *Illustrated Newspaper* saw a "silver lining" to an otherwise dark beginning to the year. Unemployment was mounting and labor agitation growing perilous. A thousand members of the Knights of Labor, an organization of half a million, struck the Gould railroad system over wage cuts and won. It was a shot across the bow, the start of what would become the "Great Upheaval." The *Illustrated*, though, looked askance and assured readers that the poor were happy with their lot and all was well; Vanderbilt was "one of the best men on earth."

On that note Miriam left for the New Orleans World's Industrial and Cotton Centennial Exposition in February 1885 with artist Charles Upham and Emily Pierce, the Denver friend who had served her so ably in court. The doctor advised quiet, but that was not to be. Joaquin Miller, her old flame and occasional lover, also came to the fair. He had just dedicated his new poetry collection, *Memorie and Rime*, to her, and the timing was right. Together they toured the Exposition with its glass-trussed exhibition hall the size of Notre Dame and specialty pavilions lit by a tall one-hundred-thousand-candlepower electric light. Miriam particularly admired the women's exhibits and was with Joaquin at the grand opening of the art gallery.

Away from the fair, she held court at the St. Charles Hotel, where she reprised her Louisiana past and rendezvoused with Miller. One morning Miriam asked poet Ella Wheeler Wilcox to breakfast with them, in part to affirm her image as a "woman's woman." Ella didn't return the favor. Mrs. Leslie, she wrote, "seemed a very tired woman in her late forties" who believed she was the inspiration behind Joaquin's "poetical genius." Joaquin, she swiped, was very "gallant and complimentary" toward her, "though I did not see any evidences of consuming passion in his attitude." She was apparently unaware of their long history of dissimulation.

Later when Miller arrived for their evening assignation, they had a much-publicized night on the town. He found her "blazing with huge diamonds" and dressed for the Carnival Ball despite the unavailability of tickets. Refusing to take no for an answer, she advanced up the stairway of the French Opera House and reigned queen of the ball in a diamond coronet and couturier satin costume. Joaquin waxed afterward: "I know of no one in history . . . so glorious as this beautiful little Creole" with "her arched lips, her eyes, her sweet baby face." If nothing else, Miller helped dispel the memory of the Marquis and restore Miriam's erotic morale. He wasn't the last.

After a detour to Cincinnati to visit her niece Carrie Wrenn, Miriam resumed her seat at Frank Leslie Publishing. The competition was at her heels. Dailies were employing ready-made stock cuts and nationally syndicated pictures, and illustrated biweekly and monthly magazines like the newly founded *Good Housekeeping* were horning in on her territory. A sensational scandal sheet, *Town Topics*, also debuted in 1885, a later thorn in her side. She bought a version of the linotype machine, marketed a fifty-cent special on Grant's life, and reinvested in her female audience, scaling up genteel-inflected advice and stories. She cut down periodicals to two weeklies and four monthlies.

By June, she was exhausted, "in search of perfect quiet." When she left for Europe she said she intended to collect material for *Frank Leslie's Pictorial Third of the Century 1851–1885* and take a vacation. She only followed through on the vacation, perhaps accompanied by a new love interest. If she first stopped in London, she would have found the Marquis in abeyance—for now. He'd met Mrs. Ada Peters as a paid entertainer at one of her Kilburn cultural parties and was in hot pursuit of the wealthy fifty-two-year-old widow. In any case, Miriam seems to have spent little time in England before leaving for Paris.

Installed at the same hotel, the Continental, was Joseph Pulitzer's younger brother, Albert, a "remarkably good-looking" man of thirty-four. Except for the age gap, they were a perfect match. Their marriage, stated the papers, was in the cards. A younger, more polished Frank Leslie, he was a journalistic powerhouse, overshadowed by his more famous brother. Brimming with self-confidence and "Hungarian vim," he had worked as a reporter on the *Sun* and James Gordon Bennett's *Herald* before founding his own newspaper in 1882, *The Morning Journal*, a breakout daily. With a shrewd sense of the market, he targeted an untapped audience, the semi-literate laboring class in search of straight-up entertainment. He devised a winning formula: a four-page tabloid-style gazette, packed with celebrity gossip and human-interest stories written in punchy, crisp prose. It sold for a penny and was an overnight success. The *Illustrated* gave Albert and his *Journal* a fulsome write-up in May. Pulitzer had earned "a rare distinction at an early age," producing a "new kind" of metropolitan newspaper that was "bright, piquant, humorous" and earning a "handsome income."

In contrast to Joseph, Albert was a bon vivant who enjoyed his wealth and lavished money on himself and friends. He liked luxury, gourmet dinners, and bespoke suits, and traveled to Paris each year for pleasure with a staff of secretaries and retainers. He understood how to "appeal to a woman's heart" and possessed precisely the qualities Miriam liked in a man—a gracious, cultivated bearing and a "suave Viennese accent." He had also written the sort of novel she appreciated, *The Romance of Prince Eugene: An Idyll in the Time of Napoleon.*

How they spent the summer isn't recorded, but he surely permitted Miriam to experience Paris *en princesse.* There would have been dinners at Grand Véfour, a shrine for gastronomes; fittings at Chavet and Worth; an opera box for Massenet's *Le Cid*; and ice cream at Tortoni's. Why the affair ended isn't clear. Miriam, though, disembarked from the *Normandie* in October in "magnificent condition." She would need to be for the year ahead.

ONCE IN MANHATTAN, she stepped into a minefield. First a minor vexation: news of her rival Joseph Pulitzer's inclusion in the Patriarch's Ball, which required a social counterstrike. She convened reporters at the Victoria to admire her cultured taste and broke out her latest Parisian costume—a black cashmere gown with a puffed velvet skirt drawn back into a "Lily Langtry" bustle that folded up like an accordion. She stood to display her "fine" figure and demonstrated her "promenade step," a graceful gait that marked "good breeding." Beyond the office, "at proper times [she was] devoted to society."

But within the office, unease pervaded the newsroom, a sense of a pending national crisis. The tensions between capital and labor had spiked once more. Twenty-three miners died in a Wilkes-Barre explosion caused by company negligence; coke-burners idled at another Pennsylvania mine; and in March fifteen thousand railroad workers struck the Southwestern Railroad, suspending six thousand miles of track and causing "confusion and chaos." The "Great Labor Strike" was gathering steam.

Miriam dodged the drama and sailed for Cuba, perhaps with the intention of assessing the prospect of a Spanish-language *Illustrated Newspaper*. Her chief object, though, seems to have been a change of scene. She toured the sights and noted with pleasure that Havana señoras put their beautiful breasts on display, as she did, in low-necked gowns at the opera. Apparently no one cabled her the news.

When she docked in New York at the end of March, the story was all over the city. *Town Topics*, the latest arrival on the weekly scene, was the brainchild of Colonel William d'Alton "W. D." Mann, a flamboyant, walrus-like rogue with a fresh take on "society journalism." His idea: expose the rascals and serve up their follies and pretentions for public consumption. The paper was an instant hit, the *National Enquirer* of the day, read by Vanderbilts and factory workers alike. The March 28 issue featured a juicy tell-all: "From Puddle to Palace," a true account of the career of the Empress of Publishing. Miriam's life had been laid bare before—in the *Territorial Enterprise* by her vindictive ex-husband eight years before—but Frank Leslie had been there to buy up copies and retaliate.

This time, she had to fend for herself against a formidable adversary with a rapier wit and a knack for soundbites. The *Topics* "Chronicler" had a field day trolling the "foul waters" of Miriam's past: the years in the "loose-girdled sisterhood," liaison with congressman Churchwell, ill-starred union with E. G., the rigged divorce, and marriage to her businessman lover whom she ruled like a "dragon." Where was "Lais" (a famous Greek courtesan) now, he asked? Clamoring for social acceptance, which had led her into to a comical affair with "a shabby, greased, and whiskered adventurer" who only wanted her "bankbook." When the little "extravaganza" ended, this "kitten" of almost sixty was left alone with her "parasites" and "venal flatterers."

The stealth smackdown opened old wounds and had long-term consequences. At nearly fifty, she was in a vulnerable place despite her bravado, without a viable love interest, an entrée into society, and her old hegemony on Publishers' Row. She squared her shoulders, feigned indifference, and armored herself with hauteur and hard-shell elitism. Her chance to display it was right around the corner. In the immediate wake of the *Town Topics* reveal, Miriam maintained an imperious silence. Then, six weeks later, Chicago blew up and she found her voice.

Chicago was a hotbed of labor tensions on the edge of mutiny. A major industrial hub, the city employed thousands of immigrant workers, largely Germans, who earned an average of $1.50 a day for a six-day, sixty-hour week. In the aftermath of the 1884 downturn and cutbacks, demands for improved working conditions accelerated, attracting socialist and anarchist activists who advocated a more combative approach to big business. The Federation of Organized Trades and Labor Unions designated May 1 as a nationwide protest for an eight-hour day. Ten thousand rallied in New York City, eleven thousand in Detroit, and as many as eighty thousand in Chicago, where a "storm of strikes" ripped through the city.

On May 3, 1886, a disturbance broke out at the McCormick Harvesting Machine Company plant. When police killed two strikers, anarchist leader August Spies called for a protest demonstration the next day. A crowd of six hundred to three thousand gathered in Haymarket Square under a light rain. The rally began peacefully; Spies stood in an open wagon and told participants that the purpose of the meeting was nonviolent. About 10:30 P.M. a police squad marched toward the wagon and ordered the mob to disperse, at which point a homemade bomb exploded in their path. The blast and ensuing gunfire killed seven policemen, four civilians, and injured scores of others.

The Haymarket Affair convulsed the country, inciting a "drama without end." Passions on both sides of the class divide flared and the immigrant and labor community came downwind of establishment prejudice and rage. Eight anarchist suspects were convicted without evidence, four of whom (including Spies) were hanged. Even measured against anti-labor censure in the mainstream press, the *Illustrated* reaction was severe. The paper excoriated the "anarchist outbreak" and stoked the hysteria, caricaturing agitators as "demented" criminals and raising fears of the spread of the "insane fury of anarchism." Mrs. Leslie was the acknowledged agent of this charged rhetoric. She found an opportunity to publicly surmount slander and stand with her patrician peers. Asked about the Haymarket conspirators, she snapped, "Worthless, discontented foreigners . . . shoot them like dogs."

The determination to live down *Town Topics* also may have contributed to the purified self-image she marketed the rest of the year. She favored the anti-saloon movement, helped collect money for a poor immigrant girl, and touted her Southern pedigree. In Europe that summer she asked a reporter from the British *Pall Mall Gazette* to her Paris hotel and told him she lived for nothing but work, "like a man without a man's enjoyment." She was an "Amazon of Journalism," too busy for recreation or romance. To dramatize the point, she officially dropped the Marquis and sent him a purse to cover his debts.

IN THE COMING months, it wouldn't be so easy to sustain this all-work chaste persona. The challenges at Frank Leslie Publishing notwithstanding—and they were formidable, with competition on the ascent—Miriam put her energies into social elevation. In 1887 she moved to even grander quarters, the Windsor Hotel, a favorite of the wealthy, and outfitted her suite with impressive furniture and status markers. Her leisured outings multiplied; she reproached women at matinees for behavior unbecoming to a "gentlewoman," reprimanded the Metropolitan Museum for showing "more money than discrimination," and applauded the absence of hats at the opera by "the wealthiest and most prominent ladies."

Nor were men out of the picture. In May, Joaquin Miller wrote a public love letter in *The Golden Era* extolling her "remarkable" career and incomparable beauty. Weeks later, she was in the thick of a new affair. He was a stunning specimen in his mid-thirties—tall, handsome, with dark eyes and a Van Dyke beard—and a reputed prince. Investigative reporter Cleveland Moffett met him at a breakfast given by Miriam at her Parisian hotel and thought Prince George Eristoff de Gourie a charming "bona fide Russian prince."

The breakfast party of six, which included a Spanish señora and Cuban grandee, was a blue-ribbon occasion with "culinary triumphs" and conversation in three languages. Mrs. Leslie told embellished stories of the Old South and the saga about Mrs. Smith's $50,000 loan. But the best raconteur was the prince, who spun riveting tales of Georgia: the twenty women ransomed each year for the Turkish sultan's harem; the beautiful wife gambled away by her husband in a ruinous card game.

The tales about himself were the problem. With an apparent tropism for titled adventurers, Miriam picked a prince with bloated pretentions and a history of petty crime. Before she fell in with Eristoff around June, he'd been arrested four times for fraud, served two prison terms, and fled to London, where he'd stolen his friend de Leuville's gold cigar case and committed a string of other misdemeanors. Nicknamed "Eely Eristoff," he was now adrift in Paris—his Russian "mother" having paid his fines and commuted his sentences.

Miriam was oblivious and checked into the Victoria Hotel with Eristoff for the celebratory week of Queen Victoria's Golden Jubilee, the fiftieth anniversary of her reign. After a quarter century, the Queen emerged from seclusion to thunderous applause and a two-day pageant of ceremonial processions and banquets.

Saturday, July 9, they set out on an afternoon drive through Hyde Park with a chaperone, Miss Ella Bennett. It was eighty-one degrees in the shade, and the landau top was folded back to catch a breeze. At the Apsley House entrance they noticed the Marquis de Leuville behind them in an open carriage. He was laughing "strangely and unpleasantly." When they turned at Queen's Gate, the Marquis pulled beside them and bowed to the Prince with an "air of sneering triumph." The carriage passed once more, and on the third try, the Marquis suddenly reared up, raised his whip, and struck the Prince across the face with the handle. A chase followed to Marble Arch, where the Marquis disappeared. "Mrs. Leslie's infidelity," said his friends, had maddened the Marquis, "who thirsted for blood." He sent Miriam a perfunctory apology, then goaded the Prince into a duel, calling him an "old man" (he was ten years younger than the Marquis) and threatening to "crush" him.

What transpired afterward is something of a mystery. According to Miriam, her appeal to the Prince's honor prevented the combat. She urged Eristoff, who insisted on revenge, not to meet the Marquis on equal terms since he didn't recognize de Leuville's inferior title. Furthermore, she didn't wish her name dragged into the feud. Her name, though, was already embroiled in the fracas and she traded on it. She told reporters the Prince had pleaded with her, "I love you," to which she'd replied, "And I do not love you. You are a splendid man and I am exceedingly fond of you, but if I ever marry, which is quite unlikely, I do not think I shall go away from my own country for a husband." As for the Prince's whereabouts, he was "called away to assume the throne of Bulgaria." Papers everywhere boldfaced the news: Mrs. Leslie "Refused a Real Prince."

Instead of "unpleasant publicity" from the affair, she "used her considerable skills to come out ahead." Almost. When she resumed work in the fall, another *Town Topics* landed on her desk. Col. Mann's send-up of the Hyde Park incident was withering. The rival suitors, Prince Ivenuff Hairystuff and "poor, devoted" Vicomte Camelote de Pacotille, had come to blows in London over Mrs. Lola Morelie, "Proprietor of *Morelie's Slopbasin* and *Morelies' Stewplate*." Explained Mrs. Morelie, "I cannot escape the havoc my marvelous features make in a man's heart." After thrashing the Prince, the Vicomte fled the scene "in a cloud of pearl powder as his padded bosom sobbed visibly."

Suspicions about the Prince's identity and past must have added insult to injury. Then a second unwelcome publication appeared: the first *Social Register*, a record of Society comprising the 3,600 best people in New York City. She—a millionaire, confirmed lady, and cultivated cosmopolite—was not listed. This called for still bolder measures. She delivered verdicts on immigrants, correct careers for women, and the proper New Year's Day conduct established by "long-inherited gentility." She announced her intention to purchase a house in Washington and engage in "president-making."

Her life story in the *Times-Picayune* swelled to mythic proportions. She might have stepped out of an American fairy tale—the treasured daughter and "family pet" of seven children, destined to be a prodigy of beauty and brilliance. Her highborn father devoted himself to her education and trained her "under the tenets of old aristocracy" in six languages, math, poetry, and art so that she became as "erudite as a doctor of laws" by thirteen. The "pink of propriety," she married at fourteen and built a triumphant career through her rare gifts and fortitude.

Syndicated accounts continued in the same vein. Reporters cried up her colossal success, radiant health sustained on four hours of sleep, and show-stealing public appearances. In December she debuted a new over-the-top costume of velvet and terra-cotta brocaded silk with a bonnet and muff to match. Her publishing empire, she bragged, was running full tilt, with expansion plans for a Mexican plant and worldwide distribution.

* * *

EITHER SHE BELIEVED her own bluster or lost sight of the terrain. Right under her nose publishers were outpacing her. Charles Dana's evening *New York Sun* succeeded beyond expectation, and Joseph Pulitzer just scored a coup with stunt journalism. Nellie Bly, his new hire, feigned insanity and spent ten days in Blackwell's Island Asylum, recording the event in a "Madhouse Series" that set journalistic records.

Miriam chose a bad time to ride the brakes in the publishing business. Emotions ran high in 1888 and an edgy, polarized public clamored for news, which came thick and fast. Instead of dissipating, the post-Haymarket paranoia spread. Apocalyptic novels, like Joaquin Miller's *Destruction of Gotham*, registered the national alarm. In Miller's futuristic dystopia, a "wicked, wild, and reckless" mob sack and torch millionaires' mansions and burn the "New Babel" to the ground. To many, Manhattan felt like a tinderbox where hostilities could erupt into an urban inferno any second. The dangerous classes, immigrants, laborers, the poor, and "reds" of every stripe were concentrated in the city where the wealth gap yawned widest.

Although it escaped Miriam's notice, an obscure police reporter was roaming among the dangerous classes and assembling a pitiless record of what he saw. In January, Jacob Riis toured the darkest slums of New York armed with a camera using magnesium flash powder. His stark photographs pictured conditions unimagined by the privileged: gaunt guttersnipes, hollow-eyed men at five-cent-a-night cribs, wasted mothers with babies, and lost souls of Bottle Alley and Rivington Dump. His shots of tumbledown tenements, cats-cradled with drying lines and silted with trash, called wealthy landlords to account—if they bothered to look.

Throughout the year, Riis worked to assure that they did. In a population of a million and a half, 1,093,701 inhabited these ghettos and numbers were on the rise. He lectured at churches and meeting halls across the boroughs, showing his images on a projecting screen accompanied by an unsparing text. The talks formed the basis of his *How the Other Half Lives* in 1889, a future catalyst of social reform.

Publications like the *Sun*, *Harper's*, and others gave Riis space and commentary, but not *Frank Leslie's*.

Meanwhile, the elite minority was growing in wealth, arrogance, and political power. While Riis photographed the destitute downtown, the social rich dined and danced at Delmonico's with ever greater one-upmanship. At the Patriarch's Ball on January 17, Ward McAllister ordered up a festivity without equal: rooms smothered in out-of-season tulips, hyacinths, and lily-of-the-valley and a damask-covered buffet board of canvasback duck and bombe glacée on silver platters. The only downside for McAllister was the company. In order to acquire the requisite number for the ball, he explained, he had to go out "among the ranks of professional men"—"lawyers, doctors, and the like"—when everyone knew "there [were] not more than four hundred properly so-designated society people in New York." The election of 1888 approached and his "people" would dictate politics and turn the Senate into a "Millionaires' Club."

Miriam upped the ante and moved a third time to the Gerlach Hotel in the fashionable Twenty-seventh Street district. The eleven-story apartment building offered elegant double suites and princely amenities with an interior that surpassed the Windsor in expense and show. If she wished to host a dinner, she had the right setting. The Gerlach contained a gold-and-pearl Louis XVI dining hall with a balcony for two orchestras, dome of jeweled lights, and a superb chef. She stamped her coat of arms on her possessions and reopened her salon on more luxurious lines.

As befit her accommodations, Miriam redoubled her patrician allegiance. She decried immigrants, running a front-cover *Popular Monthly* special on the "Immigrant Question," which called for legislation to stop the influx of paupers and suspicious aliens. She execrated Chicago strikers, unthrifty paupers, and Henry George with his absurd crusade to tax land owned by millionaires. The harsh editorial tone of 1888 was unprecedented, supplemented by engravings that assailed "foreignness, criminality, and the labor movement."

Not content with behind-the-scenes engagement, Miriam published an essay collection, *Rents in Our Robes,* to air her views and
authority. She began by pulling rank on Ward McAllister who, she
twitted, merely exposed his lack of acquaintance with timeless European "aristocratic customs" with his Four Hundred gaucheries.

An experienced *mondaine,* she took young women in hand. As
if on a reparative mission for her childhood, Miriam argued girls
should be "rosebuds," kept pure and "above suspicion" by vigilant
parents. Equality was essential, but a woman must never mistake
"liberty for license" or forget feminine graces. It was important to
manage men and love (too often fleeting) and possess a full complement of social skills.

This was not Susan B. Anthony's idea of feminism. While
mainstream feminists in 1888 were all for purity, they deplored
feminine arts, self-beautification, romance, and the cultivation of
male admiration. Far from caring about beaux, they asked women
to subdue the "tainted half of the race" and drive men from the bar-
rooms and stewpots of sin. They would have labeled Miriam a "genteel feminist," a "charm school feminist," or worse. She responded
in kind: American suffragists are "not often charming, [and] are
seldom comely" and as a rule "abhor the society of men."

Before blanket book publicity was in vogue, Miriam staged a
barnstorm for *Rents.* With the press at her command, she swamped
papers with interviews, columns, and events to promote her brand.
She exhorted American women to learn from French ladies and
admonished ingenues never to propose marriage and lose the "right
of refusal." At her Park Place office, she dropped aperçus from *Rents.*
Seated beside a vase filled with roses, she reiterated her concept of
"womanly" feminism. While a woman shouldn't say "obey" at the
altar (she was often a man's superior), she should school herself in
marital artistry and the "virtues of a wife."

In October, she staged a publicity event at the Gerlach, a "ladies'
only" reception attended by Nell Nelson, a star reporter from the

Chicago Times. Miss Nelson arrived to find the drawing room ablaze with lights from amber globes, mandolins playing in the background, and Mrs. Leslie dressed in a silver-trimmed black and white gown. Miriam ushered guests through velvet portières into her bedroom, a boudoir "fit for an empress."

The main event was the trunk show. In a corner stood an open steamer trunk gorged with the latest lingerie from Paris. The chemise "is the most womanly article in a woman's wardrobe," she instructed, flourishing a black satin corset embroidered with red dragonflies. She encouraged the ladies to rummage at their leisure. Afterward, she led the group to her Thursday evening soirée. "I never sit down," she told Miss Nelson, "because I make a better appearance on my feet" and "because I can introduce everybody and look aloft if an uncongenial lion goes by."

The lions, though, were making themselves scarce—a rare hiatus in Miriam's love life. The dailies churned up gossip about a marriage to Henry F. Gillig of the American Exchange, a travel service and bank for tourists in London and Paris. Possibly she did dally with Gillig; he was a Barnumesque figure with ambitions to make the Exchange "the grandest thing on earth." She admitted he was "a very dear friend" and invested $55,000 in his venture. Mark Twain contributed $10,000. Neither would see their money back. Gillig, it soon developed, was engaged in financial chicanery and hopelessly bankrupt by November. Miriam boasted that she saw a "great many men besides Mr. Gillig," and declined, on average, two offers of matrimony a day.

She was content with her full life and many friends and gave no thought to marriage. But in weaker moments she said otherwise. A woman's "starving heart," she confessed, cries for "sympathy and companionship in her pursuits." If she could relive her life, she lamented, she would "prefer a quiet home, obscurity, and no knowledge of the world and no rights except those of a mother and a wife."

Her heart didn't seem to be in her publishing house, either. It was becoming clear the *Illustrated* couldn't withstand the onslaught of the dailies. Pulitzer cut better deals on paper and advertising and had inside congressional connections and entrepreneurial genius. He raised $100,000 for the Statue of Liberty and was about to send Nellie Bly on an "Around the World in Eighty Days" expedition to challenge Jules Verne's fictional feat. The *Illustrated Newspaper* tried to keep pace. When the Great Blizzard struck New York on March 11, the second largest snowstorm in American history, Miriam's artists created historic images of the twenty-foot snowdrifts and panicked residents, two hundred of whom died. But the issue arrived too late, ten days after the storm.

AT THE START of the New Year, Miriam took action. She procured four partners and incorporated the publishing company with a million dollars in capital. A month later she sold the weeklies to W. J. Arkell of Judge Publishing for $300,000 with a substantial investment of her own in the company. Her object, she said, was to concentrate on the *Popular Monthly*, her best-selling property, and several minor magazines and devote more time to leisure. Her work had grown too stressful. In fact, she divested herself at a strategic moment, when weeklies were going nowhere.

News of the sale brought tributes. Columnists recounted Mrs. Leslie's wealth and prominence, and women's groups paid homage. The Illinois Woman's Press Association seated her in the "box of honor," and Ella Wheeler Wilcox gave a luncheon where her place card read "a Minerva and Fair Venus in one mold." The Topeka Printer Girls formed a "Leslie Club"; cabinet members' wives voted her one of the "twelve greatest living women in America."

Times-Picayune reporter "Vidette," who fabulized Miriam's biography two years earlier, returned for a second write-up. After a guided tour through the Gerlach and its "embarrassment of riches," she joined Mrs. Leslie in a sitting room behind the salon. A center table held a collection of Miriam's books in "handsome bindings," which she discussed with animation. "Vidette" concluded that she was the model American woman and a "paragon of versatility," as well as a writer of "very excellent English." "High renown as an author awaits her."

Miriam didn't need to put pen to paper again. She tied with Mrs. Hicks-Lord as the sixth richest woman in America and could honorably retire at fifty-three. With $3 million in safe securities, she could be a fashion icon, continental hostess, and culture connoisseur, and join the rest of the wealthy leisured ladies of her day. In the beginning she must have been tempted. She attended winter receptions, volunteered for charity, and flaunted her fashion authority. Trend trackers detailed her Bernhardt-inspired tea gown of salmon brocade and her collarless work dresses with mini-bustles. "In the new dresses from Paris," she decreed, "the bustle is scarcely perceptible." But, she cautioned, a "well-formed woman" (like herself) "can hardly dispense with a little fullness at the back of her gown." She reminded the public of her continued allure. She had "princes at her feet" and Eristoff "was nursing his broken heart on the continent."

The Prince, though, was doing neither. He had been in New York for months, occupied with heiresses at Delmonico's and other Society haunts. By February Miriam couldn't pretend he wasn't there. On the fourteenth, detectives apprehended Prince Eristoff de Gourie at the Hotel Brunswick and took him to police headquarters, where he was charged with fraud and locked in a cell overnight. The revelations the next day disgorged his whole history. Again, Miriam was cast on the mercy of the popular press and mocked. The Prince's long criminal record filled the papers, along with his numerous failed attempts to ensnare rich women.

The episode was squalid enough. He'd acquired a $500 sealskin coat from a prominent furrier on promise of payment and pawned it for $100. But, assured columnists, "There is no doubt he really is a prince . . . Mrs. Frank Leslie knows it [and] he courted her." The Marquis wasn't doing her proud in England, either, with court troubles of his own that she would discover that summer. The same month she suffered heavy losses in the Moore-Benjamin iron mines, thanks to a bad tip from her protégée Ella Wheeler Wilcox.

Whether these comedowns prompted her next move or she'd planned it all along, she embarked on a second career as an author in February. With her celebrity platform she could reach a larger audience and gain the "renown" "Vidette" promised. In any event, Miriam could not idle; she had scores to even, rivals to outshine, and more prizes to win.

On average, she produced an article a month, each a taste fiat. She decided the question of the "purity" of the French *valse*, ill-tempers in marriage, and the "right kind of girl." Her opinions, she declared, were "the fruit of much observation and study of mankind." A woman should never smoke, it discolored her teeth and repelled male admirers; nor should she wear gay colors on the street, tailor-made suits, or cheap shoes and gloves. At the theater she should come in full décolleté, covering her arms with tulle if necessary.

Her receptions at the Gerlach grew in brilliance, with professional elocutionists and vocalists to entertain. She gave a deluxe luncheon for the Centennial Celebration of Washington's inauguration with choice guests, such as New Jersey plutocrat George Shepard Page, and made a memorable entrance at the ball afterward bedecked in diamonds.

May 1 capped three days of parades and fireworks attended by thousands who watched newly-elected President Benjamin Harrison enter the city like General Washington—rowed in by twelve silk-hatted oarsmen on a barge to a twenty-one gun salute. Beneath the hoopla, the celebration was a public relations spectacle that obscured the truth. Far from a second Washington, Harrison was the stooge of fat cat businessmen who named his cabinet and stacked Congress and the courts to further their interests. The economic elites—bankers, industrialists, and trustmen—owned the President and dictated policy.

Steel magnate Andrew Carnegie provided the governing rationale. In his 1889 essay "The Gospel of Wealth," he defended the sacred law of unfettered competition and the "right of the millionaire to his millions." His solution to inequality and surplus wealth: charity to the deserving poor administered by the rich. This was already in practice in Manhattan, where Josephine Shaw Lowell, genteel commissioner of the New York Charity Organization Society, collected data on over ninety thousand "disreputable" urban poor and rationed accordingly. Handouts to the degraded class worked evil and unrest.

Disquiet, however, only increased; William Dean Howells presaged imminent calamity in his 1889 novel, *A Hazard of New Fortunes*, where neither side of the class divide comprehends the other, with tragic consequences. As he told his friend Henry James, he felt American civilization was "coming out all wrong."

A month after the Washington Centennial, Howells's fears seemed confirmed. At the exclusive South Fork Fishing and Hunting Club in the Pennsylvania Alleghenies, members had repeatedly failed to repair the three-mile dam around their recreational lake. On May 31 the dam burst during an epic rainstorm and flooded the coal and steel towns below. Over two thousand people—workingmen and their families—died in the "Johnstown Flood," igniting a major scandal and latent class rage. The club tycoons responsible for the disaster were the same capitalist giants who cut wages and enriched themselves at labor's expense.

In the near future there would be repercussions. *The Boston Weekly Globe* surveyed prominent Americans for a solution. Andrew Carnegie repeated his Social Darwinist bromides; Julia Ward Howe pressed for women's suffrage; P. T. Barnum recommended an educated electorate; others advanced land reform, improved childcare, and return to religion and a "citizen's duty." Mrs. Frank Leslie skirted the issue and suggested more art training in schools.

HER ANNUAL EUROPEAN trip took precedence. She sailed on the *City of Paris*, the first ship to cross the Atlantic in six days; a floating palace with concerts, electric ventilation, and a sumptuous bill of fare. The wind was at Miriam's back. The *Sun* listed her among the American writers whose reputations were "household words." She planned, she said, to launch a fashion magazine in London. But she did not plan on the return of the Marquis. Since their rupture over the Hyde Park incident, Miriam had every reason to believe she'd seen the last of him.

In the last two years, de Leuville had become the kept man of wealthy widow Mrs. Ada Peters, who gave him a weekly magazine, *Society Times*, pocket money, an agent, and a large flat in Albert Mansions where he entertained on a baronial scale. The Marquis, however, was outspending his income; he needed open credit and funds of his own. Due to an inheritance hitch, Mrs. Peters would lose her fortune if she remarried, which turned the Marquis's thoughts to Miriam, who he believed still loved him. His only difficulty that summer was the reemergence of Louisa Tussaud, who put her Bickley Place house on the market as the "Marquise de Leuville." Marriage to Miriam without a title might be a dealbreaker. The Marquis persisted anyway and spread the word that Mrs. Leslie had come to England expressly to marry him.

Nothing could have been further from her mind. As she explained in a *Boston Globe* essay, lightweight lovers have their uses, especially to older women who enjoy flattery and a little *passade*, but they have their "limitations." They can't be taken seriously, and once they run out of someone else's money and have to earn a living, they look pathetic, like "poor little trained poodles" or "industrious fleas." She had other priorities in London: her reputation to build and burnish. Papers throughout America reprinted her report of a weekend among the landed gentry. Her hosts, she wrote, laid out the welcome mat and provided liveried servants to anticipate every wish—snacks, wardrobe repairs, and access to the picture galleries, hot houses, stables, and library.

She also wanted to revisit her friend Jane Wilde. Jane had been busy publishing magazine pieces and books of Irish folklore, one of which, *Ancient Cures, Charms, and Superstitions*, was nearly out. But Oscar had quit his job in June as editor of *Lady's World*, and family finances were on life support. This time Miriam ordered the coachman to Jane's new address, 146 Oakley Street, a shabby ivied house in Chelsea. No servant greeted her, and she climbed a narrow dark staircase to an upper room that looked like "the kind usually let out in furnished apartments."

Jane, however, preserved appearances. She floated toward Miriam in high finery, a lavender silk gown studded with family miniatures, her hair dressed in ringlets beneath a tall lace headdress. At once, they were deep in banter and shared sentiments. Jane's commitment to gender equality had intensified; she was persuasive and impassioned and perhaps helped propel Miriam's nascent feminism. (Her donations to Elizabeth Cady Stanton and her causes began that year.) "What we chiefly want," Jane urged, "is the influence of women who think for themselves and feel for their sex."

At some point, Willie, Oscar's older brother, sauntered over, fixed his "carnal smile" on Miriam, and dialed up his charm. He told jokes, theater anecdotes—how he once shouted instructions to actors from his box—and tossed off bon mots and clever compliments. Before the end of the afternoon, Miriam had invited Willie to accompany her to America, where he would give three lectures over three months. It would "do him a deal of good," said Jane, wearied by his constant sponging, clubbing, and listless work on Fleet Street. Nothing came of the lecture tour, but Willie would be back.

ON JULY 20, 1889, Miriam left for Paris, which was in the midst of the Fourth International World's Fair. She'd hyped the Exposition in a May *Popular Monthly* cover story and wouldn't be disappointed. Even jaded fairgoers admitted it was the "most grandiose, the most dazzling, the most marvelous spectacle ever seen." In honor of the anniversary of the Revolution, the French threw the party of the century. Guidebooks advised tourists to allow ten to twenty days to see the Exposition, which covered 237 acres and contained sixty thousand exhibits from forty-three nations.

The centerpiece was the Eiffel Tower, a thousand-foot-high iron spire, an inverted champagne flute that symbolized French *gloire*. Farther down the Champ de Mars stood a second feat of iron construction—the Machinery Building, a hall the size of the Place des Vosges, with sixteen thousand exhibits inside. Miriam didn't linger there; even devout technophiles left "stupefied" by the surfeit.

She would have been drawn, instead, to the "magic carpet," the colonial pavilions, with villages representing each French possession from Tunisia to the Congo. The Belle Epoque craze for the exotic started here. Afternoons the streets came alive with Egyptian belly dancers, Javanese gamelan musicians, and Algerian Tuareg vendors. On Tuesday nights a procession wove through the pavilions—Senegalese cavalry, Vietnamese in frightening masks, veiled dancers, and a writhing Tonkin dragon.

Novelties beckoned at every turn: a telephone display where visitors listened to Opéra auditions through two earpieces (early stereophonic sound), a park that later became a prototype of Disneyland; and a reconstructed Bastille transformed into an amusement center with roller coasters and music hall acts. Despite the forward thrust of the fair, conservatism prevailed in the visual arts. The Palais des Beaux-Arts exhibited classical sculptures and naturalist/academic paintings and ignored the Impressionists. Miriam's artistic taste, considered purblind today, was mainstream: epic historical canvases, autumnal landscapes, and sentimental depictions of ascending angels and happy peasants.

Over 7,050 entries came from America. The United States made a strong showing at the Exposition: Louis Comfort Tiffany and painters John Singer Sargent and Gari Melchers won grand prizes, and Johns Hopkins and the University of California, gold medals for photography. But the real American coup was Buffalo Bill's "Wild West Show." For five months "Guillaume le Buffe" took Paris (and the ladies) by storm with a spectacular of mock battles and rodeos, with a cast of 245 cowboys, lady riders, shooters, and Indians, and 252 cattle.

Trick sharpshooter Annie Oakley was a top draw, a tiny woman in a fringed midi-skirt who shot dimes in the air and cigarettes from men's lips, and hit a playing card from thirty paces. Like Miriam, she was a Victorian deviant, a woman in a man's profession with a man-size sense of self, who forestalled criticism through a calculated feminine persona, "princess of the West." In her dress, however, Annie Oakley prefigured the future. Her calf-length skirts anticipated the new decade of less restrictive, plainer clothes adapted to women's more active lifestyles. Parisian walking dresses were already two inches off the ground, and loose silk "frocks" were on view at the fair. Miriam followed fashion, but stopped there.

That summer in Paris she collected antique Louis XV buttons, amassed corselets-gorges (the first bra) at Cadolle's, and visited Worth's for her annual fittings. The great couturier preferred curvaceous clients and richly decorated gowns cut to complement a full figure. His 1889 look suited Miriam to perfection—dresses that evoked the Medicis, with puffed sleeves to the elbow, nipped-in waists, and a smooth silhouette, all garnished with gold-beaded tulle, moiré ribbons, and satin panels. She would be his best customer this season. She also brought home a Yorkshire terrier, Zulu, arrayed in $600 worth of jewelry.

At home, she resumed her business-cum-literary career and self-promotional crusade. She reappeared at her Gerlach Thursdays, inviting a reporter to partake of a "highly enjoyable evening" and mingle with the city's glitterati. Mrs. Leslie, she wrote, "is very wealthy" and derives her income both from her periodicals and the "handsome prices" she receives from her essays. *The Pittsburgh Dispatch* named her one of the "writers of world-wide reputation." She prepared a book, *Beautiful Women*, and published two articles in quick succession: "Paris Ragpickers," a romanticized story of *chiffonniers* who found treasures in garbage dumps, and "The Best Kind of Man."

Despite her continued avowals of her contented single life, the desire for a man festered. What, she asked, was a woman to do when "pitiless middle age" descended and she required "protection and nurture"? She looked back nostalgically to Frank Leslie, a moral and physical paragon and "very tower of strength." An "Adonis" offered no support in later years, and the "selfish sybarite" was the worst possible choice—the man who drank a little too much, gambled at his club, and did deeds in questionable company unfit for a lady's ears. It was an exact portrait of Willie Wilde. Which perhaps explains why his American lecture tour never materialized—or why hers did. In another career pivot, Miriam recast herself as a professional public speaker and engaged Chicago lecture agents Thearle and Pelham to book twenty lectures for her in the coming year. The tour wasn't the victory walk she expected, and desire, she found, could play perverse tricks.

CHAPTER EIGHT

"FASCINATING WOMAN"
1890–95

THE COLD COMES early in St. Paul. Mrs. Leslie's evening wrap, a silk cloak trimmed with Siberian squirrel and white angora, was no match for a Minnesota October, forty-one degrees and falling. But the People's Church, the city's premier speaker's venue, was overheated and filled to capacity. An audience of 2,500 waited for the long-anticipated lecture by "the most brilliant woman in America," "the Queen of Journalism." At eight, the lights dimmed and Miriam strode to the lecture platform. She needed no introduction. "Ladies and Gentlemen, I am Frank Leslie."

Tonight's topic: "the Royal Leaders of Society." For her talk, one of twenty in twenty cities, she'd been paid more than any woman in the country, $200 a night plus a box-office percentage. She'd trained "like a racehorse" for the tour, and if she were successful, she planned to give a hundred more in the New Year.

She placed her right hand on the reading desk and began. The audience sat up. Few in this recently industrialized prairie town had ever seen such a display. Dressed in a white satin gown edged in black Chantilly lace with a low "empire" bodice, she blazed with diamonds—huge solitaire earrings, two hair ornaments, a dog collar, medallion, and necklace of three thousand diamonds with a secret vial for poison in a jeweled bird. On each arm she wore three heavy bracelets set in stones, and on each hand, emerald and diamond rings.

She spoke for over an hour. With "Southern gesticulations" in a British-accented contralto, she traced the history of Society's rulers from the "founder" Henry VIII to the current "gentleman's gentleman," the Prince of Wales. Only two Americans qualified: Presidents Chester A. Arthur and George Washington. The lecture, however, ended with a patriotic flourish, Joaquin Miller's poem "Columbus," dedicated to her: "He gained a world—he gave that world its grandest lesson," she declaimed, "on and on!"

The response wasn't the ovation Miriam hoped. Apart from her costume, the *St. Paul Globe* found the lecture "disappointing": Mrs. Leslie's voice was unpleasant and her "style and delivery" "amateurish." The rest of the tour encountered the same reception. Chicago, still unappeased by her call to shoot anarchists like "mad dogs," dismissed her as a cruel "animated fashion plate" and "empty-headed doll." By the time she reached Washington, so few bought tickets at Lincoln Music Hall that she demanded her guarantee money back and refused to speak. Toward mid-November, the verdict was in: "Mrs. Frank Leslie did not score her usual success in the lecture field."

On the record, she blamed managers, critics, and public taste, but privately she admitted she should have picked an American topic. She'd miscalculated. In a new decade of bootstrap moxie and nativist pride, old Europe savored of grandmother's curio cabinet. Which touched a raw nerve: Miriam was fifty-four and loath to admit it. She soaked in pine essence, put veal masks on her face, and promoted her desirability. She had "more offers of marriage than any woman in and out of the circle of the Four Hundred," and circulated an account of a young Irish devotee who broke into her cabin at sea to meet her.

That summer she capitalized on another intrigue with the Marquis de Leuville. In June he was in serious difficulties—both low in funds and on trial for intent to create a riot at a popular theater. According to his allies, Miriam deliberately led him on. She lunched with him at the Grosvenor Hotel two days after she arrived, and may or may not have met him at the Vestry and taken out a marriage license. Either way, he cabled New York that the wedding would take place in a fortnight. The day came and the Marquis appeared at the Burlington Hotel to escort her to the Registry, only to find that she'd checked out and was on the dock in Liverpool. She told reporters shipboard that she had no intention of marrying the Marquis, whose behavior was "inexplicable."

Still undeterred, de Leuville repeated the stunt that won Miriam before. He found a *Gil Blas* reporter who'd disputed Miriam's purported age of thirty-eight and provoked a duel. She played up the story. In an interview headlined "Must the Marquis Die?", she recounted an ominous portent at the Gerlach. The mirror de Leuville had given her fell from the wall and shattered as if hit by a bullet. She could never forgive herself if "anything fatal happened."

To her embarrassment, nothing did. After his opponent nicked the Marquis in the shoulder with his sword and both went off arm in arm, Miriam snorted, "He is an idiot." De Leuville retaliated by satirizing her as "Mrs. Unlessly," with infants dueling over her with baby bottles. The affair took an ugly turn. "It makes us tired," complained the *Chicago Tribune*. "We have had too much of Mrs. Frank Leslie and her Marquis [but] the world seems to enjoy laughing at them."

Miriam rebounded in November from the de Leuville contretemps and disappointing lecture tour with the publication of a gilt-engraved gift book, *Beautiful Women of Twelve Epochs*. With an idealized wash drawing of herself on the frontispiece, she profiled high-bred beauties from Druid priestesses to chaste Saxon noblewomen to Queen Anne, prefacing each with a quatrain of her own: "Great love is stronger than death/Or than the howling tempest's breath." The volume sank without a bubble; middle-class women of

1890, on the move in the workplace and public life, didn't relate to ancient noble beauties and their love dramas.

Miriam, though, remained an unreconstructed romantic. While she rallied women to storm the business world with "steady nerves" and courage, she believed "the great inescapable desire of a woman's heart is for love"—"there is really no joy so deep, so high, so all pervading in a woman's life as the joy of love." She admitted she was "looking for a husband, but he must be the right man."

On New Year's Eve, she launched her search with a grand reception for assorted notables and theater friends dressed in a beau-catcher gown embellished with pearls and gold leaf looped with diamond chains. She revised her biography to subtract twenty years from her age and attributed her distinctions to her aristocratic father who enhanced her "fatal gift of beauty" through lessons in classics and civil engineering.

She hired a Parisian introducer, Baroness Althea d'Avernas Salvador, to aid her quest. Unknown to Miriam, the Baroness, née Miss Simpson of Fairfield, Connecticut, lacked elite connections (neither she nor the Baron belonged to the *mondanité*) and was of no use that summer. Miriam kept her on the payroll for good measure and tried her luck in London. Women, she believed, possessed a "glorified instinct" for scoping out good men.

IN HER HASTE, Miriam's "glorified instinct" failed her. At Jane Wilde's 1891 soirée, she encountered Willie Wilde again, now at the end of his tether. He was deep in debt and the effects of his dissipated life were beginning to tell: his eyes were bagged, features bloated, and whiskers streaked with gray. But he could be charming if he liked and amuse friends with mimicry, recitations, bon mots, and droll anecdotes. It was in his interest to charm Mrs. Leslie and he was *en forme*. Although she pretended to equivocate, she agreed to marry him in the fall.

Willie never seems to have doubted the outcome and forged a check in her name after she left. He arrived on the S. S. *Havre* on the first of October, and three days later the wedding took place in the pastor's study at the Church of the Strangers, with Miriam in a beaded Worth ensemble of pearl gray satin with a matching bonnet. She deducted twelve years and entered her age as forty-three in the church record book, the better to approximate Willie's thirty-nine. Reverend Charles Deems, former editor of *Frank Leslie's Sunday Magazine*, officiated, and best man, Marshall P. Wilder, gave her away.

The effect of Wilder beside the six-foot-three-inch groom must have been striking. Marshall, an intimate of Miriam's and a salon regular, was "one of the world's greatest comedians" and a hunchback who stood only as high as her waist. He towered above Willie, though, in character. A striver and self-starter, Marshall pioneered a career as a legitimate actor (rather than a Barnum act) who scripted his own routines, wrote three books, and earned a fortune as a celebrity entertainer.

Wilde, however, promised to reform and work in partnership with Miriam in the publishing business. She had no concept of his idea of work. His routine on the *Daily Telegraph* was to take an assignment, walk in the park, lunch at his club with a glass of wine, stroll through the afternoon, and return to his club where he dashed off a leader in an hour before "cigar[s], bottles, [and] ballet." This was on days when he bothered to report at all.

Yet hopes ran high on October 4. Miriam had refurbished the Gerlach with a joint bedroom and dressing room for Willie and booked a wedding supper at Delmonico's. After the ceremony, the party sat down to a six-course dinner of capon, beef tenderloin, and upland plover, accompanied by four wines, Möet and Chandon champagne, and a cardinal punch. Willie tied one on and collapsed drunk on the marriage bed that night.

The binge lasted a week and brought unwelcome surprises. Bad enough that he couldn't deliver and left his false teeth on the bureau, but he was a mean drunk. Two nights after the wedding, he stumbled into the room, smashed bottles, and threatened Miriam, yelling, "Damn your soul!" and "To hell with you!" The housekeeper said she was afraid she'd wake up and find Mrs. Leslie dead. Once Miriam had a close call. On a carriage ride, they approached a precipice and Willie shouted: "I have a blankety blank good notion to drive down that embankment and break your neck." Miriam wasn't easily cowed; she consigned Willie to a separate "sleeping room" and put up a brave front.

As the weeks wore on, this became increasingly hard to do. The marriage, which she thought would generate positive publicity, had the reverse effect. The press descended like jackals, jeering at her age (she was "old enough to be his mother") and her last-gasp fourth "attempt at matrimony." She forged on, paid his double-digit liquor bills at the Lotos Club, and buried herself in business while he slept until one thirty each afternoon.

The breaking point came the first of the year. In January 1892, she assembled a hundred friends to accompany them by train to the first annual convention of the International League of Press Clubs in San Francisco. Willie began to feel alarmed for his future and sent Miriam a mea culpa sonnet beforehand, which she printed in the *Monthly*:

> Into love's water have I cast my stone,
> Where gently mirrored lay your face so fair;
> But now the rippling circles, under grown,
> Have blurred the clear gray eyes and golden hair.
> Love! Can no love for all my faults atone?
> Should the waves quiet, will you still be there?

Unmoved, Miriam put him in a separate coach car and changed her name back to Frank Leslie. She informed reporters that she would become Mrs. Wilde as soon as her husband made "for himself a name equal to my own." He was in no hurry. Mrs. Leslie, he drawled, "has made industry a study while I have reciprocated by making indolence mine."

The honeymoon, as one journalist commented, had "waned" and "the evidences of suffering and night vigils [were] on Mrs. Wilde's fine face." The strain grew more apparent throughout the trip. Willie's pique as a backstage husband intensified as Miriam's stature grew at the conference. Her speech to the League, "Reminiscences of a Woman's Work in Journalism," built a defiant case for female empowerment; not only could a woman succeed in anything she attempted, but "the good steed progress was bearing women to the front" where they were "gallop[ing] the course with men neck and neck." She concluded with a poem written for her by Joaquin Miller (now in exile, as he'd promised if she married again)—"The Mother of Men," a six verse hymn to "spotless woman," "the kingliest warrior born."

The local papers feasted on the open "War between Mrs. Frank Leslie and her Husband." Miriam told reporters that the British man was less courteous than an American "hod carrier" and dressed Willie down in public. Before the press corps, she chastised him for his inability to "distinguish" himself, and when he protested, she fleered, "I believe, Mr. Wilde, I am being interviewed, not yourself. He has been here ninety days," she pursued, "that's long enough for any man of brains to attract attention to himself. I really should have married Oscar."

At this point, Willie stood and said he'd be at the Press Club until 3:00 A.M.

"Then ring and order another room, sir," she retorted.

The press had no patience with this. California dailies portrayed her as a "short and dumpy [woman] with wrinkled and rouged" cheeks who browbeat her carefree husband. She could take only so much. On a cruise with a friend in San Diego Bay, she burst into tears over Willie's impotence, and suffered a panic attack during a sightseeing expedition. At a ruined Spanish mission, a door slammed behind her and she let out an "unearthly" scream, swearing a skeletal man had seized her in the darkness. (Freud, then studying the sexual origins of hysteria, should have been there.)

BACK IN NEW York, she pulled herself together and took action. Either Willie shaped up and earned his keep or he must go. She put the case before his mother, who surely tried to dissuade her, then cut bait. There would be consequences—none pleasant—but she was "tired," she said, "of being the bank and sick nurse for a man."

She deposited Willie with Jane in May and spent the summer of 1892 recuperating. After a pleasure tour to Venice and Trouville, she visited her actress friend Nettie Hooper in Paris and ordered a complete new wardrobe from Worth's. She took it to New York in the fall, where style-watchers raved over her Renaissance festoons, quilled sashes, and leg-o-mutton sleeves. Again, she was the most fashionably "gowned woman in New York." She defended her failed marriage at her newly opened salon as a mistake any woman might make in search of a helpmate; she deserved "sympathy not censure."

Her first-line remedy, though, was work. "Shall I tell you why [I love] hard, unending, unrequited labor?" she explained. "It is because it makes me forget myself, because it removes from me the dull, dead past with all its weight of sorrow and pain and makes me strong again." After full days at the office, she wrote seven essays in 1892 for the American Press Association. Five of these unloaded on Willie. She broke the "dirty linen" taboo and defended herself: Why should an "unhappy and wronged wife" remain silent against a domestic abuser? She should "pay up" the tyrant and broadcast his crimes. Doctors, she added with pre-Freudian insight, know that "outcries" mitigate "the effects of pain."

In one essay after another she enumerated Willie's offenses: the "water torture" she endured with his brutality, dissipation, insults, and slovenly behavior. He slopped around in disarray, smoked in the boudoir, and laughed lazily when asked not to. Marriage, she concluded, was a lottery where few won and "domestic treachery" thrived, but what was the alternative? The "bitter pangs of loneliness."

Despite her therapeutic endeavors, happiness seemed elusive by year's end. Her Louisiana "pretty boy" actor Albert Hope, whom she'd installed in the Gerlach Hotel, was arrested for forgery and default on a $10,000 loan, and surrendered a diary full of compromising entries about their relationship. Another protégé, poet Willis Ardennes Jones-Foster, got involved in a scheme to scam the Ecuadorian Consul and dragged her name into it. And Wing and Son sued her for nonpayment of a $4,700 necklace. She seemed to be in a dark stretch on fate's "iron road."

MIRIAM HOPED TO turn the page in 1893. Her essay collection *Are We All Deceivers?* was slated for publication; her play, *The Froth of Society*, scheduled to open at the Union Square Theater; and her divorce from Willie on track. (Through proof of his adultery, she'd insured he'd be unable to remarry, a law still on the books in New York and other states.) She awaited honors at the Chicago Exposition where America's leading women were to be lauded. No one could have imagined how the year would play out.

The first alarm sounded weeks before Grover Cleveland's second inauguration when the Philadelphia and Reading Railroad collapsed and touched off a run on gold. A recession, obscured by paper prosperity, had been brewing for months due to reckless rail expansion, drained gold reserves, and declining agricultural prices and exports. By June, the credit system seized up and panic set in. America was in the grip of the country's worst-ever financial depression. The stock market cratered and banks foundered, setting off a tsunami of business failures. Before the year was out, six hundred fifty banks, seventy-four railroads, and sixteen thousand business firms went under, and industrial unemployment rose to 20 percent. The human toll for the next five years was incalculable—millions were paupered and ruined.

New York was the eye of the storm. In a city already plagued with rampant poverty, the hit was catastrophic. Throughout Manhattan's Lower East Side, where unemployment stood at 35 percent, rag pickers, beggars, vendors, and tramps swarmed through narrow streets piled with animal carcasses and rotting garbage. Deaths from exposure, suicide, and starvation reached an alarming rate.

As City Hall idled and civic charities refused aid to "indolent vagrants," the fuse blew. Hunger strikes erupted downtown. Unionists and socialists clamored for governmental relief and anarchists preached insurrection. Emma Goldman, radical firebrand and "High Priestess of Anarchy," addressed three thousand in Union Square, ordering the crowd to demonstrate "before the palaces of the rich," steal bread, and "take everything by force." Class warfare ramped up and brought surges of strikes and violence throughout America.

On the other side of the income divide, fear engulfed the genteel establishment. The ruling elite demanded law and order, fomented racial and religious prejudice, and promoted tough love. The "best people" recoiled from the destitution. As did Miriam. Each day on her walks to her Sixteenth Street office, she averted her gaze from the specters of poverty and affliction. She should have paid attention. A cultural and social upheaval was in progress that would impact her life in ways she never guessed.

She also cut an unfortunate figure during the depression. Even accounting for a despair-hardened heart and her Society aspirations, her response to the national crisis was insensitive to an extreme. As a poor girl, her dis-identification with wretchedness was to be expected, but she approached brute indifference.

Unlike fellow publisher Joseph Pulitzer, who declared a war on poverty, distributed free loaves, and documented the misery; unlike heiress Lillian Wald, who founded Henry Street Settlement for the down and out; and unlike Macy's cofounder Nathan Straus, who opened five-cent stands, Miriam retreated to her suite and compiled her essay collection *Are We All Deceivers?* The publisher, Neely's

Library of Choice Literature, heralded the book as a surefire success: "The public appetite is sharp," they pronounced, for Mrs. Leslie's latest work. But she misread the moment; there was something to offend everyone.

The extent of male anxiety was her first mistake. Spurred by her Wildean ordeal, she heightened her feminist rhetoric—just when men felt imperiled by financial loss and women's entry (five million) into the workplace. She celebrated the "new order" of liberated womanhood and exhorted women to get off the fainting couch and free themselves from the "swaddling bands" of oppression. "Eminence," she charged, "is actually woman's proper position"—a besetting male terror. With traditional manhood in jeopardy, men foresaw "sexual anarchy" and a reign of battleaxes.

To worsen their apprehensions, Mrs. Leslie gave them a taste of their own medicine in *Deceivers* and ranked men like livestock. "You will find the typical Boston man," she itemized, "cold and reserved"; the New Yorker, cynical; the Westerner, hospitable and boisterous; and the Southerner, generous, romantic, and discreet, if too quick on the trigger. Men, in general, she continued, should learn to please women, perhaps at a "school of professional beaux."

She had to have foreseen the consequences. The mid-nineties male backlash was vicious. Leading authorities, led by doctors and scientists, conducted a "weaker sex" campaign and persecuted dissidents with incarcerations in "rest cure" asylums. Women were ordered to "live as domestic a life as possible" and avoid brainwork on pain of "neurasthenia." Miriam shot back: Women should tax their minds to the limit and "make [their] mark" or "die in the attempt." They were as capable as the "Great Napoleon."

By rights such philippics should have won over her female readers. Yet despite her endorsement of women's rights, she was off script. Early feminists supported a different agenda: prohibition, civic service, prudery, dress reform, and enlightened manless celibacy.

Miriam, on the other hand, argued for personal fulfillment in life, work, and love, and proposed an unfashionable Machiavellian route to power. To prevail, women should adopt protective coloration and deploy the guerrilla arts of "sympathetic charm," "fascination," soigné apparel, and "gentle deceptions." Her role models weren't calculated to please, either: "immoral" seductresses like Cleopatra, Ninon de Lenclos, and mythic Lilith, who rejected Adam's dominion in Eden for an erotic paradise of her own with revolving mates and seditious offspring. "I am afraid I am Lilith," she added imprudently. On the subjects of temperance, settlement houses, and chastity, she was silent. And although she abstained from alcohol herself, she declined to sign the temperance pledge. Sales and reviews were lackluster. "Such a book," carped critics, "is always sure of readers, but readers are not always to be rewarded for their pains."

As if she'd learned nothing from *Deceivers*, she mounted a production of her play, *The Froth of Society*, based on Alexandre Dumas's *Demi-Monde*, which she'd translated and published thirty-five years before. The farce revolves around a cheeky Parisian courtesan who schemes to dispatch a lover and marry a nobleman amid an amorous romp of deceits and subterfuges.

Pre-production, Mrs. Leslie assured the press that she'd expurgated the play, "made it polite and clean," and "placed special emphasis on purity." Suzanne, the heroine, "is not a model of virtue," she conceded, but such types—as she knew firsthand—were "perhaps not impossible in America." The house was packed at the Union Square Theater opening night, April 24, 1893, with a large Leslie claque in attendance. Nevertheless, the production was skewered as a "frothy bit of bad society" and limped through an East Coast tour.

Again, she was tone deaf to the temper of the times. The nineties marked the apogee of national prudery, with Anthony Comstock re-armed and on the warpath. Aided by the Watch and Ward Society and recent "Hicklin test," which broadened the legal definition of obscenity, his armies of suppression assailed threats to public immorality with redoubled ferocity. Vice squads boarded up nude paintings, like Luis Falero's *Twin Stars* (now displayed in the Metropolitan Museum of Art), and confiscated such smut as *The*

Canterbury Tales, Moll Flanders, Oscar Wilde's plays, and Tolstoy's *The Kreutzer Sonata.*

Behind Comstock was a broad base of American support. The Woman's Christian Temperance Union, the largest women's organization, crusaded against licentious art, dance, and plays; the American Library Association sanitized its shelves; and the respectable middle class referred to bulls as "male cows" and illegitimate babies as "children of sin." Mark Twain called Titian's *Venus with a Mirror* "the foulest, vilest, the obscenest picture the world possesses," and Theodore Roosevelt labeled Tolstoy a "sexual and moral pervert." The "Iron Maidens" of social purity ruled the day. By the time her French comedy reached Boston, Mobile, and New Orleans, burlesque versions proliferated, entitled *The Dregs of Society* and *The Fringe of the Froth of the Crust of Society.* She was mortified.

THE LONG-AWAITED COLUMBIAN Exposition failed to salve the injury. Her hopes for a star turn came to naught. The Chicago World's Fair in May commemorated the four hundredth anniversary of Columbus' voyage to the New World and surpassed all previous fairs, with six hundred acres filled with lagoons and canals and a "White City" of neoclassical whitewashed buildings. In contrast to the national turmoil, the Exposition was a monument to order and symmetry. At the central Court of Honor towered the symbol of the fair—a sixty-five-foot Hellenistic female statue with a horn of plenty and children at the base, the ideal "True Woman," the Republican Mother.

Beside the statue stood the Renaissance-inspired Women's Building, "delicate, dignified, pure, and fair to look upon." Here three hundred women, including Mrs. Leslie, convened at the World's Congress of Representative Women to read papers, network, and unite for change.

Within the pavilion, however, they were a house divided. The Lady Managers, led by socialite Mrs. Potter Palmer, advocated charity work as women's highest calling; militant suffragists urged direct political action; and the Woman's Christian Temperance Union rallied the "purer sex" to cleanse the male Augean stable. (They campaigned against images of female nudes at the fair.)

Mrs. Leslie fit nowhere under the tent. Her *Exposition Souvenir* biography was dated copy from 1888, and the paper she presented came out of left field, a paen to the "tenderly bred" new Southern woman who was making her way in business, not with "battleaxe[s]" but with "perfumed oil." In any case, neither Miriam's contribution nor the feuds among the women's factions mattered in the end. The fair's overriding theme was veneration of the domestic goddess, and the exhibits were a long tribute to woman as mother, homemaker, teacher, cook, and moral paragon.

Miriam would have felt no more welcome at the Midway Plaisance next to the Women's Building—the flip side of the neoclassical White City—where the rabble thronged the mile-long fairway gaping at belly dancers, chewing Juicy Fruit gum, and riding the two-hundred-and-sixty-five-foot Ferris wheel. The fair had been a national "sham" and letdown both for Miriam and the women's Congress.

HER TRIP TO London to deliver the divorce papers in June did nothing to lighten her mood. Though she preferred not to dwell on it, her romantic pride had suffered. The divorce from Willie Wilde, which she dispatched in 1893, had taken an unexpected toll. Almost as soon as she left him with his mother in London after their brief, stormy marriage, the newspapers struck. "I have always received the kindest treatment," she reminded reporters, "at the hands of the gentlemen of the press."

But they did not behave as gentlemen. They profiled Wilde sympathetically, aired his grievances, and went on the attack. The beleaguered Willie—an "easy-going, large-eyed Englishman"—had wedded a shrew who shackled him to her "apron strings" and treated him like her "coachman." His flight from her was the "one brilliant stroke of his life." As for Mrs. Leslie, she was ugly, wrinkled, and sixty, and unlikely to find another husband.

They hit home. Love, unfortunately, was her weak spot. Neither Willie's treachery nor her avowals of strong, independent woman-hood could staunch her desire for male adoration. And she was amid another dry spell. Her "regular," poet Joaquin Miller, had departed to the "Hights," a California aerie with a harem of acolytes, and the Marquis de Leuville was a nuisance and an embarrassment.

In hopes of a return to favor, the Marquis challenged Willie to a duel and foolishly left the weapons to Wilde, who chose hansom cabs and cab horses, each riding the other's choice. De Leuville lost; he was thrown to the pavement, kicked by his horse, and left with a broken nose and two broken ribs.

To salt the wound, American papers ran accounts of fictitious suitors, both of whom she might have welcomed: popular bachelor Senator David B. Hill and "one of the handsomest actors in New York," forty-year-old Myron Calice. She was patently "grieved" and snapped at reporters: "Why are such statements published?"

Homecoming was hard enough. Behind her was a London summer of social snubs, unrelieved by a Paris detour for new gowns. "I have suffered intensely in mind and grown thin," she said, "but I have come back to work."

SHE CAME BACK to Armageddon. The depression had deepened in 1894 and the country was on the verge, many feared, of a proletarian revolution. With mounting layoffs, beggary, and hunger, the desperate masses grew militant. One after another, labor disputes exploded into violence, from the Pennsylvania coal mines and New England silk factories to the western railroads. In Chicago, the bloody Pullman strike shut down rail traffic for two months and resulted in the intervention of fifty thousand federal troops. Coxey's Army, an embattled brigade of five hundred jobless "tramps," staged a protest march to Washington that ended in mayhem on the Capitol grounds. Panic seized the comfortable classes as armies of the unemployed fanned out across America.

Harrowing poverty invaded Manhattan. It was the "blackest winter in New York history"—arctic cold with fifteen inches of snow in one day—with unemployment topping eighty thousand and 1.1 million poor huddled in unheated hovels. Homeless "hobos" filled parks and flophouses, stretched out "like stabbed fish," more dead than alive. Ragged street urchins scavenged for food and shelter.

Amid the desolation, Miriam verged on a depression of her own. The insults and injuries of the past year had snowballed. "Happiness," she lamented, "lies on the other side of the river," and young hopes dissolve into "bitterness and ash." Love's bubble bursts, men fail women, and time is no healer for a "harsh and bitter and cruel" sorrow. "A woman with no one to love her is the most miserable of creatures" who grows either "defiant, bitter and narrow or withers and languishes like spring flowers in the east wind."

She grew more embittered and narrower in her sympathies. When asked for answers to the poverty crisis, she replied that the poor should seek respite in happy marriages and refreshment in library books at the end of the day. (City seamstresses worked fourteen hours a day, and cigar laborers, ten to eleven, for starvation wages.) Just government was the solution, not charity. And if "dire poverty" comes, she declared, a man could trust his wife to take up the "laboring oar"—this when 25 percent of working women were jobless.

Immersed in her distress, she walled off the devastation and turned to her default therapy: work. In 1894, she dashed off nine essays in quick succession. The majority were rehashed hobby horses—the wreckage of wedlock, male chivalry, and fine manners. A few, though, took a fresh stab at feminism. At her most combative, she proclaimed the demise of the "women's sphere" and heralded the "coming woman," who would revolutionize history. By the year

2000, she predicted, female doctors, lawyers, and business leaders would be commonplace.

But once more she lost the mainstream. Miriam's brand of feminism was out of sync; she refused to endorse suffrage (despite longtime contributions to Elizabeth Cady Stanton), counseled moderation, and again proposed "safe machinery," a stealth approach to empowerment. In one improvident essay, she targeted the "New Woman" movement, an advance guard of activists who should have been her allies. These outspoken radicals championed wholesale liberation—free love, birth control (which Miriam had practiced illegally), gender equality, and full participation in the world. Instead, she rebuked them as "daughters of revolt" who "repel[ed] rather than [won]."

What her work failed to achieve, Miriam tried to attain through her routine anodynes. There were the consolations of dress and self-adornment—six Worth creations of china silk and French crepe with velvet "ruffle wings," which she invited the press to admire. She fanned up her ego. She corralled reporters to puff her pedigree and "perfect foot" (modeled in terra-cotta) and flaunted her $2.5 million fortune, roughly $75 million today.

She plunged into social life. Her round of engagements accelerated: nightly dinners for friends at the Gerlach Hotel, "unusually brilliant" Thursday evenings, and a raft of women's clubs events. For all her egocentricity, she had a way with people and a gift for friendship that insured constant company. She found no "joy" that season "in a life partaken alone."

The hectic pace continued in London, where she gave morning receptions and went wherever she was invited. She put a good face on things, but the visit was a blow to her vanity. Willie Wilde, in defiance of the court order, had married Miss Sophia Lees, a younger woman, and rubbed it in. "I married for love this time," he ribbed, and credited the rumor that Mrs. Leslie wanted him back. "Too late," he said, it was "logically and legally impossible." Miriam riposted that she "could not imagine Mr. Wilde marrying a woman with no money";

the lady was forty and poor. But Miriam was forced to confront the truth bruited all over town: She'd been married for her bank balance. Afterward, Paris paled. The "pleasures [had] departed," and on her return to New York, papers noted she "had not been well."

LITTLE WONDER. WHEN she thought fate had dealt its worst, she found bad news at the office. Absorbed in her personal life, she hadn't been minding the store. The Frank Leslie business was in trouble. This wasn't a problem publicity could solve, but she tried. With media fanfare, she moved the publishing house to new headquarters on Bond Street and designed her "editorial sanctum" to resemble a Savoy suite, with Oriental carpets and sumptuous décor.

She ran a *Popular Monthly* cover story in October to promote the magazine. With full-page glamorized photographs of herself front and back, the feature recounted the *Monthly*'s illustrious history and boasted of its superior content, technology, and roster of illustrious names. Under the "inspired management" of the remarkable Mrs. Leslie, the monthly magazine remained the "best in the world."

She was four-flushing. All the hype couldn't conceal the fact that she'd lost her publishing edge. In her self-preoccupation, she'd been blindsided by a revolution in journalism. A new crop of publishers was transforming the industry and crowding out the competition with the magazine of the future.

The point man of the revolution was a dark horse. Frank Munsey, a greenhorn from Maine with a long face, tar-black eyes, and a cowcatcher mustache, had come to New York in his twenties and bombed at every publishing venture for five years. When the depression struck, he was $100,000 in debt with two failing periodicals on his hands. Desperate and out of options, he gambled on a novel concept—a magazine for the everyman that paid for itself through mass advertising.

Circulation numbers were key, and he targeted the neglected expanding population of ordinary working men and women who wanted affordable, easy-read magazines. (The "yellow" dailies, Pulit-zer's *World* and Hearst's *Journal*, had already captured this audience with boldface, sensational papers at bargain prices.)

In October 1893 he slashed the cost of his *Munsey's Magazine* from twenty-five cents to ten cents and geared content to "the people, for the people." In a brief thirty-six pages of large typeface, he gave the average public what they wanted—copious pictures, current events, advice columns, celebrity profiles, and snappy fiction. "We want stories," Munsey announced, "not weak tales of sickly senti-mentality, not pretty writing."

His bet paid off. Rivals sneered that he had the "talent of a meat packer, the morals of a money changer, and the manner of an undertaker." But no one argued with his bottom line. From 1893 to 1895, circulation jumped from sixty thousand to five hundred thou-sand and ad space boomed, covering overhead and fattening profits.

The major monthlies fell in step. *Ladies' Home Journal*, *McClure's*, *McCall's*, and *Cosmopolitan* lowered their prices to ten cents and produced magazines on the Munsey model. They hired popular authors, such as Bret Harte and Stephen Crane, and treated American themes, underclass life, and real-world stories in simple, direct prose. Like *Munsey's* they courted advertisers and reduced production costs further through streamlined machinery, conveyor systems, and increased use of photographs and linotype where compositors worked for straight wages. These were the ris-ing industry kingpins whose magazines were commandeering the market.

Miriam struggled to catch up. "A born businesswoman," she believed, "is inventive. She sees by instinct what movement is likely to be successful, and is not afraid to move without precedent." But she didn't move inventively or fast enough. She brought technology up to par with thirteen rapid-fire rotary presses that electrotyped pages onto curved metal plates and pulled the magazine into the "age of the camera" by incorporating photoengravings, half-tone reproductions, and oil-colored lithographs in her issues.

Despite her investments in technology, however, Miriam neglected the rising mass audience. Either her instinct deserted her or identification with the privileged blinded her, but she failed to refresh the magazine, leaving the format, subject matter, and twenty-five cent price unchanged. Compared to the competition, the *Monthly* looked staid and elitist. Each issue contained a hundred and twenty-eight pages of double-columned literature of the sort Munsey reviled: high-stilted prose, escapist travelogues, and sentimental stories and serialized novels about the upper class.

She was at her most obtuse in 1895—the game-changing "Year of the Magazine." The issue she prepared in the fall featured a profile on robber baron Jay Gould's daughter, romantic holidays in "Pineapple Land," and a saccharine mélange of lily flower poems and genteel melodramas. The *Popular Monthly* aimed for the polite bourgeois parlor; the new magazines, for the omnibus and the hustling masses who wanted cheap reads on hot topics at their level. Miriam's profit margins told the story. She was eyeing the door.

SHE WAS ALSO eyeing omens. Belief in the paranormal wasn't uncommon at the turn of the century. Distinguished figures— *Monthly* contributor Andrew Lang, psychologist William James, physicist Oliver Lodge, and Nobel laureate Charles Richet—took psychic phenomenon and extrasensory experiences seriously. Even professional scoffer Mark Twain championed ESP, and her old friend from Saratoga Springs, Cornelius Vanderbilt, communed daily with his deceased mother under her portrait and burned his hair clippings to ward off evil spirits.

For someone of her caliber—hard-headed, worldly, and pragmatic—Miriam would seem the last person to subscribe to paranormal beliefs. But under the circumstances, almost anyone in her place might have been unnerved. Recently she had witnessed occurrences to chill the staunchest skeptic—events that might have tapped into her memories of Louisiana voodoo, the spells of the dread loa.

In 1894 in London, she'd visited Cheiro, the famous psychic and palmist, whose findings weren't taken lightly. He foresaw the murder of a civic leader to the hour and later predicted the Titanic tragedy while the ship was in drydock. At her reading, Miriam didn't like what she heard. When she extended her hand, he saw romantic distress, mischief from "some unfavorable attachment," mental fatigue, and a major life change in her deep-grooved fate line. She was visibly disquieted. "Your possession of this mysterious skill and facility," she wrote in his autograph book, "might well inspire fear."

She didn't have to look beyond her New York apartment for a source of fear. The Gerlach Hotel, where she'd lived for a decade, seemed under a strange curse. The building was the last word in modern elegance, with a towered roof and bowed bays designed to "capture the slightest breezes in summer." A "French flat" such as Miriam's, a spacious floor-through suite, cost $360 a month (the average yearly income of most Americans). Top-of-the-line luxury living—sentineled and full-service.

Yet something sinister was at work on the premises. A fire erupted in the hundred-percent fireproof building, followed by a series of bizarre incidents. Gerland Hull, a Saratoga Springs neighbor who "moved in best society," shot himself in the head with a revolver. Afterward, crime invaded the Gerlach. A resident, Judge Henry W. Bookstaver of the Court of Common Pleas, was found beaten, bloodied, and robbed of his watch and chain on Forty-sixth Street and Fifth Avenue at 3:00 A.M. Socialite Mrs. Archibald A. Hutchinson lost a costly diamond and turquoise bracelet, which turned up in the hands of two vandals at a pawn shop next door.

The building's most famous tenant, engineer/inventor Nikola Tesla, had his own brush with the Gerlach curse. The father of modern electronic transmissions, Tesla discovered the technology responsible for fluorescent light, X-rays, robotics, laser beams, remote control, bladeless turbines, television, and radio. From the roof of the Gerlach, he received the first radio waves from his laboratory on South Fifth Avenue thirty blocks away.

He was also a man at home in the paranormal. He had supernatural visitations and "saw" the alternating current concept that inaugurated wireless communication in a vision. While reciting Goethe's *Faust* at sunset, the idea came to him in a spectral flash, and he drew the diagram with a stick in the sand. When his laboratory burned to the ground on March 13, 1895, he might well have felt the presence of malign, unseen powers in the hotel.

Miriam had her own share of untoward mishaps at the Gerlach. A newspaperwoman with impeccable references, Mary H. Martin, had arrived for an interview, and in the process, filched a diamond pin worth $500, several checks, and a "considerable sum in cash." Miss Martin, a grifter with a long history of impersonations and intrigues, was apprehended and jailed, but freed without explanation by the governor.

More alarming was an attempt on her life—and from no ordinary source. On a routine Thursday morning a few years back, she received a strange envelope at the Gerlach. Inside she found a letter, signed "Jack the Ripper," that ordered her to appear at the Hotel Marlborough with $400 in small bills or face murder and mutilation. Another alleged note from the infamous serial killer had warned city inspector Byrnes that he was "coming to the states to baffle the skill of New York's finest detectives." He was thought to be at large and the signature "xxxs" on the border of the notepaper and cockney solecisms matched the Ripper's.

Mrs. Leslie, noted reporters, was "not easily frightened, but now felt a trifle uncomfortable." She stationed patrolmen at the Gerlach and her office and hired an armed bodyguard to accompany her on the street. Many conjectured the extortionist was the same bomber who exploded a suitcase of dynamite in the office of Wall Street magnate Russell Sage, but the case was never solved. As far as anyone knew, the unapprehended Jack the Ripper was still on the loose.

If she needed a prod, this was it. In May 1895, she unloaded the *Popular Monthly*, along with *Frank Leslie's Pleasant Hours* and *Frank Leslie's Budget of Fun*, on Frederick L. Colver, who leased the publications from her for five years at an annual rate of $6,000. Colver and his syndicate, she told the press, would introduce beneficial changes to the magazines while she recuperated abroad, freed from "all worry" and "relieved of managerial cares."

On the surface, her explanation for a "long vacation" at fifty-nine seemed nothing unusual. The average life expectancy for a woman in 1900 was sixty-four years, and oil titan John D. Rockefeller retired at fifty-eight. But Miriam had no idea of fading into the sunset. She intended to recharge and attend to unfinished business. "Whenever I [am] out of sorts or in need of rest," she liked to say, "I try a change of air." Rest was going to be out of the question.

CHAPTER NINE

"LONG VACATION"
1895-98

ON MAY 25 Miriam boarded the *City of Rome* on a tide of promise. Deflecting suspicions of nervous bankruptcy and failing powers, she told reporters she'd be back in the fall to take charge. Her trip to England, she said, was chiefly to console her friend Lady Wilde, who was prostrated by her son Oscar's indictment for gross indecency. The situation was sticky: Miriam had been Oscar's chief promoter on his American tour, and his offense struck horror in Comstock's America. She rose to his defense, but the day she left, Wilde was convicted and sentenced to two years of hard labor for "corruption of the most hideous kind among young men" and a homosexual affair with Lord Alfred Douglas.

Once in London, Miriam seems to have washed her hands of the Wildes. She had nothing to gain through association with scandal or reacquaintance with Willie, who had fallen off the wagon and into debt and lived with his wife and ill mother on Oakley Street. If Miriam made her promised consolation call, it must have been awkward, since she'd stopped Lady Wilde's support checks after the divorce and Jane was down to her last shilling.

But that wasn't the purpose of her furlough in the first place. Her object was self-replenishment, an opportunity to buoy her reputation and achieve her heart's desires—true love and social acceptance. On every front she'd taken a beating. Her celebrity, she feared, was in eclipse. Before her break with the *Monthly*, she complained that the woman who "defies convention" or "publishes a newspaper has no more distinction than the first man who ate an oyster." She planned to change that.

Europe was a perfect theater of operations. While gaining continental éclat, she could avail herself of fresh social and romantic opportunities.

Miriam had grievances to settle with New York Society. Despite her best efforts, the Manhattan upper crust continued to exclude her. She'd gone to great lengths to gain their acceptance—invented a *pur-sang* pedigree, dressed like a duchess, affected aristocratic airs, rented opera boxes, frequented elite hotels, and anglicized her speech. When Ward McAllister, Mrs. Astor's watchdog, died in 1895, restrictions loosened and prospects improved. Socialite Alva Vanderbilt procured a once-tabooed divorce; Mrs. Stuyvesant Fish dined at Sherry's Restaurant among "loose women"; and former prostitute Arabella Huntington built a mansion on Fifth Avenue and was on the way to acceptance.

But the great ladies "snubb[ed] Miriam at their entertainments. She was conspicuously absent at the Society dinners, fêtes, and subscription balls and nowhere to be found among the twelve thousand five hundred names in the *Social Register* for the last eight years. The patriciate had spoken: Mrs. Leslie was still "a person one does not know"—a triple divorcée, a professional woman, a public woman, and who knows what else.

Another might have shrugged off the Astorocracy and moved on with her life and career. But Miriam's great ambition—born of early humiliations and underclass expedients—was social prominence. "Everybody," she wrote, "aspires to belong to society and to have the reputation of belonging. To be out of society is to be out of the world, and in that case we might as well be dead."

In Europe the "business of making a social splash" came easier. Society was more porous, and increasing numbers of nouveaux riches—the "Chicago Smith" clan and Pittsburgh cobbler-turned-steel boss Henry Phipps—were being "received" after a shine-up abroad. The fast track to the first circles was through marriage into the aristocracy, a growth industry. In 1895, nine American heiresses acquired titled husbands in England, not counting those who made matches on the continent. Land-poor and still suffering the effects of the recession, the nobility prospected for daughters of the new rich. Looks and breeding played no part; Count Boni de Castellane of the *ancienne noblesse* had just married Anna Gould, whose only charm (she was plain, hirsute, and vulgar) was her fortune. "In light of her dowry," said Boni, "she doesn't look bad at all."

Miriam might have thought she, too, could catch the wave. She knew romance was a long shot at sixty. But she believed the "fascinating woman" was "seldom young" and easily eclipsed ingenues with her mature charms and "secret of perpetual youth." Add to that her money—she was a millionaire with ready cash and income from rentals and investments.

SHE LEFT NOTHING to chance. She settled in "charming apartments" on Victoria Street in 1895 and opened for business. Except for a flying visit to New York in January, she concentrated her efforts on England and the Continent for the next year and a half. As a Parthian shot, she published an essay, "Heroines of Chivalry," in her final *Monthly* that celebrated the *dame galante*—the "fascinating woman" she intended to embody abroad. "Condemn her as we will," she challenged, she "reigns triumphantly through the ages."

Miriam gave it her best shot—a musicale for three hundred guests, luncheons at homes, and receptions in honor of Isadora Duse, Sarah Bernhardt, Adelina Patti, and Nellie Melba. She mingled with "quality" on the "grand drive" through Hyde Park; she toasted the Queen at a Fourth of July banquet. She took special pains with her wardrobe, affecting British gentry–style velvet jackets and coattails and wearing "splendid" heirloom pearls that had "been in her family for centuries."

Romance was harder to orchestrate. The Marquis de Leuville had dropped his suit and lived at Walsingham House surveilled by his wealthy provider Mrs. Peters. And her gentleman friend Ulysses S. Glick didn't join her as expected. Glick, a self-styled "professor" and "smooth talker," who studied for the ministry and spoke Japanese, was Miriam's steady companion in Manhattan. He squired her to dinners and plays, had free use of her carriage, and planned to buy one of her publications. The month after Miriam arrived in London, however, she learned Glick had been arrested for the theft of $334 from a wealthy businessman and false promises of land investments.

Miriam, though, kept gossip columnists busy. An American reporter spotted her at a fashionable cabaret and quizzed her about her reputed lovers. Was she to marry Arthur Wellesley, a peer and fourth Duke of Wellington? "My dear," Mrs. Leslie replied, "there is absolutely no truth whatever in the rumor." They may have trysted, but this illustrious lord possessed four titles and nineteen thousand acres of family estates and had a wife and six children. Rumors of engagement to widowed ex-president Benjamin Harrison proved equally baseless since he was on the brink of marriage to his wife's secretary, twenty-five years his junior.

Not to be discouraged, she worked on her publicity profile in the press and set her sights on Paris, with its ennobled *mondaine* and "parallel aristocracy" of ladies with a past—often elder *charmeuses*. The Baroness Salvador was there to open doors, but the Connecticut-born baroness would have been useless in the market for titles. The nobility, in reaction to the wane of the aristocracy and the rise of labor unrest and money power, had closed ranks against Americans.

Americans weren't only scorned. It was a season of xenophobia, with Jews in disfavor as well. Jewish Artillery Captain Dreyfus had been convicted and exiled to Devil's Island for life the previous January, based on a fabricated espionage case. The *ton* were vehement anti-Semites and settled differences in the Dreyfus Affair (which lasted three years in court) with pistols on riverbanks at a rate of three duels a day. None of which ruffled the smooth surface of aristocratic life—everyone affected "to understand nothing," and escaped into rarefied festivities, self-display, and ornamental décor.

The high priest of his haute circle was Count Robert de Montesquiou. An aesthete and snob who traced his ancestry to the Merovingian kings, he reigned over a phantasmagoric realm within the noblesse. He occupied an outré Quai d'Orsay mansion furnished to disorder the senses: ecclesiastical furniture, a sledge on a bear rug, a jeweled live tortoise, a dragon bed with mother-of-pearl eyes, and a curio case that contained George Sand's cigarette stub and Napoleon's chamber pot.

He looked the part. As slim as a tango dancer, with a Roman nose, waxed birdwing moustache, and penciled eyelids, he wore eccentric dandified costumes accessorized with nosegays and Liberty foulards. He wrote obscure symbolist verse, dueled, and gave sought-after soirées. Society swans like fashion idol Elisabeth Greffulhe doted on him, and Marcel Proust, one of the few outsiders admitted to his company, imitated his mannerisms (such as clapping his hand on his mouth to conceal his black teeth) and portrayed him as Baron Charlus in *Remembrance of Things Past*. He was the Marquis de Leuville with money—beyond reach.

Outside of this elect preserve, Paris was "dancing on a volcano." Explosive tensions seethed beneath the frenetic Belle Epoque gaiety: hostilities toward Jews and the Church, rumblings of war with Germany, threats from anarchists, and angry protests from workers. Change was happening too fast to assimilate.

For consolation and distraction, though, Paris was unsurpassed. A vast entertainment complex arose to accommodate the need to vent and escape where few—not even Miriam—could nurse disappointment and despair for long.

Paris was festivity on steroids. Commercial movie houses proliferated and popular plays—domestic dramas in modern dialogue and sensationalistic thrillers—drew half a million people to theaters once a week. After twenty-seven years, the city revived the "Boeuf Gras" pageant, a three-day bacchanalia climaxed by a parade of floats carrying a fat steer in a golden cage and King Carnival surrounded by cabbages and pig-masked men in bathtubs. The Champs Élysées was knee-deep in confetti.

Rich and poor alike flocked to the 264 *café-concerts* to drink, frolic, and take in the live musical acts. Miriam, who loved these "Liberty Halls," almost certainly visited the most celebrated, the Folies-Bergère. At the Folies, she would have seen the great demi-mondaine, La Belle Otero—a reincarnation of her mentor, Lola Montez. Caroline Otero, a tempestuous Spanish beauty with black gypsy eyes, a heart-shaped face, and voluptuous breasts, danced like "an uncontrolled panther in heat" and plundered men and bank accounts. In Paris that summer a Russian prince sent her a million rubles wrapped in a note: "Ruin me but do not leave me." He was at the end of a long stag line of besotted admirers, among them Willie Vanderbilt (Alva's husband), five crowned heads, business moguls, titled swells, and eight men who committed suicide over her. They made her richer than any courtesan in history.

Otero had come a long way. Born illegitimate to the village prostitute in a desolate mountain town, she was raped at eleven until her pelvis broke and escaped with a boy who taught her to dance and pimped her out. She tangoed from waterfront bars to the big time and never looked back. Decked in jewels "like a precious idol," she slept in a carved bed beneath a frescoed Sistine ceiling, drove a gilt barouche drawn by black mules, and dressed in gold-net designer extravaganzas cut within an ace of her nipples.

To watch her at the Folies was to feel the full force of her firepower. When she swiveled out in a plunge-back white satin gown, she put the "F" in flamenco, stamping and gyrating lasciviously to castanets and guitars. Onstage Miriam saw the summum of her "fascinating woman," the one before whom men submit and others "wane and pale."

Otero and the amorous anarchy of Paris might have prompted a new slant in Mrs. Leslie's essays that summer. Where was a definitive guide to female erotic empowerment in this tourbillon of cultural change and normlessness? She went to the Bibliothèque nationale to find out. There she consulted the medieval courtly love tradition with its "precise and firm" laws of desire laid down by ladies "experienced in *galanterie*," laws that were timeless and permitted women to reign supreme in romance. These ladies understood the fundamental truths—that difficulty, for instance, "exalts passion" and cannot "rest stationary"—and knew how to enamor worthy lovers.

Their strongest lure, Miriam wrote, was conversation. "Debutantes" today should take their cue and learn to speak with "improvisational verve," and fluency "on any topic." "Delightful conversation," she promised, throws a "spell."

Grace, too, must be cultivated. In a second installment, she chided the "athletic sisterhood" who barreled around on bikes in ungainly sportswear. Perhaps with Otero in mind, she commended "graciousness of movement" and "lissome" carriage. "Get strong without the insolence of strength," she instructed; then "you will be made love to as never yet."

Miriam, though, was talking to a wall. Yet again, she misjudged the zeitgeist. Her "debutantes" were off the loveseat. The new "Gibson Girls" were challenging men in sports, politics, and the workplace, and going natural. They trusted their untutored charms in romance—if they cared at all.

Miriam affected indifference and returned to self-promotion, announcing plans for a daily newspaper and forthcoming novel. She set off on an extensive European sightseeing excursion. Somewhere between Germany and Nice she fell ill and extended her holiday six months.

SHE WOULD HAVE done better to stay abroad. When she returned in August 1896, the country was on even higher boil—worsened poverty, deeper class divisions, and a rancorous election year. Miriam's French friend, Paul Bourget, toured Manhattan's "lower strata" a few months earlier and documented the wreckage. New York slums were among the worst in the world. In the hovels he encountered "frightful wretchedness" at every turn—starved families of nine in one-room basements and emaciated lodgers in "dormitor[ies] of poverty" sprawled naked without two cents for a hammock. Two-thirds of the city inhabited these pestholes and died in droves from calamities like the 1896 ten-day heatwave, where temperatures hit a hundred and twenty degrees in the tenements, killing fifteen hundred.

The poverty emergency dominated the presidential campaign. The peoples' Democratic Party backed populist candidate William Jennings Byrant, a charismatic orator who demanded governmental relief for the suffering poor and restraints on plutocratic power. Crisscrossing the country by train, he galvanized hundreds of thousands with promises of reform and free silver, thundering, "You shall not crucify mankind on a cross of gold."

Ranged against him was the Republican conservative establishment bankrolled by moneymen, the one-third of one percent who owned a sixth of the national wealth. They ran Ohio governor William McKinley on a big business platform and outspent Bryant by $7 million, spreading libels and sowing socialist fear. McKinley won by six hundred thousand votes.

Pro-capitalist conservatives held the whiphand. Legalized segregation disenfranchised the Black population; anti-strike legislation throttled labor; and high tariffs, no income tax, and the gold standard created an El Dorado for the privileged. In response, resistance from the left built exponentially, setting the stage for the Progressive movement.

Miriam underrated the resistance. She needed publicity, but not this kind. "Meg" Merrilles, a special correspondent for the *Pittsburgh Press*, was in Manhattan to cover the Christmas season and had been invited to Mrs. Leslie's holiday salon. After a spaghetti dinner at Maria's, a hangout for "press people," she appeared at the

Gerlach Hotel around midnight. Miriam greeted her at the door in "the fullest of full dress" and said, "Clothes do not make a particle of difference, my dear, we only recognize talent here."

"Meg" cased the room and surveyed the "talent": singers with "unpronounceable names," ladies in low neck, swallow-tailed men, and performers like Charles Lewis, a.k.a. "M. Quad," famous for his deadpan humor. She sipped sparkling punch from a crystal cup until 2:00 A.M., then walked down Tenth Street. There she saw a sight to "make the angels weep," a single file of "hundreds of hungry" men in the cold waiting for a free loaf of stale bread from a "charitable" baker. Incensed by the contrast, she wrote a front page "Diatribe on New York" that savaged Miriam and her salon with its "opulence of toilets" and "surplus cash," and heartless treatment of the destitute.

ANOTHER UNDERCURRENT CAUGHT Miriam unawares; the national love affair with high society was cooling and entry to the ranks, contracting. The megarich—idle, money-drunk, and uncurbed—were indulging in an orgy of exorbitant diversions and bad behavior. The mistress of revels, Mrs. Stuyvesant Fish, "Mamie," who succeeded Mrs. Astor to the throne, limited the "chosen" to favored free spenders and transformed the monde into Mardi Gras.

Mamie Fish, a short, stout matron with basset-hound eyes, specialized in insult and shock theater entertainment. She compared a friend's fountain to a horse's watering trough, called Alva Vanderbilt a "toad" to her face, and welcomed guests with, "Well, here you all are with older faces and younger clothes." She swore like a stevedore, smoked, and threw showstopper entertainments.

She gave a ball for the Prince del Drago of Corsica, a tuxedoed monkey that swung on chandeliers and hurled champagne glasses at guests; hosted a Dog's Dinner for a hundred pets, served by footmen; and a Heavenly Party with Western Union messengers dressed as angels in mini-shorts. Not to be outdone, plutocrats put on Servants' and Hobos' dinners, placed hundred-dollar bills in napkins, and hid emeralds and rubies in sandpile centerpieces for guests to scoop out with silver trowels.

The ringmaster who orchestrated these productions was of a piece with the parties—the outlandish Harry Lehr. Unlike his predecessor, Ward McAllister, Lehr didn't pretend to be wellborn. He was a penniless upstart from Baltimore without connections or an impressive appearance. Tall, scrawny, and pug-nosed, he resembled a "pig in men's clothes" and spoke in a "high falsetto voice." Yet through ingratiation and flattery, he insinuated himself into polite company and wormed his way to Newport and into the favor of Society. He fawned, amused, planned big-top parties, chose dresses for the ladies, and made himself indispensable to the jaded rich.

When the doyennes directed him to marry, he married, a Four Hundred–approved choice who removed his financial and status worries for life. The twenty-nine-year-old Elizabeth Drexel Dahlgren of the Philadelphia banking fortune accepted his offer with surprising naïveté. She had been recently widowed and should have seen the signs: Mamie Fish's wisecrack that he was "just one of us girls," and his sexless relationship with women. On their wedding night she prepared to receive him in her bridal peignoir and asked the maid to summon him. After two hours, he appeared and told her to sit down: "I do not love you," he declared, "I can school myself to be polite but that is all. The less we see of one another the better."

As to why he married her, he replied, "Dear lady, do you really know so little of the world that you have never heard of people being married for money, or did you imagine your charms placed you above such a fate?" Elizabeth bore up and maintained a "devoted couple" façade until he died twenty years later, unwilling to offend her mother, the Catholic Church, and ruling matriarchs.

The monied bachelors, meanwhile, were on a sexual bender. Prominent architect Stanford White stalked young girls and lured teenage model Evelyn Nesbit to his mirrored playroom with a red velvet swing, where he plied her with champagne until she passed out, then raped her. (Her husband later killed him in a sensational murder case.)

"Stag rackets" flourished—one of which resulted in a scandalous exposé. It was a classic men's night out among the "howling swells," an engagement party for Herbert Barnum Seeley's brother at Sherry's with a thirteen-course dinner and "hot entertainment." For dessert, belly dancer "Little Egypt" (Canadian-born Catherine Devine) leaped out of a whipped cream pie and performed a "couche couche" on the tabletop as guests hooted and pawed. She began to strip; "netherworld" exotic dancers waited in the wings to join the revels. Unluckily, police captain Whiskers Chapman was on the scene and confused the banquet door with the dressing room, where he surprised a clutch of disrobing dancers. A trial ensued, and the wealthy bachelor subculture became public for the first time. The press rained down vitriol: the "awful Seeley dinner" exposed "the utter moral rottenness of the so-called 'smart set' of Gotham."

The decisive blow was the infamous Bradley-Martin Ball. The grande dame Mrs. Bradley-Martin believed an exorbitant fancy-dress ball would generate business and benefit the paupered masses. She engaged the Waldorf and distributed details to the press on a daily basis: the *ancien régime* costumes, six thousand mauve orchids, and updated guest list. The poor weren't impressed, and some threatened to bomb the Bradley-Martin home and the ballroom.

On the appointed night, periwigged guests stepped from carriages into a heckling mob of protesters. Inside a hundred detectives disguised as liveried lackeys stood guard over the ball, where Mrs. Bradley-Martin received on a dais as Mary Stuart in black velvet robes encrusted with jewels and frothed with lace, valued today at $30,000 a yard. She led the *danse d'honneur* with John Jacob Astor, and throughout the night-long figures and quadrilles, attendees feasted on unlimited canvasback duck, British pheasant, and twenty-one delicacies. The backlash was swift. Preachers denounced them from the pulpit and public outrage forced the Bradley-Martins to leave town and take refuge at their sixty-five thousand acre Scottish estate.

* * *

ALTHOUGH MIRIAM'S EXTRAVAGANCES—small-time in comparison—escaped the cascade of censure, the sting of exclusion still rankled. She had no place in the Fish/Bradley-Martin bacchanalia, no entrée, and no hopes of one. But there was always England—a more elastic beau monde and a festival to attract the cream of the aristocracy. It was Queen Victoria's Diamond Jubilee, a celebration of her sixty-year reign, and a turning point for Miriam.

She sailed June 3, 1897, on a high note. Her star was rising once more in America where she figured prominently in the press, "looking handsome" at receptions, reciting at an Opera House event, and reading a valentine poem she composed "at eleven" to the Women's Press Club. Reporters admired her chic blue traveling suit at the pier, and in her stateroom she found an "immense bouquet" from an admirer, Marquis Alexandre Imbert de Maryed (of dubious ancestry), accompanied by a romantic verse.

In London, she went to all the Victoriana festivities—garden parties, dedications, and receptions costumed in conspicuous "fluffed out" Parisian gowns—swept up in the imperialistic fervor. She paid ten guineas for a seat at the Jubilee parade and watched troops from every colonial possession march in full-dress panoply down streets festooned with flowers, rainbow bunting, and union jacks. Thousands lined the six-mile route to cheer the Queen, who drew up the rear in an open carriage drawn by eight cream horses. On her sixtieth anniversary, her sway reached from continent to continent, over a quarter of the world's population; the day was a "Festival of the British Empire."

Mark Twain, who was there, was underwhelmed and compared the pageant to "an allegorical suggestion of the last day." But he was in the minority. Miriam, an imperialist convert, was in the right place at the right time. Americans at home kindled to the display of imperial power. The nation was disquieted, restless, and spoiling for action. The nineties' male generation feared creeping emasculation, a dread that manliness was being sapped by emboldened women and effete modern life. The antidote was physical hardship, plant-the-flag adventure, chivalric heroism, and the strenuous life. And what more perfect tonic than international expansion? American greatness required empire; "I should welcome almost any war," proclaimed then Assistant Secretary of the Navy and macho cheerleader Theodore Roosevelt.

ENTICING OPPORTUNITIES BECKONED: the South Pacific, Hawaii, and in the nick of time, a Cuban rebellion against Spain. Cuba was a fat target. There were economic advantages for sugar and coffee investments and a built-in popular sympathy for persecuted rebels interred in squalid death camps. The newspapers did the rest. In a mano a mano for circulation numbers, Pulitzer and Hearst whipped up the public war cry with screaming headlines and lurid, melodramatic stories. When the American battleship *Maine* blew up in Havana's harbor (cause disputed) in February 1898, Hearst wired: "You furnish the pictures and I'll furnish the war." Roosevelt called the reluctant McKinley a president with the "backbone of a chocolate éclair," and the "splendid little war" was on.

Miriam ignored her stake in the publishing world and the juggernaut of "yellow" papers and tabloid journals and became a featured American flag-waver. She performed Joaquin Miller's "Cuba Libre" at a St. George Hotel gala and her salons. "Comes a cry from Cuban waters," she recited, "Bid her strike! Lo, it is written—Blood for blood and life for life." She published personal recollections of the Spanish royal family with vignettes of the bigoted Queen and thirteen-year-old enfant terrible, Alfonso, who squirted water and flung sand at elder statesmen.

As the Spanish-American war sped to victory, Miriam joined the national euphoria. On the eve of her annual trip abroad Miriam intended to celebrate. America was in the imperial game and she felt she was at the top of hers. She was again "the most famous and successful woman journalist of all times," "one of the greatest women of the century." She'd just been seated at the Fortnightly Club's "table of honor," given speeches as a world business authority, and been named a "shining example" to American women. There was a national lecture tour on "Society Queens" in the works. Her retirement was on a roll. Her June 7 evening reception was to be particularly brilliant.

BY LATE AFTERNOON June 7, 1898, the heat had settled and a soft breeze eddied through the Gerlach, luffing the lace curtains and riffling tablecloth tassels. The double parlors were low-lit with gilt scones and readied for a celebratory Thursday salon—the silver trappe bowl filled with Roman punch, the sideboard laid out with caviar, and Jacqueminot roses placed on the piano. Miriam wore one of her *chef d'oeuvres*, likely a Worth reception dress laced tight at the waist with a deep-cut bodice and trained lace overskirt. She was awash in jewels—her diamond chain and earrings, bracelets inscribed "Florence" in gems, and a diamond Spanish comb in her high-waved coiffure. In a photograph taken about the time, she stands behind the velvet portieres between the two parlors, her miniature Yorkshire terrier, Chico, in the crook of her elbow. She radiates authority, strut, and triumph.

As usual, she never sat down, although her swan-bill corset would have made it difficult even if she wanted to. She circulated among her guests—assorted poets, novelists, actors, press people, European drop-ins, and a cluster of musicians in bib and tucker. As the new vice-president of the Edward Irving Darling Musical Society, Miriam invited select members, several of whom were on the program.

She threaded through the crowd "pairing off people" who shared "common affinities" or might engage in "interesting disputes." Conversational groups gathered in shoals around the room—an amber-and-gold showpiece, packed with brocaded chairs, buhl cabinets, damask-draped tables, celebrity mementos, travel souvenirs, bibelots, and baseboard-to-ceiling paintings on the walls, with a large portrait of her younger self front and center. One gallant guest noticed a heart-embroidered Aubusson rug and quipped, "The hearts, Mrs. Leslie, are even beneath your feet." "Quite their proper place," she riposted, and rapped a gloved hand in her palm to begin the concert.

The pianist was running scales in the smaller parlor while a large woman with an ostrich feather aigrette in a black pompadour leaned over the score. She was opera diva Madame Giulia Valda, familiar to everyone present and Miriam's close friend. Born Julia Wheelock in Boston to a truckman's family, she lucked into a wealthy uncle at age five who transported her to Italy to study voice with maestro Francesco Lamperti. With Lamperti she learned his "singing on the breath" method and debuted to rave reviews throughout Europe. Like Miriam, she was a giant persona and self-dramatizer with a racy past, having disposed of her first husband in a scandalous case in which she proved his impotence to the British high court in graphic detail. Now in her forties, she ran a Lamperti-Valda school in Paris and New York.

Mme. Valda nodded to the pianist to begin and sang "Je Suis Titania la Blonde," her sparkling soprano soaring through the room, with coloratura leaps, runs, and trills. Next opera legend Giuseppe del Puente reprised Carmen's "Toreador" in his strong rich baritone. Poems were read, and Marshall Wilder was enlisted to perform his comic monologue, "Baby," about an inept husband's attempt to buy ribbons for his baby—blue or pink, he doesn't care, as long as it "matches the baby." As a finale, Mme. Valda retook the stage and delivered Gilda's "Dearest Name" from Rigoletto, her "strongest opera."

Midway through the aria, a servant tapped Miriam on the shoulder and summoned her to the telephone. "Go and say and I am engaged," she shushed, "I cannot come and find out what they want."

The servant reappeared. It was urgent. Miriam motioned to Mme. Valda to continue and mouthed, "I will only be gone a moment."

At the telephone table she lifted the shaft and heard an unfamiliar voice: "It is reported on the street that the Arkell have made an assignment." This was the owner of Judge Publishing, to whom she'd sold the *Illustrated Newspaper* in 1889 and invested her savings.

She waited a beat; cranks abounded. "Are you sure the report is true?"

"Certain," he answered.

Uneasy now, she rang the Judge Building: "The head of the firm is out."

"Say that Mrs. Frank Leslie wants to speak to one of the firm and no one else."

Arkell then came on the line and confirmed the news: his Judge Publishing Company and publisher of *Leslie's* weekly was bankrupt, and her investment and retirement fund had washed away in an instant.

She sat down dumbfounded. The Arkells, it seemed, had speculated behind her back, slacked off, and been obliterated by the innovative "yellow" papers during the Spanish American War.

She had one card left to play. She dialed Frederick Colver at the *Monthly*, which itself was in a freefall thanks to the new magazine surge. Her proposition was rash, a wild gamble. Would Colver agree to incorporate the business as a stock company with herself as "president and editor of the magazine?" He agreed. Her disciples later put a heroic spin on the moment: "The little gemmed hand which hung up the receiver was the hand of Napoleon." It remained to be seen.

She returned to the music parlor where a small party lingered after Mme. Valda's performance. When Madame saw Miriam she raised her eyebrows and flashed: "Indeed, you have kept us waiting! I thought you were never coming back. I was going."

Miriam strode past her to the piano, and addressed the group: "Well, my friends, in the interim, I have lost a fortune and put myself in the way of making another."

The audience must have been at a loss. If they caught on, they surely thought she'd slipped her moorings during her "long vacation." The publishing world was a blood sport that belonged to ruthless young turks who were reinventing the industry. At sixty-two, she'd aged out of the job, lost touch, and gone to grass. When the last guest left, she walked into her boudoir, closed the open Louis Vuitton steamer trunk, and said: "The failure will change my entire life."

CHAPTER TEN

TOUT OU RIEN
1898–1917

MIRIAM'S COMMAND CENTER at the Sherry Hotel to rescue the *Popular Monthly* and her fortune looked "more like a lady's boudoir than a business office." A rose light filtered through pink curtains onto her Renaissance desk where she sat on a throne chair beneath a crystal chandelier surrounded by scented flowers. On the green-silvered wallpaper stamped with Napoleonic emblems hung bucolic oil paintings and a portrait of King Lear, the Victorian symbol of the good father.

Her boutique setting, though, was a blind to disguise operations and her perilous position. When she took over as president of the newly formed stock company, the business was down for the count. Frederick Colver, lessee of the magazine for three years, had let the *Monthly* spiral out, and Miriam's finances were worsened further by Arkell's failure at the *Illustrated Newspaper* and $46,000 in real estate losses. She saw she was "out of the swim" after her "long vacation" and was "as nervous as possible" about the siege ahead. But she steeled her resolve and didn't let on. She fitted up her rooms like a "Petit Trianon," and sailed out in "superb satins" of "watermelon pink." From her "daintily" furnished office, she hunkered down and masterminded a comeback.

If she hadn't paid attention to the magazine revolution before, she did now. She purchased an up-to-the-minute printing and binding plant and revamped the *Monthly* front to back, reducing size, cutting price, and modernizing layout with single-column pages, bold typeface, and bright visuals. "The tone and policy," she pledged, "will change," and "various novelties" introduced. For the first time in over a decade, she caught the cultural curl. In the afterglow of the Spanish-American War, the country was on a patriotic high, with Hawaii and Puerto Rico conquered and the Philippines in the offing. Every issue of the refurbished *Popular Monthly* beginning in November 1898 featured triumphal pieces on Cuban engagements and photodocumentaries of imperialist inroads in the Pacific and Caribbean. She hired marquee writers such as William Dean Howells, Henry James, and Bret Harte, and targeted a growth-market beyond the genteel parlor—the burgeoning urban white-collar middle class. Without losing her base, Miriam pulled these new readers with a high-energy mix of sports stories, breezy contemporary fiction, and a "Women of Action" series with profiles of modern "Outdoor" and "Wall Street Women." Each copy came with a gold cover and contained no more than twelve articles.

Within four months, circulation rose to two hundred thousand copies, paid subscriptions (at a dollar a year) increased six-fold, and counter sales doubled. Miriam scored a second publishing coup "unequaled in the history of periodical literature." She drew fat advertising and made her second fortune.

Emboldened by her success, she collected her syndicated essays in a volume, *A Social Mirage*, and added twenty new ones. She souped up her feminist message: Women, she charged, should break the bonds that "chained [them] to the traditional rock" of circumscribed femininity. They should demand male deference and learn "the habit of command."

On a personal note, she was more ambiguous. Out of one side of her mouth she denounced the generic man as an egocentric brute and lambasted marriage; out of the other, she praised "agreeable men" (especially Latin lovers) and celebrated marital "comfort and repose." Her inner conflict was at full torque: the charms of age versus youth; class versus claustral Society; single womanhood versus the "great craving" for love and male approval. A loveless woman, she declared, was a pathetic creature who channeled her thwarted desire into her dog or philanthropy.

PHILANTHROPY WASN'T ON Miriam's wavelength in 1899, though it should have been. The Progressive Era, a nationwide reform movement that lasted nearly twenty years, had just gained traction. The new dominant middle class—a chunk of her readers— were spearheading a social welfare crusade to address the urgent problems of poverty, immigration, class-division, growing corporate power, and wholesale corruption. Activist Jane Addams founded a model settlement house that engaged privileged women in community service; grassroots alliances legislated civic, labor, housing, and educational reforms; and a squadron of brash writers documented the extent of the mess.

Miriam's competitors were busy hiring these muckrakers for their magazines and watching numbers rise. *Munsey's* had already scooped up journalists who poked into dark corners and spotlighted establishment abuses. Frank Norris, a top contributor, was then amid an evisceration of the railroad monopoly in his novel *The Octopus*, and Ida Tarbell, who later took down Standard Oil, was a *Munsey* favorite. She was also a friend of Frederick Colver and had his ear.

In hindsight, Miriam shouldn't have gone abroad the summer of 1899. But she was exhausted: "Many people have no idea what literary work is," she explained. "I have just read 30,000 pages of manuscript before accepting a continued story." Besides, there were inducements overseas—an International Council of Women meeting and a romantic prospect. After London, where she attended private musicales and gave a party at the Tudor House for American Newspaper Women in rooms cooled by ice swans, she went straight to Paris.

THE BARONESS SALVADOR (heretofore unhelpful) promised a gentleman with potential, a neighbor who owned a villa a mile from the Salvadors' home. The Prince de Lusignan didn't belong to the Parisian "born," and perhaps held a faux title. (This was a subject of some dispute in his lifetime.) However, he was a wealthy widower of sixty-five who belonged to learned societies, founded a college, and published books on history and linguistics. He was also strikingly handsome. In a portrait painted that year, he lounges on a chair in a waistcoat sashed with a silk ribbon, the image of a stage *primo uomo*, with a Grecian nose, white goatee, and jet eyes beneath black, high-arched brows.

Ambroise Calfa owed his exotic looks to his Middle Eastern heritage. Born in Constantinople to an Armenian merchant family, he studied in Venice and moved to Paris as prefect of studies at Samuel Moorat Armenian College. He bought real estate, prospered, and in 1878 he and his two brothers claimed descent from medieval Armenia's last king of the House of Lusignan. They produced a letter from a long-lost cousin, a Russian colonel who called himself "Crown Prince of Cyprus, Jerusalem, and Armenia," and Ambroise took the title when his brother died. Seven years later, he and his wife revived the Order of St. Catherine of Mount Sinai, a twelfth-century chivalric society dedicated to the protection of pilgrims to the martyr's Egyptian shrine.

As head of the order, the Prince could induct members and confer honors. To commemorate his romance with Miriam that summer, he anointed her Grand Canoness of the Order of Chevaliers of St. Catherine. If she regarded this as a consolation prize for "Princess of Lusignan," she concealed it, and spent three weeks luxuriating at Carlsbad.

The Bohemian spa with thirteen mineral springs was famous for its healing properties, and so renowned as a last resort for the terminally ill that the "dread of Carlsbad" was a byword. Anxious to assure the public of her "perfect health" and youthful vigor, Miriam insisted she was there "not for the waters, but just for the rest." She attended Stadtpark concerts, dined at Elephant and Sanssouci, and promenaded in the statue-lined colonnades with privileged Europeans. She returned to New York on *La Touraine*, her terrier Chignito under her arm, and told reporters at the dock that she wanted to "settle down to work."

That wouldn't be so simple. While she was away, Frederick Colver, listed as a mere "Secretary and Treasurer" on the masthead, plotted sedition. He conspired with twenty-seven-year-old Ellery Sedgwick, assistant editor at *Youth's Companion*, a magazine in the *McClure's* tradition that specialized in entertainment and carried blue-chip authors like Stephen Crane. Colver might have consulted his friend Ida Tarbell, too.

Miriam suspected nothing. Nine years ago, she hired Frederick, a glib drummer with no journalistic experience or credentials, to procure ads. Pudgy and round-faced with a brilliantined black comb-over, he had shrewd eyes given to sharp, sidelong glances. He was born poor in Brooklyn and went to work at sixteen in a publishing warehouse where he hustled ads and earned enough by his twenties to start his own agency. Due to the dominance of advertising in journalism, he saved enough to buy 50 percent of Miriam's stock company. He wanted more now that the *Popular Monthly* had taken off.

The opening salvo was a request for development funds. Frugal with cash, Miriam surrendered the rest of her stock, secure in her seniority at the firm—a mistake. Soon afterward, Colver walked into her office and "talked plainly to her." It was "not enough that the magazine had been remodeled," he said, radical changes were in order, and her "day was over." As majority owner in the company he could do as he wanted, and he wanted Miriam out. He fired her as editor-in-chief and assumed the job himself in the November 1899 issue. "At last," he said, "he was able to give full expression to his own ideas without being hampered by tradition."

As it happened, he had no ideas except increased advertising and reproduced Miriam's magazine to the letter, continuing the same content and format and the "Women in Action" series. Only not so successfully. Ellery Sedgwick, his editorial advisor, was apparently unwilling or unable to exploit the blockbuster Progressive market, and after six years of red ink, Colver sold the magazine at a loss to *McClure's*.

Miriam was stupefied. She'd returned a conquering heroine who'd salvaged a dead magazine and made it pay singlehandedly, a feat few men could pull off. She cried foul and summoned the press. Colver and his cronies, she protested, took advantage of her absence abroad to trick her into ceding control, seized the company, and axed her. "Mrs. Leslie," reported the newspapers, "will go to the courts for redress."

She didn't and couldn't. Ultimately, it was just about business, the tooth-and-claw law of the marketplace, out with the old, in with the new. To on-the-make newcomers in the trade, she was an "anachronism" on Publishers' Row.

THE QUESTION FOR Miriam in 1900 was crisis management—how to rescript her defeat and spin it to her advantage. She cast her exit as an early retirement "during which she planned to put into books the thoughts and experiences of her busy life." She had other plans as well. Thanks to her business manager, Louis Cramer, who had multiplied the quarter million-dollar profit from her publications eight-fold, she was rich. She could give her social ambition full rein.

Miriam ordered a majestic gown of heavy *peau de soie* embroidered with emeralds and pearls and commissioned a flattering photograph of herself in the dress, carried by newspapers across America. Then she boarded the *City of Rome* for Europe to set the wheels in motion. The Baroness Salvador, who "attended to all her affairs," was there to greet her and expedite the business. Through discreet channels, Miriam reinvented herself as the Baroness de Bazus. Her claim to the title was based on descent from an eighteenth-century Toulouse mayor theoretically related to Phillipe Picot knighted by Louis IX. The Baron's Huguenot heirs, Miriam alleged, brought the title with them to New Orleans where it "descended through the centuries" to Miriam's deceased aunt, Eulalie Follin.

Miriam's ancestors wouldn't have recognized themselves. Roman Catholic merchants from Picardie in northern France, they settled in Charleston, South Carolina, where the family patriarch is buried in St. Mary's Catholic Cemetery. Her father, too, died Catholic. But it made a good story and if men could do it—the Marquis de Leuville, Prince Eristoff, and Prince de Lusignan—why shouldn't she? She designed a coat of arms, two crossed silver lances over a cock's head, and stamped it on all her possessions beneath the motto, "*Tout ou Rien*" (All or Nothing)." Her reclaimed French "relatives" "received [her] with open arms," and her friend Baroness Althea Salvador gave a ceremonial dinner for La Baronne de Bazus, Miriam's eighth name so far. She could swan it over the Colver crowd and enter Society.

That was going to be problematic. Society—even the peerage—was losing its heft and cachet. After Dreyfus's pardon, the gratin's rabid anti-Semitism put them in bad odor with enlightened Europeans. As Baron de Charlus gripes in Proust's *Remembrance of Things Past*, "All this Dreyfus business is destroying society." Comte de Montesquiou, the Baron's real-life counterpart, himself fell from favor when he was seen whacking women and children with his cane to escape the Bazar de la Charité fire that killed 126—an unproved allegation, but it stuck. The *monde's* royalist cause also drew scorn as the pretender, Prince Philippe, Duke of Orléans, disgraced himself in exile, engendering "undisguised contempt of both French people and foreigners."

Invested with her title, Miriam took up the faded banner of the *ancien régime*. Like the aristocratic French families who fled to the country to protest the newfangled 1900 World's Fair, she turned her back on the uncouth, garish modern century. The fair epitomized it—a monstrous shrine, in Henry Adams's view, to the god of technology and a finale to traditional values—infested with "decadent" Art Nouveau, motorcycle races, and American jazz.

On August 1, 1901, Miriam arrived in New York on the S. S. *Oceanic*, registered as Baroness de Bazus with a "B" embossed on her seventeen trunks. To an America grown increasingly disenchanted with rank, she got a chilly reception. Reporters tried "in vain to guess the nationality" of her family and took a dim view of her baronial ancestry, quoting the prices for foreign titles. To prove her case, she charted her genealogy back to the "old nobility before the French Revolution" and exhibited an "imposing parchment." At this point, the press was wise to purchased parchments and titles, but decided to wink and let her have her whim: "she is in possession of enough coin of the realm to buy any stray barony she desires," noted the papers; she'd "worked hard enough."

What she couldn't buy at any price was entrée to the best New York circles despite her aristocratic reincarnation. She shouldn't have wasted her time. The social elite at the turn of the century were in deep disrepute and self-destructing through ever more flagrant profligacy and public scandals. The attack dog behind their downfall was the same man who earlier filleted Miriam—Colonel William d'Alton Mann, the *Town Topics* publisher and "Saunterer." A corpulent, deceptively avuncular figure in a clerical frock coat with a white lumberjack beard, Mann had a single mission: to flush out and pick off the "silly fools, jackasses, and libertines" that constituted "worthless New York Society."

One by one he outed Miriam's "gods on Olympus," often by name, with a monsoon of salacious misdeeds. For a fee, he buried stories, and when his racket came to light, he opened his books and revealed bribes from high company—William Vanderbilt, Arabella Huntington, Oliver Harriman, et al. The Society Miriam yearned to join was on the way out—its carnival excesses and sins condemned by the public, its lifestyle grown unfashionably antique. They were "sailing to oblivion" on the tide of the twentieth century.

Perhaps Miriam began to glimpse this or perceived the futility of her acceptance by the gratin. Otherwise, how to explain her move from Sherry's to the Chelsea Hotel on West Twenty-third Street, an apartment complex originally designed as an egalitarian commune, with a mix of artists and "quality." She lived halfway up the red brick Victorian gothic building on the sixth floor, reached by a serpentine "grand staircase." Pier 54, the White Star Line, was just down the block—convenient for her trips abroad. But that summer she wouldn't be among the passengers.

She resumed her salon and blocked out the boiling rapids of change. The cries for reform were growing louder and addressing tenement abuses and education; the Metropolitan subway system was pounding toward completion; and Coney Island developers were hammering the last nails at the twenty-two acre Oriental-themed "Luna Park" that catered to the soda-and-frankfurter mob. Soon President McKinley would be shot and killed by a Polish anarchist at a Buffalo Pan-American Exposition, to be succeeded by Theodore Roosevelt.

BEFORE LONG, MIRIAM read her own obituary. According to the papers, she had been "ill for some time." This was her nemesis; she'd never, she bluffed, "had a sick day in her life," compliments of her gymnastic exercises, brisk rubdowns, walks, and a diet free of alcohol, caffeine, and candy. None of which saved her. By year's end, her legs and ankles began to swell, and her urine foamed, stank, and turned ochre. She took to her bed with intense abdominal pain.

Dr. William H. Thompson, member of the prestigious New York Academy of Medicine, diagnosed nephritis, a kidney inflammation treated with cold compresses and aspirin, invented in 1899. Then in a worst-case (but common) scenario, she suffered a stroke on December 22 and was conveyed to Roosevelt Hospital in critical condition. In January, deathbed bulletins appeared, and throughout spring and summer, her obituary filled the news. She wouldn't have been pleased with her death notice and its emphasis of her feminine charms over her business career. Not to mention the fact that she was alive and on the mend in New Jersey.

According to the accepted narrative, Miriam's faculties deserted her after her stroke. Her right hand trembled and her mind unraveled. But the record tells a different story. She spent the summer convalescing in Montclair, New Jersey, and was in such fettle that a reporter couldn't find her at the hotel. She was driving to Cranford sixteen miles away and "wouldn't be back until late." When she returned, she said she only had mosquitoes to complain of, which were nothing compared to fleas at an old Peruvian ball, which she recalled in colorful detail.

In September she was busy planning a magazine devoted to women and longed to "get back to editorial work." Her publicity machine prepared the ground for her reentry. She was featured among women of "position, influence, and achievement" in a new anthology and given a six-page spread in *Seen and Heard* magazine that touted her "crack-a-jack" position in the publishing world.

Miriam's women's magazine didn't materialize—just yet. But she was an active member of the Women's Press Club where she served as vice-president, and hale enough to spend her usual three months in England and France. With her customary asperity, she weighed in on British society when she came back. Gowned in lavender silk strewn with diamonds and pearls, she delivered a biting critique of mercenary international marriages and the "shameless" American heiresses who sold themselves to reprobate nobles. "The English," she jabbed, "know how to appreciate our money bags."

For a presumed invalid, she was in remarkable form. She kept a close eye on finances (too close, claimed detractors) and won damages of $64,484 against the Congress Spring Company when they tried to scam her. Her digests of *Social Mirage* essays filled papers, and her salon picked up where it left off, except that guests were B-listers and the evenings were a step into the last century. She served the same Roman punch instead of cocktails, poets recited antique, rose-petal verses, and she received *en grande tenue*. Few mentioned muckraker novels, Picasso's rose period, or the implications of Wright's recent airplane flight.

One of the company, however, brought the twentieth century with her. Feminist Carrie Chapman Catt, president of the National American Woman Suffrage Association, was hard to miss—a big-boned, imposing woman with deep-set raptor eyes and Phidian features who stood a head higher than the other women. Yet everyone seemed to miss the fact that Miriam "contrived to talk longer with her than with the other guests." Some were too busy maligning Miriam; her old protégée Ella Wheeler Wilcox complained about her deficient looks and "iceberg" cruelty, and editor Ellery Sedgwick, her *Monthly* replacement, portrayed her as a "shriveled old lady, bedizened like a Dresden china shepherdess, smirking and talking as if she were the Queen of Sheba."

CONTRARY TO THE digs that she'd "lost her attractions," she carried off a prize the summer of 1904. Despite a relapse of nephritis, she journeyed with Baroness Salvador to Le Havre, Cherbourg, and Boulogne and kept her wardrobe up to date. Somewhere, perhaps at the London festivities for Spanish King Alfonso, she donned a fresh couturier gown and met Teodoro Martel y Fernández de Córdova.

Teodoro—for once in Miriam's life—was the genuine article, a marquis from the highest tier of the Spanish aristocracy who was an esteemed poet, scholar, politician, businessman, and gentleman, known as the "Cordovan hero" for his humanitarian work. He was a distingué, still-dashing caballero with black, soulful eyes, a strong nose, and an imperial pencil mustache. Although republican in his sympathies, he was intimate with the royal family and King Alfonso, who appointed him gentleman-in-waiting and gave him a gold key to the king's bedchamber. He had been widowed for eighteen years from Countess Maria Teresa, a marquesa, and inherited from her the title to the Villaverde la Alta estates, where he divided his time between Marmolejo and Paris.

A "charming romance" ensued. As Miriam told it, he "laid violent siege for her heart," with "all the warm-blooded persistence for which his countrymen are famous." She reciprocated, having discovered at last the "best man" she despaired of finding—an *honnête homme*, a litterateur, and a genuine nobleman. "Saddest of all," she once reflected, "is love that comes 'too late.'" She was sixty-eight to his seventy-one and not in the pink of health. Yet she believed in her secret of "perpetual youth," and he was a "dream realized—the best of [her] lovers rolled into one."

Separated from her in the fall, he cabled often in 1905 and wrote her seven times a week seeking her hand in marriage. It was a needed morale boost. With his *Popular Monthly* on the skids, Colver decided to change the title to the *American Illustrated Magazine*, erasing the Leslie name from the publishing world. After fifty years, the Frank Leslie brand was obliterated from memory, and Miriam's glory days with it. She was, noted the *New York Times*, a "figure in journalism no more." "New men with new ideas," trumpeted *Printers' Ink*, now manned the business and intended to "remodel the *Monthly* on modern lines." Under the regime of the "younger generation," the magazine had "passed on to new successes." A foolhardy boast; within months, Munsey bought out the underwater publication.

When Miriam accepted Teodoro's proposal is uncertain. She kept the engagement from her closest friends, she said, because her "intended was considerably older than" herself. More likely, marital negotiations accounted for the secrecy. Although Miriam insisted "both [were] entirely disinterested" monetarily, the Marquis had debts at his Cordova Villaverde la Alta estate, and as a strict Catholic, he required permission to marry a protestant and triple divorcée. Miriam also made stipulations, including a provision that they spend half the year in Spain, the other in New York City. But every obstacle seems to have been removed, and the wedding was set for early May 1907.

In preparation, Miriam assembled a trousseau in Paris. Her photograph, perhaps designed as a wedding portrait, evinces no signs of ill health or withered old age. She looks enviously in trim, her features softened with becoming embonpoint, her large dark eyes un-creased and luminous. She holds herself straight-spined like a dancer, her hands in first position, dressed in a dotted swiss tulle gown caught at the waist with a satin cummerbund attached to a pleated train.

Paris in 1906 was champagne season. Miriam and the Marquis must have made a handsome pair on the boulevards, she in a walking dress with a picture hat veiled in an embroidered violette; he in a morning suit, top hat, and staghorn cane. Street singers lined the avenue; three circuses fringed Montmartre, new bustling sidewalk cafés spilled into the streets, and couples danced the cakewalk and tango at *tours de valse* on every corner.

As a stately elder couple, their pleasures would have been more sedate—Old World Bois outings, tea at Rumpelmayer's with foie gras sandwiches, poetry readings, theater, and soirées. Possibly he escorted Miriam to a recherché salon such as Madame de Caillavert's Sunday "conversational dinners" where Proust and cultural elites gathered to discuss her chosen topic, silenced by a porcelain bell if they spoke out of turn. America was far away—the San Francisco earthquake with five hundred dead, the noisome International Workers of the World, and the unpleasant blurb that another Baroness de Bazus surfaced in Bavaria. No matter: She anticipated a better title and position.

In the established European tradition, Teodoro might have accompanied her to the couturier for her wardrobe—morning, afternoon toilettes, indoor robes, and evening dresses—both at Worth's, which had her "form," and Jacques Doucet's, famed for frocks of filmy chiffons over pastel satin stitched with ruches, volents, and gold inserts.

Lingerie, though, was the "soul" of the trousseau. She needed two dozen ribbon-threaded *robes de nuit*, and another two dozen flounced muslin drawers, chemises, and silk petticoats. The corset was the centerpiece. Wasp waists were in fashion, with an added S-bend contour that pushed the bust forward and buttocks back. Hence the necessary armature of boned and tight-laced corsets, disguised as *objets d'art* in satin and Pompadour embroidery. Miriam ordered multiples of these, and incidentals—platinum hairpins, openwork stockings, and fans for all occasions—and shipped her purchases to New York.

IN MID-MARCH, SHE'D barely unwrapped the tissue paper before she received the news. "Death," announced the cable, "surprised [the Count of Villaverde la Alta] in Paris, March 12, 1907." For reasons that remain unclear, she waited a month to notify the press. If she anticipated raised eyebrows, she was right. After the pseudonobles in her romantic past, reporters were leery of this one, whom they misidentified as the Marquis of Campallegre.

In a preemptive strike, she marshalled reporters to interview her. She exhibited his photograph and said he told her "to place his picture in [her] drawing room and to tell the whole world that there was one Spanish gentleman who would willingly give up his life" for her. His "last words," she added, "were for her." How much they believed is another matter. Yet this time, she had truth on her side and was genuinely "broken hearted."

After ten days in Paris with the Baroness Salvador, she joined Teodoro's two daughters in Cordova and decorated his tombstone at the Villaverde la Alta. She left with his gold key to the king's bedroom, which she wore on a chain like a rosary at her waist.

Teodoro's death cut deep. As she said of another bride-to-be whose Spanish fiancé died, she was a "widow in heart, if not in

name," her loss exacerbated by an unofficial engagement and the
ebullience around her. In a bitter contrast to her grief, the country was in high spirits, off to a "bully" year of hope and rocketing
optimism. "Anything, everything," proclaimed Thomas Edison,
"is possible."

THE YEAR 1908 signaled "America's entry into the modern
world"—a revved-up machine age that left Miriam behind. The "great
multitude" eyed Model T's, put up prefab "kit homes" in months,
installed washing machines, and danced to "Sally in the Alley" on
$8.75 Victrolas. America was a global power, in possession of the
Caribbean, Latin America, and the Panama Canal, and sent a "Great
White Fleet" of sixteen battleships around the world to flaunt the fact.
Although problems remained—endemic poverty, child labor, terror-
ist bombs, and escalating violence toward African Americans—the
nation was on a celebratory, self-congratulatory spree.

Miriam proceeded with her usual trip abroad, but she "did not
enjoy London and Paris a bit," and returned early in July. The Franco-
British Exhibition, a mammoth fair of wedding cake palaces around
an artificial lake, left her cold. Designed as a trade show to celebrate
the Entente Cordiale between the two countries, the Exhibition was
nine-tenths amusement park, with attractions like the Flip Flap,
with two steel arms two hundred feet high with platforms for pan-
oramic views of the fairground. Eight million visitors of all classes
streamed in from May to October.

Unsurprisingly, Miriam was in no mood for them. The tubular
sheath dresses worn by the masses were "very indecent." They lacked
underskirts, clung to the figure, and were meant for the "young and
slender." She was neither, and she was offended. Something else,
more obscure, also contributed to her ill-humor in London. "I was
used by everybody as a pincushion," she complained, "I am full of
pinpricks." In all likelihood, the cause was de Leuville's death, which
triggered a spate of attack pieces on the Marquis, "the first of the

fraudulent nobility to deceive New York society," most conspicuously Mrs. Frank Leslie. Whatever the affront, she intended to "show people" when she got home that she was "still alive and really had ideas."

Instead, she faded from view and seemed in hibernation. But behind the scenes she mounted a rebound. She entered her age in *Who's Who* as fifty-eight, entertained "only bracing people" in London, and solicited a special correspondent to state that she looked "as young as ever this season and quite as gorgeous."

MIRIAM WAS GIRDING up for her valedictory tour. In early February she boarded the train for the grueling eighty-one-hour journey and received a hero's welcome in San Francisco. The newspapers hailed her as "one of the most interesting women in the world, one who has really done big things," and flocked to interview her at the Palace Hotel, newly rebuilt after the 1906 earthquake. Seated in the Great Garden Court beneath the three-story vaulted ceiling of iridescent glass, she recounted her career highlights and delivered her verdict on suffrage. She admired the female activists in New York, especially their leader, Mrs. Catt, who was "conducting herself with great dignity." "Ultimately," she continued, "women will gain suffrage rights," but she doubted if the time were right yet for a female president.

The city came out to fête her. The prestigious Sequoia Club hosted an "elaborate" reception, and the Alameda County Press Club staged a ballroom banquet where her old paramour Joaquin Miller gave the honorary address in an "afternoon suit" and pioneer high boots. His ardor for her had mellowed with age, but tonight he delivered a "very eloquent" tribute, winding up with a recitation of "Columbus," the poem he wrote for her. Miriam presided in a regal costume of "rarest black lace," draped in diamonds and pearl chains.

After California she planned to travel and write for a syndicate, but her work had grown dated and was no longer in demand. She did manage a visit to Europe, and brought the late Marquis's daughter, Rosaria Villaverde, home with her. The "accomplished," tactful Rosaria dealt patiently with Miriam as she upbraided a custom's officer and appeased reporters with praises of New York. She "preferred the American type of man to any other in the world."

She professed to admire the "hustling and bustling" city, but Manhattan of 1910 must have overwhelmed the delicately raised, country-bred Rosaria. The roar of midtown was so strident that the Ritz Carlton Hotel repaved Forty-seventh Street with wood blocks, and the car congestion choked thoroughfares to such an extent that the mayor proposed a Fifth-and-One-Half Avenue to divert traffic. Six more skyscrapers stabbed the horizon; department stores were vertical hives of seven thousand employees serving customers slapping racks of ready-mades.

A greater din racketed downtown. The New York population topped four and a half million, 40 percent of whom lived below Fourteenth Street in noisy, cramped tenements amid the cries of strange-voiced vendors and clashes in the street. Gangs like Little Italy's "Black Hand" sowed terror, police cracked skulls for minor infractions (street hockey and open hydrants), and criminals of every stripe were on an epic rampage. After the fall/winter season in the city, Rosaria must have been relieved to leave Mrs. Leslie and the roiling cauldron of Gotham and return to the Cordova estate.

MIRIAM'S LAST THREE years are a subject of debate. By one account she was in rapid decline, sinking into physical wreckage and advancing dementia. By another, she held on, in possession of her powers until the end. At the start, she clearly had her wits about her. During 1911, she entertained Alfonso's emissaries in Washington and made perfect sense in an interview with the "Nellie Bly of the West," journalist Ada Patterson. Sounding a century ahead of her time, Miriam advised career women to "forget their sex during office hours," not "practice allurements," and be bold—"essay new

paths." You "cannot have [an] omelet," she enjoined, "without breaking eggs."

Cloistered in her Sherman Hotel rooms (where she moved from
the old Chelsea), she didn't address the worst problem for working
women—the plight of the underpaid masses, highlighted by the
March Triangle Factory fire that incinerated 141 garment workers,
exposing the illegal violations and starvation wages. But the lot of
women was on her mind. Six times she changed her will, each with
a more-targeted, larger bequest on their behalf. Carrie Catt's name
kept coming up. She called her the "splendid general" of suffrage,
slipped her checks, and said she was with her "heart and soul."
"When I come to die," she hinted, "you find that, like yourself, I am
interested in woman's advancement."

In early January 1912 Miriam sustained a relapse and unwisely
permitted her cousin, daughter of her uncle Aristide, to stay with
her. It wasn't Annie Simons's first visit. For the past decade she'd
hovered around in the capacity of companion and occasional nurse.
While she was there, Miriam's condition deteriorated, necessitating
a three-month hospital confinement.

The next year Annie reappeared like a circling crow. This time
Miriam suffered a second stroke that left her infirm and crippled.
Paralyzed on the left side, she walked with a spastic lurch, her leg
dragging behind her, and became irascible and dictatorial with
Annie. Her cousin complained that Miriam ordered her to walk the
dog in a kimono, take coffee without cream (an extra ten cents), and
use her own linens on the bed. As impaired as she was, Miriam
might have known what she was about. "They are only after my
money," she wrote Catt.

She put the final touches to her will on May 22, 1914. All
the helping hands who surrounded her—Annie, her niece Carrie Wrenn, her nurse Mrs. Frey, masseuse Nellie Hyland, and her
three doctors—counted on legacies and didn't see her lawyer, William Cromwell, come and go. Four days later she sailed to Europe
with Mrs. Frey. Fading fast, she made a tragic figure. Onboard, she

rang for the ship's doctor twenty times a day, harassed the crew, and boasted pathetically of her worldwide fame. Baroness Salvador, another expectant beneficiary, engaged rooms for her at the Hotel Mozart for five weeks and took an adjacent room to be "constantly near her."

Once back in August, she spent three weeks in New Jersey with Carrie Wrenn, unable to "control her excrements, solid and liquid." Wrenn then brought her to New York and transferred her to Dr. John Welch, who'd agreed to give up his patients and limit his practice to Mrs. Leslie.

On September 18, 1914, a beautifully dressed, elegant young woman visited Miriam's crowded bedside. She was Marguerite Linton Glentworth, president of the New York Women's Press Club and author of the sensational *The Tenth Commandment*. Although she came on behalf of promised funds to the club, there was a personal bond. A kindred spirit, she wrote the novel Mrs. Leslie began but never finished. The heroine, a Southern stage diva, leaves the theater at the height of her career to marry Society's "wealthiest and most aristocratic" man, only to desert him for the free bohemian life she misses. Unable to resolve the conflict, she dies nonetheless in her lover's arms at the end with a "look of peace" on her face. In Marguerite's presence, Miriam had her third and final stroke.

Her obituary on September 19, 1914, was minor news. Northern France was a Götterdämmerung with the Allies slaughtered in the trenches at the First Battle of the Aisne and the Germans on a jack-booted "Race" to Belgium. Her death notice read as if she'd written it herself, recording her age as sixty-three and citing her noble French ancestry, social distinction, intellectual attainments, and wonderworking business accomplishments.

The choice of Calvary Baptist Church for the funeral is puzzling. The gothic Fifty-seventh Street behemoth was a fundamentalist stronghold, tough on moral peccadilloes, partner dancing, and marital delinquencies. The Women's Press Club and Professional Woman's League filled the pews and honorary pallbearers included

Louis Cramer and William Cromwell. Friends and relations accompanied the bier by private funeral car to Woodlawn Cemetery.

NEARLY EVERYONE HAD an eye on a piece of the estate. They were in for a surprise, Miriam's last coup de theatre. Before the seal was broken, droves of hopefuls came out of the woodwork: her Alabama aunt's children and kin, far-flung cousins, and Frank Leslie's brood from his first marriage. No one was prepared for the contents. Apart from $130,000 allocated to Rosaria Villaverde, Marguerite Glinton, and specific people and causes, she left the bulk of her two-million-dollar estate to Carrie Chapman Catt for "the furtherance of the cause of Woman's Suffrage," with no strings attached.

Her obituary might have been buried, but this was a bombshell. Mrs. Leslie, one of the least visible suffragists, donated the largest sum ever given to the vote for women—a gift never exceeded. Mrs. Catt didn't sleep the night she heard the news. The bequest could revolutionize the movement; it was an "awful responsibility," combined with the "ordeal of trying to please all the relatives." She couldn't have guessed the extent of the ordeal.

Less than a week after the Leslie will was published, fortune-seekers lunged for the spoils. Besides creditors and charities, a tribe of claimants closed in and tried to break the will. "Human nature," fleered Catt, "was never so close to pig nature and fox nature as when on the scent of money of the dead." Arthur Leslie, Alfred's son, led the charge with three other step-grandchildren, who contended their grandfather verbally promised two-thirds of the estate to them and that Miriam had no legal right to any of it.

They pooled resources and hired James Wescott, a legal sharpshooter. He dredged up old court cases and engaged a detective to track Miriam's past. On December 12, he filed papers before probate and opened Pandora's box. The history Miriam tried so hard to hide unfurled in banner headlines: "Girlhood Scandal Hidden Sixty

Years," "Mrs. Leslie of Negro Birth." The whole story poured out—dockets, documents, and testimonials. Readers learned Miriam's real age (seventy-seven) and her misadventures on the wild side: her demimonde years, Peacock shotgun marriage, sordid Squier divorce, and ten-year ménage à trois with Frank Leslie. They learned the full extent of her faked aristocratic background. Instead of Huguenot gentry, she came from a family of bounders and bankrupts with an absentee father and an unmarried mother who perhaps kept a "house of ill fame"—and perhaps wasn't her mother at all.

The parentage question "was never settled"—even after the court ruled against Leslie. Without extant records, the detective lost the trail, but the circumstantial evidence suggested Miriam's biracial origin. Her birth wasn't registered (as with mixed-race children), Charles's live-in stepdaughter in New Orleans witnessed a Black slave mother, and Susan Danforth's whereabouts were unclear at the time. In his final summation, the judge refused to withdraw "serious contention that Mrs. Leslie was the daughter of a negro slave."

Mrs. Catt's lawyer, William Cromwell of Sullivan and Cromwell, successfully crushed the biracial allegation with racist stereotypes, upheld Miriam's reputation and legitimacy, and sustained the will. But the legacy was chipped away. Suffrage wasn't a popular cause, and everyone in Miriam's retinue clawed at the estate. Her financial manager, antisuffragist Louis Cramer, demanded a bigger cut, friends piled on, and Dr. Welch requested $12,500 because Miriam was a "bad patient." The litigations were endless and dragged on in Dickensian fashion for more than six years.

In the process, her intimates—Annie Simons, Carrie Wrenn, and Baroness Salvador—eviscerated her in an attempt to prove she was non compos and corrupt when she made her last will. She was a "pervert," "sexual degenerate," "egomaniac," and stingy tyrant in her dotage. She reneged on her promises and endowed women's suffrage, they fumed, due to Carrie Catt's malign influence over Mrs. Leslie's "diseased mind." Cromwell pacified them with payoffs.

After all was said and done, Catt lost a million dollars of the original legacy in legal costs, tax assessments, and sums to claimants, auditors, executors, and Cromwell himself (equally opposed to suffrage), who collected $95,000 in fees. At the final accounting, $977,875.02 remained.

THE LEGACY

MRS. CATT, AS Miriam perceived, was a "splendid general" and wise steward of her estate. When she recovered the money in 1917, she had a weakened, splintered movement on her hands. As president of the National American Woman Suffrage Association, she faced a divided party and the slow death of her "Winning Plan" designed to centralize operations, devise strategy, and fill the war chest. Votes for women had failed in New York State in 1915—a serious setback. The day she "got the first receipts from the Leslie estate," she said, was "one of the happiest days of her life." She wheeled out her "Winning Plan."

She beefed up the New York campaign and won the state contest in 1917, doubling suffrage sympathy in America, which created the needed momentum for the Nineteenth Amendment. With the rest of the legacy she built a massive publicity machine, the Leslie Woman Suffrage Commission, a command station unlike anything the movement had been able to assemble before. Catt hired a crack staff and organized a multi-pronged offensive, with specific forces concentrated on different fronts. In a coordinated blitz, she formed departments for news releases, bulletins, propaganda films, telephone drives, "stunts services" (parades, etc.), education, anti-suffrage pushback, fundraising, and lobbying.

One of the Commission's most effective weapons was a magazine, *The Woman Citizen*, a weekly for general consumption dedicated "to Mrs. Frank Leslie's generosity toward the cause of woman's suffrage and her faith in woman's irresistible progress." Boldly laid out, picturesque, and on point, the magazine captured a broader base and popularized the vote initiative in America. It became the "leading women's publication," responsible for influencing congressmen (who got free copies) and bringing the national press to an "overwhelming" support of suffrage. Miriam's idea for a new women's magazine surpassed her dreams, and her money kept the publication solvent.

After Catt shepherded the vote for women through Congress on August 26, 1920, the Leslie Commission continued for nine years, with a leftover cache of $116,000 that funded international suffrage and the League of Women Voters. The ripple effect lasted a generation and beyond. Feminist leader Harriet Taylor Upton later wondered if women "would still be going up to the capital if [not for] Mrs. Leslie." In absentia, Miriam played her last great role onstage, scripting an exit that turbo-boosted the revolution.

Her trustee might have done more. Seventeen months before the passage of the Nineteenth Amendment, Mrs. Catt received a petition from the African American Women's Association to join the Commission. They were denied—a stark instance of the exclusion of women of color from the feminist movement. Catt lost an opportunity to mend and extend race relations for the future and concealed what she must have suspected: that her benefactor had "black blood."

Miriam believed "women should guard their secrets." This may have been among the many secrets she hid within her fantasy bulwark of invented names and personas and aristocratic pretensions. Or why she armored herself in mystery, determined to be one of "the permanent guesses of mankind." "The sphinx," Miriam said, "has the best of it every time."

Yet she didn't get the best of it from posterity. The bigger mystery surrounding Mrs. Leslie is how and why she vanished from memory. A doyenne of theater and show, she would hate to be forgotten. She will never be remembered as a champion of courageous causes and good works like the female icons of the time: Jane Addams, Harriet Tubman, Susan B. Anthony, Nellie Bly, Emma Goldman, Ida B. Wells, and others.

She was an unabashed egotist, indifferent to self-sacrificial deeds, and devil-driven for fame, rank, and power. She liked the pomps and vanities of Society and forbidden fruits of the sexual subculture. Her persona was a tissue of lies, her passions were unworthy of her: dubious men, titles, diamonds, ovations, and ostentatious displays. She was vain, bigoted, imperious, and hard-boiled.

But if she was deeply flawed and embodied some of the worst aspects of the Gilded Age, she was also leagues ahead of her time and deserves to be back in the public eye—in the pantheon of feminist pioneers. A titanic vanguard figure, she was a woman of phenomenal charisma, strength of character, and chutzpa who bulldozed social dictates and blazed the trail. She faked out the male establishment, torched prescribed femininity, and sidewinded to unimaginable power and influence. She lived large and pushed the feminist frontier—beyond the Nineteenth Amendment.

She wanted women to be fully "in the world"—visible, engaged, fulfilled, and at the forefront. Otherwise, "we might as well be dead." Chances are Miriam never thought she'd be dead to the world. A self-mythologizer, she saw herself as the legendary Lilith, the immortal gadfly and moral truant, who defied Adam's dominion and founded her own paradise, filled with "jinn" lovers and a race of "glorious," "rebellious daughters" "claiming the New World as their special domain."

ACKNOWLEDGMENTS

ON THE TRAIL of Mrs. Frank Leslie, her secrets and stories, I've been blessed with a dream team of guides, sleuths, and supporters. The late Peter Mayer's enthusiasm and vision for the book lit the path. His long, single-spaced emails packed with pointers and suggested approaches gave me my compass bearings and marching orders. My savvy agent, Lynn Nesbit, was there, too, at the get-go to spur me on. Lenny Golay, another prime mover, prodded me long ago to write about Mrs. Leslie and lent her sharp editorial eye to the project until the end. As for editors, I lucked out with Tracy Carns and Chelsea Cutchens. Editors don't come any better than Chelsea; her oversight from details to the big picture helped steer and shape the book. Copy editor Melissa Wagner, proofreader Janine Barlow, and the creative Abrams staff were nonpareil.

A master guide was Dr. Lawrence Friedman. A scholar/ philosopher and an inspired psychiatrist, he aided the investigation of Mrs. Leslie's life and times with his wise counsel and fortified me at every level. I also owe a deep debt to the late Madeleine Stern, whose *Purple Passage: The Life of Mrs. Frank Leslie* first mapped and documented the territory.

The years spent in research taught me renewed gratitude to librarians, archivists, and specialists in the field. Particular thanks to the New-York Historical Society Library, where I logged many hours in the Squier files, aided by the hospitable staff. At the South Carolina Historical Society archives, Harlan Greene, head of Special Collections, went overboard on my behalf, producing early Charleston censuses and following leads. One of those leads took me to historian Nic Butler at the Charleston County Public Library whose help can't be overestimated. He found thought-to-be lost inventories of the enslaved people who belonged to Miriam's father's first wife, as well as their marriage contract, and other crucial documents.

Still more, he made them available to me from the South Carolina Department of Archives and History, accompanied by lessons in early Charleston history, culture, and society.

Tom Nagy guided me through beautifully digitalized versions of the *Frank Leslie's Illustrated Newspaper* at Accessible Archives, and Elizabeth Watts Pope, curator of books at the American Antiquarian Society, furnished copies of rare *Lady's Journals*. Thanks, too, to the New York Public Library for its *Chimney Corner* issues and Leslie collection of photographs and materials. I had benefit, as well, of nineteenth-century music and fashion experts, soprano Kate Hurney and Gilded Age clothing authority Caroline Millbank. Douglas Anderson and J. C. Hallman, both authors and scholars of Victorian American culture and literature, were two more great advisors.

Readers and sounding boards cropped up everywhere for second opinions and insights—Catherine Hiller, Kathryn Staley, Bill Goldstein, Stuart Bennett, and Drs. Edith McNutt, Peter Buckley, and Maxine Antell.

For across-the-board support I had premier tech help from the incomparable Frank Vasquez and ongoing advice from book ace Carol Fitzgerald. I also found a continual supply chain of ideas at the Colony Club Literature and Arts Committee discussions and Monday Charleston "salons" with Belinda and Richard Gergel, Jonathan Green, Walter Fiederowicz, Autumn Phillips, et al. Courmes residents in France not only delivered mental inspiration but sustained my spirit—neighbors like Barbara Viaggio, Cristina Gastaldi, Danielle Boeri, Richard Thierry, Philippe Gamba, Carol Euzière, René Martin, Eric Cocu, and Bruno Rouganne.

To the home front, though, I owe the most. Neide Hucks, my extended family, nurtured body, mind, and soul. And my daughter, Phoebe Prioleau, spared time from an arduous pediatric psychiatry fellowship to read and reread drafts. A published poet, writer, and critic, she supplied priceless input. As for my brilliant husband, Philip, there are no words for his labors and contributions.

He worked tirelessly and selflessly without complaint, vetting concepts and sentences, dispensing medical knowledge, and critiquing every page of the book. He shouldered domestica, cleared space for my work, laughed me off cliffs, and made the long trail to Mrs. Frank Leslie both possible and a joy.

NOTES

INTRODUCTION

4 I've also used . . . : Vivian Gornick, "Vivian Gornick on the 'Forgotten' Wife of Victorian Novelist, George Meredith," *Literary Hub*, June 24, 2020, lithub.com/Vivian-gornick-on-the-forgotten-wife-of-victorian-novelist -george-meredith/.

PROLOGUE

5 She had "met . . .": "The Story of a Woman of Business," in *The National Exposition Souvenir: What America Owes to Women*, ed. Lydia Hoyt Farmer (Chicago: Charles Wells Moulton, 1893), 432.

5 Before her "long . . .": *Boston Globe*, May 20, 1895, 6.

5 She stood at . . . : *Los Angeles Herald*, February 13, 1892, 10.

6 She was "consecrated . . .": *Kansas City Times*, July 10, 1898, 13; and *Book News*, April 1893, 48.

6 Fragile and ethereal . . . : See full quote: "The bones of her cranium are thinner, smaller, and more pliant and the space to be filled by the brain is smaller." Barbara Welter, *Dimity Convictions: The American Woman in the Nineteenth Century* (Athens: Ohio University Press, 1976), 156.

6 "Should women make . . .": Quoted in Julie Husband and Jim O'Loughlin, *Daily Life in the United States 1870–1900* (Westport, CT: Greenwood Press, 2004), 101; and Tom Lutz, *American Nervousness* (Ithaca and London: Cornell University Press, 1991), 31.

6 A "true woman," . . . : Quoted in John S. Haller Jr. and Robin M. Haller, *The Physician and Sexuality in Victorian America* (New York: W. W. Norton, 1974), 98.

6 The presence of . . . : See Carl N. Degler, "What Ought to Be and What Was: Women's Sexuality in the Nineteenth Century," *American Historical Review* vol. 79, no. 5 (December 1974), 1468.

6 The Rubicon of . . . : Quoted in *Primers for Prudery*, ed. Ronald G. Walters (Englewood Cliffs, NJ: Prentice-Hall, 1974), 75 and 49.

7 Yet Mrs. Leslie . . . : Quoted in Milton Rugoff, *Prudery and Passion* (New York: W. W. Norton, 1971), 127.

7 She assumed the . . . : It had served her purposes to be an enigma and keep them guessing. "Never tell how the watch goes," she advised. "There

is no incentive to interest like mystery." Mrs. Frank Leslie, *Are We All Deceivers? The Lover's Blue Book* (Chicago: Neely, 1893), 49.

7   Who could possibly . . . : Mrs. Frank Leslie, *Rents in Our Robes* (Chicago: Clark & Co., 1888), 111.

7   "I imagined," recalled . . . : *Times-Picayune* (New Orleans), March 21, 1893, 3.

7   Instead, Mrs. Leslie . . . : Ibid.; and *Book News*, April 4, 1893, 343.

7   Her wardrobe was . . . : *Book News*, April 4, 1893, 343.

7   Even now, over sixty . . . : Mrs. Frank Leslie, *A Social Mirage* (New York: F. Tennyson Nee, 1899), 403.

7   She possessed a . . . : Farmer, *National Exposition Souvenir*, 430; and *Detroit Free Press*, November 3, 1890: 3. For an analysis of seduction expertise, see Georg Simmel, "Flirtation," in *Georg Simmel: On Women, Sexuality, and Love*, trans. and ed. Guy Oakes (New Haven: Yale University Press, 1984), 133–152.

7   A woman who . . . : Leslie, *Are We All Deceivers?*, 232.

7   "Never come down . . .": Leslie, *Social Mirage*, 397.

8   Excluded from the . . . : Farmer, *National Exposition Souvenir*, 430.

8   Mrs. Leslie occupied . . . : *Independent Record*, October 28, 1888, 3.

8   She sat at . . . : Mrs. Leslie called these aids the "subtle fascinations of the toilet table," Leslie, *Social Mirage*, 281. The full range of this equipment included "half a dozen" small crystal boxes filled with pins "of all sizes, designs and colors." A lioness figurine crouched on a tray that held hair pins, a jeweled shoehorn, button hook, hand-glass, and manicure set "fit for an empress." There would also have been a hair receiver for false extensions and curls called "rats." *Independent Record* (Helena, MT), October 28, 1888, 3.

8   At sixty-two she . . . : *Los Angeles Herald*, February 13, 1892, 10.

9   Miriam Leslie, however . . . : Leslie, *Social Mirage*, 121; and Charles Baudelaire, "In Praise of Cosmetics," *My Heart Laid Bare and Other Prose Writings* (New York: Vanguard Press, 1951), 63.

9   With luck, Annie . . . : The Matter of the Estate of Frank Leslie, also known as Mrs. Frank Leslie, also known as the Baroness de Bazus, Deceased. *Reports of Cases Heard and Determined in the Appellate Division*, vol. 175, New York Supreme Court, 1917, vol. 1, 248.

9   Mrs. Leslie found . . . : Leslie, *Rents in Our Robes*, 89.

10 The staging ground . . . : *Daily Picayune* (New Orleans), July 31, 1898, 19.

10 Around her in . . . : *Independent Record* (Helena, MT), October 28, 1888, 3.

10 For Victorian Americans . . . : Marian Fowler, *In a Gilded Cage: From Heiress to Duchess* (New York: Vintage Books, 1993), 110.

10 An elegant turnout . . . : See Valerie Steele, *Fashion and Eroticism* (New York: Oxford University Press, 1985), 120.

10 Despite her indifferent . . . : *Detroit Free Press*, November 3, 1890, 3.

10 In column after . . . : Leslie, *Are We All Deceivers?*, 271.

10 Fashion could take . . . : Ibid.

10 Tonight required "royal . . .": Ibid., 270.

11 Finally, Mrs. Leslie . . . : M. H. Dunlop, *Gilded City: Scandal and Sensation in Turn-of-the-Century New York* (New York: Perennial, 2001), 64.

11 "Jewels," she decreed . . . : Leslie, *Are We All Deceivers?*, 77.

11 Decked in precious . . . : *Huron Expositor*, December 12, 1890, 7.

11 After she attached . . . : *Detroit Free Press*, March 5, 1885, 12.

11 Platters clunked on . . . : *Independent Record* (Helena, MT), October 28, 1888, 3.

11 She swept her . . . : Quoted in Madeleine Stern, *Purple Passage: The Life of Mrs. Frank Leslie* (Norman: University of Oklahoma Press, 1953), 106; and *Detroit Free Press*, November 3, 1890, 3.

CHAPTER ONE

13 "Delicate Huguenot Exotic" . . . : Donald Dale Jackson, "Frank Leslie: Belle of the Boardroom," *Smithsonian Magazine*, November 1, 1997, www .smithsonianmag.com/history/miriam-leslie-belle-of-the-boardroom -53610628/.

13 Everyone could see . . . : Madeleine Stern, *Purple Passage: The Life of Mrs. Frank Leslie* (Norman: University of Oklahoma Press, 1953), 208; and "Mrs. Frank Leslie Born in New Orleans," *Times-Picayune*, September 20, 1914, 10.

14 The elaborate building . . . : For a description, see Stanley Clisby Arthur, *Old New Orleans* (Westminster, MA: Heritage Books, 1936), 33–234.

14 The once-manicured Jackson . . . : Quoted in Mollie Moore Davies and Ruys Smith, *Southern Queen: New Orleans in the Nineteenth Century* (London: Bloomsbury, 2011), 143.

14 Over the clatter . . . : See "French Market Celebrates 200th Anniversary," *Preservation in Print* 18, no. 4 (May 1991). Also see Joan B. Garvey and Mary Lou Widner, *Beautiful Crescent: A History of New Orleans* (Gretna, LA: Pelican Publishing Co., 2014), 149; "Sunday Morning at the French Market," old-new-orleans.com/NO_Sunday_Morning.html; and Lawrence N. Powell, *The Accidental City: Improvising New Orleans* (Cambridge, MA: Harvard University Press, 2012), 269–272 and passim.

14 Artist Charles Upham . . . : *Frank Leslie's Illustrated Newspaper*, March 31, 1883, 95.

14 Beneath tented booths . . . : Ibid.

14 Reporters found her . . . : *Times-Democrat*, February 26, 1883, 4; and *Times-Picayune*, February 26, 1883, 2.

15 Yes, she exclaimed . . . *Times-Picayune*, February 26, 1883, 2.

15 "This is my . . .": Ibid; and Mrs. Frank Leslie, *Are We All Deceivers? The Lover's Blue Book* (Chicago: Neely, 1893), 177.

15 She was "born . . .": Jackson, "Belle of the Boardroom."

15 Brought up in . . . : *Book News*, April 1893, 342.

15 The government needed . . . : "Exile Destination: St. Domingue," Acadian-Cajun Genealogy & History (website), accessed February 6, 2017, www .acadian-cajun.com/exsd.htm.

16 The Follins were . . . : The Estate of Frank Leslie, Supreme Court, 1917, vol. II, 372. Melanie Follin, Miriam's grandmother, circulated this tall tale.

16 Miriam's incurable romanticism . . . : See Madeleine Stern's highly glamorized rendition of this period in *Purple Passage*, 6. For more of these glorified versions, see Carl Carmer, *Stars Fell on Alabama* (New York: Doubleday, 1934); Albert J. Pickett, *History of Alabama and Incidentally of Georgia and Mississippi, from the Earliest Period*, vol. 1 (Sacramento, CA: Creative Partners, [1851], 2015), 633; and Emma Gelders Sterne, *Some Plant Olive Trees* (New York: Doubleday, 1934). For a true account, see Eric Sauger, *Reborn in America*, trans. Madeleine Velguth (Tuscaloosa: University of Alabama Press, 2011), 220–379, passim; "Demopolis, Alabama," Wikipedia, en.wikipedia.org/wiki/Demopolis, _Alabama; and "Vine and Olive Colony," *Encyclopedia of Alabama*, www .encyclopediaofalabama.org/article/h-1539.

16 When the settlers . . . : See "Vine and Olive Colony," *Encyclopedia of Alabama*.

17 Irregular free sex . . . : Sauger, *Reborn in America*, 296.

17 (Two resident Follin . . .): Jean Charles Auguste and Matthieu Firmin who inhabited the colony married Creoles in 1805 and 1806 respectively. See index in Sauger. "Creole" can indicate either a white or mixed-race native of Louisiana, although it came to mean primarily "people of color" by the mid- to late nineteenth century. Throughout I use "Creole" in the second sense, a person of mixed racial origin.

17 Rather than dancing . . . : Sauger, 295.

17 "Here my only . . .": Quoted ibid.

17 Miriam's father at . . . : See James E. Hagy, *Charleston South Carolina City Directories for the Years 1816, 1819, 1821, 1825, and 1829* (Baltimore: Clearfield Co., 1996), 144. I am grateful to Harlan Greene, head of the special collections at the Charleston College Library, for the identification of Charles.

Name mix-ups were common (Augustus was double-listed), but the choice is obvious. Charleston then was a mixed-race city, particularly the poorer quarter above Calhoun Street.

17 Profits sank, and . . . : For a discussion of this period, see Peter A. Coclanis, *The Shadow of a Dream: Economic Life and Death in the South Carolina Low Country 1670–1920* (New York: Oxford University Press, 1998), 111–60; and Joseph Kelly, *America's Longest Siege: Charleston, Slavery, and the Slow March toward Civil War* (New York: The Overlook Press, 2013).

18 Charleston records show . . . : The Estate of Frank Leslie, Supreme Court, 1917, vol. I, 94.

18 After her husband . . . : *Post and Courier* (Charleston, SC), December 25, 1830, 3.

18 She must have . . . : Marriage Settlement, Caroline Trescot and Charles Follin, October 2, 1830, South Carolina Department of Archives and History, 51.

18 They realized $10,780.90 . . . : The Estate of Frank Leslie, Supreme Court, 1917, vol. I, 80.

19 Her official mother . . . : See letters on exhibit from 1841–1842 in The Estate of Frank Leslie, Supreme Court, 1917, vol. II, 316–27.

19 Miriam liked to . . . : See John Joseph May, *Danforth Genealogy* (Boston: Charles H. Pope, 1902), 160–61.

19 While in the . . . : Letters, The Estate of Frank Leslie, Supreme Court, 1917, vol. II, 317 and 312.

19 Manhattan wasn't known . . . : Timothy J. Gilfoyle, *City of Eros: New York City, Prostitution, and the Commercialization of Sex, 1790–1920* (New York: Norton, 1992), 55; and Edwin G. Burrows and Mike Wallace, *Gotham: A History of New York City to 1898* (New York: Oxford, 1999), 484.

19 No birth certificate . . . : The Estate of Frank Leslie, Supreme Court, 1917, vol. I, 109.

20 The practice was . . . : Mary Chestnut, quoted in and see Curtis Harris, "The Loathsome Den—Sexual Assault on the Plantation: #MeToo," *Brave Ideas Blog*, President Lincoln's Cottage (website), December 19, 2017, www .lincolncottage.org/the-loathsome-den-sexual-assault-on-the-plantation -metoo/.

20 Records have recently . . . : For this I am immensely grateful to historian Nic Butler, PhD, of the Charleston Public Library who unearthed these documents for me and made them available during COVID lockdown. They include the sale of forty slaves by Caroline and Charles Follin, 1831, Series S213003, volume 005k, page 00498, item 00; Series S213003, volume 0050, page 00119, item 00; and "Slave Auction," *City Gazette*,

May 26, 1829, and *Southern Patriot*, May 22, 1829. Also an inventory of the personal property of Dr. John Trescot, 1820, 278; Will of Charles Carrere, 1826, Will Book G (1828–34), South Carolina Department of Archives and History, 368; and Marriage Settlement between Caroline Carrere and Charles Follin, W. I. K., ST 452, South Carolina Department of Archives and History, 48–51.

20 By the mid-nineteenth . . . : See the example of New Orleans mixed-race slave Sally Miller (b. 1817), who showed "no trace of African descent" and closely resembled Miriam. "She had long, straight black hair, hazel eyes, thin lips, and a Roman nose." Tomas Ruys Smith, *Southern Queen: New Orleans in the Nineteenth Century* (New York: Continuum, 2011), 95. Also see Martha A. Sandweiss: "People of African descent who passed as white understood that a fair complexion could conceal a mixed racial heritage," *Passing Strange: A Gilded Age Tale of Love and Deception Across the Color Line* (New York: Penguin, 2010), 141.

20 Even Charles's stepdaughter . . . : The Estate of Frank Leslie, Supreme Court, 1917, vol. I, 165.

20 He little reckoned . . . : Frederick Marryat, quoted in Burrows and Wallace, *Gotham*, 617.

21 *Longworth's Almanac* of . . . : *Longworth's New York Register and City Directory*, 1839–1840, 259.

21 By 1840, they . . . : 1840 United States Federal Census, New York Ward 14, New York, NY, Roll 307, 350.

21 Nights in the . . . : For a summary, see Burrows and Wallace, *Gotham*, 620.

22 He was "without . . .": Letter, The Estate of Frank Leslie, Supreme Court, 1917, vol. II, 318.

22 He would, however . . . : Ibid., 320.

22 "Time, my dearest," . . . : Ibid., 325.

22 She now lived . . . : Ibid., 399.

22 She nostalgically recalled . . . : Mrs. Frank Leslie, *A Social Mirage* (New York: F. Tennyson Nee, 1899), 48; and Leslie, *Are We All Deceivers?*, 197, 296.

22 Children played unsupervised . . . : See Eliza Ripley, *Social Life in Old New Orleans* (New Orleans: Cornerstone Press [1912], 2012), 2–4.

23 Before she died, . . . : Rose E. Young, *The Record of the Leslie Woman Suffrage Commission, Inc., 1917–1929* (New York: The Leslie Woman Suffrage Commission, Inc., 1929), 9.

23 Her father might have reminisced . . . : Letter, The Estate of Frank Leslie, Supreme Court, 1917, vol. II, 399.

23 He liked to . . . : Ibid.

23 One of his "old-time . . .": For details of New Orleans domestic life see Ripley, *Social Life in Old New Orleans*, 39 and passim.

23 A Mr. Ogden, presumably . . . : Letter, The Estate of Frank Leslie, Supreme Court, 1917, vol. II, 326.

23 Girls from "good . . .": See Ripley, *Social Life in Old New Orleans*, 5–11, 12.

24 Very likely, his . . . : Quoted in Stern, *Purple Passage*, 12.

24 She paid "proper . . .": Letters, The Estate of Frank Leslie, Supreme Court, 1917, vol. II, 328, 357.

24 Later Miriam preened . . . : *Times-Picayune*, March 31, 1893, 3.

24 The educational advantages . . . : Letter to Carrie Wrenn, The Estate of Frank Leslie, Supreme Court, 1917, vol. II, n.d., 392.

25 Her family, she . . . : See *Alton Evening Telegraph*, October 17, 1891, 6.

25 Charles Dickens, a . . . : Charles Dickens, *American Notes*, ed. Patricia Ingham (New York: Penguin Books, [1842], 2004), 176–80.

25 But Cincinnati was . . . : For the official account of the Cincinnati period, see Stern, *Purple Passage*, 9–10; and Frances Trollope, *Domestic Manners of the Americans* (Mineola, NY: Dover Publications, [1832] 2003), 43–56.

25 Men, complained Dickens . . . : Dickens, *American Notes*, 176; John Clubbe, *Cincinnati Observed: Architecture and History* (Columbus: Ohio State University, 1992), 167; and Trollope, *Domestic Manners of the Americans*, 27.

25 "Shakespeare, Madame, is . . .": Quoted in Trollope, *Domestic Manners of the Americans*, 49.

25 At the same . . . : For more on the benighted condition of Blacks in Cincinnati, white destitution, and the Abolition uproar, see Joanne H. O'Connell, "Understanding Stephen Collins Foster, His World and Music," doctoral dissertation, d-scholarshipitt.edu/7365/1/OConnell_ETD2007.pdf. Especially see 129. Also see John C. Teaford, *Cities of the Heartland: The Rise and Fall of the Industrial Midwest* (Bloomington: Indiana University Press, 1993), 10; and Clubbe, *Cincinnati Observed*, 168.

25 Beneath Dickens's "private . . .": Dickens, *American Notes*, 180.

26 He lectured her . . . : Letter, The Estate of Frank Leslie, Supreme Court, 1917, vol. II, 329.

26 A "crime of . . .": Ibid.

26 As for those . . . : Ibid., 334.

26 "I am sure," . . . : Ibid.

26 She should also . . . : Ibid.

26 "These qualities are . . .": Ibid.

26 Enter classes, he . . . : Letter, ibid., 332.

26 The key was . . . : Ibid.

26 With his brother . . . : Letter, ibid., 368.

26 He "should have . . .": Letter, ibid., 372.

26 "There is no . . .": Ibid.

26 A note of . . . : Letters, ibid., 330, 334.

27 She was forced . . . : Letter, ibid., 364.

27 Noel, the hope . . . : Letter, ibid., 368.

27 Miriam's cousin, Charles . . . : Letter, ibid., 334.

27 In Miriam's version . . . : Quoted in Stern, *Purple Passage*, 11.

27 "The throng and . . .": *London Times* correspondent, quoted in Burrows and Wallace, *Gotham*, 653.

27 Sharpers and con artists . . . : George G. Foster, *New York by Gas-light and Other Urban Sketches*, ed. Stuart M. Blumin (Berkeley: University of California Press, [1850] 1990), 108.

27 Cabbies cried, "Carriage . . .": Ibid., 74.

28 Instead of the . . . : See *Valentine's Manual of the City of New York* (New York: Old Colony Press, 1918), 297.

28 With him were . . . : Population Schedules of the 7th Census of the United States, 1850, New York, Ward 14, reel 551. National Archives and Records Service, accessed April 3, 2017.

28 One contemporary source . . . : *Daily Territorial Enterprise*, July 14, 1878, 4.

28 If so, it . . . : The Estate of Frank Leslie, Supreme Court, 1917, vol. I, 29; and *Territorial Enterprise*, 4.

28 Charles couldn't bail . . . : See record of his string of debts, The Estate of Frank Leslie, Supreme Court, 1917, vol. I, 175–77.

28 With a cool . . . : Ibid., 428.

29 She now professed . . . : See "Brief Memoir of the Life of Gen. Paez," *New York Herald*, July 29, 1850, 1.

29 "A woman with . . .": Leslie, *Are We All Deceivers?*, 162.

29 It was a . . . : Karen Horney, quoted in *Handbook of Interpersonal Psychoanalysis*, eds. Marylou Lionells, John Fiscalinii, and Daniel B. Stern (New York: Routledge, 1995), 350.

29 Although apologists after . . . : For more on the design and squalor of the East Tenth Street home, see "East 10th Street Historic District Designers' Report," January 17, 2012, *New York City Landmarks Preservation Commission*, ed. Mary Beth Botts, media.villagepreservation.org/wp-content/uploads/2020/03/15123117/East-10th-Street-Historic-District-NYC-LPC-Designation-Report.pdf.

30 From nether Mexico . . . : Letter from Minatitlan, December 25, 1853, The Estate of Frank Leslie, Supreme Court, 1917, vol. II, 336.

30 "Think for a . . .": Quoted in Stern, *Purple Passage*, 11.

30 "To see you . . .": Quoted ibid., 12.

30 Little wonder she . . . : Leslie, *Are We All Deceivers?*, 26, 168; Mrs. Frank Leslie, *Rents in Our Robes* (Chicago: Clark & Co., 1888), 46.

30 Seamstresses, flower-makers, map-colorers . . . : Foster, *New York by Gas-light*, 175, 229.

30 Volunteer societies like . . . : See Barbara J. Berg, *The Remembered Gate: Origins of American Feminism, 1800–1860* (New York: Oxford University Press, 1978), 223–42.

30 An estimated fifty . . . : See Gilfoyle, *City of Eros*, 55–88; and Edward K. Spann, *The New Metropolis* (New York: Columbia University Press, 1981), 248.

30 Successful demimondaines with . . . : See Foster, *New York by Gas-light*, 92–100.

31 Investigative reporters, however . . . : The Chronicler, "From Puddle to Palace," *Town Topics*, March 28, 1886, 13, 14.

31 Everywhere "stories [were] . . .": *Territorial Enterprise*, 4.

31 Girls in big . . . : Leslie, *Are We All Deceivers?*, 138.

31 Her sympathies were . . . : "The Heroines of Chivalry," *Frank Leslie's Popular Monthly*, December 1895, 653; and Alexandre Dumas Jr., *The Demimonde: A Satire on Society*, trans. Mrs. E. G. Squier (Philadelphia: J. B. Lippincott, 1858), iii.

31 And whether she . . . : *Times-Democrat*, May 31, 1908, 34.

31 Putting identities on . . . : Self-created profiteers and social counterfeits proliferated during the runaway growth of cities, immigration, and incessant mobility. See Karen Halttunen, *Confidence Men and Painted Women: A Study of Middle-Class Culture in America* (New Haven: Yale University Press, 1982) for an excellent summary. The trickster motif in American literature dates from Simon Suggs in folklore ("It's good to be tricksy in a new land"), and includes Mark Twain's Duke and Dauphine in *Huckleberry Finn* and Herman Melville's *The Confidence Man*.

31 She quickly discarded . . . : Letter, The Estate of Frank Leslie, Supreme Court, 1917, vol. II, 334.

32 A Dr. Collyer on . . . : See Foster, *New York by Gas-light*, 78–83, 107.

32 Each night an . . . : See ibid., 95.

32 Early in the . . . : Letter, The Estate of Frank Leslie, Supreme Court, 1917 , vol. II, March 16, 1854, 377.

32 But, he teased . . . : Ibid., 378.

32 Be assured: she . . . : Ibid.

32 Susan, meanwhile, spoke . . . : Leslie, *Are We All Deceivers?*, 259.

32 Contrary to her father's . . . : Letter, The Estate of Frank Leslie, Supreme Court, 1917, vol. I, 334.

32 "Within the heart . . .": Quoted in "Mrs. Frank Leslie," *Detroit Free Press*, November 3, 1890, 3.

32 Inside, she met . . . : *Territorial Enterprise Extra*, 5.

33 This continued until . . . : The Estate of Frank Leslie, Supreme Court, 1917, vol. I, 258.

33 As of 1848 . . . : "Sex Offenses," www.tcpl.org/sites/default/files/content /archive/101-117_Law.pdf, 106–107.

33 He protested his . . . : Judgment Roll, The Estate of Frank Leslie, Supreme Court, 1917, vol. I, 46.

33 Besides, the sheriff . . . : Ibid., 45; and "Sex Offenses," www.tcpl.org/sites /default/files/content/archive/101-117_Law.pdf, 107.

33 Peacock recoiled and . . . : The Estate of Frank Leslie, Supreme Court, 1917, vol. I, 66.

33 The lady just . . . : Ibid., 69.

33 The night life . . . : Foster, *New York by Gas-light*, 174 and 175, passim.

33 When they reached . . . : The Estate of Frank Leslie, Supreme Court, 1917, vol. I, 65.

34 "Do you take . . .": Ibid., 71.

34 From then on . . . : Ibid.

34 Marriage in the 1850s . . . : Berg, *The Remembered Gate*, 91–94.

34 In the world of strangers . . . : See Halttunen, *Confidence Men and Painted Women*, 47.

34 Since Peacock couldn't . . . : www.tcpl.org/sites/default/files/content /archive/101-117_Law.pdf, accessed May 14, 2017.

34 A "miscellaneous assortment . . .": Quoted in Burrows and Wallace, *Gotham*, 774.

34 Two German sisters . . . : See full account ibid., 743.

35 Around Tompkins Square . . . : Ibid., 774.

35 In Brooklyn, the . . . : See ibid., 859. My great-grandmother Harriet Mason Stevens attended one of these auctions; see Frank G. Davis, *Bucknell Alumni News*, September 1947.

35 Miriam's "Creole" looks . . . : Quoted in Sharon Hartman Strom, *Fortune, Fame, and Desire: Promoting the Self in the Long Nineteenth Century* (New York: Rowman & Littlefield, 2016), 42.

35 After he left . . . : Ibid.

35 Rumor had it . . . : *Territorial Enterprise*, 5.

35 Crowds of visitors . . . : Burrows and Wallace, *Gotham*, 670.

36 Perhaps she contributed . . . : Quoted ibid., 670.

36 On March 6, 1856, . . . : *Territorial Enterprise*, 5.

36 The Brown, Hall, . . . : Letters, The Estate of Frank Leslie, Supreme Court, 1917, vol. I, 53.

36 About this time . . . : Quoted in Strom, *Fortune, Fame, and Desire*, 42.

36 "Desolate and hopeless," . . . : Letters, The Estate of Frank Leslie, Supreme Court, 1917, vol. II, 382 and 383.

36 "What are you . . .": Letter, Ibid., 385.

36 You keep a . . . : Ibid.

37 He was on . . . : Ibid.

37 A dramatic black-Irish . . . : Quoted in Bruce Seymour, *Lola Montez: A Life* (New Haven: Yale University Press, 1996), 42; and quoted in Ishbel Ross, *The Uncrowned Queen: Life of Lola Montez* (New York: Harper & Row, 1972), 89.

37 She was, wrote . . . : *Frazer's Magazine*, quoted in Ross, *The Uncrowned Queen*, 93.

38 She was more . . . : Quoted in Seymour, *Lola Montez*, 295.

38 Noel was soon . . . : Ross, *The Uncrowned Queen*, 257.

38 She had marked . . . : Letter, The Estate of Frank Leslie, Supreme Court, 1917, vol. II, 385.

38 Dumas alerted his . . . : Quoted in Ross, *The Uncrowned Queen*, 83.

39 On July 7, 1856 . . . : Seymour, *Lola Montez*, 349.

39 It was uncertain . . . : Ibid.

39 Hearses rumbled "unceasingly" . . . : *Brooklyn Eagle*, July 16, 1856, 2.

39 At the first . . . : Letter, The Estate of Frank Leslie, Supreme Court, 1917, vol. II, 386.

39 She was out of options . . . : Foster, *New York by Gas-light*, 70.

CHAPTER TWO

41 Grief, reported the papers . . . : *Chicago Tribune*, September 20, 1856, 2.

41 Shattered by the . . . : Ibid.

41 Broken and bereaved . . . : Bruce Seymour, *Lola Montez: A Life* (New Haven, CT: Yale University Press, 1996), 351.

42 The yellow fever . . . : *New York Times*, October 29, 1856, 1.

42 "Give us liberty . . .": *Richmond Dispatch*, November 28, 1856, 2.

42 "Woman is, in . . .": Ibid.

42 On October 20 . . . : *New York Times*, October 20, 1856, 8.

42 At the station . . . : Ibid.

42 The pay at . . . : Ibid.

42 The din of repaved . . . : See complaints in the newspaper, *New York Times*, September 12, 1856, 1.

43   The woman who . . . : Quoted in Ishbel Ross, *The Uncrowned Queen: Life of Lola Montez* (New York: Harper & Row, 1972), 125.

43   "I have killed . . .": *Daily Territorial Enterprise*, July 14, 1878, 5–6.

43   "Una cara tan . . .": Letter, February 27, 1855, The Estate of Frank Leslie, Supreme Court, 1917, vol. II, 385.

43   Lola transported the . . . : *New York Times*, January 26, 1857, 6.

44   With her charge . . . : Lola Montez, *The Arts of Beauty* (New York: Chatham House reprint, 1969), 35.

44   She then taught . . . : Ibid., 64.

44   Voice training followed . . . : Ibid., 70. She was turning Miriam into a model of Erving Goffman's theory of social prestige: a clever performance determines public reception and rank. See Erving Goffman, *The Presentation of Self in Everyday Life* (Garden City, NY: Doubleday, 1959), passim.

44   In addition, a . . . : "Autobiography," *Lectures of Lola Montez* (New York: Rudd & Carleton, n.d.), 15.

44   "I am a . . .": Quoted in Ross, *The Uncrowned Queen*, 310.

44   "I could give . . .": Quoted in Seymour, *Lola Montez*, 355.

45   The "sisters" opened . . . : Quoted in Stern, *Purple Passage: The Life of Mrs. Frank Leslie* (Norman: University of Oklahoma Press, 1953), 19.

45   "This," Jenny cries . . . : Edward Stirling, *Cabin Boy* (London: Nassau Steam Press, 18–), 21.

45   As expected, the . . . : *Frank Leslie's Illustrated Newspaper*, March 7, 1857, 212–13.

46   "The younger sister," . . . : Quoted in Seymour, *Lola Montez*, 356.

46   In 1855, illustrator . . . : Quoted in Sharon Hartman Strom, *Fortune, Fame, and Desire: Promoting the Self in the Long Nineteenth Century* (New York: Rowman & Littlefield, 2016), 42–43.

46   He was, noted . . . : *Territorial Enterprise*, 6.

46   But his presence . . . : *The Story of a Penitent: Lola Montez* (New York: Protestant Episcopal Society for the Promotion of Evangelical Knowledge, 1867), 12, 25.

46   When she caught . . . : *Territorial Enterprise*, 6.

46   Miriam kept the . . . : For evidence of this, see Strom, *Fortune, Fame, and Desire*, 48.

46   She hectors, pleads . . . : Tom Taylor, *Plot and Passion: A Drama in Three Acts* (New York: Robert M. Dewitt, n.d.), 12.

47   Cornered at last . . . : Ibid., 30.

47   The Washington *Evening* . . . : *Evening Star* (Washington, DC), June 30, 1857, 2; and quoted in Stern, 22.

47 Susan might well . . . : See Susan's anxiety about money at the time. Letter, May 26, 1857, Letters, The Estate of Frank Leslie, Supreme Court, 1917, vol. II, 341.

47 "My present purpose," . . . : Letter to Evert Duyckinck, September 5, 1854, quoted in Terry A. Barnhart, *Ephraim George Squier and the Development of American Anthropology* (Lincoln: University of Nebraska Press, 2005), 214.

47 But he was . . . : Mrs. Frank Leslie, *Are We All Deceivers? The Lover's Blue Book* (Chicago: Neely, 1893), 69–70.

47 By nature choleric . . . : Quoted in Strom, *Fortune, Fame, and Desire*, 8.

48 Novelist Anthony Trollope . . . : Anthony Trollope, *The Way We Live Now*, ed. Peter Merchant (London: Wordsworth Classics [1875], 2001), 67.

48 Although he championed . . . : Samuel A. Bard (Ephraim George Squier), *Waikna; or Adventures on the Mosquito Shore* (New York: Harper & Brothers, 1855), 59 and 19.

48 It was an open . . . : Quoted in Strom, *Fortune, Fame, and Desire*, 27.

48 Artist Sam Bard . . . : Squier, *Waikna*, 102.

48 He told them . . . : E. G. Squier, letter to parents, September 10, 1857, New-York Historical Society.

48 He "cordially dislike[d]" . . . : Ibid.

48 He had known . . . : Strom, *Fortune, Fame, and Desire*, 42.

49 Miriam lay closeted . . . : E. G. Squier, letter to parents, October 18, 1857, New-York Historical Society.

49 E. G., no friend . . . : See his comparison of "Women's Rights" to chattering macaws in *Waikna*, 89, and his defense of patriarchal rule: the exemplary Poyers have "a purely patriarchal organization, in which the authority of paternity and of age was recognized in the fullest degree," 297.

49 Confined to the . . . : See Catherine E. Beecher, *A Treatise on Domestic Economy for the use of Young Ladies of Home and at School*, especially "The Peculiar Responsibilities of American Women," 10.

49 "She who makes . . .": Isabella Beeton, *Mrs. Beeton's Book of Household Management* (Ex-Classics Project, [1859–1861], 2009), 78. Curiously, Miriam would later publish this book in America.

49 Polite society filled . . . : Quoted in Stern, *Purple Passage*, 27.

49 Miriam's mother conveniently . . . : Quoted ibid.

50 "Financially, affairs are . . .": E. G. Squier, letters to parents, October 15, 1857, and December 3, 1857, New-York Historical Society.

50 Given the alternative . . . : Quoted in Strom, *Fortune, Fame, and Desire*, 49.

50 She hired a . . . : See letter, May 26, 1857, The Estate of Frank Leslie, Supreme Court, 1917, vol. II, 340.

50 For practice, she . . . : Alexandre Dumas Jr., *The Demi-monde: A Satire on Society*, trans. Mrs. E. G. Squier (Philadelphia: J. B. Lippincott, 1858), 73.

50 "You should not . . .": Ibid., 110.

50 "We passed a . . .": E. G. Squier, letter to parents, December 26, 1857, New-York Historical Society.

50 Minnie "complain[ed]" and . . . : E. G. Squier, letter to parents, March 25, 1858, New-York Historical Society.

51 "Money is very . . .": E. G. Squier, letter to parents, May 28, 1858, New-York Historical Society.

51 E. G. alerted his . . . : E. G. Squier, letter to parents, September 6, 1858, New-York Historical Society.

51 If she did . . . : E. G. Squier, letter to parents, December 31, 1858, New-York Historical Society.

51 Miriam still "suffered . . .": E. G. Squier, letters to parents, December 31, 1858, and January 30, 1859, New-York Historical Society.

51 She took solace . . . : E. G. Squier, letter to parents, June 7, 1859, New-York Historical Society. Miriam believed pets were a palliative for women in "loveless marriages." See Leslie, *A Social Mirage*, 309; and Leslie, *Are We All Deceivers?*, 267, 268.

51 The *New York Herald* . . . : *New York Herald*, August 16, 1859, 5.

52 To "keep the pot . . .": E. G. Squier, letter to parents, April 23, 1859, New-York Historical Society.

52 Again, he reported . . . : E. G. Squier, letter to parents, June 8, 1859, New-York Historical Society.

52 This time Miriam . . . : Mrs. Frank Leslie, *Rents in Our Robes* (Chicago: Clark & Co., 1888), 127.

52 In August, E. G. . . . : Jon Sterngrass, *First Resorts: Pursuing Pleasure at Saratoga Springs, Newport and Coney Island* (Baltimore, MD: Johns Hopkins Press, 2001), 22 and passim.

52 He radiated exuberance . . . : Budd Leslie Gambee Jr., *Frank Leslie and His Illustrated Newspaper, 1855–1860* (Ann Arbor: University of Michigan Department of Library Science, 1964), 2.

52 But she may . . . : *Frank Leslie's Illustrated Newspaper*, August 27, 1859, 200.

52 "Her carriage is . . .": Ibid.

53 His governing principle . . . : Quoted in Richard F. Selcer, *Civil War America: 1850 to 1875* (New York: Facts on File, 2006), 289.

54 According to the . . . : The Estate of Frank Leslie, Supreme Court, 1917, vol. I, 132.

54 Miriam, once more . . . : E. G. Squier, letter to parents, February 10, 1860, New-York Historical Society.

54 In *A Trip to Cuba* . . . : Julia Ward Howe, *A Trip to Cuba* (Boston: Tichnor and Fields, 1860), 35 and 12.

54 She even "bore . . .": E. G. Squier, letter to parents, April 10, 1860, New-York Historical Society.

54 Amid throngs of . . . : See Howe, *A Trip to Cuba*, 146–48.

55 The place to . . . : Ibid., 99. See 100–10 for details.

55 Women were welcome . . . : Ibid., 106.

55 With her sharp . . . : Leslie, *Are We All Deceivers?*, 90; and *Daily Exchange*, December 7, 1860, 4.

55 Although E. G.'s colonization . . . : E. G.'s colonization proposal was revamped in Congress to promote Honduras as a settlement for freed American slaves. See also Senator Anthony's part in this, Strom, *Fortune, Fame, and Desire*, 50.

55 The parties split . . . : "No matter how hard *Leslie's* tried to 'balance' its coverage, the publication of pictures that portrayed sectional division undermined compromise," Joshua Brown, *Beyond the Lines: Pictorial Reporting, Everyday Life, and the Crisis of Gilded Age America* (Berkeley: University of California Press, 2002), 47.

56 Otherwise, warned his . . . : Quoted in Edwin G. Burrows and Mike Wallace, *Gotham: A History of New York City to 1898* (New York: Oxford, 1999), 865.

56 Frank Leslie positioned . . . : Quoted in Brown, *Beyond the Lines*, 47.

56 "We must go," . . . : E. G. Squier, letter to parents, January 25, 1861, New-York Historical Society.

56 When Lincoln entered . . . : *Cincinnati Daily Press*, March 8, 1861, 1.

56 She went "through . . .": E. G. Squier, letter to parents, March 11, 1861, New-York Historical Society.

57 His account of . . . : *Frank Leslie's Illustrated Newspaper*, March 23, 1861, 285.

57 He pictured her . . . : Ibid.

57 Although diagnosis was . . . : E. G. had a special horror of syphilis, which he called "this disgusting disease" caused by "unrestrained licentious intercourse." See Bard, *Waikna*, 68, 244.

57 By 1861, the . . . : E. G. Squier, letter to parents, April 30, 1861, New-York Historical Society.

58 The choice between . . . : Quoted in Gambee, *Frank Leslie*, 2; and E. G. Squier, letter to parents, March 30, 1862, New-York Historical Society.

58 The next morning . . . : Quoted in Stern, *Purple Passage*, 36.

58 He placed a . . . : *Frank Leslie's Illustrated Newspaper*, February 22, 1862, 209, 214.

58 He paid E. G.'s . . . : E. G. Squier, letter to parents, April 14, 1862, New-York Historical Society.

58 Five months after . . . : Brown, *Beyond the Lines*, 48.

58 E.G.'s health had . . . : E. G. Squier, letter to parents, January 15, 1863, New-York Historical Society.

59 She eliminated dismal . . . : This raises the question of Miriam's personal response. She had been case-hardened by life and was blinkered in her passion to succeed. But how callous was she really toward the suffering? Her Southern kinswomen at this point sustained terrible losses and were lucky to own a tattered petticoat or pair of shoes. See stories of these women and the privations they endured (including shoes to wear), especially the account of Sarah Morgan in Miriam's home state, in *Heroines of Dixie: Spring of High Hopes*, ed. Katherine M. Jones (St. Simons Island, GA: Mockingbird Books, 1955), 145, 161, and passim.

59 A crass choice . . . : Quoted in *Mary Chestnut's Civil War*, ed. C. Vann Woodward (New Haven: Yale University Press, 1981), 581.

59 They wanted to . . . : *Frank Leslie's Lady's Magazine*, February, 1863, 82.

59 Miriam responded by . . . : E. G. Squier, letter to parents, March 11, 1863, New-York Historical Society.

59 Neither "would have . . .": E. G. Squier letter to parents, October 29, 1863, New-York Historical Society.

59 After a grueling . . . : Ephraim George Squier, *Peru Illustrated: Or Incidents of Travel and Exploration in the Land of the Incas* (New York: Hurst & Co., 1877), 31 and 29.

59 Shrouded in a . . . : Ibid., 46.

60 "Under a brisk . . .": "The Ladies of Lima," *Chimney Corner*, February 1865, 12. Interestingly, she lifts this passage and the whole description of houses in Lima verbatim from E. G.'s *Peru*, 42.

60 When she arrived . . . : Quoted in Stern, *Purple Passage*, 42.

60 "Scarcely ever free . . .": E. G. Squier, letter to parents, December 13, 1863, New-York Historical Society.

60 There she received . . . : Miriam Squier, letter to E. G. Squier, April 12, 1864, New-York Historical Society.

60 She teased him . . . : Ibid.

60 When she recovered . . . : "The Ladies of Lima," 13.

60 The Limeñas, noted . . . : Ibid.

60 "Poor girl," he . . . : E. G. Squier, letter to parents, December 13, 1863, New-York Historical Society.

61 "Mrs. S-r, just . . .": *Frank Leslie's Illustrated Newspaper*, September 17, 1864: 403.

61 By December 1864 . . . : See Brown, *Beyond the Lines*, 52; and *Witness to the War: First-Hand Accounts from Frank Leslie's Illustrated Newspaper*, ed. Stuart A. Murray (New York: HarperCollins, 2006), passim and 210.

61 Why, she needled . . . : Miriam Squier, letter to E. G. Squier, April 12, 1864, New-York Historical Society.

61 She doubted "[their] . . .": Ibid.

62 "If [a man] . . .": Ibid.

62 The arrangement on . . . : Ibid.

62 He brought a . . . : Strom, *Fortune, Fame, and Desire*, 53.

62 Frank kept Miriam . . . : Miriam Squier, letter to E. G. Squier, April 12, 1864, New-York Historical Society.

62 The country was . . . : Quoted in Stern, *Purple Passage*, 45; and *New York Times*, November 16, 1865, 1.

62 Miriam's *Frank Leslie's* . . . : *New York Times*, November 16, 1865, 1.

63 Behind the persona . . . : *Frank Leslie's Chimney Corner*, June 3, 1865, 10.

63 In letters to . . . : See Linda Frost, "Where Women May Speak for Themselves: Miriam Frank Leslie's 'Ladies' Conversazione,'" *Blue Pencils: Hidden Hands*, eds. Sharon M. Harvest and Ellen Gruber Garvey (Boston: Northeastern Press, 2004), 60–79.

63 "M.A.L." wrote that . . . : *Chimney Corner*, September 2, 1865, 219; and see Viola Treadwell's letter, July 1, 1865, 75.

63 "Mr. Editor" responded . . . : *Chimney Corner*, July 15, 1865, 155.

63 "That is all . . .": Ibid.

63 No small achievement . . . : See Matthew Goodman, *Eighty Days: Nellie Bly and Elizabeth Bisland's History-Making Race Around the World* (New York: Ballantine Books, 2013), 8–13.

63 He apprehended Juan . . . : E. G. Squier, letter to brother Frank, February 20, 1866, New-York Historical Society.

64 Then, in a . . . : E. G. Squier, letter to brother Frank, October 5, 1866, New-York Historical Society.

64 Moreover, his symptoms . . . : E. G. Squier, letter to brother Frank, September 12, 1866, New-York Historical Society.

64 The year 1866 . . . : *Valentine's Manual of Old New York*, ed. Henry Collins Brown (New York: Valentine's Manual, 1922), 2.

64 "Minnie," he noted . . . : E. G. Squier, letter to parents, February 19, 1867, New-York Historical Society.

64 He seems to . . . : Ibid.

65 Water poured over . . . : E. G. Squier, "Two Weeks in a British Bastille," New-York Historical Society.

65 In his misery . . . : Ibid.

65 When the constable . . . : Ibid.

65 Leslie appeared to . . . : Ibid.

65 Nor could Miriam . . . : Frank Leslie, *Appellant v. Miriam F. Leslie, and Others, Respondents. New York Court of Appeals*, vol. 13 (1883), 877.

65 Frank's sister, Mrs. Mary Ann Jubber . . . : Ibid., 878.

65 She witnessed their . . . : Ibid.

66 "That will keep . . .": Ibid., 879.

66 "Yes," replied Miriam . . . : Ibid.

66 In his collected . . . : *New York Daily Herald*, April 1, 1867, 4.

66 He thanked Miriam . . . : E. G. Squier, letter to Miriam Squier, March 8, 1867, New-York Historical Society.

66 Miriam riposted on . . . : Miriam Squier, letter to E. G. Squier, March 22, 1867; Frank Leslie, *Appellant*, vol. 13 (1883), 359–360.

66 She heard "loud . . .": Ibid., 879.

66 Once in Paris . . . : E. G. Squier, letter to brother Frank, March 28, 1867, New-York Historical Society.

66 A profligate spender . . . : Leslie, *Are We All Deceivers?*, 297.

67 A vast amusement . . . : It was as if, said one, "a gigantic fairy [had] jumbled and dumped all his theatrical sets," Victor Fournel, *Correspondent*, April 1867, n.

67 But like many Americans . . . : See Mark Twain's reaction to the Fair in *Innocents Abroad* (New York: Bantam [1869], 1964), 73–76.

67 "The Great Exhibition," . . . : "Letter from Paris," *Frank Leslie's Illustrated Newspaper*, July 13, 1867, 259. The American entry in the fine arts left him equally cold. Whistler's *White Girl*, he sneered (with the aesthetic myopia of his peers), was "horrible," painted with a "whitewash broom in one hand and a tar-brush in the other," ibid.

67 Paris, he concluded . . . : Ibid.

68 Leslie had been . . . : Ibid.; and E. G. Squier, letter to Mr. Powell, June 11, 1867, New-York Historical Society.

68 E. G. had to . . . : E. G. Squier, letter to parents, June 11, 1867, New-York Historical Society.

68 "All the people . . .": *New York Times*, June 25, 1867, 5.

68 Guests descended a . . . : Ibid.

68 Hidden orchestras serenaded . . . : *Frank Leslie's Illustrated Newspaper*, July 13, 1867, 258.

68 "Only the pen . . .": M. Marx, quoted in Edward Legge, *The Comedy and Tragedy of the Second Empire: Paris Society in the Sixties* (New York: Harper & Bro., 1911), 76.

68 The next day . . . : E. G. Squier, letter to Mr. Powell, June 11, 1867, New-York Historical Society.

68 As they toured . . . : *Appellant v. Miriam F. Leslie*, vol. 13 (1883), 881.

68 At the Hotel . . . : Ibid., 880.

68 In Rome they . . . : Ibid.

69 "Here they are," . . . : Ibid.

69 When Mrs. Jubber . . . : Ibid., 881.

69 Pity, she said . . . : Ibid.

69 The subject was . . . : Leslie, *Are We All Deceivers?*, 114.

CHAPTER THREE

71 "Domestic Treachery": Mrs. Frank Leslie, *Are We All Deceivers? The Lover's Blue Book* (Chicago: Neely, 1893), 288.

72 "Wealth and poverty," . . . : "Along the Hudson River at New York," *Atlantic Monthly*, July, 1868, 4.

72 After the "established . . .": Henry James, "Daisy Miller," *Daisy Miller and Washington Square*, intro. Jennie A. Kassanoff (New York: Barnes & Noble Classics, [1879] 2004), 76; see Joe O'Connell, "Delmonico Steak: A Mystery Solved," *Steak Perfection*, November 2003, www.steakperfection.com /delmonico/Steak.html.

73 Cornelius Vanderbilt, the . . . : Quoted in Matthew Josephson, *The Robber Barons* (New York: Harcourt, 1962), 15.

74 The extent was . . . : Ted Curtis Smythe, *The Gilded Age Press: 1865–1900* (Westport, CT: Praeger, 2003), 13, and see 10–13, 18–19.

76 Mme. Demorest, regarded . . . : Edwin G. Burrows and Mike Wallace, *Gotham: A History of New York City to 1898* (New York: Oxford, 1999), 960.

76 The February 1868 . . . : *Intelligencer* (Anderson, SC), February 5, 1868, 2.

76 It also carried . . . : *Frank Leslie's Illustrated Newspaper*, March 26, 1870, 19.

77 He returned the . . . : See account in *Detroit Free Press*, July 21, 1868, 3.

77 "I am afraid," . . . : *Philadelphia Evening Telegraph*, August 18, 1869, 5.

77 Miriam could not . . . : *Buffalo Commercial*, August 5, 1868, 1.

78 The ten-day train . . . : Quoted in Stansfer, "E. G. Squier and HIRP," *Hispanic Historic Review*, February 1966, 26.

78 For starters, he . . . : David Dixon Porter, letter to E. G. Squier, July 13, 1869, New-York Historical Society.

78 E. G. settled instead . . . : See *New York Daily Herald*, April 18, 1870: 6. Squier biographies traditionally assume he played an important role in Central American affairs at the time, as Honduran minster resident and chargé d'affaires in Washington.

78 He started . . . : David Dixon Porter, letter to E. G. Squier, July 13, 1869, New-York Historical Society.

79 "The changes in . . .": E. G. Squier, letter to parents, January 12, 1869, New-York Historical Society.

79 For practical purposes . . . : *Deceivers*, 205. On the luxury of hotels and of not "having a kitchen cabinet to fight today," see Mrs. Frank Leslie, *Rents in Our Robes* (Chicago: Clark & Co., 1888), 90.

80 She enriched the . . . : *Chimney Corner*, June 1, 1867, 10.

80 She brightened the . . . : *Intelligencer* (Anderson, SC), February 5, 1868, 2.

80 She made it . . . : See *Frank Leslie's Lady's Magazine*, July 1868, 23.

80 A novice could . . . : Ibid., March 1869, 172–73.

80 An evangelist of . . . : Ibid., April 1869, 240.

81 Columns advised women . . . : Ibid., August 1869, 105.

81 Secreted in squibs . . . : Ibid., January 1869, 75.

82 Her platform raised . . . : See Victoria Woodhull, "A Speech on the Principles of Social Freedom," *The Victoria Woodhull Reader*, ed. Madeleine B. Stern (Weston, MA: M & S Press, 1974), 23.

82 Mary Louise Booth published . . . : *Harper's Bazar*, June 12, 1869, 379.

82 A patriarchal diehard . . . : See Joshua Brown, *Beyond the Lines: Pictorial Reporting, Everyday Life, and the Crisis of Gilded Age America* (Berkeley: University of California Press, 2002), 104–12, for a summary of Leslie's treatment of women in the *Illustrated Newspaper*.

82 He despised Sorosis . . . : *Frank Leslie's Illustrated Newspaper*, March 16, 1872, 1.

82 The "modern Amazon," . . . : Ibid.

82 Better, in Miriam's . . . : Leslie, *Rents in Our Robes*, 111.

83 They sailed on . . . : This was the preferred liner of the Theodore Roosevelt family. The Scotia turns up in *Twenty Thousand Leagues under the Sea*, where it resists collision with its watertight compartments, and in *The Legend Begins*, Sherlock Holmes's ship of choice.

83 Instead of languishing . . . : E. G. Squier, letter to brother Frank, May 26, 1870, New-York Historical Society.

83 E. G. called her . . . : Ibid.

83 Twice Mrs. Jubber entered . . . : Frank Leslie, *Appellant v. Miriam F. Leslie, and Others, Respondents*, New York Court of Appeals, vol. 13 (1883), 833.

84 He had the . . . : Ibid.

84 She distinctly heard . . . : Ibid., 834.

84 Soon after he . . . : E. G. Squier, letters to brother Frank Squier, May 26, 1870 and July 4, 1870, New-York Historical Society.

84 She fatigued easily . . . : E. G. Squier, letter to brother Frank, June 8, 1870, New-York Historical Society.

85 Prosper Merimée compared . . . : Quoted in Allistair Horne, *La Belle France* (New York: Vintage/Random House, 2006), 268–69.

85 Within its gilded . . . : Quoted in Pascal Boissel, *Grand-Hôtel Café de la Paix: Two Centuries of Parisian Life*, trans. George Mutch (Italy: Éditions Italiques, 2004), 65.

85 "I could well . . ." : Ibid.

86 At the finale . . . : Jacques Offenbach, *La Grande-Duchesse de Gérolstein*, www.opera-arias.com/offenbach/grande-duchesse-gerolstein/libretto/.

86 From his box . . . : Quoted in Rupert Christensen, *Paris Babylon* (New York: Viking, 1994), 70.

86 Miriam's health foundered . . . : E. G. Squier, letter to brother Frank, June 16, 1870, New-York Historical Society.

86 He was "much . . .": Ibid.

86 When E. G. and . . . : For a description, see *Frank Leslie's Illustrated Newspaper,* September 10, 1870.

86 As the guest . . . : *Frank Leslie's Illustrated Newspaper*, July 30, 1870.

87 By June 28, the . . . : Ibid.

87 E. G. felt abused . . . : E. G. Squier, letter to brother Frank, June 16, 1870, New-York Historical Society.

87 She "detest[s] England," . . . : E. G. Squier, letter to brother Frank, August 18, 1870, New-York Historical Society.

87 "We're in a . . .": Quoted in Horne, *La Belle France*, 272.

87 Yet "despite the . . .": E. G. Squier, letter to brother Frank, September 9, 1870, New-York Historical Society.

88 In spite of . . . : E. G. Squier, letter to parents, March 1, 1871, New-York Historical Society.

88 E. G.'s income from . . . : E. G. Squier, letter to brother Frank, August 1, 1870, New-York Historical Society.

88 His friend Admiral . . . : David Dixon Porter, letter to E. G. Squier, October 12, 1870, New-York Historical Society.

88 But she prepared . . . : E. G. Squier, letter to brother Frank, October 2, 1870, New-York Historical Society.

88 Critics applauded her . . . : *Frank Leslie's Illustrated Newspaper*, March 16, 1871, 2.

88 Miriam's friend Jane . . . : "Frank Leslie as a Friend," *Frank Leslie's Lady's Journal*, February 7, 1880, 210.

88 Miriam targeted a . . . : *Once a Week*, March 4, 1871, 1.

89 Under oath, E. G . . . : *Leslie v. Leslie*, Frank Leslie against Sarah Ann Leslie, 1871, New York Common Pleas, Hall of Records, New York City.

89 Miriam testified in . . . : Ibid.

89 "Let some such . . .": Quoted in Christensen, 333.

90 Such feminine outrages . . . : *Frank Leslie's Illustrated Newspaper*, July 8, 1871, 267.

90 As the *Illustrated* . . . : Ibid., July 30, 1870, 306; and James D. McCabe, *Lights and Shadows of New York* (Philadelphia: National Publishing Company, 1872), 685.

90 Forty thousand poor . . . : See McCabe, 687.

90 To a nervous . . . : Burrows and Wallace, *Gotham*, 1008.

91 He was a . . . : In a cartoon of the Tammany Ring, his cronies assail Frank Leslie "what pretends to be a friend of ours." *New York Times*, July 19, 1872, 1.

91 At a festive . . . : "The Voice of the Clam," June 17, 1871, New-York Historical Society.

91 Afterward, Leslie planted . . . : "Sketch of a Great Publishing House," *Springfield Journal*, July 8, 1871, 4.

91 She renamed the . . . : Business Statement, *Frank Leslie's Lady's Journal*, February 1880, 210.

91 Her ingenue learned . . . : *Frank Leslie's Lady's Journal*, November 25, 1871, 24 and 28.

91 "This is our . . .": Ibid., 26.

92 And the "Gossip" . . . : *Frank Leslie's Lady's Journal*, March 28, 1874, 307.

92 At the same . . . : See Robert Tomes, *The Bazar Book of Decorum* (New York: Harper & Brothers, 1870), 171.

92 She had massive. . . : See McCabe, 142 and 144 and passim; and George Ellington, *The Women of New York* (New York: New York Book Co., 1869), 28–41.

92 With the *Journal's* . . . : *Frank Leslie's Lady's Journal*, November 25, 1871, 17.

92 "A lady," pronounced . . . : Ibid., May 18, 1872, 1.

92 Deftly shifting the . . . : Ibid., September 27, 1873, 305.

92 At one level . . . : Ibid., November 25, 1871, 19.

93 Like whaling heiress . . . : For more about the fascinating Hetty Green, see Janet Wallach, *The Richest Woman in America: Hetty Green in the Gilded Age* (New York: Anchor Books, 2012).

93 Exploiting this to . . . : *Frank Leslie's Lady's Journal*, December 6, 1873, 50. Also see editorials November 25, 1875, 19; and July 4, 1874, 114. A few years later Miriam returned to this theme in *Rents in Our Robes* and

deplored the state of daughters of the new rich who are "not taught to work" or manage their affairs, 12.

93 "How few marriages . . .": *Frank Leslie's Lady's Journal*, July 4, 1874, 114.

93 Every woman, she . . . : *Frank Leslie's Lady's Journal*, May 18, 1872, 2.

93 E. G. had become . . . : See E. G. Squier, letter to parents, October 11, 1871, New-York Historical Society.

94 One terrifying night . . . : Quoted in Madeleine Stern, *Purple Passage: The Life of Mrs. Frank Leslie* (Norman: University of Oklahoma Press, 1953), 63; and *Appellant v. Miriam F. Leslie*, 1883, vol. 13, 109.

94 He'd recognized Dewitt . . . : For an account of how Hitchcock remained a "journeyman artist in New York rather than an immortalized one" due to E. G.'s betrayal, see Sharon Hartman Strom, *Fortune, Fame, and Desire: Promoting the Self in the Long Nineteenth Century* (New York: Rowman & Littlefield, 2016), 55.

94 But E. G. had . . . : *Territorial Enterprise*, 8.

94 Prostitution had become . . . : See Ellington, *Women of New York*, 264.

94 A rouged matron . . . : I am indebted to George Ellington's detailed account of one of these visits in *Women of New York*, 197–201.

95 The artists testified . . . : Quoted in Stern, *Purple Passage*, 64; and see Squier v. Squire, Miriam Florence Squier against Ephraim George Squier, Superior Court of the City of New York, Divorce Records, vol. 35, 164–84.

95 "Mrs. Squier tells . . .": Douglas Campbell, letter to E. G. Squier, April 25, 1873, New-York Historical Society.

95 Humiliated and livid . . . : E. G. Squier, letter to Douglas Campbell, June 5, 1873, New-York Historical Society.

96 He had "surrendered . . .": Ibid.

96 The affair, he . . . : Ibid.

96 "My mouth shall . . .": Ibid.

CHAPTER FOUR

97 "The Grand Seigneur . . ." : Quoted in Joshua Brown, *Beyond the Lines: Pictorial Reporting, Everyday Life, and the Crisis of Gilded Age America* (Berkeley: University of California Press, 2002), 151.

97 With the last . . . : *Wheeling Daily Intelligencer* (West Virginia), August 15, 1874, 1.

97 Comstock, the purity . . . : Quoted in Edwin G. Burrows and Mike Wallace, *Gotham: A History of New York City to 1898* (New York: Oxford, 1999), 1015.

98 Congress appointed him . . . : See ibid., 1016, 1017; and Margaret A. Blanchard, "The American Urge to Censor: Freedom of Express vs. the Desire to Sanitize," *William and Mary Review*, vol. 33, 1992, 748.

98 Finally in mid-January . . . : Quoted in Joshua Brown, "*The Days' Doings*: The Gilded Age in the Profane Pictorial Press," reprinted paper from the American Studies Association Annual Meeting, October 17, 2003, josh-brownnyc.com/daysdoings/index.htm.

98 The women of . . . : *National Republican*, January 13, 1873: 4; and *Knoxville Daily Chronicle*, July 21, 1872, 2.

98 In his notebook . . . : Brown, "*Days' Doings.*"

98 Armed with warrants . . . : Quoted in Milton Rugoff, *Prudery and Passion* (New York: W. W. Norton, 1971), 125.

99 "The epidemic of . . .": George Templeton Strong, "October 27, 1873," *The Diary of George Templeton Strong*, Allan Nevins and Milton Halsey Thomas, eds. (Seattle: University of Washington Press, 1952), 396.

99 One broker called . . . : Quoted in Burrows and Wallace, *Gotham*, 1021.

99 A "mad terror" . . . : *Nation*, quoted in Michael A. Bellesiles, *1877: America's Year of Living Violently* (New York: The New Press, 2010), 4.

99 "The storm, which . . .": *Frank Leslie's Illustrated Newspaper*, October 11, 1873, 70.

100 Frank paid her . . . : See John Oller, *American Queen* (New York: Da Capo Press, 2014) for the fate of Miriam's contemporary, Kate Chase Sprague, who divorced her husband and ended up isolated and poor in a dilapidated farm selling eggs from door to door.

100 Miriam later recalled . . . : "Egotistic Frank Leslie," *Indianapolis Sentinel*, November 7, 1890, 4.

100 To be sure . . . : *Wheeling Intelligencer*, September 15, 1874, 1.

100 They refurbished the . . . : *Detroit Free Press*, November 3, 1890, 3.

100 They embarked on . . . : *Territorial Enterprise* Extra, July 14, 1878, 9.

100 Newspapers attributed his . . . : See *Buffalo Daily Courier*, August 28, 1874, 1; *Brooklyn Union* (New York), August 19, 1874, 2; and *Democrat and Chronicle* (Rochester, NY), August 24, 1874, 3.

101 And wherever she . . . : Mrs. Frank Leslie, *Rents in Our Robes* (Chicago: Clark & Co., 1888).

101 "All or most . . .": Mrs. Frank Leslie, *Are We All Deceivers? The Lover's Blue Book* (Chicago: Neely, 1893), 79.

101 "More money was . . .": *Territorial*, 9.

101 Wherever they "obtain[ed] . . .": Ibid.

102 "We knew," snooted . . . : Ward McAllister, *Society As I Have Found It* (Cassell, 1890), 217.

103 Finally Miriam and . . . : *Territorial*, 9.

103 The "high-toned" met . . . : Ibid.

103 Throughout, the Leslies . . . : *Town Topics*, March 28, 1886, 14.

103 Miriam would harbor . . . : Leslie, *Are We All Deceivers?*, 76, 81.

104 The pauper/tramp, argued . . . : *Frank Leslie's Illustrated Newspaper*, August 5, 1876: 354–355. See also "A Villainous Tramp Repulsed by a Plucky Woman," in his *The Days' Doings*, June 12, 1875, 9.

104 Frank's own coachman . . . : See *New York Daily Herald*, February 12, 1874, 4.

104 He repaved the . . . : *New York Herald*, July 13, 1874, 3.

104 The maroon and . . . : See ibid.; and *Grange Advance*, October 7, 1874: 10.

104 After two seasons . . . : Quoted Joaquin Miller in Stern, *Purple Passage*, 74.

104 A journalist sent . . . : *Cincinnati Enquirer*, August 18, 1877, 5.

105 Joaquin Miller is . . . : M. M. Marberry, *Splendid Poseur: Joaquin Miller— American Poet* (New York, Thomas Y. Crowell, 1953), 121.

106 "It helps sell . . .": Quoted in Frances and McGovern, eds., "Joaquin Miller, The Poet of the Sierras," *Literary Traveler*, February 1, 2000, www .literarytraveler.com/articles/joaquin-miller-the-poet-of-the-sierras/.

106 Joaquin always called . . . : "Mrs. Frank Leslie," *Golden Era*, May, 1887, 181–82.

106 In Joaquin's version . . . : Juanita J. Miller, *My Father: C. H. Joaquin Miller* (Oakland, CA: Tooley-Towne, 1941), 90.

107 The Byronic artist/hero . . . : Joaquin Miller, *The One Fair Woman* (New York: G. W. Dillingham, 1876), 490.

107 She is his . . . : Ibid., 82, 403.

107 Thou shalt walk . . . : *Frank Leslie's Illustrated Newspaper*, May 6, 1876, 142.

107 After six months . . . : Leslie, *Are We All Deceivers?*, 64; and see Leslie, *Rents in Our Robes*, 27.

107–108 Some women, though . . . : Leslie, *Rents in Our Robes*, 49; and *Ladies' Home Journal*, May, 1890, 90.

108 They want a . . . : Leslie, *Rents in Our Robes*, 46.

108 Nothing, she must . . . : Leslie, *Rents in Our Robes*, 22.

108 He was roughly . . . : Leslie, *Are We All Deceivers?*, 45–46, 52, 24, 60.

108 "The handsome man," . . . : Ibid.

108 He serialized Joaquin's . . . : *Frank Leslie's Illustrated Newspaper*, February 12, 1876, 362.

108 Joaquin who had . . . : Quoted in Stern, *Purple Passage*, 74.

110 His plump Sicilian . . . : Roderick J. Barman, *Citizen Emperor: Pedro II and the Making of Brazil 1875–1891* (Stanford, CA: Stanford University Press, 1999), 128.

110 Ahead of them, . . . : The single tribute to African Americans at the Exposition was the statue by Italian Francesco Pezzica, which offered a mordent

commentary on the real status of Blacks at the fair. None were included in construction crews, despite 70 percent Black unemployment in Philadelphia. Frederick Douglass was refused his designated place on the platform until Roscoe Conkling intervened.

111 They arrived by . . . : *Buffalo Commercial*, June 23, 1876, 2; and *Times* (Philadelphia), July 28, 1876, 2.

111 Bedizened in chaps . . . : *Frank Leslie's Historical Register of the United States Centennial Exhibition of 1876*, ed. Frank G. Norton (New York: Frank Leslie's Publishing House, 1877, 126 and 128.

111 Later, Dom Pedro thanked . . . : Quoted in *Times* (Philadelphia), July 28, 1876, 2.

111 "Good taste," the . . . : Quoted in Barman, *Citizen Emperor*, 279.

111 The depression had . . . : John Leng, *America in 1876* (England: Dundee Advertiser, 1877), 318.

112 Frank Leslie counted among . . . : See *Frank Leslie's Illustrated Newspaper*, July 15, 1876, 301 for the engraving.

113 "This lady," wrote . . . : *Cincinnati Enquirer*, October 1, 1876, 10.

113 Her hair, he . . . : Ibid.

113 The Centennial, he . . . : Quoted in Bellesiles, *1877*, 18.

113 Editors routinely received . . . : "Journalists," Leslie wrote, "are undoubtedly paid for party work." He then argues that stump speakers, even preachers, indulge in the same practice. See *Frank Leslie's Illustrated Newspaper*, July 8, 1876, 282.

113 The conflict centered . . . : Quoted in Bellesiles *1877*, 40.

114 The losers in . . . : Tilden was the Rothchild's attorney—on the side of money interests; Hayes, "the bank owner's dummy." Quoted in Bellesiles, *1877*, 20. Both candidates favored an end to Reconstruction and removal of federal troops, the only protection against racist terrorism.

114 The national "fit . . .": "Encouraging Business Prospects," *Frank Leslie's Illustrated Newspaper*, March 3, 1877, 418.

115 Onboard they found . . . : Mrs. Frank Leslie, *California: a Pleasure Trip from Gotham to the Golden Gate* (NY: G. W. Carleton & Co. Publishers, 1877), 19.

115 "Anarchy," stated the . . . : Quoted in Robert V. Bruce, *1877: Year of Violence* (New York: Bobbs-Merrill, 1959, reprint Chicago: Ivan R. Dee, 1989), 33.

115 She had put . . . : Leslie, *Are We All Deceivers?*, 99.

115 She would enjoy . . . : Leslie, *California: a Pleasure Trip*, title.

115 She sank into . . . : Ibid., 19.

115 Although the city . . . : Ibid., 26, 30, 32, 33.

115 The train resembled . . . : Ibid., 35.

115 The Ute Pass . . . : Ibid., 58, 59, 65.

116 The "dirty and . . .": Ibid., 275.

116 "All we wanted . . .": Quoted in Bellesiles, *1877*, 72.

116 The rallying cry . . . : Quoted ibid., 67.

116 At the Salt . . . : Leslie, *California*, 82.

116 He was a . . . : Ibid., 97.

116 When he attempted . . . : Ibid., 97.

116 "I'm sure not," . . . : Ibid.

116 She pressed on . . . : Ibid.

117 He cast her . . . : Ibid.

117 From Utah, the . . . : Ibid., 105.

117 Profiteer William Sharon won . . . : Ibid., 133.

117 Thirty guests sat . . . : Ibid., 121.

117 Two other San Francisco . . . : Ibid., 182.

118 She visited the . . . : Ibid., 139, 141.

118 She watched pigtailed . . . : Ibid., 149.

118 "The poor creatures," . . . : Ibid., 165.

118 In a rare . . . : Ibid., 145.

118 En route Miriam . . . : Ibid., 201.

119 The place, she . . . : Ibid., 277.

119 Nothing in sight . . . : Ibid., 278.

119 The book appeared . . . : *Hartford Courant*, December 19, 1877, 2; and *Sun*, April 17, 1878, 2.

120 There's evidence novelist . . . : Quoted in Stern, 234–35. She acknowledges that at the least Austin "helped Mrs. Leslie with the book." Inside Jane's copy of *California,* her daughter crossed out the author's name and wrote: "She did *not*! My Mother wrote it *all*! From a few very poor, *very* poor notes of Mrs. Leslie's."

120 Though he decried . . . : Quoted in Brown, *Beyond the Lines*, 160.

121 Somehow she wheedled . . . : *Frank Leslie's Illustrated Newspaper,* May 4, 1878, 147.

121 Again she assumed . . . : Ibid.

121 The Spanish moss . . . : Ibid.

121 They, too, would . . . : *Frank Leslie's Illustrated Newspaper,* June 29, 1878, 288 and 290.

122 New York could never . . . : *Frank Leslie's Popular Monthly,* August, 1878, 550.

122 Here people treated . . . : Ibid.

122 At Las Cañas, Don . . . : Ibid., 419.

122 Miriam observed children . . . : Ibid., 423 and 424.

122 A "negress" ladled . . . : Ibid., 423.

122 If "all slaves . . .": Ibid.

122 But as she . . . : Ibid., 418.

122 All the while . . . : Ibid., 422.

123 Boys in segregated . . . : See Ibid., 547.

123 "A prison," Miriam . . . : Ibid., 552.

123 A fearsome "negress" . . . : Ibid. 555.

123 The "milder maniacs" . . . : Ibid., 556.

123 Then she and her . . . : Ibid, 559.

CHAPTER FIVE

125 "A Bitter Pill": Quoted in "Frank Leslie's Pluck," *San Francisco Chronicle*, January 14, 1892, 3.

125 When Miriam boarded . . . : *Frank Leslie's Illustrated Newspaper*, May 4, 1878, 147.

125 After "quite a scuffle," . . . : *Inter Ocean* (Chicago), January 31, 1878, 4.

126 But in August . . . : See "Sharp Practice and Libel," *Frank Leslie's Illustrated Newspaper*, September 8, 1877, 3.

127 Anti-vice czar . . . : "The Wickedest Woman in New York," *Leavenworth Daily Commercial* (Kansas), November 6, 1868, 1.

127 Throughout *California: A* . . . : Mrs. Leslie, *California*, 278; and *Frank Leslie's Illustrated Newspaper*, April 27, 1878, 125.

127 Miriam had forgotten . . . : E. G. Squier, letter to Douglas Campbell, June 5, 1873, New-York Historical Society.

128 And Virginia City . . . : Mrs. Frank Leslie, *California: a Pleasure Trip from Gotham to the Golden Gate* (NY: G. W. Carleton & Co. Publishers, 1877), 277, 278, 280.

128 Rollin M. Daggett, editor of . . . : Quoted in Madeleine Stern, *Purple Passage: The Life of Mrs. Frank Leslie* (Norman: University of Oklahoma Press, 1953), 93.

128 They were a . . . : *Territorial Enterprise Extra*, 4.

128 Every word of . . . : Ibid.

128 Born out of . . . : Ibid.

128 She led Squier . . . : Ibid.

129 "Was there ever . . .": Ibid., 10.

129 "On the whole," . . . : E. G. Squier, letter to parents, September 11, 1878, New-York Historical Society.

129 Uxorious and gullible . . . : Quoted in Stern, *Purple Passage*, 95.

129 Fashion edicts came . . . : *Frank Leslie's Lady's Magazine*, October, 1878, 270.

129 Women in the . . . : *Frank Leslie's Lady's Magazine,* October 1878, see "Guardian Angel," 166; "Ora Pro Nobis, A Fair Young Wife at her Orisons," 266 and "Morning Prayer," 301; September 1878, see "Too Late," 190, "A Cruel Letter," 200, and "A Fatal Letter"; July 1878, 50.

129 A true man . . . : See Ibid., 255; and November 1878, "Married Men," 397.

129 If false rumors . . . : *Frank Leslie's Lady's Magazine,* October 1878, 296.

129 A victim of . . . : *Frank Leslie's Lady's Magazine,* November 1878, 378.

131 His twin palace . . . : Quoted in Greg King, *Season of Splendor: The Court of Mrs. Astor in Gilded Age New York* (Hoboken, NJ: John Wiley, 2009), 145.

131 Asked why she . . . : Eric Homberger, *Mrs. Astor's New York: Money and Social Power in a Gilded Age* (New Haven: Yale University Press, 2002), 193.

132 Her "astorimperious" manner . . . : Quoted in Jerry E. Patterson, *The First Four Hundred: Mrs. Astor's New York in the Gilded Age* (New York: Rizzoli, 2000), 65.

132 If the tiny . . . : See Jack Beatty's excellent *Age of Betrayal* for more on the wealth gap. The 1880 census found that 25,000 people owned one-half of the national wealth, and 250,000, 75 to 80 percent. *Age of Betrayal: The Triumph of Money in America 1865–1900* (New York: Random House, 2008), 200.

132 There was a . . . : Henry George, *Progress and Poverty* (New York: Robert Schalkenbach Foundation, 2008 [San Francisco: W. M. Hinton, 1879], 10.

132 The average worker . . . : See *Bulletin of the Department of Labor,* #18, September, 1898, 698.

132 The same year . . . : Quoted in Alan Trachtenberg, *The Incorporation of America* (New York: Farrar, Straus and Giroux, 2007), 70, 73.

132 Over twenty thousand . . . : See partial coverage, *Frank Leslie's Illustrated Newspaper,* May 3, 1879, 131.

133 Even equilibrist Frank . . . : *Frank Leslie's Illustrated Newspaper,* October 25, 1879, 118.

133 For the rest . . . : *Frank Leslie's Lady's Magazine,* February, 1879, 102; and See *Frank Leslie's Lady's Magazine,* January 1879, 73 and 70.

133 Doubling down on . . . : "The Pine-Apple Trade in the Bahamas," *Frank Leslie's Illustrated Newspaper,* June 21, 1879, 268.

134 Frank's letters to . . . : *Philadelphia Inquirer,* April 18, 1879, 3.

134 He concluded by . . . : Ibid.

134 "Mr. Leslie," reported . . . : Ibid.

134 The May 3 edition . . . : *Frank Leslie's Illustrated Newspaper,* May 3, 1879, 131.

134 At Interlaken, he . . . : *Boston Post,* August 6, 1879, 3; and *St. Joseph Weekly Gazette* (MO), June 26, 1879, 6.

134 He replenished Miriam's . . . : *Boston Post,* August 6, 1879, 3.

134 Heedless of the . . . : *St. Joseph Weekly Gazette* (MO), June 26, 1879: 6; and *Boston Post*, August 27, 1879, 3.

134 First, their French . . . : *Sun* (New York) August 1, 1879, 1.

134 Three weeks later . . . : *New York Times*, August 27, 1879, 8.

135 Frank's personal history . . . : *Burlington (VT) Free Press*, December 19, 1879, 3.

135 "His action against . . .": *Democrat and Chronicle*, Rochester, NY, December 1, 1879: 3.

135 He charged the . . . : *Brooklyn Daily Eagle*, November 24, 1879, 4.

135 "Put your finger . . .": *Tennessean*, January 14, 1880, 3.

136 In her version . . . : Ibid.

136 He drew her . . . : Ibid.

136 In the same . . . : *St. Joseph Weekly Gazette* (MO), May 7, 1885, 12.

136 Although Miriam insisted . . . : See *New York Times*, February 15, 1880, 5.

136 "There is no . . .": Ibid.

136 Though moribund, he . . . : Ibid.

137 As she recalled . . . : *Detroit Free Press*, November 3, 1890, 3.

137 In the obituary . . . : *New York Times*, January 11, 1880, 2.

137 "Only the rich," . . . : James D. McCabe, Jr., *New York by Gaslight* (Philadelphia: Hubbard Bros, 1882, rpt. New York: Greenwich House, 1984), 232.

137 Funerals were exorbitant . . . : Ibid. And see *Medical Advance*, vols. 11–12, 1882, 179: "Funerals cost two and one-half times more money annually than would buy the grounds and buildings of all the universities and colleges in America. Funerals cost in 1880 enough money to pay the liabilities of all the commercial failures in the US during the same year, and give each bankrupt a capital of $8,630 with which to resume business," 179.

138 One of them . . . : *Observer*, January 17, 1880, 2.

138 Gone was the . . . : Mrs. Frank Leslie, *Are We All Deceivers? The Lover's Blue Book* (Chicago: Neely, 1893), 69.

139 Embalming had just . . . : James D. McCabe, *Lights and Shadows of New York* (Philadelphia: National Publishing Company, 1872), 232.

139 Never, wrote one . . . : *Times-Picayune*, January 17, 1880, 2.

139 Frank's son Henry . . . : Ibid.

139 At the sight . . . : Ibid.

140 Covering every doctrinal . . . : "The Consecration of a Grave," Burial II, *The Book of Common Prayer and Administration of the Sacraments and Other Rites and Ceremonies of the Church According to the Use of the Episcopal Church*, 503.

140 Later, Miriam erected . . . : See lot 109–10, Woodlawn Cemetery.

141 She placed his . . . : *Frank Leslie's Popular Monthly*, March, 1880, 262.

141   "Mrs. Leslie," pronounced . . . : *Onaga Democrat* (Onaga, KS), January 29, 1880, 4.

141   Her one-room attic . . . : Robert A. M. Stern, Thomas Mellins, and David Fishman, *New York 1880: Architecture and Urbanism in the Gilded Age* (New York: Monacelli Press, 1999), 578; and *New York Daily Tribune*, October 2, 1900, 4.

141   She knew, she . . . : Ibid.

142   When she traveled . . . : McCabe, *Lights and Shadows*, 187.

142   Conductors were brusque . . . : Ibid.

142   They refused seats . . . : Mrs. Frank Leslie, *Rents in Our Robes* (Chicago: Clark & Co., 1888), 42 and 45.

142   She described one . . . : Mrs. Frank Leslie, *A Social Mirage* (New York: F. Tennyson Nee, 1899), 152.

142   Playing into Gilded . . . : Frank Leslie, *Appellant v. Miriam F. Leslie and Others, Respondents, New York Supreme Court General Term, Surrogates Court,* case on appeal, vols. II and III (New York: E. O'Keefe, 1881), 681 and 254.

142   A procession of . . . : Ibid.

142   "She completely fascinated . . .": *New York Times*, April 15, 1880: 3, and see "The Mysteries of Mind," *Frank Leslie's Illustrated Newspaper*, June 11, 1881, 246 for prevailing belief in this idea.

142   The court was . . . : See Bram Dijkstra, *Idols of Perversity: Fantasies of Feminine Evil in Fin-de-Siecle Culture* (New York: Oxford University Press, 1976), 272–401; Judith Fryer, "Temptress," *Faces of Eve: Women in the Nineteenth-Century American Novel* (New York: Oxford University Press, 1976), 27–84; Nina Auerbach, "Angels and Demons," *Woman and the Demon: The Life of a Victorian Myth* (Cambridge: Harvard University Press, 1982), 63–108 and passim.; and Nel Noddings, "The Devil's Gateway," *Women and Evil* (Berkeley: University of California Press, 1989), 35–58.

143   Under her seductive . . . : Frank Leslie, *Appellant v. Miriam F. Leslie, New York Supreme Court*, 449.

143   Most viciously, she . . . : Ibid., 2.

143   Such iniquity was . . . : Quoted in John S. Haller Jr. and Robin M. Haller, *The Physician and Sexuality in Victorian America* (New York: W. W. Norton, 1974), 84, and see effect of desertion of the home circle for the workplace on women, 235.

143   Her brazen adultery . . . : Frank Leslie, *Appellant v. Miriam F. Leslie, New York Supreme Court*, 307.

143   Stephen J. Cox, a . . . : Ibid., see 418–19.

143   He said Miriam . . . : Ibid., 117. She also confessed to her brother-in-law, Frank Squier, that she had "never been his wife" after their Peru expedition.

143   Once he saw . . . : Ibid., 49.

143   "Their conduct," she . . . : Ibid., 828.

144   She believed in . . . : Leslie, *Social Mirage*, 228.

144   A past mistress . . . : *Town Topics*, March 28, 1886, 14.

144   As the session . . . : Leslie, *Social Mirage*, 231.

144   Throughout the hearing . . . : *New York Times*, April 15, 1880, 3; and quoted in Stern, 100.

144   Thundered Fullerton, "To . . .": Frank Leslie, *Appellant v. Miriam F. Leslie, New York Supreme Court*, 88.

144   At Bergen Point . . . : Ibid., 213.

145   In clipped, schoolmistress . . . : Ibid., 751.

145   During their regular . . . : Ibid., 695.

145   She remembered his . . . : Ibid., 682.

145   The opposition objected . . . : Ibid., 699, 702. She and Mrs. Pierce often "talked over" these scenes, so it wouldn't be surprising, given the stakes, if she improved on her friend's script.

145   While Miriam wept . . . : Ibid., 675, 680.

145   She disobeyed her . . . : Ibid., 675.

145   "For the sake . . .": Ibid.

145   Afterward, Mr. Leslie . . . : Ibid., 677.

146   She continued to . . . : Ibid., 688.

146   His last words . . . : Ibid., 692.

146   The December 18 . . . : *Frank Leslie's Illustrated Newspaper*, December 18, 1880, 246.

146   They summed up . . . : *Frank Leslie, Appellant vs. Miriam F. Leslie, New York Supreme Court*, 142. See an example of his damaged reputation in the *Grenola Argus* (KS), February 18, 1881, 3: His sons came out badly, but "Frank Leslie, however, could hardly have expected any other result. His example taught his child fraud and licentiousness."

146   With the blessing . . . : See Charles Daly, *Reports of Cases Argued and Determined in the Court of Common Pleas, for the City and County of New York* (NY: Banks and Brothers Law Publishers, 1885), 82.

146   "She had no . . .": "The Story of a Woman of Business," in *The National Exposition Souvenir: What America Owes to Women*, ed. Lydia Hoyt Farmer (Chicago: Charles Wells Moulton, 1893), 432.

147   "No," she flashed . . . : *Canton Advocate* (SD), October 12, 1882, 4.

147   She spent the . . . : *New York Daily Tribune*, October 2, 1900, 4; and see Esther Crain, "A Cold, Sick Winter in New York," *Ephemeral New York*, January 13, 2010, https//ephemeralnewyork.wordpress.com/2010/01/13 /a-cold-sick-winter-in-new-york-city/.

147   "If poverty [comes] . . .": Leslie, *Social Mirage*, 233.

147 But there must . . . : Farmer, *What America Owes to Women*, 432.

147 By spring the . . . : Ibid.

147 She "knew of . . .": *Canton Advocate*, October 12, 1882, 4.

147 She later winced . . . : Leslie, *Social Mirage*, 306.

147 She felt like . . . : *Bushton News* (KS), November 16, 1900, 2.

148 Women, by definition . . . : See Haller and Haller, *Physician and Sexuality in Victorian America*, 40.

148 Devotee Joaquin Miller . . . : "Mrs. Frank Leslie," *Golden Era*, May, 1887, 182.

149 By her own . . . : *Bushton News*, November 16, 1900, 2.

149 To breathe was . . . : *New York Times*, June 29, 1881, 8.

149 "It was a . . .": *San Francisco Examiner*, January 14, 1892, 3.

149 She waged a . . . : Farmer, 431.

149 In a June 18 . . . : *Frank Leslie's Illustrated Newspaper*, June 18, 1881, 262.

150 Looking back, she . . . : *Canton Advocate* (SD), October 12, 1882, 4.

CHAPTER SIX

151 "Queen of Park . . .": Madeleine Stern, *Purple Passage: The Life of Mrs. Frank Leslie* (Norman: University of Oklahoma Press, 1953), 104.

152 As he told . . . : George Alfred Townsend, "Days of Gloom in the White House," *Frank Leslie's Popular Monthly*, September, 1881, 264–65.

152 At the Baltimore . . . : *Evening Star*, July 28, 1881, 1.

152 The president threw . . . : Quoted in Howard Markel, "The Dirty, Painful Death of a President James A. Garfield," PBS News Hour, September 16, 2016, www.pbs.org/newshour/health/dirty-painful-death-president.

152 As the police . . . : Quoted in *Frank Leslie's Illustrated Newspaper*, July 16, 1881, 335.

152 "I knew," she . . . : *Bushton News* (KS), November 16, 1900, 2.

153 He mugged for . . . : *Evening Star* (Washington, DC), July 2, 1881, 19.

153 After all, he . . . : *Frank Leslie's Illustrated Newspaper*, July 16, 1881, 335.

153 She procured a . . . : *Frank Leslie's Illustrated Newspaper*, July 30, 1881, 362.

154 In early fall . . . : Quoted in Stern, *Purple Passage*, 105.

154 Overnight her feat . . . : Quoted ibid., 104.

154 She was suddenly . . . : *Frank Leslie's Illustrated Newspaper*, July 30, 1881, 358.

154 In an artful . . . : Quoted in Stern, *Purple Passage*, 106; and *Pensacolian* (FL), May 30, 1885, 6.

154 Businessmen found her . . . : Ibid.

155 A contemporary print . . . : James Cehphas Derby, *Fifty Years Among Authors, Books, and Publishers* (Hartford, CT: M. A. Winters Hatch, 1886), 696.

155 By the end . . . : *Frank Leslie's Illustrated Newspaper*, July 30, 1881, 358.

155 "It was a . . .": Quoted in *Ladies' Home Journal*, May 1890, 3.

155 Determined to "make . . .": Mrs. Frank Leslie, *Are We All Deceivers? The Lover's Blue Book* (Chicago: Neely, 1893), 125; and *Ladies' Home Journal*, May 1890, 3.

155 Soon after her . . . : *Inter Ocean* (Chicago), September 3, 1891, 9.

155 A titled Euro-version . . . : Mrs. Frank Leslie, *Rents in Our Robes* (Chicago: Clark & Co., 1888), 46.

156 Her friend, writer . . . : See Braddon's fictional portrait of him as Baron de Cazalet in *Mount Royal* (London: John and Robert Maxwell, 1882), 263. In this novel, he is seen as a "gorgeous" dandy, "notorious duelist," and "Don Juan" who lays siege to the heroine, Christabel Tregonell, 239, 250, and 263 . And see passim., 234–303.

156 When he saw . . . : *Democrat and Chronicle*, March 22, 1884, 3.

156 He paced the. . . : Ibid.

156 She was overworked . . . : Leslie, *Rents in Our Robes*, 8.

156 She also yearned . . . : Leslie, *Rents in Our Robes*, 8. For her bitter view of the "soap bubble" of romantic love, see Mrs. Frank Leslie, *A Social Mirage* (New York: F. Tennyson Nee, 1899), 7; Leslie, *Rents in Our Robes*, 51; and Leslie, *Are We All Deceivers?*, 84, 288. Her contradictory need for love appears in *Ladies' Home Journal*, May 1890, 3, and *Social Mirage*, 308: "A woman, she wrote, with no one to love her is the most miserable of creatures."

156 Intensity, she also . . . : Leslie, *Are We All Deceivers?*, 53.

156 She was a . . . : Le Marquis de Leuville, "To Florence," *Poems and Aelia from Entre-Nous* (New York: American News Company, 1884), frontispiece.

156 He was with . . . : See *Inter Ocean* (Chicago), September 3, 1881, 9.

157 In a diplomatic . . . : See Joshua Brown, *Beyond the Lines: Pictorial Reporting, Everyday Life, and the Crisis of Gilded Age America* (Berkeley: University of California Press, 2002), 177; and *Frank Leslie's Illustrated Newspaper*, June 10, 1882, 243. The *Illustrated* returned to reporting on the labor movement in 1882 and far exceeded competitors in the number and scope of its treatment of strikes, parades, conventions, etc. for seven years.

157 Coverage of the . . . : *Frank Leslie's Illustrated Newspaper*, September 16, 1882, 55.

157 While condemning the . . . : Ibid., September 2, 1882, 18.

157 Editorials praised American . . . : *Frank Leslie's Illustrated Newspaper*, August 5, 1882, 369. See cover caricature of Italian strike breaker and

"Russian Jews at Castle Garden." The year 1882 saw a massive increase in immigration, primarily unskilled single men escaping "La Misera" in Italy and Jews fleeing Russian pogroms and persecution.

157 In February she . . . : *Frank Leslie's Popular Monthly*, March 1882, 383.

158 Mirroring elite tastes . . . : *Frank Leslie's Popular Monthly*, March 1882, 382.

158 "Wealth and material . . .": Ibid.

158 On the subject . . . : *Frank Leslie's Popular Monthly*, February, 254.

158 The "fastidious" social . . . : *Frank Leslie's Popular Monthly*, May, 638.

158 "As if Lady . . .": Ibid.

158 She ended with . . . : Ibid.

158 She chided further . . . : Ibid.

159 One of his first calls . . . : Quoted in Lloyd Lewis and Henry Justin Smith, *Oscar Wilde Discovers America 1882* (New York: Harcourt Brace, 1936), 155., 32 and Oscar Wilde, *A Woman of No Importance, Oscar Wilde: The Importance of Being Earnest and Other Plays* (London: Penguin, 1988), Act 3, Scene 1, 116.

159 Affecting an Aesthetic . . . : Quoted in Lewis and Smith, *Oscar Wilde Discovers*, 35.

159 On cue, he . . . : Ibid.; and quoted in Richard Ellman, *Oscar Wilde* (New York: Vintage Books, 1987), 160.

159 By the time . . . : Ibid., 35.

159 The cultural lights . . . : Quoted in Ellman, *Oscar Wilde*, 160.

159 A poem, he said . . . : Quoted in Lewis and Smith, *Oscar Wilde Discovers*, 58.

160 Colonel Morse, his . . . : *Frank Leslie's Illustrated Newspaper*, January 21, 1882, 382.

160 But the lecture . . . : Quoted in Michele Mendelssohn, *Making Oscar Wilde* (London: Oxford University Press, 2018), 75.

160 Audiences at Harvard . . . : See *Harper's Weekly*, January 28, 1882, cover; and *Washington Post*, January 22, 1882, 4.

160 Vaudeville comedians and . . . : Lewis and Smith, *Oscar Wilde Discovers*, 374.

160 A *Nation* critic . . . : See Col. Higginson's attack and discussion of the homosexual attacks in Mendelssohn, *Making Oscar Wilde*, 131–32, 150.

160 He toyed with . . . : Quoted in Lewis and Smith, *Oscar Wilde Discovers*, 332.

160 Wilde put a . . . : Quoted in Mendelssohn, *Making Oscar Wilde*, 138.

160 She plugged his . . . : *Frank Leslie's Illustrated Newspaper*, January 21, 1882, 381, 382; and see *Frank Leslie's Illustrated Newspaper*, February 18, 1882, 443.

160 The *ton* didn't . . . : See Lewis and Smith, *Oscar Wilde Discovers* about the cold-shoulder he received from high society, 45, 60, and passim.

160 Finally, box-office . . . : Quoted in Mendelssohn, *Making Oscar Wilde*, 137.

161 Miriam said she . . . : Quoted in Lewis and Smith, *Oscar Wilde Discovers*, 444.

161 He'd decided, he . . . : Quoted, Ibid.

161 His "mission to . . .": Quoted in *New York Tribune*, January 10, 1883, 4; and quoted in Lewis and Smith, *Oscar Wilde Discovers*, 442.

161 As they parted . . . : Quoted in Lewis and Smith, *Oscar Wilde Discovers*, 444.

161 Joaquin Miller described . . . : *Times–Picayune*, January 9, 1883, 2.

161 By the end . . . : *National Republican* (Washington, DC), January 27, 1883, 5.

162 An advertising-age . . . : See nine-page, double columned feature in *Frank Leslie's Popular Monthly*, August, 1883, 129–38.

162 She was the . . . : Ibid., 131.

162 Both "ladylike" and . . . : Ibid.

162 "They all touch . . .": Quoted in Stern, *Purple Passage*, 108.

162 "I am ashamed . . .": Quoted in Derby, *Fifty Years Among Authors*, 696.

162 In two years . . . : Quoted in Stern, *Purple Passage*, 109.

162 She was "young . . .": *Benton Weekly Record* (Fort Benton, MT), June 23, 1883, 1; and quoted in Stern, *Purple Passage*, 109.

162 She could espouse . . . : See *Frank Leslie's Illustrated Newspaper*, February 10, 1883; and the following editorials that year: *Frank Leslie's Illustrated Newspaper*, August 4, 1883, 386; October 27, 1883, 146. On women: *Frank Leslie's Illustrated Newspaper*, February 17, 1883, 426; March 17, 1883, 50; June 2, 1883, 230.

163 Alva, an ambitious . . . : Quoted in Greg King, *Season of Splendor: The Court of Mrs. Astor in Gilded Age New York* (Hoboken, NJ: John Wiley, 2009), 56.

163 The "famous editress" . . . : *Times-Picayune*, January 21, 1883, 3; and *Tennessean*, February 4, 1883, 12.

163 She had come . . . : *Times-Picayune*, February 26, 1883, 2.

163 Fast-forwarding to her . . . : Ibid. and in the August *Frank Leslie's Popular Monthly*, 1883, issue she reinforced this with a description of herself, 135.

164 Reporters hailed her . . . : See *Times-Picayune*, February 26, 1883, 2; and *Juaniata Sentinel & Republican* (Mifflintown, PA), March 28, 1883, 4; and *Times-Picayune*, March 6, 1883, 2.

164 To interviewers she . . . : *Times-Picayune*, March 3, 1883, 4.

165 The extravaganza cost . . . : For a fuller accounts of the ball see Susannah Broyles, "Vanderbilt Ball—How a Costume Ball Changed New York Elite Society," *New York Stories*, Museum of the City of New York, August 6, 2013, blog.mcny.org/2013/08/06/vanderbilt-ball-how-a-costume-ball

-changed-new-york-elite-society/; and Sara Donati, "Vanderbilt Costume Ball," The Gilded Hour, thegildedhour.com/vanderbilt-costume-ball/.

165   Some newspaper critics . . . : See *Evening Star* (Washington, DC), April 4, 1883, 7; and *Chicago Tribune*, March 23, 1883, 11.

166   After the ball . . . : Quoted in King, *Season of Splendor*, 65.

168   He made the . . . : See full account in Dick Weindling and Marianne Colloms, *The Marquis de Leuville: A Victorian Fraud?* (Gloustershire: The History Press, 2012), loc. 234, www.historypress.co.uk.

168   With Louisa's encouragement . . . : See reviews, ibid., loc. 537–64.

169   He subtracted ten . . . : *Chicago Tribune*, October 27, 1883, 16.

169   As she admitted . . . : Leslie, *Are We All Deceivers?*, 263.

169   Few at the . . . : Quoted in *Times Herald* (Port Huron, MI), August 20, 1883, 4.

169   "Many people of . . .": *Frank Leslie's Illustrated Newspaper*, July 7, 1883, 323.

169   The highlight of . . . : Quoted in *San Francisco Examiner*, January 14, 1892, 3.

169   By eighteen, Jane . . . : Quoted in Eleanor Fitzsimons, "Jane Wilde," *Wilde's Women* (New York: The Overlook Press, 2015), 29.

169   Flamboyant free spirit . . . : Quoted in Fitzsimons, *Wilde's Women*, 31.

170   When she rapped . . . : For a description of these salons from multiple perspectives, see Eleanor Fitzsimons, "Speranza's Saturdays," *Wilde's Women*, 130–43.

171   Jane would have . . . : Quoted ibid., 140, 141.

171   Afterward, Miriam called . . . : *San Francisco Examiner*, January 14, 1892, 3; and Lady Jane Wilde, *Essays and Stories* (New York and London: Keller-Farmer Co., 1907), 24–25.

171   She continued: "With . . .": Lady Jane Wilde, *Essays and Stories*, 24–25.

172   Jane said, "Mrs. . . .": Quoted in Stern, 113.

172   Perhaps he read . . . : Quoted in Ellman, *Oscar Wilde*, 223.

172   Perhaps de Leuville rose . . . : Le Marquis de Leuville, *Poems and Aelia from Entre-Nous* (New York: American News Company, 1885), 104.

172   The dispute, according to rumor . . . : Quoted in Weindling and Collin, *Marquis de Leuville*, loc. 905.

172   "When a woman . . .": *Buffalo Evening News*, July 11, 1883, 6.

173   Belle Epoque Paris . . . : Quoted in Walter Benjamin, "Paris, Capital of the Nineteenth Century," in *Charles Baudelaire*, trans. Henry Zohn (London: Verso, 1989).

173   "On the boulevards," . . . : Quoted in Émile Bergerat and Vanesssa R. Schwartz, *Spectacular Realities: Early Mass Culture in Fin-de-Siècle Paris* (Berkeley: University of California Press, 1998), 21.

174   As she explained . . . : *Detroit Free Press*, March 5, 1885, 12.

174   "The diamonds are . . .": Ibid.

174   These notorious *grandes* . . . : See especially, Anon., *Pretty Women of Paris* (London: Wordsworth Editions, 1996 [1883]), passim.

174   *Nana,* based on . . . : Émile Zola, *Nana,* trans. Douglas Parmée (New York: Oxford University Press, 2009 [1880]), 27.

175   Nor could she . . . : See Charles Culliford Boz Dickens, *Dickens's Dictionary of Paris 1883: An Unconventional Handbook* (London: Macmillan & Co., 1883), 125, 251, and 255.

175   Select private salons . . . : See Alb, *Living Paris and France* (Paris: Galignani [1885]. 1889), 5.

175   With de Leuville on . . . : Quoted in Bergerat and Schwartz, *Spectacular Realities,* 109.

175   He produced a . . . : See *Le Soir* story, quoted in *Daily Kansas Herald* (Lawrence, KS), August 13, 1883, 3.

175   Unsuspected by Miriam . . . : See Westminster Diocesan Archives cited in "References," en.wikipedia.org/wiki/thomas_John_Capel, accessed August 9, 2020.

175   After the luncheon . . . : See *Frank Leslie's Illustrated Newspaper,* September 8, 1883, 44.

175   Three days later . . . : *Wood Country Reporter* (Grand Rapids, WI), July 19, 1883, 7.

175   To compound his . . . : *Times Herald* (Port Huron, MI), August 20, 1883, 4.

176   A seasoned Lothario . . . : Anthony Trollope, *The Small House at Allington,* intro. Julian Thompson (New York: Penguin Books, 2005 [1864]), 668.

176   The story, "A . . .": See *Evening Star* (Washington, DC), October 13, 1883, 7.

CHAPTER SEVEN

177   "Cheated by Sentiment": Mrs. Frank Leslie, *A Social Mirage,* 35.

177   The Victoria Hotel . . . : Tom Miller, "The Lost Victoria Hotel—Fifth Avenue and 27th Street," *Daytonian in Manhattan* (blog), February 3, 2014, daytoninmanhattan.blogspot.com/2014/02/the-lost-victoria-hotel-fifth -avenue.html.

177   Newspapers throughout the . . . : *Boston Globe,* March 19, 1884, 5.

177   According to reports . . . : *Tennessean* (Nashville), March 21, 1884, 8.

177   Both gave exclusives . . . : See *Boston Globe,* March 19, 1884, 5.

178   As for herself . . . : Ibid.

178   Now engaged in . . . : See *National Tribune* (Washington, DC), April 3, 1884, 5.

178   His secret: an . . . : See *Inter Ocean* (Chicago), April 13, 1884, 6.

178   If the press . . . : See *National Tribune* (Washington, DC), April 3, 1884, 50.

178 In June Miriam . . . : See *Leavenworth (KS) Standard*, June 1, 1884, 1.

178 She was "indifferent . . .": *Hoxie (KS) Sentinel*, October 2, 1884, 1.

178 She would be . . . : Eric Homberger, *Mrs. Astor's New York: Money and Social Power in a Gilded Age* (New Haven: Yale University Press, 2002), 206.

178 Mrs. Leslie responded . . . : *Frank Leslie's Illustrated Newspaper*, September 13, 1884, 50.

179 The Leslie company . . . : *Weekly Town Talk* (Alexandria, LA), January 4, 1884, 3.

179 They were the . . . : *Hoxie (KS) Sentinel*, October 2, 1884, 1.

179 At one of . . . : There was no Naples Society for the Encouragement of Art—only one in Warsaw—and he doesn't turn up in the 1884 roster of the International Literary and Artistic Association. His one authentic membership was the Royal Historical Society of London where, as a fellow, he pledged a future contribution.

180 After the first . . . : *Boston Globe*, December 17, 1884, 5.

180 "He had fully . . .": Ibid.

180 Sickles, the evening's . . . : *Detroit Free Press*, December 18, 1884, 2.

180 "Simply a matter . . .": Ibid.

180 He leaned his . . . : Ibid.

180 "Call tomorrow," said . . . : Ibid.

181 Mrs. Leslie said she . . . : Ibid.

181 The legacy, in . . . : *Atchison (KS) Daily Patriot*, January 28, 1885, 1.

181 Miriam promptly announced . . . : *Buffalo Morning Express*, March 10, 1885, 4.

181 As she put . . . : Mrs. Frank Leslie, *Are We All Deceivers? The Lover's Blue Book* (Chicago: Neely, 1893), 52.

181 She was "prostrated," . . . : Dick Weindling and Marianne Colloms, *The Marquis de Leuville: A Victorian Fraud?* (Gloustershire: The History Press, 2012), loc. 1150.

181 Joining the chorus . . . : *Baxter Springs (KS) News*, January 31, 1885, 4.

181 In business, said interviewers . . . : *San Francisco Chronicle*, October 15, 1885, 1; and *Topeka (KS) Daily Capital*, April 30, 1885, 6.

181 "Her face," raved . . . : *Canton Independent-Sentinel* (Canton, PA), April 17, 1885, 6.

181 She endorsed Liebig's . . . : *Boston Globe*, March 16, 1885, 4.

181 The *Illustrated* saw . . . : *Frank Leslie's Illustrated Newspaper*, January 3, 1885, 322.

182 The *Illustrated*, though . . . : See *Frank Leslie's Illustrated Newspaper*, September 26, 1885, 90, and October 17, 1885, 135.

182 One morning Miriam . . . : *San Francisco Chronicle*, November 15, 1885, 1.

182 Mrs. Leslie, she wrote . . . : Ella Wheeler Wilcox, *The Worlds and I* (New York: George H. Doran, 1918), 131, 132.

182 Joaquin, she swiped . . . : Ibid., 132.

182 He found her . . . : Joaquin Miller, "Mrs. Frank Leslie," *Golden Era*, May 1887, 182.

182 Joaquin waxed afterward . . . : Ibid., 182–83.

183 By June, she . . . : *Times-Picayune*, July 21, 1885, 2.

183 When she left . . . : See *Times-Picayune*, June 4, 1885, 6.

183 Installed at the . . . : James Palmer, "Albert Pulitzer: Notes on the Lesser-Known Pulitzer Brother," Pulitzer Prize website, www.pulitzer.org/page /albert-pulitzer-notes-lesser-known-pulitzer-brother, 3.

183 Their marriage, stated . . . : See *Richmond Dispatch*, June 17, 1885, 2, for this widely distributed story.

183 Brimming with self-confidence . . . : Palmer, "Albert Pulitzer," 3.

184 Pulitzer had earned . . . : *Frank Leslie's Illustrated Newspaper*, May 2, 1885, 173–74.

184 He understood how . . . : Palmer, "Albert Pulitzer," 6, 7.

184 Miriam, though, disembarked . . . : *Times-Picayune*, October 18, 1885, 51.

184 She convened reporters . . . : *Topeka State Journal* (KS), January 7, 1886, 1.

184 She stood to . . . : *Oskaloosa (KS) Independent*, January 16, 1886, 1.

185 Beyond the office . . . : *Burlington (VT) Free Press*, March 9, 1886, 2.

185 Twenty-three miners died . . . : *Frank Leslie's Illustrated Newspaper*, March 20, 1886, 71.

185 The *Topics* "Chronicler" . . . : *Town Topics*, March 28, 1886, 13, 14.

186 Where was "Lais" . . . : Ibid., 14.

186 Clamoring for social acceptance . . . : Ibid.

186 When the little . . . : Ibid.

186 Ten thousand rallied . . . : James Green, *Death in Haymarket* (New York: Anchor Books, 2006), 161.

187 The Haymarket Affair . . . : Ibid., 10.

187 The paper excoriated . . . : *Frank Leslie's Illustrated Newspaper*, May 15, 1886, 194, August 7, 1886, 386, and August 14, 1886, 407.

187 Mrs. Leslie was . . . : See Joshua Brown, *Beyond the Lines: Pictorial Reporting, Everyday Life, and the Crisis of Gilded Age America* (Berkeley: University of California Press, 2002), 204.

187 Asked about the . . . : Quoted in *Sterling Standard* (IL), October 23, 1890, 7.

187 She favored the . . . : See *Leavenworth (KS) Times*, September 19, 1886, 3.

187 In Europe that . . . : *Pall Mall Gazette*, August 28, 1886, 1.

187 She was an . . . : Ibid.

188 Her leisured outings . . . : *Frank Leslie's Illustrated Newspaper,* January 8, 1887, 355, May 21, 1887, 215, and April 30, 1887, 163.

188 In May, Joaquin . . . : Miller, *The Golden Era,* May 1887, 182–83.

188 Investigative reporter Cleveland . . . : *Sunday Truth* (Buffalo), July 2, 1887, 3.

188 The breakfast party . . . : Ibid.

189 He was laughing . . . : Weindling and Collin, *Marquis de Leuville,* loc. 72.

189 When they turned . . . : Ibid.

189 "Mrs. Leslie's infidelity," . . . : Ibid., loc. 1516; and *Pittsburgh Daily Post,* July 16, 1887, 7.

189 He sent Miriam . . . : Weindling and Collin, *Marquis de Leuville,* loc. 1529.

189 She told reporters . . . : *Chicago Tribune,* September 10, 1887, 5.

189 As for the . . . : Ibid.

189 Papers everywhere boldfaced . . . : Ibid.

189 Instead of "unpleasant . . .": *Sun* (New York), September 10, 1887, 2.

189–90 The rival suitors, Prince . . . : Quoted in Weindling and Collin, *Marquis de Leuville,* loc. 1491.

190 Explained Mrs. Morelie . . . : Ibid.

190 After thrashing the . . . : Ibid.

190 She delivered verdicts . . . : See *Frank Leslie's Illustrated Newspaper,* December 31, 1887, 331 and see 330. See December 3, 1887, 242–43.

190 She announced her intention . . . : *Harrisburg* (PA) *Telegraph,* August 29, 1887, 2.

190 She might have . . . : *Times-Picayune,* November 27, 1887, 12.

190 Her highborn father . . . : Ibid.

190 The "pink of . . .": Ibid.

190 In December she . . . : See *Morning Call* (Paterson, NJ), December 21, 1887, 7.

190 Her publishing empire . . . : See *Sunday Truth* (Buffalo, NY), July 17, 1887, 3; and *Harrisburg Telegraph,* August 29, 1887, 2.

191 In Miller's futuristic . . . : Joaquin Miller, *The Destruction of Gotham* (New York: Funk & Wagnell's, 1886), 12.

191 In a population . . . : See "Statistics Bearing on the Tenement Problem," Appendix, Jacob Riis, *How the Other Half Lives,* 1890, www.bartleby.com /208/26.html.

192 At the Patriarch's . . . : See *New York Times,* January 18, 1888, 1.

192 In order to . . . : Quoted in *Chicago Tribune,* April 5, 1888, 4.

192 She stamped her . . . : See *St. Louis Post-Dispatch,* October 28, 1888, 20.

192 She decried immigrants . . . : See *Frank Leslie's Popular Monthly,* March, 1888, 260–267.

192   She execrated Chicago . . . : See *Frank Leslie's Illustrated Newspaper,* October 20, 1888, 55, February 25, 1888, 19, December 8, 1888, 262, and December 29, 1888, 331.

192   The harsh editorial . . . : Brown, *Beyond the Lines,* 203.

193   She began by . . . : Leslie, *Rents in Our Robes,* v.

193   As if on . . . : Ibid., 9, 14.

193   Equality was essential . . . : Ibid., 109.

193   It was important . . . : See ibid., 27.

193   Far from caring . . . : France E. Willard, *How to Win: A Book for Girls* (1888) in ed. Aileen S. Kraditor, *Up from the Pedestal: Selected Writings in the History of Feminism* (Chicago: Quadrangle Books, 1968), 318.

193   She responded in . . . : *Chicago Tribune,* February 5, 1888, 27.

193   She exhorted American . . . : *Buffalo Times,* November 14, 1888, 3.

193   Seated beside a . . . : *Standard Union* (Brooklyn, NY), October 25, 1888, 2.

193   While a woman . . . : Ibid.

193   In October, she . . . : Reporter Helen Cusak-Carvalho, who used the byline Nell Nelson, had just gone undercover in Chicago city factories and written an explosive series, "City Slave Girls," which ran from July 30 to August 27. See "City Slave Girls," *Chicago Times,* July 30–August 27, 1888.

194   Miriam ushered guests . . . : *St. Louis Post-Dispatch,* October 28, 1888, 20.

194   The chemise "is . . .": Ibid.

194   "I never sit . . .": Ibid.

194   Possibly she did . . . : Quoted in *New Haven Evening Register,* April 17, 1888, www.twainquotes.com. Accessed 12/28/2019.

194   She admitted he . . . : *Buffalo Evening News,* March 23, 1888, 5.

194   Miriam boasted that . . . : *Semi-Weekly Spokesman-Review* (Spokane, WA), April 19, 1888, 7.

194   A woman's "starving . . .": *Standard Union* (Brooklyn), October 25, 1888, 2.

194   If she could . . . : *Buffalo Times,* November 14, 1888, 3.

195   When the Great . . . : See *Frank Leslie's Illustrated Newspaper* "Blizzard" issue, March 24, 1888, 82.

195   The Illinois Woman's . . . : *Inter Ocean* (Chicago), February 13, 1889, 3; and *Star Tribune* (Minneapolis, MN), January 27, 1889, 10.

195   The Topeka Printer . . . : *Assumption Pioneer* (Napoleonville, LA), January 26, 1888, 2; and *Saint Paul Globe,* January 6, 1889, 4.

195   After a guided . . . : *Times-Picayune,* January 6, 1889, 16.

195   A center table . . . : Ibid.

195   "Vidette" concluded that . . . : Ibid.

196   "High renown as . . .": Ibid.

196 Trend trackers detailed . . . : See *Indiana State Sentinel* (Indianapolis), January 9, 1889, 6; and *Record Union* (Sacramento, CA), January 26, 1889, 3.

196 "In the new . . .": *Times* (Philadelphia), January 27, 1889, 12.

196 But, she cautioned . . . : Ibid.

196 She had "princes . . .": *Times-Picayune*, January 6, 1889, 16; and *Hutchinson (KS) News*, January 13, 1889, 4.

196 But, assured columnists . . . : *Brooklyn Eagle*, February 20, 1889, 6.

197 She decided the . . . : "The French Waltz," *Independent-Record* (Helena, MT), February 10, 1889, 3; "Whimsical Women," *Pittsburgh Dispatch*, February 17, 1889, 14; and "Girls of the Period," *Times* (Philadelphia), March 24, 1889, 12.

197 Her opinions, she . . . : *Pittsburgh Dispatch*, February 17, 1889, 14.

197 A woman should . . . : See *Buffalo Evening News*, December 29, 1889, 5.

197 In his 1889 . . . : Andrew Carnegie, "Wealth," *North American Review*, June 1889, www.swarthmore.edu/SocSci/rbannis1/AIH19th/Carnegie.html.

198 This was already . . . : Edwin G. Burrows and Mike Wallace, *Gotham: A History of New York City to 1898* (New York: Oxford, 1999), 1158–61.

198 As he told . . . : Quoted in *A Hazard of New Fortunes*, ed. Philip Lopate (New York: Penguin, 2001 [1889–1890]), intro. xii.

198 Andrew Carnegie repeated . . . : *Boston Weekly Globe*, April 17, 1889, 7.

198 The *Sun* listed . . . : *Atlanta Constitution*, June 2, 1889, 17.

199 As she explained . . . : Reprinted in *Brooklyn Citizen*, June 30, 1889, 10.

199 They can't be . . . : Ibid.

199 Papers throughout America . . . : See *Roxboro Courier* (NC), July 4, 1889, 1.

200 No servant greeted . . . : Quoted in Eleanor Fitzsimons, *Wilde's Women* (New York: The Overlook Press, 2015), 137.

200 "What we chiefly . . .": Quoted ibid., 141.

200 At some point . . . : Quoted in Max Beerbohm in Mary M. Lago and Karl Beckson, eds., *Max and Will: Max Beerbohm and William Rothenstein, Their Friendship and Letters, 1893–1945* (Cambridge, MA: Harvard University Press, 1975), 21.

200 It would "do . . .": Quoted in Joy Melville, *Mother of Oscar* (London: Allison & Busby, 1994), 227.

200 Even jaded fairgoers . . . : Quoted in Lucien Biart in Charles Rearick, *Pleasures of the Belle Epoque* (New Haven, CT: Yale University Press, 1985), 120.

201 Miriam didn't linger . . . : Joris-Karl Huysmans, quoted ibid.

201 She would have . . . : Quoted in Arthur Chandler, "Revolution: The Paris Exposition Universelle, 1889," from *World's Fair Magazine*, 1986, vol. 7, no. 1, www.arthurchandler.com/paris-1889-exposition.

202 She reappeared at . . . : *Atlanta Constitution*, November 24, 1889, 5.

202 Mrs. Leslie, she . . . : Ibid.

202 The *Pittsburgh Dispatch* . . . : *Pittsburgh Dispatch*, November 9, 1889, 4.

202 What, she asked . . . : Mrs. Frank Leslie, "The Best Kind of Man," *St. Louis Post-Dispatch*, November 7, 1889, 8.

203 She looked back . . . : Ibid.

203 An "Adonis" offered . . . : Ibid.

CHAPTER EIGHT

205 "Fascinating Woman" . . . : Mrs. Frank Leslie, *Are We All Deceivers? The Lover's Blue Book* (Chicago: Neely, 1893), 223.

205 An audience of . . . : *St. Paul Globe* (MN), October 12, 1890, 10; and *Star Tribune* (Minneapolis), October 20, 1890, 4.

205 She needed no . . . : *St. Paul Globe*, October 22, 1890, 2.

205 She'd trained "like . . .": *Philadelphia Inquirer*, November 9, 1890, 4.

206 With "Southern gesticulations" . . . : *Star Tribune*, October 20, 1890, 4.

206 The lecture, however, . . . : Joaquin Miller, "Columbus" in Edmund Clarence Stedman, *An American Anthology* (Boston: Houghton Mifflin, 1900), 798.

206 Apart from her . . . : *St. Paul Globe*, October 22, 1890, 4.

206 Chicago, still unappeased . . . : *Chicago Tribune*, October 20, 1890, 1.

206 Toward mid-November . . . : *Sioux City Journal* (IA), November 17, 1890, 4.

206 She had "more . . .": *Times-Union* (Brooklyn), March 22, 1890, 9.

207 She told reporters . . . : Weindling and Colloms, *The Marquis de Leuville*, loc. 2182.

207 She could never . . . : Ibid., quoted, loc. 2260.

207 After his opponent . . . : Ibid, quoted, loc. 2193.

207 De Leuville retaliated . . . : Ibid., loc. 2248.

207 "It makes us . . .": Ibid., loc. 2269; and *Chicago Tribune*, August 30, 1890, 9.

207 With an idealized . . . : Mrs. Frank Leslie, *Beautiful Women of Twelve Epochs* (New York: The Gostlith & England Co., 1890), n.p.

208 While she rallied . . . : *Ladies' Home Journal*, May 1890, 3; and *Anaconda Standard* (MT), November 3, 1890, 3.

208 She admitted she . . . : *Anaconda Standard*, November 3, 1890, 3.

208 She revised her . . . : *Wilkes-Barre (PA) Times Leader*, July 21, 1891, 2.

208 Women, she believed, . . . : "Money and Marriage," *Pittsburgh Dispatch*, January 19, 1890, 20.

209 Marshall, an intimate . . . : Susan Schweik, "Marshall Wilder and Disability Performance History," *Disability Studies Quarterly* 30, no. 3/4 (2010), dsq-sds.org/article/view/1271/1294.

209 His routine on . . . : *Boston Globe*, March 20, 1892, 23.

209 Two nights after . . . : Quoted in Madeleine Stern, *Purple Passage: The Life of Mrs. Frank Leslie* (Norman: University of Oklahoma Press, 1953), 159.

210 On a carriage . . . : *Buffalo Evening News*, April 17, 1894, 1.

210 The press descended . . . : Quoted in Stern, *Purple Passage*, 156.

210 Willie began to . . . : *Frank Leslie Popular Monthly*, December, 1891, 763.

210 She informed reporters . . . : Quoted in *Los Angeles Times*, June 24, 1892, 6.

210 Mrs. Leslie, he drawled . . . : *Western Spirit* (KS), April 22, 1892, 1.

210 The honeymoon, as . . . : *Sioux City Journal* (IA), January 4, 1892, 3.

211 Her speech to . . . : *Los Angeles Times*, January 22, 1892, 6.

211 She concluded with . . . : Joaquin Miller, "The Mother of Men," *MacLean's Magazine*, July 1, 1912, 32.

211 The local papers . . . : *San Francisco Examiner*, February 18, 1892, 3.

211 Miriam told reporters . . . : *Los Angeles Times*, January 24, 1892, 6.

211 Before the press . . . : *San Francisco Examiner*, February 18, 1892, 3.

211 "He has been . . .": Ibid.

211 "Then ring and . . .": Ibid.

211 California dailies portrayed . . . : *Mail* (Stockton, CA), January 26, 1892, 3.

211 At a ruined . . . : *Buffalo Morning News*, February 7, 1892, 2.

212 There would be . . . : *Selma (AL) Times*, August 23, 1893, 3.

212 Again, she was . . . : *Atchison (KS) Daily Globe*, September 14, 1892, 2.

212 She defended her . . . : *Chicago Tribune*, August 24, 1892, 4.

212 "Shall I tell . . .": Interview in the *Detroit Free Press*, quoted in *Cloverdale Reveille* (CA), October 1, 1892, 1.

212 "It is because . . .": Ibid.

212 She broke the . . . : *St. Joseph Herald* (MO), December 6, 1892, 8.

212 She should "pay . . .": Ibid.

212 Doctors, she added . . . : Ibid.

212 In one essay . . . : See "To Reform a Man," *Vermont Farm Journal*, October 1, 1892, 2; and "Unhappy Marriages," *Atchison (KS) Daily Globe*, October 19, 1892, 3.

212 Marriage, she concluded, . . . : "Single or Double?" *Akron (OH) Daily Democrat*, December 30, 1892, 3.

212 Her Louisiana "pretty . . .": *Pittsburgh Dispatch*, December 18, 1891, 12.

213 She seemed to . . . : "Good Mottoes," *St. Joseph Herald*, December 16, 1892, 8.

214 As City Hall . . . : Edwin G. Burrows and Mike Wallace, *Gotham: A History of New York City to 1898* (New York: Oxford University Press, 1999), 1188.

214 Emma Goldman, radical . . . : Quoted in Emma Goldman, *Living My Life* (New York: Alfred A. Knopf, 1931), 123.

214 The publisher, Neely's . . . : Quoted in Stern, *Purple Passage*, 166.

215 She celebrated the . . . : Leslie, *Are We All Deceivers?*, 111.

215 "Eminence," she charged . . . : Ibid., 104.

215 With traditional manhood . . . : Quoted in George Gissing, Elaine Show-alter, *Sexual Anarchy: Gender and Culture at the Fin de Siècle* (New York: Viking, 1990), 2.

215 "You will find . . .": Leslie, *Are We All Deceivers?*, 20, 22–25.

215 Men, in general . . . : Ibid., 264.

215 Women were ordered . . . : Quoted in David E. Shi, *Facing Facts: Realism in American Thought and Culture 1850–1920* (New York: Oxford University Press, 1995), 92.

215 Miriam shot back . . . : Leslie, *Are We All Deceivers?*, 128.

215 They were as . . . : Ibid., 162.

215 To prevail, women . . . : Ibid., 227, 279.

215 Her role models . . . : Ibid., 228.

216 "I am afraid . . .": Ibid., 111.

216 "Such a book . . .": *Writer*, June 1893, 126.

216 Pre-production, Mrs. . . . : *Times-Picayune*, March 21, 1893, 3; and *Evening World* (New York), April 25, 1893, 4.

216 Suzanne, the heroine . . . : *Times-Picayune*, March 21, 1893, 3.

216 Nevertheless, the production . . . : Quoted in Stern, *Purple Passage*, 167.

216 The nineties marked . . . : Anthony Comstock stalked peddlers of prurience with a vengeance. One of his victims was Ida Craddock, a women's rights freethinker, who wrote pro-sex manuals and authored such books as *The Wedding Night* and *Heavenly Bridegrooms*. After two arrests by Comstock—the last, in 1902, resulting in a sentence of life imprisonment—she killed herself.

216 The Woman's Christian . . . : For more on late nineteenth-century views of female sexuality and its impact on feminists see John S. Haller Jr. and Robin M. Haller, *The Physician and Sexuality in Victorian America* (New York: W. W. Norton, 1974), passim; and *Primers for Prudery*, ed. Ronald G. Walters (Englewood Cliffs, NJ: Prentice-Hall, 1974), passim.

217 Mark Twain called . . . : Quoted in Milton Rugoff, *Prudery and Passion* (New York: W. W. Norton, 1971), 117, 129.

217 The "Iron Maidens" . . . : Quoted ibid., 313.

217 Beside the statue . . . : Quoted in Alan Trachtenberg, *The Incorporation of America* (New York: Farrar, Straus and Giroux, 2007), 221.

218 Her *Exposition Souvenir* . . . : Mrs. Frank Leslie, "The Southern Woman—Past and Present," in *The National Exposition Souvenir: What America*

Owes to Women, ed. Lydia Hoyt Farmer (Chicago: Charles Wells Moulton, 1893), 150.

218 Miriam would have . . . : See "The World's Fair Cosmopolis," *Frank Leslie Popular Monthly*, October, 1893, 415.

218 The Fair had been a national . . . : Quoted in Bellamy, *The Incorporation of America*, 215.

218 "I have always received . . .": *Los Angeles Herald*, March 7, 1895, 6.

218 The beleaguered Willie . . . : *San Francisco Call*, June 8, 1893, 10.

218 His flight from . . . : *Memphis Commercial*, June 21, 1893, 4.

219 To salt the . . . : *Boston Globe*, September 16, 1893, 2.

219 She was patently . . . : *Selma (AL) Times*, August 23, 1893, 3.

219 "I have suffered intensely . . .": *Freeman's Journal* (Dublin), September 29, 1893, 7.

219 It was the . . . : Esther Crain, *The Gilded Age in New York 1870–1910* (New York: Black Dog & Leventhal, 2016), 120.

220 Homeless "hobos" filled . . . : Stephen Crane, "An Experiment in Misery," 1894 public.wsu.edu/_campbelld/crane/experim.htm.

220 "Happiness," she lamented . . . : *Kansas Christian Advocate*, July 21, 1894, 2; and "Mrs. Frank Leslie as a Preacher and Teacher," American Press Association, *Northern Advocate* (Whangarei, New Zealand), December 2, 1893, 3.

220 Love's bubble bursts . . . : *Topeka (KS) Mail*, August 31, 1894, 6.

220 "A woman with . . .": *Nashville American*, January 21, 1894, 11.

220 When asked for . . . : See *Eugene (OR) Guard*, December 14, 1894, 2.

220 (City seamstresses worked . . .): For more on the suffering of the working poor, see Paul Bourget's 1894 account in *Outre-Mer—Impressions of America* (New York: Charles Scribner's, 1896), 179–180, 193.

220 And if "dire . . .": *Akron (OH) Daily Democrat*, February 2, 1894, 4.

220 At her most . . . : *Democrat and Chronicle* (Rochester, NY), July 4, 1894, 7; and *Wilkes-Barre (PA) Times Leader, Evening News*, January 20, 1894, 7.

220 Miriam's brand of . . . : *Democrat and Chronicle*, July 4, 1894, 7.

221 Instead, she rebuked . . . : *Akron (OH) Daily Democrat*, June 5, 1894, 2.

221 There were the . . . : *Topeka (KS) Daily Capital*, November 13, 1894, 6.

221 She corralled reporters . . . : *Press* (Kansas City, KS), January 1894, 7.

221 Her round of . . . : *Standard Union* (Brooklyn), January 6, 1894, 7.

221 She found no . . . : *Daily Leader* (Lexington, KY), October 29, 1893, 2.

221 "I married for . . .": *Detroit Free Press*, April 13, 1894, 2.

221 "Too late," he said . . . : *Boston Globe*, April 27, 1894, 2.

221 Miriam riposted that . . . : *Los Angeles Herald*, April 13, 1894, 1.

221 The "pleasures [had] . . .": *Weekly News* (Wilkes-Barre), September 29, 1894, 2.

222   With media fanfare . . . : *Frank Leslie's Popular Monthly*, October, 1894, 396.

222   Under the "inspired . . .": Ibid., 386.

222   In October 1893 . . . : Frank Munsey, quoted in John Simkin, "Munsey's Magazine," *Spartacus Educational*, September 1997, spartacus-educational .com/USAmunseys.htm.

223   "We want stories," . . . : Quoted in Theodore Peterson, *Magazines of the Twentieth Century* (Urbana: University of Illinois Press), 15.

223   Rivals sneered that . . . : Quoted ibid., 4.

223   "A born businesswoman," . . . : *Ladies' Home Journal*, May 1890, 3.

224   When she extended . . . : Cheiro, *Language of the Hand* (New York: The DeVinne Press, 1894), 102.

225   "Your possession of . . .": Ibid., 190.

225   The building was . . . : Tom Miller, "The 1883 Hotel Gerlach—nos. 49–55 West 27th Street," *Daytonian in Manhattan*, September 5, 2013, daytonin-manhattan.blogspot.com/2014/02/the-lost-victoria-hotel-fifth-avenue .html.

225   A "French flat" . . . : "The Modern New York Apartment House," *Frank Leslie's Illustrated Newspaper*, December 8, 1888, 265.

225   Gerland Hull, a . . . : Miller, "The 1883 Hotel Gerlach."

226   A newspaperwoman with . . . : *New York Times*, December 13, 1893, 1.

226   Another alleged note . . . : "Mrs. Wilde's Scare," *Harrisburg Star Independent*, December 9, 1891, 2.

226   Mrs. Leslie, noted . . . : Ibid.

226   Colver and his . . . : *Boston Globe*, May 20, 1895, 6; and *Ottawa Journal* (Ontario, Canada), Mary 23, 1895, 5.

227   On the surface . . . : *Boston Globe*, May 20, 1895, 6.

227   "Whenever I [am] . . .": *Boston Post*, January 18, 1893, 2; and Mrs. Frank Leslie, *Rents in Our Robes* (Chicago: Clark & Co., 1888), 127.

CHAPTER NINE

229   "Long Vacation": *Boston Globe*, May 20, 1895, 6.

229   Her trip to . . . : See *Atlantic Constitution*, May 23, 1895, 3.

229   She rose to . . . : Quoted in in Richard Ellman, *Oscar Wilde* (New York: Vintage Books, 1987), 477.

230   Before her break . . . : *Topeka (KS) Mail*, June 14, 1895, 6.

230   She'd gone to . . . : She peppered her speech with "my dears," and affected a British pronunciation of "wimming" for "women," for instance. *Huron Expositor*, December 12, 1890, 7.

230   But the great . . . : Mrs. Frank Leslie, *Are We All Deceivers? The Lover's Blue Book* (Chicago: Neely, 1893), 76.

230 The patriciate had . . . : Homberger, *Mrs. Astor's New York*, 206; and Mary Cable, *Top Drawer: American High Society from the Gilded Age to the Roaring Twenties* (New York: Antheneum, 1984), 118.

230 "Everybody," she wrote . . . : Leslie, *Are We All Deceivers?*, 80.

231 In Europe the . . . : Homberger, *Mrs. Astor's New York*, 20.

231 "In light of . . .": Quoted in Franco Cologni and Eric Nussbaum, *Platinum By Cartier: Triumph of the Jeweler's Art* (New York: Harry Abrams, 1995), 9.

231 But she believed . . . : Mrs. Frank Leslie, "Attractive Women: They Need Not Be Pretty or Young," Leslie, *Are We All Deceivers?*, 223, 224; and "Heroines of Chivalry," *Frank Leslie Popular Monthly*, December 1895, 653.

231 She settled in . . . : *Buffalo Courier*, June 7, 1896, 18.

231 "Condemn her as . . .": "The Heroines of Chivalry," *Frank Leslie Popular Monthly*, December 1895, 653.

231 She took special . . . : *Inter Ocean* (Chicago), August 3, 1896, 3.

232 Glick, a self-styled . . . : *Los Angeles Herald*, July 30, 1895, 9.

232 "My dear," Mrs. Leslie . . . : *Buffalo Courier*, June 7, 1896, 18.

232 Not to be . . . : Stephen Clarke, *Dirty Bertie: An English King Made in France* (London: Arrow Books, 2014), 14. Also see Cornelia Otis Skinner for the acceptance of divorcees, demi-castors in *Elegant Wits and Grandes Horizontales* (Boston: Houghton Mifflin, 1962), 228.

233 None of which . . . : Quoted in Barbara W. Tuchman, *The Proud Tower: A Portrait of the World Before the War: 1890–1914* (New York: Ballantine Books, 1962), 193.

233 Outside of this . . . : Georges Montorgueil, *Vie des Boulevards* (UK: British Library, Historical Print Editions, 1896), 226.

234 Miriam, who loved . . . : Mrs. Leslie, "Social Slang of Paris," *A Social Mirage* (New York: F. Tennyson Nee, 1899), 348 and more on the subject, 347–48.

234 Caroline Otero, a . . . : Quoted in Arthur H. Lewis, *La Belle Otero* (New York: Trident Press, 1967), 34.

234 In Paris that . . . : Quoted ibid., 74.

234 Decked in jewels . . . : Quoted ibid., 182.

234 Onstage Miriam saw . . . : Leslie, *Are We All Deceivers?*, 229, 232.

235 There she consulted . . . : "The Courts of Love," *Monmouth Press* (NJ), June 22, 1895, 7. The psychologist Havelock Ellis, whom Miriam read at the time, was writing a comprehensive study of the "Art of Love" tradition that would be published a few years later. See *Studies in the Psychology of Sex* (New York: Random House, 1906), vol. 2, 507–75.

235 These ladies understood . . . : Ibid.

235 Their strongest lure . . . : Seigneur de Brantome, *Lives of Fair and Gallant Women*, trans. A. R. Allison (New York: Liveright, 1933, originally published circa 1584–1599), 164, and see his "Of the Power of Speech in Love," 162–67.

235 "Debutantes" today should . . . : "Good Conversation," *Harrisburg Telegraph*, March 14, 1896, 3.

235 "Delightful conversation," she . . . : Ibid.

235 In a second . . . : "The Woman Athlete," *Interior Journal* (Stanford, KY), January 10, 1896, 4.

235 Perhaps with Otero . . . : Ibid.

235 "Get strong without . . .": Ibid.

236 In the hovels . . . : Paul Bourget, *Outre-Mer—Impressions of America* (New York: Charles Scribner's, 1896), 181.

236 Crisscrossing the country . . . : Quoted in Paul Boyer, Joseph E. Kett, et al., *The Enduring Vision: A History of the American People*, vol. II, 7th ed. (Boston: Wadsworth, 2011), 613.

236 After a spaghetti . . . : "Gimme a Gift," *Pittsburgh Press*, December 20, 1896, 17.

237 Miriam greeted her . . . : Ibid.

237 "Meg" cased the . . . : Ibid.

237 There she saw . . . : Ibid.

237 Incensed by the . . . : Ibid.

237 She compared a . . . : Quoted in Greg King, *Season of Splendor: The Court of Mrs. Astor in Gilded Age New York* (Hoboken, NJ: John Wiley, 2009), 85, 86.

238 Tall, scrawny, and . . . : Quoted ibid., 106.

238 She had been . . . : Quoted ibid., 108.

238 After two hours . . . : Elizabeth Drexel Lehr, *King Lehr and the Gilded Age* (Bedford, MA: Applewood Books, 1935), 45.

238 As to why . . . : Ibid.

239 It was a . . . : M. H. Dunlop, *Gilded City: Scandal and Sensation in Turn-of-the-Century New York* (New York: Perennial, 2001), 170.

239 The press rained . . . : Quoted ibid., 176.

239 The decisive blow . . . : For a good account of the ball, see Dunlop, *Gilded City*, 20–36.

240 Her star was . . . : *San Francisco Call*, March 7, 1897, 30; and *New York Times*, February 14, 1897, 5. The whole poem reads:

The good St. Valentine is here.
He pulled me roughly by the ear.

And waking in a great affright
In haste I rose and struck a light.
"Come," said the saint, "a letter write
To him you love this very night,
And on my way I'll take it there.
Said I: "Here I've no ink nor pen."
Then from behind his ear he drew
A pen not quite so good as mine,
And from his pocket—only think,
A little bottle full of ink,
A sheet of paper. So you see,
The good old saint has brought to thee
My likeness so large and bright,
I am sure will give you great delight.

240 Reporters admired her . . . : *Kansas Star*, June 3, 1897, 1.

240 In London, she . . . : *Daily Herald* (Ohio), June 9, 1897, 8.

240 Mark Twain, who . . . : Mark Twain, "Queen Victorian's Jubilee," reprint, *San Francisco Examiner*, June 23, 1897, in *A Tramp Abroad and Other Travels*, Library of Congress, 1052.

241 American greatness required . . . : Quoted in Boyer, Kett, et al., *Enduring Vision*, 616.

241 When the American . . . : Quoted in kcatfish, "You furnish the pictures and I'll furnish the war.," Medium, November 28, 2014, medium.com /covilian-military-intelligence-group/you-furnish-the-pictures-and-ill -furnish-the-war-67de6coe1210.

241 Roosevelt called the . . . : Quoted in Edwin G. Burrows and Mike Wallace, *Gotham: A History of New York City to 1898* (New York: Oxford, 1999), 1215; and John Hay, quoted in Boyer, Kett, et al., *Enduring Vision*, 620.

241 "Comes a cry . . .": Joaquin Miller, "Cuba Libre," *The Complete Poetical Works of Joaquin Miller* (San Francisco: Whitaker & Ray, 1897), 253.

241 She published personal . . . : See *News-Palladium* (MI), May 23, 1898, 2.

241 She was again . . . : Quoted in Madeleine Stern, *Purple Passage: The Life of Mrs. Frank Leslie* (Norman: University of Oklahoma Press, 1953), 135, 139.

242 She'd just been . . . : *Clarion-Ledger* (MI), June 16, 1898, 1; and *Los Angeles Herald*, May 8, 1898, 17.

242 She threaded through . . . : *Harrisburg Telegraph* (PA), March 4, 1896, 3.

243 One gallant guest . . . : Quoted in Stern, *Purple Passage*, 125.

243 "Quite their proper . . .": Ibid.

243 With Lamperti she . . . : See Daniel Shigo, "Column of Breath," Shigo Voice Studio, April 21, 2019, www.shigovoicelessons.com/voicetalk//2019 /04/column-of-breath.html.

243 Poems were read . . . : Marshall Wilder, "Stories about Baby," *Edison Amberol Record*, cylinder, four minutes, December 1908.

243 As a finale, . . . : *New York Times*, June 26, 1886, 5.

243 "Go and say . . .": *Times-Picayune*, July 31, 1898, 19.

243 Miriam motioned to . . . : Ibid.

244 At the telephone . . . : Ibid.

244 She waited a beat . . . : Ibid.

244 "Certain," he answered . . . : Ibid.

244 Uneasy now, she . . . : Ibid.

244 "Say that Mrs. Frank Leslie . . .": Ibid.

244 Would Colver agree . . . : Ibid.

244 Her disciples later . . . : Ibid.

244 When Madame saw . . . : Ibid.

244 Miriam strode past . . . : Ibid.

245 When the last . . . : Quoted in *Logansport Reporter* (IN), June 22, 1898, 7.

CHAPTER TEN

247 Miriam's command center . . . : *North Adams Transcript* (MA), December 14, 1898, 7.

247 She saw she . . . : *Times-Picayune*, July 31, 1898, 9.

247 She fitted up . . . : *North Adams Transcript*, December 14, 1898, 7.

248 And from her . . . : *Times-Picayune*, July 31, 1898, 9.

248 "The tone and . . .": *Santa Fe Monitor*, September 29, 1898, 1.

248 Miriam scored a . . . : Quoted in Madeleine Stern, *Purple Passage: The Life of Mrs. Frank Leslie* (Norman: University of Oklahoma Press, 1953), 172.

248 She souped up . . . : Mrs. Frank Leslie, *A Social Mirage* (New York: F. Tennyson Nee, 1899), 331.

248 They should demand . . . : Mrs. Leslie, "The Helplessness of Women," ibid., 306.

249 Out of one . . . : Ibid. See: "Deceits of Love," 218, "The Agreeable Man," 350–60, "About Marriage," 87.

249 Her inner conflict . . . : Ibid. See: "Woman's Youth," 185, "A Plea for Artificialities," 119, "The Society Girl as a Wife," 206.

249 But she was . . . : *Brooklyn Daily Eagle*, August 27, 1899, 36.

251 The Bohemian spa . . . : See Ignaz Kraus, M.D., *Carlsbad: Its Thermal Springs and How to Use Them* (London: Trübner & Co., 1887), 122.

251 Anxious to assure . . . : *Brooklyn Daily Eagle*, August 27, 1899, 36.

251 She returned to . . . : Ibid.
251 Soon afterward, Colver . . . : Charles L. Benjamin, "The 'American Illustrated Magazine' and Its Publisher," *Printers' Ink,* vol. 52, 1905, 38.
251 It was "not . . .": Ibid., 38.
252 "At last," he . . . : Ibid., 37.
252 "Mrs. Leslie," reported . . . : *Dayton Herald,* October 2, 1900, 1.
252 To on-the-make newcomers . . . : Stern, 173.
252 She cast her . . . : *Marietta Daily Leader,* October 18, 1900, 2.
253 The Baroness Salvador . . . : *New York Supreme Court, Appellate Division, First Department in the matter of the Application of Baroness Althea Salvador to Set Aside the Decree Dated December 7, 1914 Admitting Probate the Last Will and Testament of Frank Leslie, Deceased 1920,* 32.
253 The Baron's Huguenot . . . : *Kenosha (WI) News,* September 5, 1901, 2.
253 Her reclaimed French . . . : Ibid.
253 As Baron de Charlus . . . : Quoted in Tuchman, *Proud Tower,* 195.
253 The *monde's* royalist . . . : *Chicago Tribune,* August 18, 1901, 11.
254 Reporters tried "in . . .": *Sheridan (IN) News,* August 2, 1901, 2.
254 To prove her . . . : *Kenosha (WI) News,* August 5, 1901, 2.
254 At this point . . . : *Buffalo Times,* July 29, 1901, 3.
254 A corpulent, deceptively . . . : Quoted in Greg King, *Season of Splendor: The Court of Mrs. Astor in Gilded Age New York* (Hoboken, NJ: John Wiley, 2009), 409.
254 One by one . . . : Mrs. Frank Leslie, *Are We All Deceivers? The Lover's Blue Book* (Chicago: Neely, 1893), 92.
255 They were "sailing . . .": King, *Season of Splendor,* 423.
255 According to the . . . : *Semiweekly Billings Gazette* (MT), December 24, 1901, 8.
255 This was her . . . : Mrs. Frank Leslie, "How Women should Care for Health," in *Rents in Our Robes* (Chicago: Clark & Co., 1888), 69.
256 She was driving . . . : *St. Louis Post Dispatch,* July 6, 1902, 1.
256 In September she . . . : *Brooklyn Citizen,* September 29, 1902, 5.
256 She was featured . . . : "Mrs. Leslie: Successful Business Woman and Publisher," *Woman: Her Position, Influence and Achievement Throughout the Civilized World from the Garden of Eden to the Twentieth Century,* ed. William C. King (Springfield, MA: The King-Richardson Co., 1902), 450; and *Seen and Heard,* March 20, 1901, 36.
256 Gowned in lavender . . . : See *Indianapolis Star,* August 17, 1903: 6.
256 "The English," she . . . : Ibid.
257 Yet everyone seemed . . . : Mary Gray Peck, *Carrie Chapman Catt: A Biography* (New York: H. W. Wilson, 1944), 225.

257 Some were too . . . : Ella Wheeler Wilcox, *The Worlds and I* (New York: George H. Doran, 1918), 313; and Ellery Sedgwick, *The Happy Profession* (Boston: Little, Brown, 1946), 89.

257 Contrary to the . . . : Wilcox, *Worlds and I*, 131.

258 A "charming romance" . . . : *Washington Post*, April 20, 1907, 12.

258 As Miriam told . . . : Ibid.

258 "Saddest of all," . . . : Leslie, *Social Mirage*, 261.

258 Yet she believed . . . : Leslie, *Are We All Deceivers?*, 224; and Stern, *Purple Passage*, 178.

258 She was, noted . . . : *New York Times*, July 23, 1905, 30.

258 "New men with . . .": Charles L. Benjamin, "The 'American Illustrated Magazine' and Its Publisher," *Printers' Ink*, vol. 52, 1905, 35.

258 Under the regime . . . : *New York Times*, July 23, 1905, 30.

258 She kept the . . . : *Washington Post*, April 20, 1907, 12.

258 Although Miriam insisted . . . : Ibid.

260 Lingerie, though, was . . . : Quoted in Hebe Dorsay, *Age of Opulence: The Belle Epoque in the Paris Herald 1890–1914* (New York: Harry N. Abrams, 1986), 129.

260 "Death," announced the . . . : Quoted in Manuel Perales Solís, "Los Condes de Villaverde la Alta," Lugar de Marmolejo (website), 2013, lugardemarmolejo.wixsite.com/marmolejo/en-blanco-c21uw.

260 She exhibited his . . . : *Washington Post*, April 20, 1907, 12.

260 His "last words," . . . : Ibid.

260 Yet this time, . . . : *Hawaiian Star*, June 3, 1907, 5.

260 As she said . . . : Leslie, *Social Mirage*, 400.

261 "Anything, everything," proclaimed . . . : Quoted in Jim Rasenberger, "1908," *Smithsonian Magazine*, January 2008, www.smithsonianmag.com/history/1908-7683115.

261 The year 1908 . . . : Ibid.

261 The "great multitude" . . . : Ibid.

261 Miriam proceeded with . . . : *Topeka State Journal*, July 23, 1908, 7.

261 The tubular sheath . . . : *St. Louis Post Dispatch*, July 23, 1908, 2.

261 They lacked underskirts . . . : Ibid.

261 "I was used . . .": *Topeka State Journal*, July 23, 1908, 7.

261 In all likelihood, . . . : *Lafourche Comet* (LA), April 23, 1908, 3.

261 Whatever the affront . . . : *Topeka State Journal*, July 23, 1908, 7.

262 She entered her . . . : *Sioux City Journal*, July 18, 1909, 20.

262 The newspapers hailed . . . : *San Francisco Call*, February 10, 1910, 3.

262 She admired the . . . : Ibid.

262 "Ultimately," she continued . . . : Ibid.

262 The prestigious Sequoia . . . : *Oakland Tribune*, February 26, 1910, 11.

262 His ardor for . . . : Ibid.

262 Miriam presided in . . . : Ibid.

262 The "accomplished," tactful . . . : *Oakland Tribune*, August 26, 1910, 12. For an account of Miriam's altercation with the custom's officer, see ibid.

263 She "preferred the . . .": *Ada News* (OK), September 1, 1910, 6.

263 She professed to . . . : Ibid.

263 Gangs like Little . . . : For a full account of this vice culture, see Mike Wallace, *Greater Gotham: A History of New York City from 1898–1919* (New York: Oxford University Press, 2017), 583–647.

263 Sounding a century . . . : "Hints to Business Women by a Baroness: the Former Mrs. Frank Leslie Tells How to Succeed," *Idaho Statesman*, April 30, 1911, 3.

264 You "cannot have . . .": *Caucasian* (LA), April 30, 1911, 2.

264 She called her . . . : *Winfield Courier* (KS), December 29, 1910, 11.

264 "When I come . . .": Rose E. Young, *The Record of the Leslie Woman Suffrage Commission, Inc., 1917–1929* (New York: The Leslie Woman Suffrage Commission, Inc., 1929).

264 Her cousin complained . . . : See *Surrogates' Court Reports, New York County, New York Supreme Court Case on Appeal, January 17, 1917, testimony Mrs. Carrie Wrenn.*

264 "They are only . . .": Young, *Woman Suffrage Commission*.

264 Onboard, she rang . . . : See *Supreme Court Appellate Division, The Application of Baroness Althea Salvador to set aside the decreed dated the 7th day of December 1914, admitting to probate the last will and testament of Frank Leslie, deceased,* Papers on Appeal from Order, 1920, 9.

265 Baroness Salvador, another expectant . . . : Salvador says this was 1912, but the date had to have been the last trip since Miriam didn't go abroad that year or the next; ibid., 31.

265 Once back in . . . : *Surrogates' Court Reports, January 17, 1917, testimony Mrs. Carrie Wrenn,* 77.

265 The heroine, a . . . : Marguerite Linton Glentworth, *The Tenth Commandment* (Boston: Lee and Shepard, 1902), 20.

265 Unable to resolve . . . : Ibid., 368.

266 Apart from $130,000 . . . : Young, *Woman Suffrage Commission*.

266 The bequest would . . . : Quoted in *Windsor Star* (Ontario), November 21, 1914, 10.

266 "Human nature," fleered . . . : Young, *Woman Suffrage Commission*.

266 The history Miriam . . . : *Topeka Daily Capital*, January 19, 1915, 1; and *Detroit Free Press*, December 18, 1915, 1.

267 Instead of Huguenot . . . : The Estate of Frank Leslie, Supreme Court, 1917, vol. I, 29.

267 The parentage question . . . : Young, *Woman Suffrage Commission.*

267 In his final . . . : Ibid.

267 Her financial manager . . . : *Boston Globe,* December 19, 1915, 5.

267 She was a . . . : *Surrogates' Court Reports, New York County, New York Supreme Court Case on Appeal, January 17, 1917, testimony Mrs. Carrie Wrenn,* 77.

267 She reneged on . . . : Ibid.

EPILOGUE

269 The day she . . . : Young, *Woman Suffrage Commission.*

269 "One of the . . .": *Woman Citizen,* June 16, 1917, 4.

269 It became the . . . : Young, *Woman Suffrage Commission.*

269 Feminist leader Harriet . . . : Quoted in Joan Marie Johnson, "New Yorker Mrs. Frank Leslie's Million Dollar fit to Women's Suffrage," *Gotham: A Blog for Scholars of New York City,* November 14, 2017, www.gothamcenter .org/blog/new-yorker-mrs-frank-leslies-million-dollar-gift-to-womens -suffrage.

270 Miriam believed "women . . .": Leslie, *Are We All Deceivers?,* 50.

270 Or why she . . . : Quoted in Maurice Baring, Joanna Richardson, *Sarah Bernhardt and Her World* (New York: Putnam, 1977), 74.

270 "The sphinx," Miriam said . . . : Leslie, *Social Mirage,* 327.

271 She wanted women . . . : Ibid., 172; and Leslie, *Are We All Deceivers?,* 79.

271 A self-mythologizer, she . . . : Leslie, *Are We All Deceivers?,* 105, 106.

WORKS CITED

SELECTED NEWSPAPERS AND JOURNALS

Frank Leslie's Illustrated Newspaper
Frank Leslie's Lady's Magazine and Gazette of Fashion
Frank Leslie's Lady's Journal
Frank Leslie's Chimney Corner
Frank Leslie's Illustrated Historical Register of the Centennial Exposition, 1876
The Days' Doings
Town Topics: The Journal of Society
Daily Territorial Enterprise (Virginia City, NV)
The Ladies' Home Journal
Munsey's Magazine
Times-Picayune
Harper's Weekly, A Journal of Civilization
New York Times
Boston Globe
New-York Tribune
San Francisco Chronicle
San Francisco Examiner
Post and Courier (Charleston, SC)
Detroit Free Press
Inter Ocean (Chicago)
Evening Star (Washington, DC)
Chicago Tribune
Pittsburgh Press
North Adams Transcript (MA)
St. Louis Post-Dispatch

SELECTED COURT CASES

New York Supreme Court General Term-Second Department. Surrogate's Court. Frank Leslie vs. Miriam F. Leslie and Others. Case on Appeal, vols. II and III. New York: E. O'Keefe, 1881.

Daly, Charles P. *In the Matter of the Assignment of Frank Leslie to Isaac W. England for the Benefit of Creditors, Reports of Cases Argued and Determined in the Court of Common Pleas*, February 14, 1881, vol. X. New York: Banks and Brothers, Law Publishers, 1885, pp.76–91.

Superior Court of the City of New York. Miriam Florence Squier against Ephraim George Squier, Divorce Records, vol. XXXV, pp. 169–184.

New York Supreme Court Appellate Division-First Department in the Matter of the Estate of Frank Leslie also known as Mrs. Frank Leslie, also known as Baroness de Bazus. Papers, Case and Record on Appeal, vols. I and II. New York: Middleditch Co, 1917.

Surrogates' Court and Reports, New York County, New York Supreme Court Case on Appeal, testimony Mrs. Carrie Wrenn, January 17, 1917, p. 77.

Surrogates' Court New York County in the Application of Baroness Althea Salvador to set aside the decree dated the 7th day of December, 1914, admitting to probate the Last Will and Testament of Frank Leslie, deceased and In the matter of the application of Henrietta R. Hurlbut, as Administratrix of the Goods, Chattels and Credits of the Baroness Althea Salvador, to revive the said Application of said Baroness Salvador, who is now deceased, July 26, 1920.

BOOKS BY MRS. FRANK LESLIE

Leslie, Mrs. Frank. *Are We All Deceivers? The Lover's Blue Book.* London and New York: F. Tennyson Neely, 1892–1896.

———. *Beautiful Women of Twelve Epochs.* New York: Gast Art Press, 1890.

———. *California: A Pleasure Trip from Gotham to the Golden Gate.* New York: G. W. Carleton & Co., 1877.

———. *Rents in Our Robes.* Chicago, New York, San Francisco: Belford, Clarke & Co., 1888.

———. *A Social Mirage.* London, New York, and Chicago: F. Tennyson Neely, 1899.

Squier, Mrs. E. G., trans. *The Demi-Monde: A Satire on Society from the French of Alexandre Dumas, Jr.* Philadelphia: J. B. Lippincott, 1858.

———, trans. *Travels in Central America: Including Accounts of Some Regions Unexplored since the Conquest, from the French of the Chevalier Arthur Morelet.* New York: Leypoldt, Holt & Williams, 1871.

ARTICLES AND BOOKS CITED

Alb. [Richard Whiteing]. *Living Paris and France: A Guide to Manners, Monuments, Institutions, and the Life of the People.* London: Ward and Downey, 1889 and Paris: Galignani, 1889.

Anonymous. *The Pretty Women of Paris.* Reprint 1883. London: Wordsworth Editions, 1996.

Arthur, Stanley Clisby. *Old New Orleans: A History of the Vieux Carré, Its Ancient and Historical Buildings.* Westminster, MD: Heritage Books, 1936.

Auerbach, Nina. *Woman and the Demon: The Life of a Victorian Myth*. Cambridge, MA: Harvard University Press, 1982.

Barman, Roderick J. *Citizen Emperor: Pedro II and the Making of Brazil 1875–1891*. Stanford, CA: Stanford University Press, 1999.

Barnhart, Terry A. *Ephraim George Squier and the Development of American Anthropology*. Lincoln: University of Nebraska Press, 2005.

Baudelaire, Charles. "In Praise of Cosmetics." *My Heart Laid Bare and Other Prose Writings*. New York: Vanguard Press, 1951.

Beatty, Jack. *Age of Betrayal: The Triumph of Money in America 1865–1900*. New York: Vintage, 2008.

Beecher, Catherine E. *A Treatise on Domestic Economy for the Use of Young Ladies of Home and at School*. Boston: March, Capen, Lyon & Webb, 1841.

Beerbohm, Max. *Max and Will: Max Beerbohm and William Rothenstein, Their Friendship and Letters, 1893–1945*. Edited by Mary M. Lago and Karl Beckson. Cambridge, MA: Harvard University Press, 1975.

Beeton, Isabella. *Mrs. Beeton's Book of Household Management*, vol. 1. Reprint, 1859–1860. Ex-classics Project, 2009.

Bellesiles, Michael A. *1877: America's Year of Living Violently*. New York: The New Press, 2010.

Benjamin, Charles L. "The 'American Illustrated Magazine' and Its Publisher: 'Leslie's Monthly' a Thing of the Past—How the Character of the Magazine has been Changed and Why the New Name is to be Adopted." *Printers' Ink*, vol. 52, 1905: 35–39.

Benjamin, Walter. "Paris, Capital of the Nineteenth Century," *Charles Baudelaire: A Lyric Poet in the Era of High Capitalism*. Translated by Henry Zohn. London: Verso, 1989.

Berg, Barbara J. *The Remembered Gate: Origins of American Feminism. The Woman and the City, 1800–1860*. New York: Oxford University Press, 1978.

Bergerat, Émile, and Vanessa R. Schwartz. *Spectacular Realities: Early Mass Culture in Fin-de-Siècle Paris*. Berkeley: University of California Press, 1998.

Blanchard, Margaret A. "The American Urge to Censor: Freedom of Expression vs. the Desire to Sanitize—From Anthony Comstock to 2 Live Crew." *William & Mary Law Review*, vol. 33, 1992: 741–851.

Boissel, Pascal. *Grand-Hôtel Café de la Paix: Two Centuries of Parisian Life*. Translated by George P. Mutch. Italy: Éditions Italiques, 2004.

Botts, Mary Beth, ed. "East 10th Street Historic District Designation Report," January 17, 2012. New York City Landmark Preservation Commission. media.villagepreservation.org/wp-content/uploads/2020/03/15123117/East-10th-Street-Historic-District-NYC-LPC-Designation-Report.pdf.

Bourget, Paul. *Outre-mer: Impressions of America*. New York: Charles Scribner's Sons, 1895.

Boyer, Paul S., Clifford E. Clark Jr., Karen Halttunen, Joseph E. Kett, Neal Salisbury, Harvard Sitkoff, and Nancy Woloch. *The Enduring Vision: A History of the American People, Volume II: Since 1865*, 7th edition. Boston: Wadsworth, 2011.

Braddon, Mary Elizabeth. *Mount Royal: A Novel*. London: John and Robert Maxwell, 1882.

Brantome, Seigneur de. *Lives of Fair and Gallant Ladies*. Translated by A. R. Allison. Reprint, 1584–1599. New York: Liveright, 1933.

Brown, Henry Collins, ed. *Valentine's Manual of the City of New York, 1917–1918*. New York: Old Colony Press, 1918.

Brown, Henry Collins, ed. *Valentine's Manual of Old New York*. New York: Valentine's Manual, 1922.

Brown, Joshua. "The Days' Doings: The Gilded Age in the Profane Pictorial Press," paper, American Studies Association Annual Meeting, Hartford, CT, October 17, 2003. www.joshbrownnyc.com/daysdoings/index.htm.

Brown, Joshua. *Beyond the Lines: Pictorial Reporting, Everyday Life, and the Crisis of Gilded Age America*. Berkeley: University of California Press, 2002.

Broyles, Susannah. "Vanderbilt Ball—How a Costume Ball Changed New York Elite Society." *New York Stories*, Museum of the City of New York, August 6, 2013. blog.mcny.org/2013/08/06/vanderbilt-ball-how-a-costume-ball-changed-new-york-elite-society/.

Burrows, Edwin G., and Mike Wallace. *Gotham: A History of New York City to 1898*. New York: Oxford University Press, 1999.

Cable, Mary. *Top Drawer: American High Society from the Gilded Age to the Roaring Twenties*. New York: Atheneum, 1984.

Carmer, Carl. *Stars Fell on Alabama*. New York: Doubleday, 1934.

Carnegie, Andrew. "Wealth." *North American Review*, no. 391, June 1889: 653–665.

Chandler, Arthur. "Revolution: The Paris Exposition Universelle, 1889." *World's Fair Magazine*, vol. 7, no. 1, 1986. www.arthurchandler.com/paris-1889-exposition.

Cheiro. *Cheiro's Language of the Hand: A Complete Practical Work on the Sciences of Cheirognomy and Cheiromancy, Containing the System, Rules, and Experience of Cheiro the Palmist*. New York: The DeVinne Press, 1894.

Chesnut, Mary. *Mary Chesnut's Civil War*. Edited by C. Vann Woodward. New Haven: Yale University Press, 1981.

Christensen, Rupert. *Paris Babylon: The Story of the Paris Commune*. New York: Viking, 1994.

Clarke, Stephen. *Dirty Bertie: An English King Made in France*. London: Arrow Books, 2014.

Clubbe, John. *Cincinnati Observed: Architecture and History*. Columbus: Ohio State University Press, 1992.

Coclanis, Peter A. *The Shadow of a Dream: Economic Life and Death in the South Carolina Low Country 1670–1920*. New York: Oxford University Press, 2013.

Cologni, Franco, and Eric Nussbaum. *Platinum by Cartier: Triumph of the Jewelers' Art*. New York: Abrams, 1995.

Crain, Esther. *The Gilded Age in New York, 1870–1910*. New York: Black Dog & Leventhal, 2016.

Crane, Stephen. "An Experiment in Misery." *New York Press*, April 22, 1894. public.wsu.edu/~campbelld/crane/experim.htm.

Degler, Carl N. "What Ought to Be and What Was: Women's Sexuality in the Nineteenth Century." *American Historical Review*, vol. 79, no. 5, December 1974: 1468.

Derby, James Cephas. *Fifty Years Among Authors, Books and Publishers*. Hartford, CT: M. A. Winter & Hatch, 1886.

Dickens, Charles. *American Notes for General Circulation*. London: Chapman and Hall, 1842. Reprinted and edited by Patricia Ingram. New York: Penguin, 2004.

Dickens, Charles Culliford Boz. *Dickens's Dictionary of Paris, 1883: An Unconventional Handbook*. London: Macmillan & Company, 1883.

Dijkstra, Bram. *Idols of Perversity: Fantasies of Feminine Evil in Fin-de-Siècle Culture*. New York: Oxford University Press, 1986.

Donati, Sara. "Vanderbilt Costume Ball" *Historical Fiction by Sara Donati*. thegildedhour.com/vanderbilt-costume-ball/.

Dorsay, Hebe. *Age of Opulence: The Belle Epoque in the Paris Herald, 1900–1914*. New York: Abrams, 1987.

Dunlop, M. H. *Gilded City: Scandal and Sensation in Turn-of-the-Century New York*. New York: Perennial, 2001.

Ellington, George. *The Women of New York: or, The Under-world of the Great City*. New York: New York Book Company, 1869.

Ellis, Havelock. *Studies in the Psychology of Sex*, vol. 2. New York: Random House, 1906.

Ellmann, Richard. *Oscar Wilde*. New York: Vintage Books, 1988.

Farmer, Lydia Hoyt, ed. *The National Exposition Souvenir: What America Owes to Women*. Buffalo, Chicago, and New York: Charles Wells Moulton, 1893.

Fitzsimons, Eleanor. *Wilde's Women: How Oscar Wile Was Shaped by the Women He Knew*. New York: The Overlook Press, 2016.

Foster, George G. *New York by Gas-Light and Other Urban Sketches.* Reprint, 1850. Edited by Stuart M. Blumin. Berkeley: University of California Press, 1990.

Fowler, Marian. *In a Gilded Cage: From Heiress to Duchess.* New York: Vintage Books, 1993.

Fryer, Judith. *Faces of Eve: Women in the Nineteenth-Century American Novel.* New York: Oxford University Press, 1976.

Gambee, Budd Leslie, Jr. *Frank Leslie and His Illustrated Newspaper 1855–1860.* Ann Arbor: University of Michigan Department of Library Science, 1964.

Garvey, Joan B., and Mary Lou Widner. *Beautiful Crescent: A History of New Orleans.* Gretna, LA: Pelican Publishing, 2012.

George, Henry. *Progress and Poverty.* San Francisco: W. H. Hinton, 1879. Reprint. New York: Robert Schalkenbach Foundation, 2008.

Gilfoyle, Timothy J. *City of Eros: New York City, Prostitution, and the Commercialization of Sex, 1790–1920.* New York: W. W. Norton, 1992.

Glentworth, Marguerite Linton. *The Tenth Commandment: A Romance.* Boston: Lee and Shepard, 1902.

Goffman, Erving. *The Presentation of the Self in Everyday Life.* Garden City, NY: Doubleday, 1959.

Goldman, Emma. *Living My Life.* New York: Alfred A. Knopf, 1931.

Goodman, Matthew. *Eighty Days: Nellie Bly and Elizabeth Bisland's History-Making Race Around the World.* New York: Ballantine Books, 2013.

Green, James. *Death in the Haymarket: A Story of Chicago, the First Labor Movement and the Bombing that Divided Gilded Age America.* New York: Anchor Books, 2007.

Hagy, James W. *Charleston, South Carolina, City Directories for the Years 1816, 1819, 1822, 1825, and 1829.* Baltimore: Clearfield Company, 1996.

Haller, John S., Jr., and Robin M. Haller. *The Physician and Sexuality in Victorian America.* New York: W. W. Norton, 1974.

Haltunen, Karen. *Confidence Men and Painted Women: A Study of Middle-Class Culture in America, 1830–1870.* New Haven: Yale University Press, 1982.

Harvest, Sharon M., and Ellen Gruber Garvey, eds. *Blue Pencils and Hidden Hands: Women Editing Periodicals, 1830–1910.* Boston: Northeastern Press, 2004.

Homberger, Eric. *Mrs. Astor's New York: Money and Social Power in a Gilded Age.* New Haven: Yale University Press, 2002.

Horne, Alistair. *La Belle France: A Short History.* New York: Vintage, 2006.

Howe, Julia Ward. *A Trip to Cuba.* Boston: Ticknor and Fields, 1860.

Howells, William Dean. *A Hazard of New Fortunes.* New York: Harper, 1880. Reprinted with introduction by Phillip Lopate. New York: Penguin, 2001.

Husband, Julie, and Jim O'Loughlin. *Daily Life in the Industrial United States, 1870–1900*. Westport, CT: Greenwood Press, 2004.

James, Henry. *Daisy Miller and Washington Square*. New York: Harper, 1880. Reprinted with introduction by Jennie A. Kasanoff. New York: Sterling, 2004.

Johnson, Joan Marie. "New Yorker Mrs. Frank Leslie's Million Dollar Gift to Women's Suffrage." *The Gotham Center for New York City History*, November 14, 2017. www.gothamcenter.org/blog/new-yorker-mrs-frank-leslies-million-dollar-gift-to-womens-suffrage.

Jones, Katherine M., ed. *Heroines of Dixie: Spring of High Hopes*. St. Simons Island, GA: Mockingbird Books, 1955.

Josephson, Matthew. *The Robber Barons: The Great American Capitalists, 1861–1901*. New York: Harcourt, 1962.

Kelly, Joseph. *America's Longest Siege: Charleston, Slavery, and the Slow March Toward Civil War*. New York: The Overlook Press, 2013.

King, Greg. *A Season of Splendor: The Court of Mrs. Astor in Gilded Age New York*. Hoboken, NJ: John Wiley, 2009.

King, William C., ed. "Mrs. Frank Leslie: Successful Business Woman and Publisher." *Woman: Her Position, Influence, and Achievement Throughout the Civilized World—Her Biography, Her History from the Garden of Eden to the Twentieth Century*. Springfield, MA: The King-Richardson Company, 1902.

Kraditor, Aileen S. *Up from the Pedestal: Selected Writings in the History of Feminism*. Chicago: Quadrangle Books, 1968.

Kraus, Ignaz, M.D. *Carlsbad: Its Thermal Springs and Baths and How to Use Them*. London: Trübner & Company, 1887.

Legge, Edward. *The Comedy and Tragedy of the Second Empire: Paris Society in the Sixties*. New York: Harper & Brothers, 1911.

Lehr, Elizabeth Drexel. *King Lehr and the Gilded Age*. Philadelphia: J. B. Lippincott, 1935. Reprint. Bedford, MA: Applewood Books, 2005.

Leng, Sir John. *America in 1876: Pencillings During a Tour in the Centennial Year: With a Chapter on the Aspects of American Life*. England: Dundee Advertiser Office, 1877.

Leuville, William Redivivus Oliver de Lorncourt, Marquis de. *Poems and Aelia from "Entre-Nous."* New York: American News Company, 1884.

Lewis, Arthur H. *La Belle Otero*. New York: Trident Press, 1967.

Lewis, Lloyd, and Henry Justin Smith. *Oscar Wilde Discovers America, 1882*. New York: Harcourt Brace, 1936.

Lionells, Marylou, John Fiscalini, Carola H. Mann, and Donnel B. Stern, eds. *Handbook of Interpersonal Psychoanalysis*. New York: Routledge, 1995.

Longworth's American Almanac, New-York Register and City Directory, 1839–1840. New York: Thomas Longworth, 1839.

Lutz, Tom. *American Nervousness, 1903: An Anecdotal History*. Ithaca, NY: Cornell University Press, 1991.

Marberry, M. M. *Splendid Poseur: Joaquin Miller—American Poet*. New York: Thomas Y. Crowell, 1953.

McAllister, Ward. *Society As I Have Found It*. London: Cassell, 1890.

McCabe, James D., Jr. *Lights and Shadows of New York Life; or, the Sights and Sensations of the Great City*. Philadelphia: National Publishing Company, 1872.

———. *New York By Gaslight: A Work Descriptive of the Great American Metropolis*. Philadelphia: Hubbard Brothers, 1882. Reprint. New York: Greenwich House, 1984.

McGovern, Francis. "Joaquin Miller, The Poet of the Sierras," *Literary Traveler*, February 1, 2000. www.literarytraveler.com/articles/joaquin-miller-the-poet-of-the-sierras/.

Melville, Herman. *The Confidence-Man: His Masquerade*. New York: Miller and Holman, 1857. Reprinted with introduction by Stephen Matterson. New York: Penguin, 1991.

Melville, Joy. *Mother of Oscar: The Life of Jane Francesca Wilde*. London: Allison & Busby, 1999.

Mendelssohn, Michèle. *Making Oscar Wilde*. Oxford, UK: Oxford University Press, 2018.

Miller, Joaquin. *The Complete Poetical Works of Joaquin Miller*. San Francisco: Whitaker & Ray, 1897.

———. *The Destruction of Gotham*. New York: Funk & Wagnalls, 1886.

———. "The Mother of Men." *MacLean's Magazine*, July 1, 1912: 32.

———. "Mrs. Frank Leslie." *Golden Era*, vol. 36, no. 5, May 1887: 180–183.

———. *The One Fair Woman*. New York: G. W. Dillingham, 1876.

Miller, Juanita J. *My Father: C. H. Joaquin Miller, Poet*. Oakland, CA: Tooley-Towne, 1941.

Miller, Tom. "The 1883 Hotel Gerlach—Nos. 49–55 West 27th Street." *Daytonian in Manhattan*, September 5, 2013. daytoninmanhattan.blogspot.com/2013/09/the-1883-hotel-gerlach-nos-49–55-west.html.

———. "The Lost Victoria Hotel—Fifth Avenue and 27th Street," *Daytonian in Manhattan*, February 3, 2014. daytoninmanhattan.blogspot.com/2014/02/the-lost-victoria-hotel-fifth-avenue.html.

Montez, Lola. *The Arts of Beauty; or Secrets of a Lady's Toilet with Hints to Gentlemen on the Art of Fascinating*. New York: Dick & Fitzgerald, 1858. Reprint. Chatham House, 1969.

———. "Autobiography." *Lectures of Lola Montez, Countess of Landsfeld*. Edited by Charles Chauncey Burr. New York: Rudd & Carleton, 1859.

————. *The Story of a Penitent: Lola Montez*. New York: Protestant Episcopal Society for the Promotion of Evangelical Knowledge, 1867.

Montorgueil, Georges. *Lie Vie des Boulevards*. UK: British Library, Historical Print Editions, 1896.

Murray, Stuart A. P., ed. *Witness to the Civil War: First-Hand Accounts from Frank Leslie's Illustrated Newspaper*. New York: Smithsonian, 2006.

Noddings, Nel. *Women and Evil*. Berkeley, CA: University of California Press, 1989.

Norton, Frank G., ed. *Frank Leslie's Historical Register of the United States Centennial Exhibition, 1876*. New York: Frank Leslie's Publishing House, 1877.

Oller, John. *American Queen: The Rise and Fall of Kate Chase Sprague, Civil War "Belle of the North" and Gilded Age Woman of Scandal*. New York: Da Capo Press, 2014.

Palmer, James. "Albert Pulitzer: Notes on the Lesser-Known Pulitzer Brother." *The Pulitzer Prizes*. www.pulitzer.org/page/albert-pulitzer-notes-lesser-known-pulitzer-brother.

Patterson, Jerry E. *The First Four Hundred: Mrs. Astor's New York in the Gilded Age*. New York: Rizzoli, 2000.

Peck, Mary Gray. *Carrie Chapman Catt: A Biography*. New York: H. W. Wilson, 1944.

Peterson, Theodore. *Magazines in the Twentieth Century*. Urbana: University of Illinois Press, 1956.

Pickett, Albert J. *History of Alabama and Incidentally of Georgia and Mississippi, from the Earliest Period*, vol. 1. Charleston, SC: Walker and James, 1851. Reprint. Sacramento, CA: Creative Media Partners, 2015.

Powell, Lawrence N. *The Accidental City: Improvising New Orleans*. Cambridge, MA: Harvard University Press, 2012.

Rasenberger, Jim. "1908." *Smithsonian Magazine*, January 2008. www.smithsonianmag.com/history/1908-7683115/.

Reardick, Charles. *Pleasures of the Belle Epoque*. New Haven: Yale University Press, 1985.

Richardson, Joanna. *Sarah Bernhardt and Her World*. New York: Putnam, 1977.

Riis, Jacob. *How the Other Half Lives: Studies Among the Tenements of New York*. New York: Charles Scribner's Sons, 1890.

Ripley, Eliza. *Social Life in Old New Orleans, Being Recollections of My Girlhood*. New York and London: D. Appleton & Company, 1912. Reprint. New Orleans: Cornerstone Press, 2012.

Ross, Ishbel. *The Uncrowned Queen: Life of Lola Montez*. New York: Harper & Row, 1972.

Rugoff, Milton. *Prudery and Passion: Sexuality in Victorian America*. New York: Putnam, 1971.

Sandweiss, Martha A. *Passing Strange: A Gilded Age Tale of Love and Deception Across the Color Line*. New York: Penguin, 2010.

Sauger, Eric. *Reborn in America: French Exiles and Refugees in the United States and the Vine and Olive Adventure, 1815–1865*. Translated by Madeleine Velguth. Tuscaloosa: University of Alabama Press, 2011.

Schweik, Susan. "Marshall P. Wilder and Disability Performance History." *Disability Studies Quarterly*, vol. 30, no. 3/4, 2010. dsq-sds.org/article/view/1271/1294.

Sedgwick, Ellery. *The Happy Profession*. Boston: Little, Brown, 1946.

Selcer, Richard F. *Civil War America, 1850 to 1875*. New York: Facts on File, 2006.

Seymour, Bruce. *Lola Montez: A Life*. New Haven: Yale University Press, 1996.

Shi, David E. *Facing Facts: Realism in American Thought and Culture, 1850–1920*. New York: Oxford University Press, 1995.

Shigo, Daniel. "Column of Breath," *Shigo Voice Studio*, September 29, 2015. www.shigovoicelessons.com/voicetalk//2015/09/column-of-breath.html.

Showalter, Elaine. *Sexual Anarchy: Gender and Culture at the Fin de Siécle*. New York; Viking, 1990.

Simkin, John. "Munsey's Magazine." *Spartacus Educational*, September 1997. spartacus-educational.com/USAmunseys.htm.

Simmel, Georg. *Georg Simmel: On Women, Sexuality, and Love*. Translated and edited by Guy Oakes. New Haven: Yale University Press, 1984.

Skinner, Cornelia Otis. *Elegant Wits and Grandes Horizontals*. Boston: Houghton Mifflin, 1962.

Smith, Thomas Ruys. *Southern Queen: New Orleans in the Nineteenth Century*. London: Bloomsbury, 2011.

Smythe, Ted Curtis. *The Gilded Age Press: 1865–1900*. Westport, CT: Praeger, 2003.

Social Register, 1887. Reprint. New York: Social Register Association, 1986.

Solís, Manuel Perales. "Los Condes de Villaverde la Alta." Pedro J. Delgado Guerrea, *Lugar de Marmolejo*, 2012. lugardemarmolejo.wixsite.com/marmolejo/en-blanco-c21uw.

Spann, Edward K. *The New Metropolis: New York City, 1840–1857*. New York: Columbia University Press, 1981.

Squier, Ephraim George. *Peru Illustrated: Or Incidents of Travel and Exploration in the Land of the Incas*. New York: Hurst & Company, 1877.

————. (Samuel A. Bard). *Waikna; Or Adventures on the Mosquito Shore*. New York: Harper & Brothers, 1855.

Stansifer, C. L. "E. George Squier and Honduran Interoceanic Railroad Project," *Hispanic Historic Review*, vol. 46, no. 1, February 1966: 1–27.

Steele, Valerie. *Fashion and Eroticism: Ideals of Feminine Beauty from the Victorian Era to the Jazz Age*. New York: Oxford University Press, 1985.

Stern, Madeleine B. *Purple Passage: The Life of Mrs. Frank Leslie*. Norman: University of Oklahoma Press, 1953.

Stern, Robert A. M., Thomas Mellins and David Fishman. *New York 1880: Architecture and Urbanism in the Gilded Age*. New York: Monacelli Press, 1999.

Sterne, Emma Gelders. *Some Plant Olive Trees*. New York: Doubleday, 1934.

Sterngasse, Jon. *First Resorts: Pursuing Pleasure at Saratoga Springs, Newport, and Coney Island*. Baltimore: Johns Hopkins University Press, 2001.

Stirling, Edward. *Cabin Boy: A Drama in Two Acts*. London: Nassau Steam Press, 1846.

Strom, Sharon Hartman. *Fortune, Fame, and Desire: Promoting the Self in the Long Nineteenth Century*. New York: Rowman & Littlefield, 2016.

Strong, George Templeton. *The Diary of George Templeton Strong*. Edited by Allan Nevins and Milton Halsey Thomas. Seattle: University of Washington Press, 1952.

Taylor, Tom. *Plot and Passion: A Drama in Three Acts*. New York: Robert M. Dewitt, 1853.

Teaford, Jon C. *Cities of the Heartland: The Rise and Fall of the Industrial Midwest*. Bloomington: Indiana University Press, 1993.

Tomes, Robert. *The Bazar Book of Decorum: The Care of the Person, Manners, Etiquette, and Ceremonials*. New York: Harper & Brothers, 1870.

Trachtenberg, Alan. *The Incorporation of America: Culture and Society in the Gilded Age*. New York: Farrar, Straus, and Giroux, 2007.

Trollope, Anthony. *The Small House at Allington*. London: Smith, Elder, 1864. Reprinted with introduction by Julian F. Thompson. New York: Penguin, 2005.

————. *The Way We Live Now*. London: Chapman & Hall, 1875. Reprinted and edited by Peter Merchant. London: Wordsworth Classics, 2001.

Trollope, Frances Milton. *Domestic Manners of the Americans*. London: Whittaker, Treacher, 1832. Reprint. Mineola, NY: Dover, 2003.

Tuchman, Barbara W. *The Proud Tower: A Portrait of the World Before the War: 1890–1914*. New York: Ballantine Books, 1962.

Twain, Mark. *Adventures of Huckleberry Finn (Tom Sawyer's Comrade)*. New York: Charles L. Webster, 1885.

————. *Innocents Abroad; or, the New Pilgrims' Progress.* Hartford, CT: American Publishing Company, 1869. Reprint. New York: Bantam Books, 1964.

————. *A Tramp Abroad.* Hartford, CT: American Publishing Company, 1880.

Wallace, Mike. *Greater Gotham: A History of New York City from 1898 to 1919.* New York: Oxford University Press, 2017.

Wallach, Janet. *The Richest Woman in America: Hetty Green in the Gilded Age.* New York: Anchor Books, 2012.

Walters, Ronald G. *Primers for Prudery: Sexual Advice to Victorian America.* Englewood Cliffs, NJ: Prentice-Hall, 1974.

Weindling, Dick, and Marianne Colloms. *The Marquis de Leuville: A Victorian Fraud?* ebook. Gloustershire, UK: The History Press, 2012. www.historypressco.uk.

Welter, Barbara. *Dimity Convictions: The American Woman in the Nineteenth Century.* Athens: Ohio University Press, 1976.

Wilcox, Ella Wheeler. *The Worlds and I.* New York: George H. Doran, 1918.

Wilde, Lady Jane. *Essays and Stories.* New York and London: Keller-Farmer Company, 1907.

Wilde, Oscar. "A Woman of No Importance." *The Importance of Being Earnest and Other Plays.* London: Penguin, 1988.

Wilder, Marshall P. "Stories About the Baby." *Edison Amberol Record,* cylinder, four minutes, December 1908.

Woodhull, Victoria. "A Speech on the Principles of Social Freedom." *The Victoria Woodhull Reader.* Edited by Madeleine B. Stern. Weston, MA: M & S Press, 1974.

Woodyard, Chris, ed. *The Victorian Book of the Dead.* Dayton, OH: Kestrel, 2014.

Young, Rose. *The Record of the Leslie Woman Suffrage Commission, Inc., 1917–1929.* New York: The Leslie Woman Suffrage Commission, Inc., 1929.

Zola, Émile. *Nana.* Translated by Douglas Parmée. Reprint 1880. New York: Oxford University Press, 2009.

SELECTED REFERENCE BOOKS

Albrecht, Donald, and Jeannine Falino, eds. *Gilded New York: Design, Fashion, and Society.* New York: Museum of the City of New York, Monacelli Press, 2013.

Banta, Martha. *Imaging American Women: Idea and Ideals in Cultural History.* New York: Columbia University Press, 1987.

Blum, Stella, ed. *Victorian Fashions and Costumes from Harper's Bazar 1867–1898.* New York: Dover, 1973.

Brands, H. W. *The Reckless Decade: America in the 1890s.* Chicago: University of Chicago Press, 1995.

Bussler, Mark. *New York City in the 19th Century: A Dramatic Collection of Images.* Inecom, 2019.

Cady, Edwin H., and David L. Frazier, eds. *The War of the Critics over William Dean Howells.* Evanston, IL: Row, Peterson, 1962.

Calhoun, Charles W., ed. *The Gilded Age: Perspectives on the Origins of Modern America.* Lanham, MD: Rowman & Littlefield, 2007.

Campbell, W. Joseph. *The Year That Defined American Journalism: 1897 and the Clash of Paradigms.* New York and London: Routledge, 2006.

Clinton, Catherine, and Christine Lunardini. *The Columbia Guide to American Women in the Nineteenth Century.* New York: Columbia University Press, 1999.

Craven, Wayne. *Gilded Mansions: Grand Architecture and High Society.* New York: Norton, 2009.

Cunnington, C. Willett. *English Clothing in the Nineteenth Century.* Reprint. New York: Dover, 1990.

Flexner, Eleanor, and Ellen Fitzpatrick. *Century of Struggle: The Woman's Rights Movement in the United States.* Cambridge: Harvard University Press, 1996.

Gale, Robert L. *The Gay Nineties in America: A Cultural Dictionary of the 1890s.* Westport, CT: Greenwood Press, 1992.

Grafton, John. *New York in the Nineteenth Century: 317 Engravings from Harper's Weekly and Other Contemporary Sources.* New York: Dover, 1977.

Greenwood, Janette Thomas. *The Gilded Age: A History in Documents.* New York: Oxford University Press, 2000.

Homberger, Eric. *The Historical Atlas of New York City: A Visual Celebration of 400 Years of New York City's History.* New York: Henry Holt, 1994.

Kasson, John F. *Rudeness & Civility: Manners in Nineteenth-Century Urban America.* New York: Farrar, Straus, and Giroux, 1990.

Lears, Jackson. *Rebirth of a Nation: The Making of Modern America, 1877–1920.* New York: Harper Perennial, 2009.

Lewis, Arnold, James Turner, and Steven McQuillin. *The Opulent Interiors of the Gilded Age: All 203 Photographs from "Artistic Houses," with New Text.* Mineola, NY: Dover, 1987.

McCutcheon, Marc. *The Writer's Guide to Everyday Life in the 1800s.* Cincinnati: Writer's Digest Books, 1993.

Olian, Joanne, ed. *Victorian and Edwardian Fashions from "La Mode Illustrée."* Mineola, NY: Dover, 1998.

Pfeffer, Miki. *Southern Ladies and Suffragists: Julia Ward Howe and Women's Rights at the New Orleans World's Fair.* Jackson: University of Mississippi Press, 2014.

Schlereth, Thomas J. *Victorian America: Transformations in Everyday Life, 1876–1915*. New York: Harper Perennial, 1991.

Schlup, Leonard C., and James G. Ryan, eds. *Historical Dictionary of the Gilded Age*. Armonk, NY, and London: M. E. Sharpe, 2003.

Shrock, Joel. *The Gilded Age: American Popular Culture Through History*. Westport, CT: Greenwood Press, 2004.

Traxel, David. *1898: The Birth of the American Century*. New York: Vintage, 1998.

The Universal Self-Instructor and Manual of General Reference: A Facsimile of the 1883 Edition. Introduction by Annette K. Baxter. New York: Winter House, 1970.

Trager, James. *The New York Chronology: The Ultimate Compendium of Events, People, and Anecdotes from the Dutch to the Present*. New York: HarperCollins, 2003.

Waller, George. *Saratoga: Saga of an Impious Era*. New York: Bonanza Books, 1966.

Ware, J. Redding. *Ware's Victorian Dictionary of Slang and Phrase*. Oxford, UK: Oxford University Press, 2013.

Wells, Richard A. *Manners Culture and Dress in the Best American Society*. Cleveland, OH: American Publishing, 1891.

INDEX